Thomas Jefferson

An Anthology

T0385542

Thomas Jefferson

An Anthology

Edited by

Peter S. Onuf

University of Virginia

BRANDYWINE PRESS • St. James, New York

ISBN 1-881089-57-6

Telephone Orders: 1-800-345-1776

To
My students at the University of Virginia

They make Jefferson worth rereading,
year after year

CONTENTS

CHAPTER FIVE: The Revolution of 1800 173

Thomas Jefferson

An Anthology

Making Sense of Jefferson*

In 1960, Merrill Peterson concluded in his book *The Jefferson Image in the American Mind* that Thomas Jefferson had finally, belatedly ascended to a crucial "place in the symbolical architecture of this nation." It was now possible for scholars to take the measure of the man. "The scholarly wish to possess Jefferson for himself might never be realized," Peterson wrote, "but a Jefferson about whom politicians cease to contend, whose ideas suffer drastic erosion from all sides, and whose own history proves to be a rewarding field of study in itself—this figure invites the true scholar and begs the true historical discovery." In the academy, observed Peterson, the multiple Jeffersons of the party polemicists were already giving way to a new image of the culture hero—"the civilized man" with his multiplicity of interests and achievements.[1]

Peterson looked forward to the elaboration of a scholarly, nonpartisan Jefferson image. Historians no longer saw American history as a great, ongoing struggle between Jeffersonian democrats and Hamiltonian aristocrats, the "people" and the "interests." Indeed, as Peterson showed, this genealogy of the parties had always been somewhat suspect, and the confusion became complete when Democratic New Dealers invoked Jefferson's "progressive spirit" to justify their neo-Hamiltonian programs of state intervention: "After the Roosevelt Revolution, serious men stopped yearning for the agrarian utopia, politicians (and most historians too) laid aside the Jefferson-Hamilton dialogue, and almost no one any longer maintained the fiction that American government was run, or ought to be run, on the Jeffersonian model." The "disintegration of the Jeffersonian philosophy of government heralded the ultimate canonization of Jefferson."[2]

Peterson's *Jefferson Image* is superb cultural history but poor prophecy. This is not to say that historians have neglected Jefferson. When Peterson wrote, Dumas Malone was moving into high gear with his definitive six volume biography, *Jefferson and His Time* (1948–81).[3] The greatest monument to Jefferson scholarship, the comprehensive edition of the *Papers of Thomas Jefferson*, continues its stately progress, a full half century after it was

---

*This introduction is in part an updating of the author's "The Scholar's Jefferson," *William and Mary Quarterly*, L (1993), 671–699.

1. Merrill Peterson, *The Jefferson Image in the American Mind* (New York, 1960), 447, 453–454, 395–420.

2. Ibid., 375–376.

3. Dumas Malone, *Jefferson and His Time*, 6 vols. (Boston, 1948–81). See Merrill D. Peterson, "Dumas Malone: An Appreciation," *William and Mary Quarterly*, 3d ser., XLV (1988), 237–252.

launched.[4] Meanwhile, writing about Jefferson for both scholarly and general audiences has expanded exponentially.[5] Yet Jefferson's image is as controversial now as it ever has been.

Peterson underestimated the capacity of scholars to divide into hostile "parties," regardless of the state of party conflict in the larger political culture. The old history of the parties not only distorted Jefferson's image but also deflected more fundamental questions about the new nation's character. Identifying with either Jefferson or Alexander Hamilton reinforced the faith of historians and politicians alike in the vitality and future prospects of the American political system. But the proliferating "new" histories of the 1960s and 1970s opened up profound and troubling questions about the course of American history as advocates of new approaches and methodologies sought to reconstruct the field as a whole—in ways involving and affecting the image of Jefferson.

For students of Revolutionary and early national America, Jefferson remains a fascinating and contested figure. It is not simply a question of his ubiquity, or the massiveness of his archives or the historiographical tendency to revise the revisionists. The compulsion to characterize Jefferson reflects the convergence of important trends in the discipline and in the larger culture. The discrepancy between his idealistic professions and his membership in Virginia's slaveholding planter elite presents an interpretative challenge—and provokes scholars to moral judgments.

Controversy over the Jefferson image became particularly intense in the 1990s. In *The Long Affair*, the Irish writer Conor Cruise O'Brien explicitly challenges Jefferson's "place" in the nation's "symbolical architecture," portraying his subject as a philosophical terrorist and slaveholding racist.[6] While most critics denounced O'Brien for his interpretative excesses, well-received studies by respected scholars also questioned Jefferson's standing in the pantheon. Joseph J. Ellis's prize-winning *American Sphinx*, the best single-volume biography now available, focuses on the psychological strategies that enabled Jefferson to sustain a dangerously adolescent idealism that at least squinted toward terrorism.[7] Echoing another of O'Brien's arguments, Pauline Maier's *American Scripture* downplays Jefferson's role of "author" of the Declaration of Independence: in countless communities across the continent, ordinary Americans drafted their own declarations,

---

4. *The Papers of Thomas Jefferson*, ed. Julian P. Boyd et al. (Princeton, N.J., 1950–), has regained momentum under more recent editors. The most recently published volume, XXVII (1997), takes Jefferson to the end of his tenure of secretary of state in December 1793.

5. See Frank Shuffelton's "Bibliographic Essay" in Peterson, ed., *Thomas Jefferson: A Reference Biography* (New York, 1986), 453–479. The most complete bibliographies are Shuffelton, *Thomas Jefferson, Annotated Bibliography of Writings About Him, 1826–1980* (New York, 1983), and *Thomas Jefferson, 1989–1990: An Annotated Bibliography* (New York, 1990). The Shuffelton bibliographies are now on-line, at http://etext.lib.virginia.edu/jefferson/bibliog/.

6. Conor Cruise O'Brien, *The Long Affair: Thomas Jefferson and the French Revolution* (Chicago, 1996).

7. Joseph J. Ellis, *American Sphinx: The Character of Thomas Jefferson* (New York, 1997), 127–128.

anticipating and shaping the document Jefferson wrote and that the Continental Congress edited into its familiar, "scriptural" form. These writers all ask whether Jefferson really deserves his exalted position among the revolutionary founders, an even more urgent question in the wake of DNA tests suggesting the strong possibility that he conducted a long-standing sexual relationship with his slave Sally Hemings.[8]

For most commentators today, Jefferson's fitness for a national icon has been cast as a question of character. Though this certainly reflects our current predispositions, it is fair to suggest that Jefferson brought the character question on himself, for character was his own constant concern. He devoted his political life to exposing the secret machinations of "monocrats" and "aristocrats" while establishing a new republican regime based on "natural"—authentic and responsive—representation. Though he was an advocate of transparency, his modes of self-presentation left his private life opaque and elusive. The impulse to unmask Jefferson, to make sense out of his complex career, is a mark of his continuing significance in our public culture.[9]

The Character Issue

The Revolutionary period was a crucial transitional moment for Western moral theory and practice. This was the time when a universal human nature became recognized—or constructed—and when natural philosophers naturalized racial (and gender) differences. "Equality" and "nature," the key premises of Jeffersonian thought, were contemporaneous constructs. The appropriation and elaboration of these ideas helped Jefferson and his Revolutionary colleagues solve compelling problems as they established a new republic on the periphery of the "civilized" world, but it inevitably raised new ones.[10]

The dissonance of planter privilege with enlightened theory constitutes an illuminating text for this broad political and ideological transfor-

---

8. Eugene Foster et al., "Jefferson fathered slave's last child," *Nature*, 396 (5 Nov. 1998), 27–28. The title of this piece is misleading, as Foster emphasized in a subsequent communication: it is at least theoretically possible that someone else with Jefferson's DNA could account for the match between Jefferson's descendants and the descendants of Eston Hemings, one of Sally's children. Foster et al., "The Thomas Jefferson paternity case," ibid., 397 (7 Jan. 1999).

9. For further discussion see Jan E. Lewis and Peter S. Onuf, "American Synecdoche: Thomas Jefferson as Image, Icon, Character, and Self," *American Historical Review* 103 (1998), 125–136.

10. David Brion Davis, *The Problem of Slavery in Western Culture* (Ithaca, N.Y., 1966) and *The Problem of Slavery in the Age of Revolution, 1770–1823* (Ithaca, N.Y., 1975), 169–184; Winthrop Jordan, *White over Black: American Attitudes Toward the Negro, 1550–1812* (Chapel Hill, N.C., 1968), 429–481. See also Jack P. Greene, "All Men Are Created Equal: Some Reflections on the Character of the American Revolution," in Greene, *Imperatives, Behaviors, and Identities: Essays in Early American Cultural History* (Charlottesville, Va., 1992), 236–267; Charles A. Miller, *Jefferson and Nature: An Interpretation* (Baltimore, 1988); Thomas L. Haskell, "Capitalism and the Origins of the Humanitarian Sensibility, Part I," *AHR*, XC (1985), 339–361.

mation. The ways in which Jefferson resolved or perhaps more accurately simply lived with these conflicting demands constitute his "character." That character, for all its fascination, many present-day scholars find discomfiting, if not repellent. Jefferson's inner life, insofar as it can be recovered, manifests little evidence of distress, so thoroughly did he rationalize and repress his wants and griefs. Peterson writes that Jefferson was "an impenetrable man," a conclusion echoed in the title of Ellis's *Sphinx*.[11] A generation ago, when Fawn Brodie offered an "intimate history" of Jefferson, making what turns out to be a plausible case for the relationship with Sally Hemings, she was roundly castigated for unsubstantiated and implausible speculations.[12] But more recent writers, however they weighed in on the Hemings question, have operated under the assumption that the real Jefferson *can* be known. The most successful of these works, Andrew Burstein's *The Inner Jefferson*, a sensitive study of Jefferson as a literary sentimentalist, and Annette Gordon-Reed's *Thomas Jefferson and Sally Hemings*, an eloquent and exhaustive reconsideration of the evidence and arguments concerning the relationship, show that this will be no easy task, for these two Jeffersons don't seem to have too much in common.[13] But the effort to put Jefferson back together again, to make sense of his character, has already yielded impressive results. Denial of the possibility of Jefferson's miscegenous relationship—and of the centrality of slaveholding in all aspects of his life—has been the major obstacle to understanding. This obstacle has now been removed.

We know Jefferson better, but where does that leave us? Jefferson's characteristically judgmental frame of mind, along with the dualistic, not to say Manichaean, view of the world it reveals, tempts historians to judge him in turn, sometimes very harshly, on moral grounds. Critics underscore the discrepancy between the Declaration's appeal to natural rights and Jefferson's failure to do anything about slavery, at Monticello or anywhere else. However successful historians may be in explaining this apparent contradiction, Jefferson will continue to be a controversial figure as long as race remains the great and unresolved "American dilemma."[14] There is a

---

11. For Peterson's "mortifying confession" that Jefferson "remains for me, finally, an impenetrable man," see *Thomas Jefferson and the New Nation: A Biography* (New York, 1970), viii.

12. Fawn Brodie, *Thomas Jefferson: An Intimate History* (New York, 1974). The most extensive refutation of her charges is Virginius Dabney, *The Jefferson Scandals: A Rebuttal* (New York, 1981). For a fascinating account of this controversy and further citations see Scot A. French and Edward L. Ayers, "The Strange Career of Thomas Jefferson: Race and Slavery in American Memory, 1943–1993," in Onuf, ed., *Jeffersonian Legacies*, 418–456.

13. Andrew Burstein, *The Inner Jefferson: Portrait of a Grieving Optimist* (Charlottesville: University Press of Virginia, 1995); Annette Gordon-Reed, *Thomas Jefferson and Sally Hemings: An American Controversy* (Charlottesville, 1997).

14. The vast literature on Jefferson and slavery includes Robert McColley, *Slavery and Jeffersonian Virginia* (Urbana, Ill., 1964; 2d ed., 1973); William Cohen, "Thomas Jefferson and the Problem of Slavery," *Journal of American History*, LVI, (1969), 503–526; John Chester Miller, *The Wolf by the Ears: Thomas Jefferson and Slavery* (New York, 1977); Paul Finkelman, "Jefferson and Slavery: 'Treason Against the Hopes of the World,' " in Onuf, ed., *Jeffersonian Lega-*

powerful moral animus in present-day writing on the subject—an animus that sometimes strains scholarly standards of dispassionate investigation. But it would be a mistake to reject this literature as presentist, as it is a mistake to dismiss forays into Jefferson's private life as prurient and unseemly.[15] There is a powerful integrative impulse in both enterprises. It is precisely because historians want to make sense of Jefferson, because they want to grasp exactly what it was that the Revolutionary founders intended and accomplished, that they are contesting this terrain so passionately.

The slavery problem, for Revolutionaries generally and Jefferson in particular, has especially complicated our understanding of the Revolutionary transformation and brought moral questions to the fore. Why did Jefferson never take steps to dissociate himself—or, more to the point, his slaves—from the horns of his dilemma? Surely, nobody knew better than Jefferson, the revolutionary reformer, that exceptional, unnatural historical conditions are subject to change? Thus we confront the difficult image of the democratic founder who professed a profound hostility to slavery but could never extricate himself from an institution that guaranteed the welfare and well-being of his "country," Virginia.

Republicanism and Liberalism

Jefferson has always inspired controversy, among friends as well as foes. In his own lifetime, even Jeffersonians could invoke the master's authority for dizzyingly various ends. At his death, Peterson reports, his eulogists were hard-pressed to make sense out of him: "he remained an enigma, a figure of contradiction, a man of many faces."[16] For us, Jefferson's contradictions should be an opening to understanding. Consciousness of our own ambivalent situation—at the far side of the modernity Jefferson helped invent—should enable us to construct a more dynamic and compelling Jefferson image from the contradictory influences and impulses of a long life.

Exponents of the republican synthesis set the stage for a more complex and satisfying view of Jefferson by resituating him in the Revolutionary narrative. Their Jefferson is a champion not of liberal progress but of

---

cies, 181–221; Alexander O. Boulton, "The American Paradox: Jeffersonian Equality and Racial Science," *American Quarterly*, 47 (1995); Finkelman, *Slavery and the Founders: Race and Liberty in the Age of Jefferson* (Armonk, N.Y., 1996); and Onuf, "'To Declare Them a Free and Independant People:' Race, Slavery, and National Identity in Jefferson's Thought." *Journal of the Early Republic* 18 (1998), 1–46.

15. On "presentism" see Douglas L. Wilson, "Thomas Jefferson and the Character Issue," *Atlantic Monthly*, CCLXX (Nov. 1992), 62.

16. Peterson, *Jefferson Image*, 13. For a sampling of attitudes toward Jefferson among his contemporaries see the collection edited by Jack McLaughlin, *To His Excellency Thomas Jefferson: Letters to a President* (New York, 1991).

a revival of the ancient Athenian or Roman republic, conceived as an aristocracy of virtuous, educated citizens engaged in an ongoing politics, friendship, and intellectual conversation. Viewing Jefferson as a republican on these terms associates him with the Real Whigs in eighteenth-century British politics and in general with opposition to corruption, particularly the corruption supposedly endemic to British policy toward the colonies and corrosive of republican simplicity and virtue. A Jefferson of this sort would have little in him of John Locke, the spokesman for liberal political and scientific modernity. The liberty appropriate to classical republican aristocrats, of course, could translate into the egalitarian liberty proclaimed by modern liberal politics; and the learned intellectual discourse among republican citizens could become the scientific inquiry prized by modern liberalism. All this might synthesize the two Jeffersons who appear in recent historiography and explain perhaps how Jefferson the republican did contribute to the forming of an intellectual modernity he may not have imagined. But that synthesis is up to students of Jefferson who want to make it.

While the republican revisionists challenged the conventional depiction of Jefferson as the forward-looking inventor of American nationality,[17] they assigned him a conspicuous role as a history-minded defender of colonial rights and privileges.[18] Lance Banning's *The Jeffersonian Persuasion*, published in 1978, and Drew R. McCoy's *The Elusive Republic*, which appeared two years later, pointed Jefferson backward, emphasizing the anachronistic premises of his political thought and—more explicitly in McCoy's work—his confused and agonizing encounter with modernity.[19] In doing so, both writers betrayed an ambivalence about Jefferson's influence on the new American political order and about the salience of Jeffersonianism—with its legacy of Real Whig paranoia about abuses of governmental power—for the constructive tasks of state making in the new republic.

---

17. The key text is Bernard Bailyn, *The Ideological Origins of the American Revolution* (Cambridge, Mass., 1967). For progress reports on the historiography see Robert E. Shalhope, "Toward a Republican Synthesis: The Emergence of an Understanding of Republicanism in American Historiography," *WMQ*, 3d ser., XXIX (1972), 49–80, and "Republicanism in Early American Historiography," ibid., XXXIX (1982), 334–356; Joyce Appleby, ed., "Republicanism in the History and Historiography of the United States," special issue of *American Quarterly*, XXXVII (Fall 1985). For a provocative if perhaps premature postmortem see Daniel T. Rodgers, "Republicanism: The Career of a Concept," *JAH*, LXXIX (1992), 11–38.

18. See particularly the seminal contributions of H. Trevor Colbourn, "Thomas Jefferson's Use of the Past," *WMQ*, 3d ser., XV (1958), 56–70, and *The Lamp of Experience: Whig History and the Intellectual Origins of the American Revolution* (Chapel Hill, N.C., 1965), 158–184.

19. Lance Banning, *The Jeffersonian Persuasion: Evolution of a Party Ideology* (Ithaca, N.Y., 1978); Drew R. McCoy, *The Elusive Republic: Political Economy in Jeffersonian America* (Chapel Hill, N.C., 1980). Forrest McDonald, who argues most forcefully for Alexander Hamilton's modernizing political economy, is an enthusiastic exponent of the republicanized version of Jefferson. McDonald, *The Presidency of Thomas Jefferson* (Lawrence, Kans., 1976); *Alexander Hamilton: A Biography* (New York, 1979).

The revisionists' mixed feelings about Jeffersonianism is a function of their understanding of America's imminent transition toward a recognizably modern, liberal capitalist regime. For them, Jefferson was important, for better or worse, because he was oblivious to the shape of things to come. Critics have challenged the revisionists' displacement of the liberal tradition and their portrayal of Jefferson as a man at odds with his times.[20] Exponents of liberalism recast the Revolution in progressive, forward-looking terms, with Jefferson taking the lead role. Joyce Appleby's *Capitalism and a New Social Order*, which came out in 1984, seeks to remove Jefferson and his followers from the republican synthesis. Her Jeffersonians are not the fearful oppositionists depicted by Banning and McCoy but champions of a progressive "reconceptualization of human nature," Lockeans in politics and Smithians in economics. Embracing capitalism, the great solvent of the traditional order, they reject the authority of history. "This rejection of the past," Appleby concludes, "constitutes the most important element in the ideology of the victorious Jeffersonian Republicans."[21]

The echoes of the party struggles of the 1790s thus still reverberate in the academy. The quarrel now, as then, centers on the fundamental character of the new American regime. But it does not follow that we are doomed to perpetual reenactment of our primal political drama. In fact, exponents and critics of the republican synthesis have reached a working, if somewhat begrudging, consensus on once controversial questions. The liberal and republican Jeffersons may look in opposite directions, but they share a sense of the world-historical significance of the American Revolution.[22] Similarly, both Jeffersons offer a radical critique of the corruption of the old regime, inspired in the one case by an enlightened, liberal vision of the future and in the other by an idealized, republican vision of the past. Finally, the questions of character, virtue, and the relation between self-interest and the public good were equally central to republicanism and emergent liberalism—if these isms can be

20. See particularly Michael P. Zuckert, *Natural Rights and the New Republicanism* (Princeton, 1994) and Zuckert, *The Natural Rights Republic: Studies in the Foundation of the American Political Tradition* (Notre Dame, 1996).

21. Appleby, *Capitalism and a New Social Order: The Republican Vision of the 1790s* (New York, 1984), 81, 83, 79. Appleby's essays—including "The 'Agrarian Myth' in the Early Republic" (1982) and "What Is Still American in the Political Philosophy of Thomas Jefferson" (1982)—are collected in *Liberalism and Republicanism in the Historical Imagination* (Cambridge, 1992). For a sympathetic account of Jeffersonian political economy see John R. Nelson, Jr., *Liberty and Property: Political Economy and Policymaking in the New Nation, 1789–1812* (Baltimore, 1987).

22. On the importance of historical consciousness in the civic humanist tradition see particularly J. G. A. Pocock, *The Machiavellian Moment: Florentine Political Thought and the Atlantic Republican Tradition* (Princeton, N.J., 1975). Jay Fliegelman suggests that participants in the scholarly debate over the historical consciousness of putatively republican or liberal Revolutionary Americans "may be seen as schematizing a number of the late eighteenth-century dialectics" that he explores in *Declaring Independence: Jefferson, Natural Language, and the Culture of Performance* (Stanford, 1993), 186–187.

meaningfully distinguished at this period—and were particularly compelling at a time of political upheaval.[23]

The debate over republicanism thus has given us a better understanding of the range and relevance of political discourse in Revolutionary America. Since the advent of the republican synthesis, we have moved not in circles but in a closing spiral, liberal critics building on the revisionists' achievements and revisionists recasting republicanism in ways that accommodate and explain the radical initiatives and innovations that constituted revolutionary change. Revolutionary talk—a medley of appeals to hopes and fears, patriotic sacrifice and class interest, cosmopolitan aspirations and localist prejudices—was essential to the processes of mobilizing resistance, sustaining popular commitments, and constructing and legitimating new governments.[24] As a writer, Jefferson was fluent in all these idioms. His words bridged the great divide between an enlightened, elitist republic of letters and a new world of popular political speech in a democratizing republican society.

The implications of these historiographical developments for Jefferson's image are strikingly apparent in Gordon Wood's The Radicalism of the American Revolution, published in 1992.[25] Wood sees republicanism as a terminal phase of the "monarchical" old regime that prepared the way for a thoroughgoing democratization of American society. Genteel, enlightened republicans like Jefferson—poised on the cusp of modernity and facing both ways—were central figures in the Revolutionary transformation. Wood's Jefferson does not play the same central role in the history of American democracy as Appleby's Jefferson. For Wood, democratization is a great social and cultural transformation, precipitated by a Revolutionary republican elite whose assaults on the old regime jeopardized their own class position. Radicalism tells the story of democratic progress—the story first told by Jefferson, and then about him—in an appropriately ironic fashion, replete with unintended consequences. Jefferson and his fellow Revolutionaries were transitional figures, ambivalent about the radical changes they unleashed. From this perspective, Jefferson's ambivalence

23. For discussion of these diverse sources see Richard Vetterli and Gary Bryner, In Search of the Republic: Public Virtue and the Roots of American Government (Totowa, N.J., 1987), and the essay by Jean Yarbrough, "The Constitution and Character: The Missing Critical Principle?" in Herman Belz et al., eds., To Form a More Perfect Union: The Critical Ideas of the Constitution (Charlottesville, Va., 1992), 217–249. On Jefferson and character see Yarbrough, American Virtues: Thomas Jefferson on the Character of a Free People (Lawrence, Kan., 1998).

24. Onuf, "Reflections on the Founding: Constitutional Historiography in Bicentennial Perspective," WMQ, 3rd ser., 46 (1989), 341–375. For the ideological diversity of the founding era see James T. Kloppenberg, "The Virtues of Liberalism: Christianity, Republicanism, and Ethics in Early American Political Discourse," JAH, LXXIV (1987), 9–33; and Isaac Kramnick, "The 'Great National Discussion': The Discourse of Politics in 1787," WMQ, 3d ser., XLV (1988), 3–22.

25. The Radicalism of the American Revolution (New York, 1992). Wood's account of republicanism here departs significantly from his earlier emphasis on its "classical" premises in The

and inconsistency seem less the hallmarks of a flawed or superficial character than evidence of his central position in the new nation's drama, subject to the conflicting tendencies that made the Revolution radical.[26]

As the quintessential republican, Jefferson both embodied and envisioned fundamental changes in American society. It was his responsiveness to the historical moment, not his originality, that brought him to the fore. The conflicts and tensions Wood delineates are readily apparent throughout Jefferson's writings.

Herbert Sloan's explication of the 6 September 1789 letter to James Madison is a good example of what we can learn from a close reading of a Jefferson text. Jefferson here developed the "principle that the earth belongs to the living," that "by the law of nature, one generation is to another as one independent nation to another." No generation, he told Madison, was entitled to impose a burden of debt on its successors or to "make a perpetual constitution, or even a perpetual law." Jefferson's conversations with revolutionary reformers in France, his ongoing and deeply troubling experience with indebtedness, the centrality of the debt problem in the Real Whig oppositionist thought he espoused, and his passionate commitment to generational self-determination all contributed to this extraordinary formulation of a radical democratic constitutionalism. Sloan's point is that the historical contingencies were crucially important, and that for Jefferson the political was personal and the personal political. "In our effort to understand his letter to Madison," Sloan writes, we should not attempt to "isolate" the "private Jefferson [from] the Jefferson of high politics."[27]

Next to the Declaration of Independence, the Jefferson text that has most fascinated scholars is his *Notes on the State of Virginia.*[28] What is most remarkable about the literature on this omnium gatherum, never-completed bag of a book is the extraordinary range of formal interpretative schemes—legal, natural scientific, pedagogic, and others—that have been offered by critical readers.[29] That all these readings make some sense is indicative of the richness of the *Notes;* they also suggest that Jefferson did

---

Creation of the American Republic, 1776–1787 (Chapel Hill, N.C., 1969), esp. 46–90. On the break between classical and modern republicanism see Rahe, *Republics Ancient and Modern: Classical Republicanism and the American Revolution* (Chapel Hill, N.C., 1992), 573–616.

26. On Jefferson's disillusionment with democratic society see Wood's essay, "The Trials and Tribulations of Thomas Jefferson," in Onuf, ed., *Jeffersonian Legacies,* 395–417.

27. Herbert Sloan, "'The Earth Belongs in Usufruct to the Living,'" in Onuf, ed., *Jeffersonian Legacies,* 281–315, quotation on 282. For a fuller discussion of the debt problem see Sloan's *Principle and Interest: Thomas Jefferson and the Problem of Debt* (New York, 1995). The letter is reprinted in Chapter 3 (p. 127).

28. The most authoritative edition now in print is *Notes on the State of Virginia,* ed. William Peden (Chapel Hill, N.C., 1955). Excerpts, including the Queries cited in this paragraph, are reprinted in Chapter 2.

29. A sample of some of the more interesting essays includes Lee Quinby, "Thomas Jefferson: The Virtue of Aesthetics and the Aesthetics of Virtue," *AHR,* LXXXVII (1982), 337–356; Mitchell Breitweiser, "Jefferson's Prospect," *Prospects,* X (1985), 315–352; Robert A. Ferguson, "'Mysterious Obligation': Jefferson's Notes on the State of Virginia," *American Literature,* LII

not have the same control over his multiple voices that he usually displayed in his correspondence. In this extraordinary effort to conjure up in words his society and his place in it, the personal and the political are powerfully, and sometimes painfully, juxtaposed. Nothing, for example, could have been more painful and troubling than the radically incompatible characterizations of Virginia agriculturalists as virtuous and independent yeoman farmers (Query XIX, "Manufactures") and as despotic slave owners (Query XVIII, "Manners"). That Jefferson was profoundly troubled by an institution that violated the premises of his political philosophy and jeopardized the future of the commonwealth is apparent in his invocation of a "just" God, whose "justice cannot sleep for ever."

An undercurrent of malaise pervades the Notes and is by no means confined to the discussions of race and slavery. Jefferson's inventories and descriptions are offered in a hopeful, progressive spirit that anticipates a glorious future for Virginia and for America. Yet despair shadows this hope—despair that is not simply an expression of his chronic anxieties about popular slothfulness and ignorance but is more deeply grounded in a devastating judgment on himself and his slave owning countrymen.[30] The "numbing" process Lucia Stanton describes in his life with his own slaves, the scientific racism of the natural philosopher so conspicuously displayed in the Notes, and—in later life—righteous indignation at the crypto-Federalist centralizers who would "enslave" Virginia under the pretense of liberating her slaves are ways Jefferson would find to suspend or deflect that judgment. However much he suppressed his knowledge of his slaves' humanity or denied his own despotic impulses in a regime of benevolent rationality, the problem would never go away. It was a problem that writing the Notes—the great effort to represent his country to Europeans, to his countrymen, above all to himself—had brought to the fore. This was the tragic counterpoint, the lengthening shadow of Jefferson's great project to smash the despotism of the old regime and spread universal enlightenment through words—the liberating words that articulated natural rights principles, the words by which free men signified and constituted the affectionate, durable bonds of republican government.

Jefferson's story cannot be reduced to lifelong advocacy of a single principle. Looking both ways—toward an idealized Saxon past and toward a progressively enlightened future—Jefferson invites wildly contradictory

---

(1980), 381–406; Harold Hellenbrand, "Roads to Happiness: Rhetorical and Philosophical Design in Jefferson's Notes on the State of Virginia," *Early American Literature*, XX (1985), 3–23; Pamela Regis, "Jefferson and the Department of Man," in Regis, *Describing Early America: Bartram, Jefferson, Crèvecoeur, and the Rhetoric of Natural History* (DeKalb, Ill., 1992), chap. 3; and James W. Ceaser, *Reconstructing America: The Symbol of America in Modern Thought* (New Haven, 1997), 43–65.

30. Greene emphasizes the reformist thrust of Jefferson's *Notes on Virginia* and his contributions to "a positive sense of collective self for Virginia and Virginians" in "The Intellectual Reconstruction of Virginia in the Age of Jefferson," in Onuf, ed., *Jeffersonian Legacies*, 225–253, quotation on 250.

characterizations of his political thought.[31] What gave his project coherence, Jay Fliegelman convincingly argues in *Declaring Independence*, published in 1993, was a coincidental revolution in rhetoric and sensibility. Fliegelman's Jefferson is "a witness to, and conflicted participant in, a new affective understanding of the operations of language, one that reconceives all expression as a form of self-expression, as an opportunity as well as an imperative to externalize the self, to become self-evident."[32] Our lack of sympathy with Jefferson bespeaks our failure to appreciate the psychological tensions this imperative entailed: his poor performances in public speaking revealed a sensitive self-consciousness to the contradictory claims of self-construction and self-presentation in a democratizing political world. Jefferson's life at Monticello, as well as his performances on the great stage of public life, suggests ongoing inner conflicts—and ironic if not tragic outcomes—in full measure.

Self and Society

Jefferson's "self-evident" ideas about equality and natural society reflected the strenuous efforts of an ambitious young man to overcome arbitrary and artificial obstacles to his personal progress. Through reading, writing, and reflection, the bookish provincial sought to construct an intellectually consistent character and a satisfying image of himself in the world.[33] His almost monastic regimen enabled him to convert to an advantage his rustic isolation in Albemarle County: through his intellectual attainments, the natural philosopher gained access to the centers of enlightenment and power. Jefferson savored polite company and learned conversation, but these were the fruits of lifelong labors in the privacy of his study. A rigorous process of self-construction constituted the premise of the sociability he so cherished. It would be a sociability quickly associated with the republican tradition that imagines a patrician commonwealth, its citizens participating in a continuing life of discussion.

Jefferson's juvenile encounters with classical philosophy provided the models and texts that shaped his development. The classics did not merely

31. For treatments of Jefferson's political thought that demonstrate the range of interpretative possibilities see David N. Mayer, *The Constitutional Thought of Thomas Jefferson* (Charlottesville, 1994), and Richard K. Matthews, *The Radical Politics of Thomas Jefferson: A Revisionist View* (Lawrence, Kan., 1984). Throughout a long, turbulent career, Mayer's Jefferson remains a Real Whig constitutionalist; Matthews's Jefferson, a democratic radical. Garrett Ward Sheldon discusses Jeffersonian "liberalism" in the context of the imperial crisis and his "republicanism" in the setting of Revolutionary reform in Virginia; Sheldon, *The Political Philosophy of Thomas Jefferson* (Baltimore, 1991). In *Jefferson's Empire: The Language of American Nationhood* (Charlottesville, 2000), I emphasize the importance of federalism.
32. Fliegelman, *Declaring Independence*, 2. Jefferson's problems with public speaking are suggestively elaborated in successive sections on Patrick Henry, the great orator of the Revolution, and on "Social Leveling and Stage Fright," 94–140.
33. For a good introduction to Jeffersonian thought see Daniel J. Boorstin, *The Lost World of Thomas Jefferson*, with a new preface (Chicago, 1981; orig. pub., 1948). On Jefferson's reading see Douglas L. Wilson, "Jefferson's Library," and Meyer Reinhold, "The Classical World,"

offer philosophical consolations or a refuge from the real world. The Epicureans provided practical guidance in restraining unruly passions under a personal regime of balance and moderation. Jefferson's agenda in reading the classics was to make sense of his circumstances and to secure a philosophical ground for his forward-looking personal and political projects. The philosophers' injunctions to self-control, the life of reason, and the passionate friendship of enlightened souls—all constituted a script for self-making and world-making.[34]

However much Jefferson mined classical sources for building materials, nothing could be more modern than his self-construction project. He was no retrograde pastoralist; nor when he celebrated "those who labour in the earth [as] the chosen people of God" was he invoking the disinterested virtue of classical citizenship: he was talking about his rights-conscious neighbors.[35] The citizen's participation in affairs of state was not an end itself for Jefferson but a means of curbing state power. Jefferson did not have much good to say about cities, but this was because these were the prime sites for old regime corruption, not because he rejected urbanity itself or the progress of commercial civilization.[36] Yet it would be a mistake to conclude that Jefferson's modern uses of classical sources made him— or any of his fellow citizens in the Enlightenment's republic of letters—a fully modern man. Where Jefferson was most self-consciously modern—his apotheosis of reason, his naturalistic epistemology, his crusade for universal enlightenment and liberation—is where he now seems most characteristically a man of his time, not ours.[37]

Paul K. Conkin argues that Jefferson's intellectual quest was grounded in Judeo-Christian cosmology and inspired by hopes for the progressive enlightenment of his countrymen. His laborious compilations of Bible extracts that were free from the mystifications of priestcraft represented his

in Peterson, ed., *Jefferson, A Reference Biography*, 157–179, 135–156; Charles B. Sanford, *Thomas Jefferson and His Library: A Study of His Literary Interests and of the Religious Attitudes Revealed by Relevant Titles in His Library* (Hamden, Conn., 1977); Wilson, "Jefferson and the Republic of Letters," in Onuf, ed., *Jeffersonian Legacies*, 50–76; and Burstein, *The Inner Jefferson*, 42–67.

34. On Jefferson and the philosophers see Karl Lehmann, *Thomas Jefferson, American Humanist* (New York, 1947); Carl J. Richard, "A Dialogue with the Ancients: Thomas Jefferson and Classical Philosophy and History," *Journal of the Early Republic*, IX (1989), 431–455; and Richard, *The Founders and the Classics: Greece, Rome, and the American Enlightenment* (Cambridge, Mass., 1994).

35. Wilson, "The American *Agricola*: Jefferson's Agrarianism and the Classical Tradition," *South Atlantic Quarterly*, LXXX (1981), 339–354; Paul Rahe, "Thomas Jefferson's Machiavellian Political Science," *The Review of Politics*, 57 (1995), 449–481. Wilson's piece is an important corrective to Leo Marx's influential account of Jeffersonian pastoralism in *The Machine in the Garden: Technology and the Pastoral Ideal* (New York, 1964). The Jefferson quotation is from Query XIX of *Notes*, reprinted in Chapter 2 (p. 89).

36. Onuf, *Jefferson's Empire*, chap. 2; Thomas Bender, *Toward an Urban Vision: Ideas and Institutions in Nineteenth Century America* (Lexington, Ky., 1975), 3–51.

37. Charles A. Miller, *Jefferson and Nature*. See also Joyce Appleby's *Without Resolution: The Jeffersonian Tensions in American Nationalism*, Harmsworth Inaugural Lecture (Oxford, 1992). The "Jeffersonian tension," she writes, results from the "confounding of facts and ideals. America's natural-rights philosophy did not just express aspirations; it purported to explain reality"; ibid., 17.

lifelong effort to reconcile this cosmology with his fundamental ethical values and philosophical commitments.[38] Thus he came to view "Jesus as the foremost moral reformer in human history," Eugene Sheridan writes, and this "demythologized," primitive Christianity was—or should have been—the bedrock of republican virtue.[39] Jefferson, in this respect at least, was profoundly out of tune with his countrymen. His prediction that "there is not a *young man* now living in the United States who will not die an Unitarian" could not have been further from the mark.[40] Blinded by faith in reason, he was baffled by the spread of evangelical sects that preyed, he thought, on popular credulity and ignorance. "I am of a sect by myself, as far as I know," he ruefully concluded in 1819.[41]

Jefferson sought to harmonize the gospels with classical philosophy and ethics in order to promote enlightenment and republican government. Ideally, his labors would set an example for others, but their primary function was to construct and reinforce his sense of himself; his sense of self was predicated on preserving his privacy and remaining "a sect by myself." Jefferson had no interest in publicizing his religious views or in aligning himself with anybody else's sect: throughout his life he was hostile to organized religion. The tension between his efforts to achieve harmony in society and politics—the philosophical ground and expression of Jefferson's conception of natural sociability—and the imperatives of privacy and personal autonomy was characteristic. The sentimentalist who espoused authenticity and transparency was always reluctant to expose his most serious thoughts.

Analysis of Jefferson's reading habits gets us closer to his fundamental values and assumptions. A fire that destroyed the family home Shadwell and most of the young Jefferson's personal papers left little evidence about his early life. This lacuna helps explain why his personality seems so elusive, for biographers generally shape their subjects' character from the homely details of their early years. But we do know quite a bit about the presumably formative reading experiences of the bookish young Jefferson,

38. Paul K. Conkin, "Religious Pilgrimage of Jefferson," in Onuf, ed., *Jeffersonian Legacies*, 19–49, quotation at *Jefferson's Extracts from the Gospels: "The Philosophy of Jesus" and "The Life and Morals of Jesus,"* ed. Dickinson W. Adams, *The Papers of Thomas Jefferson*, 2d ser. (Princeton, N.J., 1983). The fullest treatment is Sanford, *The Religious Life of Thomas Jefferson* (Charlottesville, Va., 1984). For a discussion of the drafting of Jefferson's first compilation (Apr. 1803) see Constance B. Schulz, "'Of Bigotry in Politics and Religion': Jefferson's Religion, the Federalist Press, and the Syllabus," *Virginia Magazine of History and Biography*, XCI (1983), 73–91. The Syllabus is reprinted in Chapter 5 (p. 188).

39. Sheridan, "Introduction," *Jefferson's Extracts from the Gospels*, 3–42, quotation at 42.

40. Jefferson to Dr. Benjamin Waterhouse, 26 June 1822, reprinted in Chapter 6 (p. 247).

41. Jefferson to Ezra Stiles Ely, 25 June 1819, quoted in Sheridan, "Introduction," *Jefferson's Extracts from the Gospels*, 42. For discussion of how Jefferson edited "The Life and Morals of Jesus" to promote his "ideals of social harmony and democracy" see Susan Bryan, "Reauthorizing the Text: Jefferson's Scissor Edit of the Gospels," *Early Am. Lit.*, XXII (1987), 19–42, quotation on 30. On the progress of evangelical religion in this period that emphasizes surprising affinities with Jeffersonianism see Nathan O. Hatch, *The Democratization of American Christianity* (New Haven, Conn., 1989).

painstakingly reconstructed in Douglas L. Wilson's edition of the Literary Commonplace Book. Jefferson's extracts from his reading of the 1760s and early 1770s began with classical authors and English poets he read before 1763, continued from 1762 to 1766 with his law studies and "most of the Greek entries," and concluded with his immersion in "poetry, classical and contemporary," during the period from 1768 to 1772 or 1773 when he set up his legal practice. Thereafter, as the imperial crisis deepened, poetry gave way to history and politics. Wilson suggests that the Literary Commonplace Book was "a deeply personal notebook with direct connections to the emotional events and preoccupations of [Jefferson's] formative years."[42]

In the pages of his commonplace book, the young philosopher first confronted disappointment in love and the death of a beloved friend; here he first rehearsed the great contest between Head and Heart.[43] Jefferson's commonplacing, Kenneth A. Lockridge argues, reveals his deepest conflicts. Lockridge reads the cluster of misogynistic extracts as Jefferson's "tirades" against his mother's domination and against female power generally; they express pervasive anxieties—and "patriarchal rage"—characteristic of a provincial gentry-in-the-making. Rhys Isaac culls the same materials for the "stories" out of which Jefferson fashioned an idealized conception of domesticity that resolved or suppressed his adolescent conflicts.[44]

The adult Jefferson had little time for poetry or for exploring the darker recesses of his psyche. But, as Burstein shows in *The Inner Jefferson*, the enlightened autodidact continued to fashion himself—and his world—through a regimen of reading and writing.[45] Jefferson's legal practice thus constituted the crucial link between adolescent reading and adult writing.[46] Reading opened up the great world for Jefferson; writing enabled him to take a leading role in its revolutionary transformation. Yet he always longed to return to Monticello, where the never-ending process of building-up and tearing-down engaged his deepest interest—and drained his financial resources. Jefferson's sense of himself was most fully ex-

---

42. "Introduction," *Jefferson's Literary Commonplace Book*, ed. Wilson, *The Papers of Thomas Jefferson*, 2d ser. (Princeton, N.J., 1989), 3–20, quotations on 8, 15–16. See also Wilson, "Thomas Jefferson's Early Notebooks," *WMQ*, 3d ser., XLII (1985), 433–452.

43. For the famous dialogue between "Head" and "Heart," see Jefferson to Maria Cosway, 12 October 1786, reprinted in Chapter 3 (p. 108).

44. Kenneth A. Lockridge, *On the Sources of Patriarchal Rage: The Commonplace Books of William Byrd and Thomas Jefferson and the Gendering of Power in the Eighteenth Century* (New York, 1992); Rhys Isaac, "The First Monticello," in Onuf, ed., *Jeffersonian Legacies*, 77–108.

45. Burstein, *The Inner Jefferson*, passim.

46. Dewey, *Thomas Jefferson, Lawyer* (Charlottesville, Va., 1986); on Jefferson's reading as a student see 9–17. Though he never appeared in court after August 1774, the honing of "his forensic and writing skills" and the "assurance" he gained as a lawyer set the stage for his public career. The revisal of the laws was the centerpiece of his reform program for republican Virginia. See Peterson, *Jefferson and the New Nation*, 97–165, and Hellenbrand, *The Unfinished Revolution: Education and Politics in the Thought of Thomas Jefferson* (Newark, Del., 1990). For a sampling of the laws reported by Jefferson's committee, see Chapter 1 (p. 47).

pressed in the construction of his mountaintop home and of the family life it contained. Isaac suggests that Jefferson sought to create "a place both of intimate domesticity and of more comprehensive sociability . . . of contemplative retreat and of continuing resort." The tension between Jefferson's private and his public world was prefigured in these intentions.[47] In later life that tension was most fully expressed in his reaction to the rancorous partisanship that came to characterize national politics in the 1790s. As Jefferson moved forward on the public stage, Jan Lewis argues, he was constantly drawn back to the consolations of Monticello and the love of his daughters and their families. The adult Jefferson's domestic idyll, his storied home, mobilized youthful fantasies to salve the wounds of public life.[48] But as countless friends, allies, and admirers visited Monticello, daughter Martha complained that Jefferson's sociability compromised the private enjoyment of his family life. The tension was basic to Jefferson's self-conception and to his ongoing negotiations with the world that defined him.[49]

Jack McLaughlin's history of Monticello's construction offers glimpses into Jefferson's private life and character. Other lives were also involved in this project, as McLaughlin's discussion of the workforce reveals.[50] Isaac suggests that Jefferson's vision of domestic bliss depended not only on exploiting the unremitting labor of his slaves but also on suppressing the African-Virginian songs and stories he had heard as a child.[51] Lucia Stanton in her important new work on the slave community at Monticello explores the relationships between Jefferson and his slaves. Stanton reconstructs the circles of the African-American community at Monticello, moving outward from the light-skinned Hemingses, who were said to have been relatives of Jefferson's wife and dominated the most skilled and trusted positions, to the industrial workers Jefferson directly supervised, and to the great majority of agricultural laborers supervised by overseers. What is remarkable about these circles is Jefferson's instrumental approach to them, the general absence of affect and human feeling that his

---

47. Isaac, "First Monticello," 90.

48. Lewis, "'The Blessings of Domestic Society': Thomas Jefferson's Family and the Transformation of American Politics," in Onuf, ed., *Jeffersonian Legacies*, 109–146. On the importance of "home" to Virginians of in this period see Lewis, *The Pursuit of Happiness: Family and Values in Jefferson's Virginia* (New York, 1983), 210: "The strands of evangelical religion, republican belief, and domestic thought combine; in the era after the American Revolution, the pursuit of happiness took men and women home."

49. His answer to the privacy problem was to recapitulate it by retreating periodically from Monticello to the other home he built for himself sixty miles away at Poplar Forest.

50. Jefferson's slaves "poured their energies into an edifice that epitomized the taste and refinement of the class that enslaved them and of the man whose ringing phrases had declared freedom for all mankind"; McLaughlin, *Jefferson and Monticello: The Biography of a Builder* (New York, 1988), 94–145, quotation on 145. See also the suggestive comments in Breitweiser, "Jefferson's Prospect," 317: "Jefferson's instrumental innovations at Monticello are aimed at projecting a *sprezzatura* that denies the labor that permits Monticello to be: it is a magic place."

51. Isaac, "First Monticello," 100–101.

very occasional expressions of sentiment only cast into relief. Most concerned with sustaining orderly conditions and maximizing productivity, Jefferson did not sentimentalize slave ownership. The contrast with his ideas about domesticity and sociability within the circles of his white family and friends could not be starker.[52]

Jefferson's life at Monticello was predicated on the fundamental distinction between white domesticity and black slavery. His voluminous correspondence provided the crucial link between home and wider world and a more expansive social setting for his "self-fashioning."[53] Letter writing was also—and above all else—the medium of extending and sustaining his widening circle of friends, the practical expression of the sociability that grounded his political philosophy and shaped his political practice.[54] As he told his future foe Noah Webster, Jr., in 1790, "No republic is more real than that of letters."[55]

The Jefferson archive provides extraordinarily rich testimony to his affectionate feelings for his vast network of friends. Jefferson addresses his correspondent as an "equal"; his concessions to the correspondent's predilections—or gender—presume a common ground to be illuminated and developed in future correspondence.[56] In other words, the letter itself—a tender or reaffirmation of friendship between equals—is both means and end for Jefferson, the practical embodiment of the republican idea. But the connection between letter writing, self-expression, and the fractious political life of the new American republic was troublesome for Jefferson. As Wilson observes, the imperatives of partisan politics led Jefferson to secrecy and concealment: "He could conscript others to pseudonymous pamphleteering and newspaper writing," and "he could even speak past his correspondents to an interested posterity . . . but he seems to have

---

52. Lucia Stanton, "'Those Who Labor for My Happiness': Thomas Jefferson and His Slaves," in Onuf, ed., *Jeffersonian Legacies*, 147–180. She makes good use of James A. Bear and Stanton, eds., *Thomas Jefferson's Memorandum Books*, *The Papers of Thomas Jefferson*, 2d ser., 2 vols. (Princeton, 1997).

53. See Burstein, *The Inner Jefferson*; Wilson, "Jefferson and the Republic of Letters," 50–76; and Robert Dawidoff, "Man of Letters," in Peterson, ed., *Jefferson: A Reference Biography*, 181–198. For a study of self-fashioning that emphasizes the importance of language see Stephen Greenblatt, *Renaissance Self-Fashioning: From More to Shakespeare* (Chicago, 1980).

54. For a good example of how Jefferson sought to build political alliances through correspondence, see his letter to Elbridge Gerry, 26 January 1799, reprinted in Chapter 4 (p. 163).

55. Jefferson to Webster, 4 Dec. 1790, in Boyd, ed., *Jefferson Papers*, XVIII, 132. Garry Wills may have overrated Hutcheson's influence, and underrated Locke's, in explicating the Declaration, but he is certainly right to emphasize the social aspect of "happiness" in his *Inventing America: Jefferson's Declaration of Independence* (New York, 1978), 149–164, 248–265. On the importance of "feelings" and "sympathetic identification" as fundamental social bonds see Fliegelman, *Declaring Independence*, 35–65.

56. According to Frank Shuffelton, the "republic of letters" could only claim "to universality . . . if it allowed for the participation of both genders, although ideally it would allow for the expression in one person of that postconventional morality able to shift with ease from the viewpoint of one to the other"; Shuffelton, "In Different Voices: Gender in the American Republic of Letters," *Early Am. Lit.*, XXV (1990), 301. See also Burstein, *The Inner Jefferson*, chap. 4.

found it next to impossible to direct his writing squarely at the public."[57] However "real" it might be to Jefferson, the "republic" that he constituted through his correspondence had to be preserved inviolate—as he guarded the privacy of his home—from the conflicts of political life. At the same time, Jefferson's correspondence—like his home—constituted the center of a busily social and deeply political world. It was a paradox, like so many in Jefferson's life, that could be reconciled only by denial—in this case, denial that Jefferson and his allies pursued their own interested ends through partisan political action.

The relationship between Jefferson's two "republics" was less a problem for Jefferson the visionary reformer than for Jefferson the statesman-politician. As Harold Hellenbrand argues in his book on Jefferson and education, Jefferson could fashion acceptable roles for himself as the proponent of republican enlightenment that did not violate his fundamental principles. By thinking of the republic "in familial terms," and not the terms of self-promotion and partisan interests, he could sustain an apolitical conception of republican leadership. Hellenbrand asserts that Jefferson "thought of his policies as instruments of moral improvement that were understandable as such by reason. He functioned as the father/teacher in the republic; in his rhetoric, he played the role of the nation's mentor."[58]

The mentor role figures prominently in Jefferson's correspondence. It helped resolve one of the most troubling and dangerous questions of his personal and political life: how to establish an affectionate relationship between the generations that did not compromise the equality and moral autonomy of necessarily dependent sons. The authority of the mentor is temporary and contingent; it is based on the sentimental, familial premise that the good father sublimates self-interest on behalf of the child. If monarchy and aristocracy are simply the most extreme, legally institutionalized forms of generational tyranny, the fundamental republican imperative of equality demands the ultimate elimination of public debts, periodic constitutional revision, and self-denying father-mentors who equip their sons for an enlightened future. This self-denial is a form of self-construction: Jefferson expected republican fathers (who would not be "aristocrats") to take the essential role in the parade of generations (the progress of civilization) as exemplars and teachers who would wield parental love and filial gratitude to make their own sons into self-controlled, self-constructing republican fathers. There is more bourgeois father than "Patriot King" (who, after all, never abdicates) in this conception of republican leadership.[59]

57. Wilson, "Jefferson and the Republic of Letters," 73.
58. Hellenbrand, *Unfinished Revolution*, 121. For further discussion of Jefferson's educational thought see Pangle and Pangle, *Learning of Liberty*, chaps. 6, 13; and Joseph F. Kett, "Education," in Peterson, ed., *Jefferson: A Reference Biography*, 233–251.
59. On the influence of Bolingbroke's ideas about patriot kingship on the first presidents, including Jefferson, see Ralph Ketcham, *Presidents above Parties* (Chapel Hill, N.C., 1984). The

Letter writing defined the parameters of Jefferson's world. He assumed different voices in performing different roles as a correspondent, but all expressed his fundamental belief in progress: his young charges would achieve a self-disciplined happiness; his countrymen would see their own true interests more clearly; and enlightenment would expand across the world. Historians who look for disclosures of an authentic self behind these many voices and roles will be frustrated. Jefferson's self is in his writing, and his fundamental commitments to equality, consent, and civility inform all his varied self-representations.

Statecraft

Jefferson's writings exercise a continuing fascination because they reflect and represent fundamental, unresolved problems in his political thought and practice as well as his private life. Our sense of these problems is not simply a function of anachronistic moralizing. Jeffersonian contradictions were abundantly apparent to contemporaries who were excluded or resisted inclusion in the widening circle of Republican friends who seized the reins of power in the electoral "Revolution of 1800." These contradictions would also become apparent to Jefferson's legatees, if not to Jefferson himself, as the nation blundered into a second, nearly disastrous war with Britain.

The discrepancies between Jefferson's idealized vision of the republic and his performances in office have been the subject of a large critical literature. Following the lead of critics in Jefferson's own time, Leonard Levy has emphasized the disjunction between his libertarian precepts and his resort to governmental coercion to muzzle—or at least chill—Federalist editors and, much more dangerously, to enforce his disastrous embargo on foreign trade in 1807 and 1808.[60] John Larson argues persuasively that the strict constructionist constitutionalism that served the Republicans so well in opposition crippled their efforts to promote the internal improvements they knew were essential to securing a fragile union.[61] Even Appleby, Jefferson's most eloquent proponent today, worries that the "fusion of democracy and capitalism" over which Jefferson originally presided has "raised formidable barriers to the public oversight of economic affairs"

---

logical incompatibility of these conceptions of paternal authority is more apparent in retrospect than in the experience of Revolutionary Americans. For analyses of the generational problem in this period see Fliegelman, *Prodigals and Pilgrims: The American Revolution against Patriarchal Authority* (New York, 1982), esp. 40–51, on "pedagogues," and Melvin Yazawa, *From Colonies to Commonweath: Familial Ideology and the Beginnings of the American Republic* (Baltimore, 1985), esp. 131–132 on Jefferson's educational ideas.

60. Leonard Levy, *Jefferson and Civil Liberties: The Darker Side* (Cambridge, Mass., 1963). See also Burton Spivak, *Jefferson's English Crisis: Commerce, Embargo, and the Republican Revolution* (Charlottesville, Va., 1979).

61. John Larson, "Jefferson's Union and the Problem of Internal Improvements," in Onuf, ed., *Jeffersonian Legacies*, 340–369. See also Joseph H. Harrison, Jr., "Sic Et Non: Thomas Jefferson and Internal Improvement," *J. Early Republic*, VII (1987), 335–349.

and to the continuing vitality and viability of the "democratic forms" that were liberating in his time.[62]

The ascendancy of a strict constructionist constitutionalism born of a fear of power subverted positive government for public purposes, but Jeffersonians could overcome their constitutional scruples when the purposes seemed sufficiently compelling. The Louisiana Purchase is the prime case in point, violating the fundamental principles that were, as Henry Adams writes, "the breath of his political life.[63] There were always exceptions and limits to the principles that Jeffersonians articulated in such absolute, unlimited terms. What would come to be called the new nation's "manifest destiny" to spread across the continent thus trumped any lingering concerns about the rights of native Americans or, for that matter, of neighboring European colonies under the law of nations.[64]

The most pernicious aspect of Jeffersonian foreign policy, Robert W. Tucker and David C. Hendrickson argue in *Empire of Liberty*, was the conflation of a vaulting idealism with a willingness to employ any means, however devious, to promote American interests. Self-righteous "moralism . . . not only constituted the central aspect of [Jefferson's] diplomatic outlook but is also identifiable as the primary corrupting factor within it." "Unable to adjust to the existing world," Jeffersonians set the pattern for the characteristically American oscillation between "withdrawal from that world" and "the attempt to reform it by imposing one's will on it."[65] Paradoxically, this self-deluding "idealism" justified a disregard for the rights of others, even—as in the case of the black rebels of Santo Domingo—when they invoked the Jeffersonian rhetoric of self-determination.

The theme that runs through all such attacks on Jefferson's record is that inflated, idealistic rhetoric was at odds with realistic assessments of policy alternatives, authorized massive disregard for the rights of others at home and abroad, and precluded the development of the kind of civic life that could alone secure the promise of republican self-government to future generations. The critics' juxtaposition of Jefferson's words and deeds points to some of the central interpretative issues. Whatever else he

---

62. Appleby, "Jefferson and His Complex Legacy," in Onuf, ed., *Jeffersonian Legacies*, 1–16, quotation at 15.

63. Henry Adams, *History of the United States of America during the First Administration of Thomas Jefferson*, 2 vols. (New York, 1889), bk. 2, 89.

64. Albert K. Weinberg, *Manifest Destiny: A Study of Nationalist Expansionism in American History* (Baltimore, 1935), 11–42; Alexander DeConde, *This Affair of Louisiana* (Baton Rouge, La., 1976). For a nuanced account of Jeffersonian Indian policy, emphasizing the unintended consequences of good intentions, see Bernard W. Sheehan, *Seeds of Extinction: Jeffersonian Philanthropy and the American Indian* (Chapel Hill, 1973); see also Onuf, *Jefferson's Empire*, chap. 1.

65. Robert W. Tucker and David C. Hendrickson, *Empire of Liberty: The Statecraft of Thomas Jefferson* (New York, 1990), 179, 247. For another powerful indictment of Jeffersonian foreign policy, emphasizing the distorting effects of Jefferson's Anglophobia and a doctrinaire commitment to commercial sanctions, see Doron S. Ben-Atar, *The Origins of Jeffersonian Commercial Policy and Diplomacy* (London, 1992). A less critical and more balanced account of Jeffersonian foreign policy, focusing on the importance of securing the union, appears in James E. Lewis, Jr., *The American Union and the Problem of Neighborhood: The United States and the Collapse of the Spanish Empire, 1783–1829* (Chapel Hill, 1998).

was, Jefferson was no hypocrite in the conventional sense; as an exponent of "natural speech" and "self-evident" truths, he did not deploy glittering phrases with a cynical, instrumental disregard for what he took to be their meanings.[66] The disjunction of speech and act, so apparent to us, does not necessarily reveal a flawed character. It is nonetheless true that the self Jefferson fashioned and the ways he constructed and conceived his private world and public career have had momentous, often unintended, and sometimes tragic implications and consequences.

Jefferson's antipathy to political life—"a dreary scene where envy, hatred, malice, revenge and all the worse passions of men are marshalled, to make one another as miserable as possible"—is well known. If Jefferson was the father of the first modern political party, it was not a paternity he happily acknowledged.[67] When, at his first inaugural, he said, "we are all republicans, we are all federalists," he was seeking to overcome and banish party divisions. Parties were anathema to Jefferson because they set up artificial and corrupt barriers among representatives of the people who should be acting together for the common good. Ominously, party divisions tended to replicate and exacerbate sectional animosities. Jefferson therefore invoked a transcendent commitment to "Federal and Republican principles, our attachment to union and representative government."[68]

Good republicans fostered peace and harmony, not the violent animosities that partisans promoted and exploited. Partisanship, the antithesis and negation of friendship, jeopardized the affectionate bonds that sustained republican government. But Jeffersonian ideas of friendship and sociability, though hostile to party, also contributed to Jefferson's great successes in party leadership. As James Sterling Young shows in *The Washington Community*, a social history of the process of governance in the new national capital, Jefferson had a genius for drawing congressmen into his charmed circle and for achieving his political goals through indirection and gentle persuasion. "Friendship"—the close personal ties of congressional agents who took charge of key legislation, the receptive predisposition of his dinner guests—was instrumental, the functional equivalent of a more complex, and inevitably hierarchical, party organization.[69]

The "irony" of Jefferson's antipartisan politics, Michael Lienesch sug-

---

66. Fliegelman, *Declaring Independence*.

67. Jefferson to Martha Jefferson Randolph, 8 February 1798, quoted and discussed in Lewis, "Blessings of Domestic Society," 114. The best account of the political culture of the 1790s is Joanne B. Freeman, "Affairs of Honor: Political Combat and Political Culture in the Early American Republic" (Ph.D. dissertation, University of Virginia, 1997). See also Richard Hofstadter, *The Idea of a Party System* (Berkeley and Los Angeles, Calif., 1970), 122–128; and Robert M. S. McDonald, "Jefferson & America: Episodes in Image Formation" (Ph.D. dissertation, University of North Carolina, 1998).

68. Jefferson's First Inaugural Address, 4 March 1801, reprinted in Chapter 5 (p. 175).

69. James Sterling Young, *The Washington Community, 1800–1828* (New York, 1966), 128–131, 163–181. See also Noble E. Cunningham, Jr., *The Process of Government Under Jefferson* (Princeton, N.J., 1978), and McDonald, *Presidency of Thomas Jefferson*.

gests, was that it intensified partisanship by opening up the political process and identifying popular sovereignty with "organized public opinion." This new sort of partisanship was supposed to merge governors and governed, representatives and represented, thus achieving the kind of transparency and authenticity that "natural language" would bring to public discourse.[70] Thus, when Republican oppositionists called for a return to the "principles of the revolution of 1776," they were seeking to show things as they really were, to unmask the villains, and to enable good republicans to recognize one another. Their own motives were self-evidently above reproach, for they sought only to restore the affectionate bonds of union on which the survival of the republic depended.[71]

For modern skeptics, such claims can only seem disingenuous and cynical—as they did in Jefferson's time to his Federalist opponents. But Jeffersonians were simply projecting into the realm of popular politics the precepts of the enlightened republic of letters. They believed that a true representation of the people's will was a powerful revolutionary force that would ultimately banish the mystifications and misrepresentations that sustained monarchical rule. The republican millennium was postponed during the 1790s, it was true, as artful aristocrats exploited popular credulity and used the new federal government to pander to selfish interests. Such setbacks did not deter the Jeffersonians but drove them to redouble their efforts to expose the malign motives of insidious opponents who merely pretended to be republicans. The conviction that Federalist machinations jeopardized the survival of the republic was powerfully confirmed by blatant assaults on civil liberties in the Alien and Sedition acts. Intoxicated with their own power, or so it seemed to strict republicans, Federalists stripped off their own disguises—and stood condemned.

Revisionist historians have illuminated the hopes and fears that animated Jefferson and his followers. Jeffersonian visions of the progress of political civilization were counterposed to chronic anxieties for the future of republican government. Imaginary networks of conspirators against liberty constituted the model—perhaps more accurately, the antitype—for the Revolutionary band of brothers who had fought for Independence and now, as the "particular friends" of Jefferson and Madison, sought to redeem republican government from its secret enemies. The darker, fearful side of this Jeffersonian Persuasion has been delineated by Lance Banning. More recently, Gordon Wood and Jay Fliegelman have emphasized the progressive and optimistic dimensions of Revolutionary thought

---

70. Michael Lienesch, "Thomas Jefferson and the American Democratic Experience: The Origins of the Partisan Press, Popular Political Parties, and Organized Public Opinion," in Onuf, ed., *Jeffersonian Legacies*, 316–339; Fliegelman, *Declaring Independence.*
71. James Morton Smith, *Freedom's Fetters: The Alien and Sedition Laws and American Civil Liberties* (Ithaca, N.Y., 1956). On the crisis of the late 1790s, see also Stanley Elkins and Eric McKitrick, *The Age of Federalism* (New York, 1993) and James Roger Sharp, *American Politics in the Early Republic: The New Nation in Crisis* (New Haven, 1993).

and sensibility.[72] Implicit in the unmasking of political enemies was the promise of a world without masks, a politics of authenticity and feeling in which interests and motives would be transparent and a true, unmediated representation would be possible. The goal was unattainable, even when the monocrats were routed: politicians would simply learn to wear more democratic masks as they appealed to an expanding electorate.

The American founders are celebrated for their gritty realism, for their immunity to the utopian aspirations that corrupted and destroyed the French Revolution. Their revolutionary optimism was predicated not on the exercise but on the restraint of power. The contrast between the American Revolution of 1776—or Jefferson's "Revolution of 1800"—and the bloody debacle in France is certainly striking. If Jefferson occasionally gave vent to sanguinary sentiments, he showed no inclination to extermi-nate his enemies when he gained power: "let them stand undisturbed as monuments of the safety with which error of opinion may be tolerated where reason is left free to combat it."[73]

The glib explanation for the peaceful transfer of power is that this was yet another instance—albeit a happy one—of the characteristically Jeffer-sonian discrepancy between talk and action. But Jefferson remained con-stitutionally averse to the abuse of power, an aversion that his years in opposition reinforced. The point of his "Revolution" was to banish forever the possibility that the power of the central government would jeopardize the rights of states or citizens. Such consolidation of authority was incom-patible with liberty, and liberty was the basis of union. Recognizing the primacy of these affectionate ties and committed to the fundamental prin-ciples of equality and consent, the triumphant Republicans would exer-cise power only to secure the broader sphere of natural society and free exchange against the depredations of the privileged and corrupt.

Conclusion

Grounded in the cosmopolitan aspirations of a young provincial who sought citizenship in the great republic of letters, Jefferson's vision of re-publican government was both an extrapolation of conventional Enlight-enment ideas about civility and sociability and a projection of his own ever-expanding circle of friends. Political life could be seen as a conversation among friends, recognizing diverse perspectives and interests while they sought a common ground and a common good. Similarly, a harmonious union of free states in America was predicated on the mutual interest and natural sociability of liberty-loving republicans, not on the energetic gov-ernment favored by Federalists—or even on the party organization that

---

72. Banning, *Jeffersonian Persuasion*. See also Gordon S. Wood, "Conspiracy and the Para-noid Style: Causality and Deceit in the Eighteenth Century," *WMQ*, 3d ser., XXXIX (1982), 401–441; Wood, *Radicalism of the American Revolution* and "Trials and Tribulations of Thomas Jefferson"; Fliegelman, *Declaring Independence*.

73. Jefferson's First Inaugural Address, 4 March 1801, reprinted in Chapter 5 (p. 175).

Republicans had to develop in order to counter Federalist corruption.[74] In its most extravagant formulation, the fulfillment of Jefferson's project would see the nations of the world substitute peaceful, mutually beneficial exchange for violent conflict.[75]

But the republic in Jefferson's mind was never the same thing as the real republic he was instrumental in creating, and the discrepancy has become increasingly apparent. Simply to sketch the bold outlines of Jefferson's hopes for himself and his world is to invite mockery and derision. Peace on earth is no more in prospect now than it was in the dangerous days when Jefferson and Madison stumbled into war. The federal union has survived, but it bears little resemblance to Jefferson's union. And the collapse of the union during the Civil War and the subsequent transformation of the federal system are traceable to Jefferson's commitment to upholding the rights of slave states, a commitment that reflected his personal failure to take any effective steps against the institution of slavery. So, too, impasse and incapacity in politics today can be blamed on the diffusion of authority, the suspicion of power, and the disjunction between the private pursuit of happiness and the intensely public life of the commonweal that Jeffersonianism authorized.

Yet these indictments of Jefferson and his legacy follow a Jeffersonian script. Our own skepticism about words and deeds hearkens back to Republican efforts to unmask the nefarious Federalist foe. But historians are now more inclined to direct this Jeffersonian skepticism at the Jeffersonians themselves. What could be more outrageously spurious than to claim, as Jeffersonians did, to speak for the people or to invoke the authority of natural language, affectionate feelings, and self-evident principles? Manipulators of public opinion, they traded in empty words; self-effacement disguised vaulting (or sordid) ambitions. If Jefferson could not acknowledge his true motives or moral lapses, most conspicuously as a slave owner, that simply makes him more of a monster of self-deception.

The present-day discomfort with Jefferson is a challenge to historical interpretation and self-reflection. Nothing is more Jeffersonian about our approach to him than to raise questions about his character as well as his statecraft. As Fliegelman suggests, the search for a natural republican language—and politics—was bound to fail: sentimentalism gave way to cyni-

74. Recent contributions to the history of federalism include Richard E. Ellis, *The Union at Risk: Jacksonian Democracy, States' Rights and the Nullification Crisis* (New York, 1987), and Peter B. Knupfer, *The Union as It Is: Constitutional Unionism and Sectional Compromise, 1787–1861* (Chapel Hill, N.C., 1991).

75. For a balanced account of Jefferson's thinking about war and peace see Reginald C. Stuart. *The Half-Way Pacifist: Thomas Jefferson's View of War* (Toronto, 1978). On Jefferson's hopes for peace through trade see Peterson, "Jefferson and Commercial Policy, 1783–1793," *WMQ*, 3d ser., XXII (1965), 584–610. On the history of federal theory and of the development of Jeffersonian-Madisonian ideas about union see Peter S. Onuf and Nicholas G. Onuf, *Federal Union, Modern World: The Law of Nations in an Age of Revolutions, 1776–1814* (Madison, Wisc., 1993); Lewis, *The American Union and the Problem of Neighborhoods;* Onuf, *Jefferson's Empire;* and David C. Hendrickson, *The Ideological Origins of American Internationalism, 1754–1861* (forthcoming).

cism as the politics of authenticity subverted itself.[76] The "real" Jefferson will continue to elude and resist judgment. A greater measure of self-consciousness about our indebtedness to Jefferson—even in criticizing him—will not resolve the controversy he continues to inspire. But it should enable us to see him more clearly in his own context.

Jefferson's great political project, his struggle against despotic rule, expressed and confirmed his fundamental commitment to the self-evident principles of his political credo. In a revolutionary world of tenuous and shifting loyalties, secret enemies and doubtful friends, this commitment defined a common ground, the only solid foundation for a durable union of liberty-loving republicans. Historians will argue about the sources of republican principles and about their unifying or divisive effects in the dynamic context of revolutionary political change. But we should never forget that neither American independence, nor the union of American states, nor the democratization of American political and social life was preordained. No one was more conscious of the fragility of the American experiment than Jefferson himself. As Gordon Wood writes, the "democratic revolution he had contributed so much to bring about" left him mystified and uncomprehending. The discrepancy between his vision of the new nation's glorious future and the actual course of its development was—or should have been—increasingly evident in his declining years. A perennial optimist, Jefferson could sustain his "sublime faith in the people" only by averting his gaze from the vulgarity and busy-ness of the rising generation.[77]

Jefferson's optimism, his belief in the liberating power of words, his faith in man's natural sociability and capacity for self-government inspire as much incredulity as assent. If his ideas now circulate as the debased coin of our democratic culture, they were real for Jefferson and revolutionary for his times. As Joyce Appleby contends, "Jefferson boldly levitated himself out of his social milieu and trained his great learning on the real problem of liberty at the end of the eighteenth century: how to make good on the Enlightenment promise that men, born with a capacity for benign self-direction, could work out their own destinies and bring into existence a world that reflected the fulfillment of desire rather than a compromise with despair."[78] The promise has not been fulfilled, even for the empowered and hopeful beneficiaries of the new dispensation. But that is America's story as much as it was Jefferson's. As long as that story is worth telling, Jefferson will continue to occupy a crucial place in our nation's history and "symbolical architecture."

---

76. Insofar as self-expression, the great imperative of the new politics of feeling, "is prescribed and determined by a set of rules and expectations, the natural self that is ostensibly revealed is, in fact, concealed by or collapsed into a theatricalized self-construction"; Fliegelman, *Declaring Independence*, 2–3 and 164–172 (on self-effacement). I have borrowed the phrase "politics of authenticty" from Marshall Berman's study of Rousseau, *The Politics of Authenticity: Radical Individualism and the Emergence of Modern Society* (New York, 1970).

77. Wood, "Trials and Tribulations of Thomas Jefferson," 412–413.

78. Appleby, "Jefferson and His Complex Legacy," 4–5.

CHAPTER ONE

Revolutionary Statesman

Thomas Jefferson came of age during the exciting years when Britain's American colonies began to resist imperial rule. Born on 13 April 1743 in Albermarle County, where his father Peter was a land surveyor and local leader in this developing piedmont region, Jefferson was well placed to launch a brilliant career. Through his mother, Jane Randolph Jefferson, he was well connected with Virginia's leading families. A precocious student, Jefferson attended the College of William and Mary from 1760 to 1762 and studied law with George Wythe, the brightest light of the Virginia bar. By 1769, he had established an extensive, potentially lucrative law practice, been elected to the House of Burgesses, and begun building his beloved mountaintop home, Monticello. In 1772 he married the wealthy young widow, Martha Wayles Skelton. Two of their daughters would survive to adulthood: Martha, born in 1772, and Maria, who came six years later. Jefferson's wife Martha died in September 1782, possibly from complications brought on by the birth in May of another daughter, Lucy Elizabeth, who died in 1784.

As a Burgess, Jefferson quickly made his mark in drafting legislation and in writing, most notably through his influential pamphlet, *A Summary View* (document 1 below). His services were rewarded by election to the Second Continental Congress in 1775, where he took a leading role in drafting some of the most important revolutionary state papers, including the Declaration of Independence (document 4). But for Jefferson, the establishment of republican governments in the new United States constituted the chief business of the American Revolution. He had little interest in military matters or aptitude for them and was, by all accounts, a poor public speaker. His contributions would be in the committee room, not on the battlefield. Three years' service in the Virginia legislature culminated in the Revisal of the Laws (document 6), a herculean codification of state law for which he was mainly responsible, and in his election to the office of governor. But his governorship, from June 1779 to June 1787, was not the glorious capstone of his career of republican reformer. A British expeditionary force led by Benedict Arnold met little resistance when it invaded the state in early 1781, driving the state government out of Richmond and Jefferson from his home in Charlottesville. Though suggestions that he was personally responsible for this debacle were ultimately refuted by the legislature, the embittered Jefferson left office under a cloud (document 7).

Jefferson's consolation in these troubled months was to return to his studies and cultivate the friendship of enlightened acquaintances such as the Frenchman Chastellux (document 8). Through his engagement with the "republic of letters," Jefferson helped link America's revolutionary experiment with Enlightenment hopes for the progress of civilization.

* * * * * * * * * *

1. A Summary View of the Rights of British America, July–August 1774.

For the Virginia Convention of August 1774, Jefferson (hereafter TJ) drafted the "Summary View" as instructions for the colony's delegation to the Continental Congress. Illness kept him from attending the Convention in person and he was not chosen as a member of the seven-man delegation. But his draft instructions caused a sensation. Though not officially adopted by the Convention, they were published anonymously under this title in Williamsburg and subsequently in Philadelphia and England. The early and widespread knowledge that Jefferson was author, however, led to numerous other, even more important writing assignments.

Resolved, that it be an instruction to the said deputies, when assembled in general congress with the deputies from the other states of British America, to propose to the said congress that an humble and dutiful address be presented to his majesty, begging leave to lay before him, as chief magistrate of the British empire, the united complaints of his majesty's subjects in America; complaints which are excited by many unwarrantable encroachments and usurpations, attempted to be made by the legislature of one part of the empire, upon those rights which God and the laws have given equally and independently to all. To represent to his majesty that these his states have often individually made humble application to his imperial throne to obtain, through its intervention, some redress of their injured rights, to none of which was ever even an answer condescended; humbly to hope that this their joint address, penned in the language of truth, and divested of those expressions of servility which would persuade his majesty that we are asking favours, and not rights, shall obtain from his majesty a more respectful acceptance. And this his majesty will think we have reason to expect when he reflects that he is no more than the chief officer of the people, appointed by the laws, and circumscribed with definite powers, to assist in working the great machine of government, erected for their use, and consequently subject to their superintendance. And in order that these our rights, as well as the invasions of them, may be laid more fully before his majesty, to take a view of them from the origin and first settlement of these countries.

To remind him that our ancestors, before their emigration to America, were the free inhabitants of the British dominions in Europe, and possessed a right which nature has given to all men, of departing from the country in which chance, not choice, has placed them, of going in quest of new habitations, and of there establishing new societies, under such laws and regulations as to them shall seem most likely to promote public happiness. That their Saxon ancestors had, under this universal law, in like manner left their native wilds and woods in the north of Europe, had possessed themselves of the island of Britain, then less charged with inhabitants, and had established there that system of laws which has so long been the glory and protection of that country. Nor was ever any claim of superiority or dependence asserted over them by that mother country from which they had migrated; and were such a claim made, it is believed that his majesty's subjects in Great Britain have too firm a feeling of the rights derived to them from their ancestors, to bow down the sovereignty of their state before such visionary pretensions. And it is thought that no circumstance has occurred to distinguish materially the British from the Saxon emigration. America was conquered, and her settlements made, and firmly established, at the expence of individuals, and not of the British public. Their own blood was spilt in acquiring lands for their settlement, their own fortunes expended in making that settlement effectual; for themselves they fought, for themselves they conquered, and for themselves alone they have right to hold. Not a shilling was ever issued from the public treasures of his majesty, or his ancestors, for their assistance, till of very late times, after the colonies had become established on a firm and permanent footing. That then, indeed, having become valuable to Great Britain for her commercial purposes, his parliament was pleased to lend them assistance against an enemy, who would fain have drawn to herself the benefits of their commerce, to the great aggrandizement of herself, and danger of Great Britain. Such assistance, and in such circumstances, they had often before given to Portugal, and other allied states, with whom they carry on a commercial intercourse; yet these states never supposed, that by calling in her aid, they thereby submitted themselves to her sovereignty. Had such terms been proposed, they would have rejected them with disdain, and trusted for better to the moderation of their enemies, or to a vigorous exertion of their own force. We do not, however, mean to under-rate those aids, which to us were doubtless valuable, on whatever principles granted; but we would shew that they cannot give a title to that authority which the British parliament would arrogate over us, and that they may amply be repaid by our giving to the inhabitants of Great Britain such exclusive privileges in trade as may be advantageous to them, and at the same time not too restrictive to ourselves. That settlements having been thus effected in the wilds of America, the emigrants thought proper to adopt that system of laws under which they had hitherto lived in the mother country, and to continue their union with her by submitting themselves to the same common sovereign, who was thereby made the central link connecting the several parts of the empire thus newly multiplied.

But that not long were they permitted, however far they thought themselves removed from the hand of oppression, to hold undisturbed the rights thus acquired, at the hazard of their lives, and loss of their fortunes. A family of princes was then on the British throne, whose treasonable crimes against their people brought on them afterwards the exertion of those sacred and sovereign rights of punishment reserved in the hands of the people for cases of extreme necessity, and judged by the constitution unsafe to be delegated to any other judicature. While every day brought forth some new and unjustifiable exertion of power over their subjects on that side the water, it was not to be expected that those here, much less able at that time to oppose the designs of despotism, should be exempted from injury.

Accordingly that country, which had been acquired by the lives, the labours, and the fortunes, of individual adventurers, was by these princes, at several times, parted out and distributed among the favourites and followers of their fortunes, and, by an assumed right of the crown alone, were erected into distinct and independent governments; a measure which it is believed his majesty's prudence and understanding would prevent him from imitating at this day, as no exercise of such a power, of dividing and dismembering a country, has ever occurred in his majesty's realm of England, though now of very antient standing; nor could it be justified or acquiesced under there, or in any other part of his majesty's empire.

That the exercise of a free trade with all parts of the world, possessed by the American colonists, as of natural right, and which no law of their own had taken away or abridged, was next the object of unjust encroachment. Some of the colonies having thought proper to continue the administration of their government in the name and under the authority of his majesty king Charles the first, whom, notwithstanding his late deposition by the commonwealth of England, they continued in the sovereignty of their state; the parliament for the commonwealth took the same in high offence, and assumed upon themselves the power of prohibiting their trade with all other parts of the world, except the island of Great Britain. This arbitrary act, however, they soon recalled, and by solemn treaty, entered into on the 12th day of March, 1651, between the said commonwealth by their commissioners, and the colony of Virginia by their house of burgesses, it was expressly stipulated, by the 8th article of the said treaty, that they should have "free trade as the people of England do enjoy to all places and with all nations, according to the laws of that commonwealth." But that, upon the restoration of his majesty king Charles the second, their rights of free commerce fell once more a victim to arbitrary power; and by several acts of his reign, as well as of some of his successors, the trade of the colonies was laid under such restrictions, as shew what hopes they might form from the justice of a British parliament, were its uncontrouled power admitted over these states. History has informed us that bodies of men, as well as individuals, are susceptible of the spirit of tyranny. A view of these acts of parliament for regulation, as it has been affectedly called, of the American trade, if all other evidence were removed out of the case, would undeniably evince the truth of this observation. Besides the duties they impose on our articles of export and import, they prohibit our going to any markets northward of Cape Finesterre, in the kingdom of Spain, for the sale of commodities which Great Britain will not take from us, and for the purchase of others, with which she cannot supply us, and that for no other than the arbitrary purposes of purchasing for themselves, by a sacrifice of our rights and interests, certain privileges in their commerce with an allied state, who in confidence that their exclusive trade with America will be continued, while the principles and power of the British parliament be the same, have indulged themselves in every exorbitance which their avarice could dictate, or our necessities extort; have raised their commodities, called for in America, to the double and treble of what they sold for before such exclusive privileges were given them, and of what better commodities of the same kind would cost us elsewhere, and at the same time give us much less for what we carry thither than might be had at more convenient ports. That these acts prohibit us from carrying in quest of other purchasers the surplus of our tobaccoes remaining after the consumption of Great Britain is supplied; so that we must leave them with the British merchant for whatever he will please to allow us, to be by him reshipped to foreign markets, where he will reap the benefits of making sale of them for full value. That to heighten still the idea of parliamentary justice, and to shew with what moderation they are like to exercise power, where themselves are to feel no part of its weight, we take leave to mention to his majesty certain other acts of British parliament, by which they would prohibit us from manufacturing for our own use the articles we raise on our own lands with our own labour. By an act passed in the 5th Year of the reign of his late majesty king George the second, an American subject is forbidden to make a hat for himself of the fur which he has taken perhaps on his own soil; an instance of despotism to which no parrallel can be produced in the most arbitrary ages of British history. By one other act, passed in the 23d year of the same reign, the iron which we make we are forbidden to manufacture, and heavy as that article is, and necessary in every branch of husbandry, besides commission and insurance, we are to pay freight for it to Great Britain, and freight for it back again, for the purpose of supporting not men, but machines, in the island of Great Britain. In the same spirit of equal and impartial legislation is to be viewed the act of parliament, passed in the 5th year of the same reign, by which American lands are made subject to the demands of British creditors, while their own lands were still continued unanswerable for their debts; from which one of these conclusions must necessarily follow, either that justice is not the same in America as in Britain, or else that the British parliament pay less regard to it here than there. But that we do not point out to his majesty the injustice of these acts, with intent to rest on that principle the cause of their nullity; but to shew that experience confirms the propriety of those political principles which exempt us from the jurisdiction of the British parliament. The true ground on which we declare these acts void is, that the British parliament has no right to exercise authority over us.

That these exercises of usurped power have not been confined to instances alone, in which themselves were interested, but they have also intermeddled with the regulation of the internal affairs of the colonies. The act of the 9th of Anne for establishing a post office in America seems to have had little connection with British convenience, except that of accommodating his majesty's ministers and favourites with the sale of a lucrative and easy office.

That thus have we hastened through the reigns which preceded his majesty's, during which the violations of our right were less alarming, because repeated at more distant intervals than that rapid and bold succession of injuries which is likely to distinguish the present from all other periods of American story. Scarcely have our minds been able to emerge from the astonishment into which one stroke of parliamentary thunder has involved us, before another more heavy, and more alarming, is fallen on us. Single acts of tyranny may be ascribed to the accidental opinion of a day; but a series of oppressions, begun at a distinguished period, and pursued unalterably through every change of ministers, too plainly prove a deliberate and systematical plan of reducing us to slavery.

That the act passed in the 4th year of his majesty's reign, intitled "An act for granting certain duties in the British colonies and plantations in America, &c."

One other act, passed in the 5th year of his reign, intitled "An act for granting and applying certain stamp duties and other duties in the British colonies and plantations in America, &c."

One other act, passed in the 6th year of his reign, intituled "An act for the better securing the dependency of his majesty's dominions in America upon the crown and parliament of Great Britain;" and one other act, passed in the 7th year of his reign, intituled "An act for granting duties on paper, tea, &c." form that connected chain of parliamentary usurpation, which has already been the subject of frequent applications to his majesty, and the houses of lords and commons of Great Britain; and no answers having yet been condescended to any of these, we shall not trouble his majesty with a repetition of the matters they contained.

But that one other act, passed in the same 7th year of the reign, having been a peculiar attempt, must ever require peculiar mention; it is intituled "An act for suspending the legislature of New York." One free and independent legislature hereby takes upon itself to suspend the powers of another, free and independent as itself; thus exhibiting a phoenomenon unknown in nature, the creator and creature of its own power. Not only the principles of common sense, but the common feelings of human nature, must be surrendered up before his majesty's subjects here can be persuaded to believe that they hold their political existence at the will of a British parliament. Shall these governments be dissolved, their property annihilated, and their people reduced to a state of nature, at the imperious breath of a body of men, whom they never saw, in whom they never confided, and over whom they have no powers of punishment or removal, let their crimes against the American public be ever so great? Can any one reason be assigned why 160,000 electors in the island of Great Britain should give law to four millions in the states of America, every individual of whom is equal to every individual of them, in virtue, in understanding, and in bodily strength? Were this to be admitted, instead of being a free people, as we have hitherto supposed, and mean to continue ourselves, we should suddenly be found the slaves, not of one, but of 160,000 tyrants, distinguished too from all others by this singular circumstance, that they are removed from the reach of fear, the only restraining motive which may hold the hand of a tyrant.

That by "an act to discontinue in such manner and for such time as are therein mentioned the landing and discharging, lading or shipping, of goods, wares, and merchandize, at the town and within the harbour of Boston, in the province of Massachusetts Bay, in North America," which was passed at the last session of British parliament; a large and populous town, whose trade was their sole subsistence, was deprived of that trade, and involved in utter ruin. Let us for a while suppose the question of right suspended, in order to examine this act on principles of justice: An act of parliament had been passed imposing duties on teas, to be paid in America, against which act the Americans had protested as inauthoritative. The East India company, who till that time had never sent a pound of tea to

America on their own account, step forth on that occasion the assertors of parliamentary right, and send hither many ship loads of that obnoxious commodity. The masters of their several vessels, however, on their arrival in America, wisely attended to admonition, and returned with their cargoes. In the province of New England alone the remonstrances of the people were disregarded, and a compliance, after being many days waited for, was flatly refused. Whether in this the master of the vessel was governed by his obstinancy, or his instructions, let those who know, say. There are extraordinary situations which require extraordinary interposition. An exasperated people, who feel that they possess power, are not easily restrained within limits strictly regular. A number of them assembled in the town of Boston, threw the tea into the ocean, and dispersed without doing any other act of violence. If in this they did wrong, they were known and were amenable to the laws of the land, against which it could not be objected that they had ever, in any instance, been obstructed or diverted from their regular course in favour of popular offenders. They should therefore not have been distrusted on this occasion. But that ill fated colony had formerly been bold in their enmities against the house of Stuart, and were now devoted to ruin by that unseen hand which governs the momentous affairs of this great empire. On the partial representations of a few worthless ministerial dependents, whose constant office it has been to keep that government embroiled, and who, by their treacheries, hope to obtain the dignity of the British knighthood, without calling for a party accused, without asking a proof, without attempting a distinction between the guilty and the innocent, the whole of that antient and wealthy town is in a moment reduced from opulence to beggary. Men who had spent their lives in extending the British commerce, who had invested in that place the wealth their honest endeavours had merited, found themselves and their families thrown at once on the world for subsistence by its charities. Not the hundredth part of the inhabitants of that town had been concerned in the act complained of; many of them were in Great Britain and in other parts beyond sea; yet all were involved in one indiscriminate ruin, by a new executive power, unheard of till then, that of a British parliament. A property, of the value of many millions of money, was sacrificed to revenge, not repay, the loss of a few thousands. This is administering justice with a heavy hand indeed! and when is this tempest to be arrested in its course? Two wharfs are to be opened again when his majesty shall think proper. The residue which lined the extensive shores of the bay of Boston are forever interdicted the exercise of commerce. This little exception seems to have been thrown in for no other purpose than that of setting a precedent for investing his majesty with legislative powers. If the pulse of his people shall beat calmly under this experiment, another and another will be tried, till the measure of despotism be filled up. It would be an insult on common sense to pretend that this exception was made in order to restore its commerce to that great town. The trade which cannot be received at two wharfs alone must of necessity be transferred to some other place; to which it will soon be followed by that of the two wharfs. Considered in this light, it would be an insolent and cruel mockery at the annihilation of the town of Boston.

By the act for the suppression of riots and tumults in the town of Boston, passed also in the last session of parliament, a murder committed there is, if the governor pleases, to be tried in the court of King's Bench, in the island of Great Britain, by a jury of Middlesex. The witnesses, too, on receipt of such a sum as the governor shall think it reasonable for them to expend, are to enter into recognizance to appear at the trial. This is, in other words, taxing them to the amount of their recognizance, and that amount may be whatever a governor pleases; for who does his majesty think can be prevailed on to cross the Atlantic for the sole purpose of bearing evidence to a fact? His expences are to be borne, indeed, as they shall be estimated by a governor; but who are to feed the wife and children whom he leaves behind, and who have had no other subsistence but his daily labour? Those epidemical disorders, too, so terrible in a foreign climate, is the cure of them to be estimated among the articles of expence, and their danger to be warded off by the almighty power of parliament? And the wretched criminal, if he happen to have offended on the American side, stripped of his privilege of trial by peers of his vicinage, removed from the place where alone full evidence could be obtained, without money, without counsel, without friends, without exculpatory proof, is tried before judges predetermined to condemn. The cowards who would suffer a countryman to be torn from the bowels of their society, in order to be thus offered a sacrifice to parliamentary tyranny, would merit that everlasting infamy now fixed on the authors of the act! A clause for a similar purpose had been introduced into an act, passed in the 12th year of his majesty's reign, intitled "An act for the better securing and preserving his majesty's dockyards, magazines, ships, ammunition, and stores;" against which, as meriting the same censures, the several colonies have already protested.

That these are the acts of power, assumed by a body of men, foreign to our constitutions, and unacknowledged by our laws, against which we do, on behalf of the inhabitants of British America, enter this our solemn and determined protest; and we do earnestly entreat his majesty, as yet the only mediatory power between the several states of the British empire, to recommend to his parliament of Great Britain the total revocation of these acts, which, however nugatory they be, may yet prove the cause of further discontents and jealousies among us.

That we next proceed to consider the conduct of his majesty, as holding the executive powers of the laws of these states, and mark out his deviations from the line of duty: By the constitution of Great Britain, as well as of the several American states, his majesty possesses the power of refusing to pass into a law any bill which has already passed the other two branches of legislature. His majesty, however, and his ancestors, conscious of the impropriety of opposing their single opinion to the united wisdom of two houses of parliament, while their proceedings were unbiassed by interested principles, for several ages past have modestly declined the exercise of this power in that part of his empire called Great Britain. But by change of circumstances, other principles than those of justice simply have obtained an influence on their determinations; the addition of new states to the British empire has produced an addition of new, and sometimes opposite interests. It is now, therefore, the great office of his majesty, to resume the exercise of his negative power, and to prevent the passage of laws by any one legislature of the empire, which might bear injuriously on the rights and interests of another. Yet this will not excuse the wanton exercise of this power which we have seen his majesty practise on the laws of the American legislatures. For the most trifling reasons, and sometimes for no conceivable reason at all, his majesty has rejected laws of the most salutary tendency. The abolition of domestic slavery is the great object of desire in those colonies, where it was unhappily introduced in their infant state. But previous to the enfranchisement of the slaves we have, it is necessary to exclude all further importations from Africa; yet our repeated attempts to effect this by prohibitions, and by imposing duties which might amount to a prohibition, have been hitherto defeated by his majesty's negative: Thus preferring the immediate advantages of a few African corsairs to the lasting interests of the American states, and to the rights of human nature, deeply wounded by this infamous practice. Nay, the single interposition of an interested individual against a law was scarcely ever known to fail of success, though in the opposite scale were placed the interests of a whole country. That this is so shameful an abuse of a power trusted with his majesty for other purposes, as if not reformed, would call for some legal restrictions.

With equal inattention to the necessities of his people here has his majesty permitted our laws to lie neglected in England for years, neither confirming them by his assent, nor annulling them by his negative; so that such of them as have no suspending clause we hold on the most precarious of all tenures, his majesty's will, and such of them as suspend themselves till his majesty's assent be obtained, we have feared, might be called into existence at some future and distant period, when time, and change of circumstances, shall have rendered them destructive to his people here. And to render this grievance still more oppressive, his majesty by his instructions has laid his governors under such restrictions that they can pass no law of any moment unless it have such suspending clause; so that, however immediate may be the call for legislative interposition, the law cannot be executed till it has twice crossed the atlantic, by which time the evil may have spent its whole force.

But in what terms, reconcileable to majesty, and at the same time to truth, shall we speak of a late instruction to his majesty's governor of the colony of Virginia, by which he is forbidden to assent to any law for the division of a county, unless the new county will consent to have no representative in assembly? That colony has as yet fixed no boundary to the westward. Their western counties, therefore, are of indefinite extent; some of them are actually seated many hundred miles from their eastern limits. Is it possible, then, that his majesty can have bestowed a single thought on the situation of those people, who, in order to obtain justice for injuries, however great or small, must, by the laws of that colony, attend their county court, at such a distance, with all their witnesses, monthly, till their litigation be determined? Or does his majesty seriously wish, and publish it to the world, that his subjects should give up the glorious right of representation, with all the benefits derived from that, and submit themselves the absolute slaves of his sovereign will? Or is it rather meant to confine the legislative body to their present numbers, that they may be the cheaper bargain whenever they shall become worth a purchase.

One of the articles of impeachment against Tresilian, and the other judges of Westminister Hall, in the reign of Richard the second, for which they suffered death, as traitors to their country, was, that they had advised the king that he might dissolve his parliament at any time; and succeeding kings have adopted the opinion of these unjust judges. Since the establishment, however, of the British constitution, at the glorious revolution, on its free and antient principles, neither his majesty, nor his ancestors, have exercised such a power of dissolution in the island of Great Britain; and when his majesty was petitioned, by the united voice of his people there, to dissolve the present parliament, who had become obnoxious to them, his ministers were heard to declare, in open parliament, that his majesty possessed no such power by the constitution. But how different their language and his practice here! To declare, as their duty required, the known rights of their country, to oppose the usurpations of every foreign judicature, to disregard the imperious mandates of a minister or governor, have been the avowed causes of dissolving houses of representatives in America. But if such powers be really vested in his majesty, can he suppose they are there placed to awe the members from such purposes as these? When the representative body have lost the confidence of their constituents, when they have notoriously made sale of their most valuable rights, when they have assumed to themselves powers which the people never put into their hands, then indeed their continuing in office becomes dangerous to the state, and calls for an exercise of the power of dissolution. Such being the causes for which the representative body should, and should not, be dissolved, will it not appear strange to an unbiassed observer, that that of Great Britain was not dissolved, while those of the colonies have repeatedly incurred that sentence?

But your majesty, or your governors, have carried this power beyond every limit known, or provided for, by the laws: After dissolving one house of representatives, they have refused to call another, so that, for a great length of time, the legislature provided by the laws has been out of existence. From the nature of things, every society must at all times possess within itself the sovereign powers of legislation. The feelings of human nature revolt against the supposition of a state so situated as that it may not in any emergency provide against dangers which perhaps threaten immediate ruin. While those bodies are in existence to whom the people have delegated the powers of legislation, they alone possess and may exercise those powers; but when they are dissolved by the lopping off one or more of their branches, the power reverts to the people, who may exercise it to unlimited extent, either assembling together in person, sending deputies, or in any other way they may think proper. We forbear to trace consequences further; the dangers are conspicuous with which this practice is replete.

That we shall at this time also take notice of an error in the nature of our land holdings, which crept in at a very early period of our settlement. The introduction of the feudal tenures into the kingdom of England, though antient, is well enough understood to set this matter in a proper light. In the earlier ages of the Saxon settlement feudal holdings were certainly altogether unknown; and very few, if any, had been introduced at the time of the Norman conquest. Our Saxon ancestors held their lands, as they did their personal property, in absolute dominion, disencumbered with any superior, answering nearly to the nature of those possessions which the feudalists term allodial. William, the Norman, first introduced that system generally. The lands which had belonged to those who fell in the battle of Hastings, and in the subsequent insurrections of his reign, formed a considerable proportion of the lands of the whole kingdom. These he granted out, subject to feudal duties, as did he also those of a great number of his new subjects, who, by persuasions or threats, were induced to surrender them for that purpose. But still much was left in the hands of his Saxon subjects; held of no superior, and not subject to feudal conditions. These, therefore, by express laws, enacted to render uniform the system of military defence, were made liable to the same military duties as if they had been feuds; and the Norman lawyers soon found means to saddle them also with all the other feudal burthens. But still they had not been surrendered to the king, they were not derived from his grant, and therefore they were not holden of him. A general principle, indeed, was introduced, that "all lands in England were held either mediately or immediately of the crown," but this was borrowed from those holdings, which were truly feudal, and only applied to others for the purposes of illustration. Feudal holdings were therefore but exceptions out of the Saxon laws of possession, under which all lands were held in absolute right. These, therefore, still form the basis, or ground-work, of the common law, to prevail wheresoever the exceptions have not taken place. America was not conquered by William the Norman, nor its lands surrendered to him, or any of his successors. Possessions there are undoubtedly of the allodial nature. Our ancestors, however, who migrated hither, were farmers, not lawyers. The fictitious principle that all lands belong originally to the king, they were early persuaded to believe real; and accordingly took grants of their own lands from the crown. And while the crown continued to grant for small sums, and on reasonable rents; there was no inducement to arrest the error, and lay it open to public view. But his majesty has lately taken on him to advance the terms of purchase, and of holding to the double of what they were; by which means the acquisition of lands being rendered difficult, the population of our country is likely to be checked. It is time, therefore, for us to lay this matter before his majesty, and to declare that he has no right to grant lands of himself. From the nature and purpose of civil institutions, all the lands within the limits which any particular society has circumscribed around itself are assumed by that society, and subject to their allotment only. This may be done by themselves, assembled collectively, or by their legislature, to whom they may have delegated sovereign authority; and if they are alloted in neither of these ways, each individual of the society may appropriate to himself such lands as he finds vacant, and occupancy will give him title.

That in order to enforce the arbitrary measures before complained of, his majesty has from time to time sent among us large bodies of armed forces, not made up of the people here, nor raised by the authority of our laws: Did his majesty possess such a right as this, it might swallow up all our other rights whenever he should think proper. But his majesty has no right to land a single armed man on our shores, and those whom he sends here are liable to our laws made for the suppression and punishment of riots, routs, and unlawful assemblies; or are hostile bodies, invading us in defiance of law. When in the course of the late war it became expedient that a body of Hanoverian troops should be brought over for the defence of Great Britain, his majesty's grandfather, our late sovereign, did not pretend to introduce them under any authority he possessed. Such a measure would have given just alarm to his subjects in Great Britain, whose liberties would not be safe if armed men of another country, and of another spirit, might be brought into the realm at any time without the consent of their legislature. He therefore applied to parliament, who passed an act for that purpose, limiting the number to be brought in and the time they were to continue. In like manner is his majesty restrained in every part of the empire. He possesses, indeed, the executive power of the laws in every state; but they are the laws of the particular state which he is to administer within that state, and not those of any one within the limits of another. Every state must judge for itself the number of armed men which they may safely trust among them, of whom they are to consist, and under what restrictions they shall be laid.

To render these proceedings still more criminal against our laws, instead of subjecting the military to the civil powers, his majesty has expressly made the civil subordinate to the military. But can his majesty thus put down all law under his feet? Can he erect a power superior to that which erected himself? He has done it indeed by force; but let him remember that force cannot give right.

That these are our grievances which we have thus laid before his majesty, with that freedom of language and sentiment which becomes a free people claiming their rights, as derived from the laws of nature, and not as the gift of their chief magistrate: Let those flatter who fear; it is not an American art. To give praise which is not due might be well from the venal, but would ill beseem those who are asserting the rights of human nature. They know, and will therefore say, that kings are the servants, not the proprietors of the people. Open your breast, sire, to liberal and expanded thought. Let not the name of George the third be a blot in the page of history. You are surrounded by British counsellors, but remember that they are parties. You have no ministers for American affairs, because you have none taken from among us, nor amenable to the laws on which they are to give you advice. It behoves you, therefore, to think and to act for yourself and your people. The great principles of right and wrong are legible to every reader; to pursue them requires not the aid of many counsellors. The whole art of government consists in the art of being honest. Only aim to do your duty, and mankind will give you credit where you fail. No longer persevere in sacrificing the rights of one part of the empire to the inordinate desires of another; but deal out to all equal and impartial right. Let no act be passed by any one legislature which may infringe on the rights and liberties of another. This is the important post in which fortune has placed you, holding the balance of a great, if a well poised empire. This, sire, is the advice of your great American council, on the observance of which may perhaps depend your felicity and future fame, and the preservation of that harmony which alone can continue both to Great Britain and America the reciprocal advantages of their connection. It is neither our wish, nor our interest, to separate from her. We are willing, on our part, to sacrifice every thing which reason can ask to the restoration of that tranquillity for which all must wish. On their part, let them be ready to establish union and a generous plan. Let them name their terms, but let them be just. Accept of every commercial preference it is in our power to give for such things as we can raise for their use, or they make for ours. But let them not think to exclude us from going to other markets to dispose of those commodities which they cannot use, or to supply those wants which they cannot supply. Still less let it be proposed that our properties within our own territories shall be taxed or regulated by any power on earth but our own. The God who gave us life gave us liberty at the same time; the hand of force may destroy, but cannot disjoin them. This, sire, is our last, our determined resolution; and that you will be pleased to interpose with that efficacy which your earnest endeavours may ensure to procure redress of these our great grievances, to quiet the minds of your subjects in British America, against any apprehensions of future encroachment, to establish fraternal love and harmony through the whole empire, and that these may continue to the latest ages of time, is the fervent prayer of all British America!

2. Virginia Resolutions on Lord North's Conciliatory Proposal, 10 June 1775. *In February the British Prime Minister Lord North proposed that if the colonies made grants to Parliament to support their governments and the common defense, the ministry would not impose any tax or revenue measure for those purposes. Governor Lord Dunmore convened the House of Burgesses in June to hear these proposals; TJ was the draftsman for the response, adopted by the committee of the whole and presented to Dunmore on 12 June, the day after TJ left Williamsburg to join the Continental Congress in Philadelphia. The Burgesses concluded that the proposal of Lord Chatham (William Pitt) to repeal all of Parliament's controversial legislation respecting America was the only possible basis of reconciliation.*

Resolved, that it is the Opinion of this Committee that an Address be presented to his Excellency, the Governor, to inform him that we have taken into our Consideration the joint Address of the two Houses of Parliament, his Majesty's Answer, and the Resolution of the Commons which his Lordship has been pleased to lay before us. That wishing nothing so sincerely as the perpetual continuance of that brotherly love which we bear to our fellow subjects of *Great Britain* and still continuing to hope and believe that they do not approve the measures which have so long oppressed their brethren in *America,* we were pleased to receive his *Lordship's* notification that a benevolent tender had at length been made by the british House of Commons towards bringing to a good end our unhappy disputes with the Mother Country: that next to the possession of liberty, we should consider such Reconciliation the greatest of all human blessings. With these dispositions we entered into consideration of that Resolution: we examined it minutely; we viewed it in every point of light in which we were able to place it; and with pain and disappointment we must ultimately declare it only changes the form of oppression, without lightening its burthen. That we cannot close with the terms of that Resolution for these Reasons.

Because the British Parliament has no right to intermeddle with the support of civil government in the Colonies. For us, not for them, has government been instituted here; agreeable to our Ideas provision has been made for such Officers as we think necessary for the administration of public affairs; and we cannot conceive that any other legislature has a right to prescribe either the number or pecuniary appointments of our Offices. As a proof that the Claim of Parliament to interfere in the necessary Provisions for support of civil Government is novel and of a late Date we take leave to refer to an Act of our Assembly passed so long since as the thirty second Year of the Reign of King *Charles* the second intituled *An Act for raising a public Revenue and for the better support of the Government of this his Majesty's Colony of Virginia.* This Act was brought over by Lord Culpeper then Governor under the great Seal of *England* and was enacted in the name of the "King's most excellent Majesty by and with the Consent of the General Assembly."

Because to render perpetual our exemption from an unjust taxation, we must saddle ourselves with a perpetual tax adequate to the expectations and subject to the disposal of Parliament alone. Whereas, we have right to give our money, as the Parliament does theirs, without coercion, from time to time, as public exigencies may require, we conceive that we alone are the judges of the condition, circumstances, and situation of our people, as the Parliament are of theirs. It is not merely the mode of raising, but the freedom of granting our Money for which we have contended. Without this we possess no check on the royal prerogative, and what must be much lamented by dutiful and loyal subjects, we should be stript of the only means, as well of recommending this Country to the favour of our most gracious Sovereign as of strengthening those bands of Amity with our fellow subjects which we would wish to remain indissoluble.

Because on our undertaking to grant money as is proposed, the Commons only resolve to forbear levying pecuniary taxes on us; still leaving unrepealed their several Acts passed for the purposes of restraining the trade and altering the form of Government of the Eastern Colonies; extending the boundaries and changing the Government and Religion of *Quebec;* enlarging the jurisdiction of the Courts of Admiralty, and taking from us the right of trial by jury; and transporting us into other Countries to be tried for criminal Offences. Standing armies too are still to be kept among us, and the other numerous grievancies of which ourselves and sister Colonies separately and by our representatives in General Congress have so often complained, are still to continue without redress.

Because at the very time of requiring from us grants of Money they are making disposition to invade us with large Armaments by Sea and land, which is a stile of asking gifts not reconcileable to our freedom. They are also proceeding to a Repetition of injury by passing acts for restraining the commerce and fisheries of the Provinces of *New England,* and for prohibiting the Trade of the other Colonies with all parts of the world except the Islands of *Great Britain, Ireland,* and the *West Indies.* This seems to bespeak no intention to discontinue the exercise of this usurped Power over us in future.

Because on our agreeing to contribute our proportion towards the common defence, they do not propose to lay open to us a free trade with all the world: whereas to us it appears just that those who bear equally the burthens of Government, should equally participate of it's benefits. Either be content with the monopoly of our trade, which brings greater loss to us and benefit to them than the amount of our proportional contributions to the common defence; or, if the latter be preferred, relinquish the former, and do not propose, by holding both, to exact from us double contributions. Yet we would remind Government that on former emergencies when called upon as a free People, however cramped by this monopoly in our resources of wealth, we have liberally contributed to the common defence. Be assured then that we shall be generous in future as in past times, disdaining the shackles of proportion when called to our free station in the general system of the Empire.

Because the proposition now made to us involves the interest of all the other Colonies. We are now represented in General Congress, by members approved by this House where our former Union it is hoped will be so strongly cemented that no partial Application can produce the slightest departure from the Common cause. We consider ourselves as bound in Honor as well as Interest to share in one general Fate with our Sister Colonies, and should hold ourselves base Deserters of that Union, to which we have acceded, were we to agree on any Measures distinct and apart from them.

To observe that there was indeed a plan of accomodation offered in Parliament, which tho' not entirely equal to the terms we had a right to ask, yet differed but in few Points from what the General Congress had held out. Had Parliament been disposed sincerely as we are to bring about a reconciliation, reasonable men had hoped that by meeting us on this ground something might have been done. Lord *Chatham's* bill on the one part and the terms of the Congress on the other would have formed a basis for negotiation which a spirit of accomodation on both sides might perhaps have reconciled. It came recommended too from one whose successful experience in the art of Government should have ensured to it some attention from those to whom it was tendered. He had shown to the world that *Great Britain* with her Colonies, united firmly under a just and honest government, formed a power which might bid defiance to the most potent enemies. With a change of Ministers however a total change of measures took place; the component parts of the empire have from that moment been falling asunder, and a total annihilation of its weight in the political scale of the World seems justly to be apprehended.

To declare that these are our sentiments on this important subject, which we offer only as an individual part of the whole empire. Final determination we leave to the General Congress now sitting, before whom we shall lay the Papers his Lordship has communicated to us. To their Wisdom we commit the improvement of this important advance; if it can be wrought into any good, we are assured they will do it. To them also we refer the discovery of that proper method of representing our well founded grievancies which his Lordship assures us will meet with the attention and regard so justly due to them. For ourselves, we have exhausted every mode of application which our invention could suggest as proper and promising. We have decently remonstrated with Parliament; they have added new injuries to the old: we have wearied our King with supplication, he has not deigned to answer us: We have appealed to the native honour and justice of the British nation; their efforts in our favour have been hitherto ineffectual. What then remains to be done? That we commit our injuries to the even-handed justice of that being who doth no wrong, earnestly beseeching him to illuminate the Councils and prosper the endeavors of those to whom America hath confided her hopes; and thro' their wise direction we may again see reunited the blessings of Liberty, property, and Union with *Great Britain.*

3. To John Randolph, Monticello, 25 August 1775. *The Loyalist John Randolph (1727–1784), a distant relative of TJ and a prominent lawyer, was the King's Attorney in Virginia until his political exile to Britain. Randolph's son Edmund became a leader in the new state and national governments. TJ was completing the purchase of a violin he had long admired; the purchase superseded an earlier agreement that the first of the two men to die would leave to the survivor either books (in TJ's case) or the violin and music (in Randolph's).*

I received your message by Mr. Braxton & immediately gave him an order on the Treasurer for the money which the Treasurer assured me should be answered on his return. I now send the bearer for the violin & such music appurtaining to her as may be of no use to the young ladies. I beleive you had no case to her. If so, be so good as to direct Watt Lenox to get from Prentis's some bays or other coarse woollen to wrap her in & then to pack her securely in a wooden box. I am sorry the situation of our country should render it not eligible to you to remain longer in it. I hope the returning wisdom of Great Britain will, ere long, put an end to this unnatural contest. There may be people to whose tempers and dispositions contention is pleasing, and who, therefore, wish a continuance of confusion, but to me it is of all states but one, the most horrid. My first wish is a restoration of our just rights; my second, a return of the happy period, when, consistently with duty, I may withdraw myself totally from the public stage, and pass the rest of my days in domestic ease and tranquillity, banishing every desire of ever hearing what passes in the world. Perhaps (for the latter adds considerably to the warmth of the former wish), looking with fondness towards a reconciliation with Great Britain, I cannot help hoping you may be able to contribute towards expediting this good work. I think it must be evident to yourself, that the Ministry have been deceived by their officers on this side of the water, who (for what purpose I cannot tell) have constantly represented the American opposition as that of a small faction, in which the body of the people took little part. This, you can inform them, of your own knowledge, is untrue. They have taken it into their heads, too, that we are cowards, and shall surrender at discretion to an armed force. The past and future operations of the war must confirm or undeceive them on that head. I wish they were thoroughly and minutely acquainted with every circumstance relative to America, as it exists in truth. I am persuaded, this would go far towards disposing them to reconciliation. Even those in Parliament who are called friends to America, seem to know nothing of our real determinations. I observe, they pronounced in the last Parliament, that the Congress of 1774 did not mean to insist rigorously on the terms they held out, but kept something in reserve, to give up; and, in fact, that they would give up everything but the article of taxation. Now, the truth is far from this, as I can affirm, and put my honor to the assertion. Their continuance in this error may, perhaps, produce very ill consequences. The Congress stated the lowest terms they thought possible to be accepted, in order to convince the world they were not unreasonable. They gave up the monopoly and regulation of trade, and all acts of Parliament prior to 1764, leaving to British generosity to render these, at some future time, as easy to America as the interest of Britain would admit. But this was before blood was spilt. I cannot affirm, but have reason to think, these terms would not now be accepted. I wish no false sense of honor, no ignorance of our real intentions, no vain hope that partial concessions of right will be accepted, may induce the Ministry to trifle with accommodation, till it shall be out of their power ever to accommodate. If, indeed, Great Britain, disjointed from her colonies, be a match for the most potent nations of Europe, with the colonies thrown into their scale, they may go on securely. But if they are not assured of this, it would be certainly unwise, by trying the event of another campaign, to risk our accepting a foreign aid, which, perhaps, may not be attainable, but on condition of everlasting avulsion from Great Britain. This would be thought a hard condition, to those who still wish for reunion with their parent country. I am sincerely one of those, and would rather be in dependence on Great Britain, properly limited, than on anyother nation on earth, or than on no nation. But I am one of those, too, who, rather than submit to the rights of legislating for us, assumed by the British Parliament, and which late experience has shown they will so cruelly exercise, would lend my hand to sink the whole Island in the ocean.

If undeceiving the Minister, as to matters of fact, may change his disposition, it will, perhaps, be in your power, by assisting to do this, to render service to the whole empire, at the most critical time, certainly, that it has ever seen. Whether Britain shall continue the head of the greatest empire on earth, or shall return to her original station in the political scale of Europe, depends, perhaps, on the resolutions of the succeeding winter. God send they may be wise and salutary for us all. I shall be glad to hear from you as often as you may be disposed to think of things here. You may be at liberty, expect, to communicate some things, consistently with your honor, and the duties you will owe to a protecting nation. Such a communication among individuals, may be mutually beneficial to the contending parties. On this or any future occasion, if I affirm to you any facts, your knowledge of me will enable you to decide on their credibility; if I hazard opinions on the dispositions of men or other speculative points, you can only know they are my opinions. . . .

4. A Declaration by the Representatives of the United States of America, in General Congress Assembled, 4 July 1776. *Following the unanimous resolution of the Virginia Convention on 15 May, Richard Henry Lee offered a resolution to Congress on 7 June on behalf of independence. Congress proceeded, on 11 June, to appoint a five-man committee, including TJ, John Adams, Benjamin Franklin, Roger Sherman, and Robert R. Livingston, to report a declaration. The draft reported by the committee had been prepared by TJ, with editorial suggestions by Adams and Franklin. More extensive changes were made when the committee's draft was debated in Congress on 2–4 July. When he drafted his autobiography (in January–July 1821) he compared his text with Congress's, concluding that most of these changes were for the worse. In the text below, passages from TJ's draft that were deleted from the document approved by Congress are italicized in brackets; additions by Congress are underlined.*

When in the course of human events it becomes necessary for one people to dissolve the political bands which have connected them with another, and to assume among the powers of the earth the separate & equal station to which the laws of nature and of nature's God entitle them, a decent respect to the opinions of mankind requires that they should declare the causes which impel them to the separation.

We hold these truths to be self-evident: that all men are created equal; that they are endowed by their creator with [*inherent and*] <u>certain</u> inalienable rights; that among these are life, liberty, & the pursuit of happiness: that to secure these rights, governments are instituted among men, deriving their just powers from the consent of the governed; that whenever any form of government becomes destructive of these ends, it is the right of the people to alter or abolish it, & to institute new government, laying it's foundation on such principles, & organizing it's powers in such form, as to them shall seem most likely to effect their safety & happiness. Prudence indeed will dictate that governments long established should not be changed for light & transient causes; and accordingly all experience hath shown that mankind are more disposed to suffer while evils are sufferable, than to right themselves by abolishing the forms to which they are accustomed. But when a long train of abuses & usurpations [*begun at a distinguished period and*] pursuing invariably the same object, evinces a design to reduce them under absolute despotism, it is their right, it is their duty to throw off such government, & to provide new guards for their future security. Such has been the patient sufferance of these colonies; & such is now the necessity which constrains them to [*expunge*] <u>alter</u> their former systems of government. The history of the present king of Great Britain is a history of [*unremitting*] <u>repeated</u> injuries & usurpations, [*among which appears no solitary fact to contradict the uniform tenor of the rest but all have*] <u>all having</u> in direct object the establishment of an absolute tyranny over these states. To prove this let facts be submitted to a candid world [*for the truth of which we pledge a faith yet unsullied by falsehood*].

He has refused his assent to laws the most wholesome & necessary for the public good.

He has forbidden his governors to pass laws of immediate & pressing importance, unless suspended in their operation till his assent should be obtained; & when so suspended, he has utterly neglected to attend to them.

He has refused to pass other laws for the accommodation of large districts of people, unless those people would relinquish the right of representation in the legislature, a right inestimable to them, & formidable to tyrants only.

He has called together legislative bodies at places unusual, uncomfortable, and distant from the depository of their public records, for the sole purpose of fatiguing them into compliance with his measures.

He has dissolved representative houses repeatedly [*& continually*] for opposing with manly firmness his invasions on the rights of the people.

He has refused for a long time after such dissolutions to cause others to be elected, whereby the legislative powers, incapable of annihilation, have returned to the people at large for their exercise, the state remaining in the meantime exposed to all the dangers of invasion from without & convulsions within.

He has endeavored to prevent the population of these states; for that purpose obstructing the laws for naturalization of foreigners, refusing to pass others to encourage their migrations hither, & raising the conditions of new appropriations of lands.

He has [*suffered*] obstructed the administration of justice [*totally to cease in some of these states*] by refusing his assent to laws for establishing judiciary powers.

He has made [*our*] judges dependant on his will alone, for the tenure of their offices, & the amount & paiment of their salaries.

He has erected a multitude of new offices [*by a self assumed power*] and sent hither swarms of new officers to harass our people and eat out their substance.

He has kept among us in times of peace standing armies [*and ships of war*] without the consent of our legislatures.

He has affected to render the military independant of, & superior to the civil power.

He has combined with others to subject us to a jurisdiction foreign to our constitutions & unacknowledged by our laws, giving his assent to their acts of pretended legislation for quartering large bodies of armed troops among us; for protecting them by a mock-trial from punishment for any murders which they should commit on the inhabitants of these states; for cutting off our trade with all parts of the world; for imposing taxes on us without our consent; for depriving us in many cases of the benefits of trial by jury; for transporting us beyond seas to be tried for pretended offences; for abolishing the free system of English laws in a neighboring province, establishing therein an arbitrary government, and enlarging it's boundaries, so as to render it at once an example and fit instrument for intro-ducing the same absolute rule into these [*states*] colonies; for taking away our charters, abolishing our most valuable laws, and altering fundamen-tally the forms of our governments; for suspending our own legislatures, & declaring themselves invested with power to legislate for us in all cases whatsoever.

He has abdicated government here [*withdrawing his governors, and declaring us out of his allegiance & protection*] by declaring us out of his pro-tection, and waging war against us.

He has plundered our seas, ravaged our coasts, burnt our towns, & destroyed the lives of our people.

He is at this time transporting large armies of foreign mercenaries to compleat the works of death, desolation & tyranny already begun with circumstances of cruelty and perfidy scarcely paralleled in the most bar-barous ages, & totally unworthy the head of a civilized nation.

He has constrained our fellow citizens taken captive on the high seas to bear arms against their country, to become the executioners of their friends & brethren, or to fall themselves by their hands.

He has excited domestic insurrection among us, & has endeavored to bring on the inhabitants of our frontiers the merciless Indian savages, whose known rule of warfare is an undistinguished destruction of all ages, sexes, & conditions [*of existence.*

He has incited treasonable insurrections of our fellow-citizens, with the allure-ments of forfeiture & confiscation of our property.

He has waged cruel war against human nature itself, violating it's most sacred rights of life and liberty in the persons of a distant people who never offended him, captivating & carrying them into slavery in another hemisphere, or to incur miser-able death in their transportation thither. This piratical warfare, the opprobium of INFIDEL powers, is the warfare of the CHRISTIAN king of Great Britain. Deter-mined to keep open a market where MEN should be bought & sold, he has prosti-tuted his negative for suppressing every legislative attempt to prohibit or to restrain this execrable commerce. And that this assemblage of horrors might want no fact of distinguished die, he is now exciting those very people to rise in arms among us, and to purchase that liberty of which he has deprived them, by murdering the people on whom he also obtruded them: thus paying off former crimes committed against the LIBERTIES of one people, with crimes which he urges them to commit against the LIVES of another.]

In every stage of these oppressions we have petitioned for redress in the most humble terms: our repeated petitions have been answered only by repeated injuries.

. A prince whose character is thus marked by every act which may define a tyrant is unfit to be the ruler of a free people [*who mean to be free. Future ages will scarcely believe that the hardiness of one man adventured, within the short compass of twelve years only, to lay a foundation so broad & so undisguised for tyranny over a people fostered & fixed in principles of freedom.*]

Nor have we been wanting in attentions to our British brethren. We have warned them from time to time of attempts by their legislature to extend [*a*] an unwarrantable jurisdiction [*over these our states*] us. We have reminded them of the circumstances of our emigration & settlement here, [*no one of which could warrant so strange a pretension: that these were effected at the expense of our own blood & treasure, unassisted by the wealth or the strength of Great Britain: that in constituting indeed our several forms of government, we had adopted one common king, thereby laying a foundation for perpetual league & amity with them: but that submission to their parliament was no part of our constitution, nor ever in idea, if history may be credited: and,*] we <u>have</u> appealed to their native justice and magnanimity [*as well as to*] <u>and we have conjured them by</u> the ties of our common kindred to disavow these usurpations which [*were likely to*] <u>would inevitably</u> interrupt our connection and correspondence. They too have been deaf to the voice of justice & of consanguinity. [*and when occasions have been given them, by the regular course of their laws, of removing from their councils the disturbers of our harmony, they have, by their free election, re-established them in power. At this very time too they are permitting their chief magistrate to send over not only soldiers of our common blood, but Scotch & foreign mercenaries to invade & destroy us. These facts have given the last . stab to agonizing affection, and manly spirit bids us to renounce forever these unfeeling brethren. We must endeavor to forget our former love for them, and hold them as we hold the rest of mankind, enemies in war, in peace friends. We might have been a free and a great people together; but a communication of grandeur & of freedom it seems is below their dignity. Be it so, since they will have it. The road to happiness & to glory is open to us too. We will tread it apart from them, and*] <u>We must, therefore,</u> acquiesce in the necessity which denounces our [*eternal*] separation <u>and hold them as we hold the rest of mankind, enemies in war, in peace friends!</u>

We therefore the representatives of the United States of America in General Congress assembled do in the name & by authority of the good people of these [*states*] <u>colonies</u> [*reject & renounce all allegiance & subjection to the kings of Great Britain & all others who may hereafter claim by, through or under them: we utterly dissolve all political connection which may heretofore have subsisted between us & the people or parliament of Great Britain: & finally we do assert & declare these colonies to be free & independent states,*] <u>solemnly publish & declare that these united colonies are & of right ought to be free & independent states; that they are absolved from all allegiance to the British crown, and that all political connection between them & the state of Great Britain is, & ought to be, totally dissolved;</u> & that as free & independent states they have full power to levy war, conclude peace, contract alliances, establish commerce & to do all other acts & things which independent states may of right do.

And for the support of this declaration, <u>with a firm reliance on the protection of divine providence</u> we mutually pledge to each other our lives, our fortunes, & our sacred honor.

5. To Edmund Pendleton, Philadelphia, 26 August 1776. *Edmund Pendleton (1734–1803) was a leading lawyer and statesman in colonial and revolutionary Virginia. First elected to the Burgesses in 1752, he was a mainstay of the Virginia Conventions (1774–1776) and a member of the First Continental Congress; he would subsequently serve as the presiding judge of Virginia's highest court, the Supreme Court of Appeals, from 1778 until his death. In this letter TJ is defending* *his proposals for the new Virginia constitution set forth in draft proposals that had arrived too late in Williamsburg to shape the document adopted by Pendleton and the Convention on 29 June. TJ's dissatisfaction with the Virginia Constitution of 1776 spurred his lifelong commitment to state constitutional reform; it is also clear from his exchanges with Pendleton and other Virginians that TJ considered developments in the states fundamentally important to the success of the revolution.*

You seem to have misapprehended my proposition for the choice of a Senate. I had two things in view: to get the wisest men chosen, & to make them perfectly independent when chosen. I have ever observed that a choice by the people themselves is not generally distinguished for it's wisdom. This first secretion from them is usually crude & heterogeneous. But give to those so chosen by the people a second choice themselves, & they generally will chuse wise men. For this reason it was that I proposed the representatives (& not the people) should chuse the Senate, & thought I had notwithstanding that made the Senators (when chosen) perfectly independant of their electors. However I should have no objection to the mode of election proposed in the printed plan of your committee, to wit, that the people of each county should chuse twelve electors, who should meet those of the other counties in the same district & chuse a senator. I should prefer this too for another reason, that the upper as well as lower house should have an opportunity of superintending & judging of the situation of the whole state & be not all of one neighborhood as our upper house used to be. So much for the wisdom of the Senate. To make them independent, had proposed that they should hold their places for nine years, & then go out (one third every three years) & be incapable for ever of being re-elected to that house. My idea was that if they might be re-elected, they would be casting their eye forward to the period of election (however distant) & be currying favor with the electors, & consequently dependant on them. My reason for fixing them in office for a term of years rather than for life, was that they might have in idea that they were at a certain period to return into the mass of the people & become the governed instead of the governor which might still keep alive that regard to the public good that otherwise they might perhaps be induced by their independance to forget. Yet I could submit, tho' not so willingly to an appointment for life, or to any thing rather than a mere creation by & dependance on the people. I think the present mode of election objectionable because the larger county will be able to send & will always send a man (less fit perhaps) of their own county to the exclusion of a fitter who may chance to live in a smaller county.—I wish experience may contradict my fears.—That the Senate as well as lower [or shall I speak truth & call it upper] house should hold no office of profit I am clear; but not that they should of necessity possess distinguished property. You have lived longer than I have and perhaps may have formed a different judgment on better grounds; but my observations do not enable me to think integrity is the characteristic of wealth. In general beleive the decisions of the people, in a body, will be more honest & more disinterested than those of wealthy men: & I can never doubt an attachment to his country in any man who has his family & peculium in it:—Now as to the representative house which ought to be so constructed as to answer that character truly. I was for extending the right of suffrage (or in other words the rights of a citizen) to all who had a permanent intention of living in the country. Take what circumstances you please as evidence of this, either the having resided a certain time, or having a family, or having property, any or all of them. Whoever intends to live in a country must wish that country well, & has a natural right of assisting in the preservation of it. Think you cannot distinguish between such a person residing in the country & having no fixed property, & one residing in a township whom you say you would admit to a vote.—The other point of equal representation I think capital & fundamental. am glad you think an alteration may be attempted in that matter.—The fantastical idea of virtue & the public good being a sufficient security to the state against the commission of crimes, which you say you have heard insisted on by some, assure you was never mine. It is only the sanguinary hue of our penal laws which I meant to object to. Punishments I know are necessary, & I would provide them, strict & inflexible, but proportioned to the crime. Death might be inflicted for murther & perhaps for treason if you would take out of the description of treason all crimes which are not such in their nature. Rape, buggery &c—punish by castration. All other crimes by working on high roads, rivers, gallies &c. a certain time proportioned to the offence. But as this would be no punishment or change of condition to slaves (me miserum!) let them be sent to other countries. By these means we should be freed from the wickedness of the latter, & the former would be living monuments of public vengeance. Laws thus proportionate & mild should never be dispensed with. Let mercy be the character of the lawgiver, but let the judge be a mere machine. The mercies of the law will be dispensed equally & impartially to every description of men; those of the judge, or of the executive power, will be the eccentric impulses of whimsical, capricious designing man. . . .

6. Revisal of the Laws, 1776–1779. *In November 1776 TJ was named to head a committee of the House of Delegates, also including Edmund Pendleton, George Wythe, George Mason, and Thomas Ludwell Lee, to revise Virginia's laws in light of the recent break with Britain. The revisors were not content with such minor changes in existing laws as expunging references to royal authority, but offered an ambitious code, in the form of 126 proposed bills, that embodied TJ's vision of republican reform. Many of the bills (such as number 79, For the More General Diffusion of Knowledge, excerpted below) proved too radical for the delegates. By early 1779, when the committee moved rapidly to complete its report, Lee had died and Mason had retired to private life. Wythe, TJ's beloved law teacher, was given primary responsibility for reviewing English statutes still in force in Virginia, Pendleton was assigned Virginia statutes, and TJ took on the most daunting challenge: to reduce the colony's common law to a coherent set of bills. After the committee's report was submitted on 18 June, the delegates moved to enact only a few of the bills. When the war was over, the legislature resumed deliberations on the report, enacting about half of the bills, among them the famous number 82, For Establishing Religious Freedom; many of the remaining bills were adopted in subsequent years. TJ's interests in republican law reform covered an extraordinary range of top-*

ics, *from education to the institution of slavery to changes in Virginia's land laws that would prevent the emergence of aristocracy. In the first selection below, TJ offers his own commentary on the committee's work; a small sample of the proposed bills follows.*

A. From Jefferson's Autobiography, Written 6 January–29 July 1821.

We thought, that on this subject a systematical plan of general education should be proposed, and I was requested to undertake it. I accordingly prepared three bills for the Revisal, proposing three distinct grades of education, reaching all classes. 1. Elementary schools for all children generally, rich and poor. 2. Colleges for a middle degree of instruction, calculated for the common purposes of life, and such as would be desirable for all who were in easy circumstances. And 3d. an ultimate grade for teaching the sciences generally, & in their highest degree. The first bill proposed to lay off every county into Hundreds or Wards, of a proper size and population for a school, in which reading, writing, and common arithmetic should be taught; and that the whole state should be divided into 24 districts, in each of which should be a school for classical learning, grammar, geography, and the higher branches of numerical arithmetic. The second bill proposed to amend the constitution of Wm. & Mary College, to enlarge it's sphere of science, and to make it in fact an University. The third was for the establishment of a library. These bills were not acted on until the same year '96. and then only so much of the first as provided for elementary schools. The College of Wm. & Mary was an establishment purely of the Church of England, the Visitors were required to be all of that Church; the Professors to subscribe it's 39 Articles, it's Students to learn it's Catechism, and one of its fundamental objects was declared to be to raise up Ministers for that church. The religious jealousies therefore of all the dissenters took alarm lest this might give an ascendancy to the Anglican sect and refused acting on that bill. Its local eccentricity too and unhealthy autumnal climate lessened the general inclination towards it. And in the Elementary bill they inserted a provision which completely defeated it, for they left it to the court of each county to determine for itself when this act should be carried into execution, within their county. One provision of the bill was that the expenses of these schools should be borne by the inhabitants of the county, every one in proportion to his general tax-rate. This would throw on wealth the education of the poor; and the justices, being generally of the more wealthy class, were unwilling to incur that burthen, and I believe it was not suffered to commence in a single county. I shall recur again to this subject towards the close of my story, if I should have life and resolution enough to reach that term; for I am already tired of talking about myself.

The bill on the subject of slaves was a mere digest of the existing laws respecting them, without any intimation of a plan for a future & general emancipation. It was thought better that this should be kept back, and attempted only by way of amendment whenever the bill should be brought on. The principles of the amendment however were agreed on, that is to say, the freedom of all born after a certain day, and deportation at a proper age. But it was found that the public mind would not yet bear the proposition, nor will it bear it even at this day. Yet the day is not distant when it must bear and adopt it, or worse will follow. Nothing is more certainly written in the book of fate than that these people are to be free. Nor is it less certain that the two races, equally free, cannot live in the same government. Nature, habit, opinion has drawn indelible lines of distinction between them. It is still in our power to direct the process of emancipation and deportation peaceably and in such slow degree as that the evil will wear off insensibly, and their place be pari passu filled up by free white laborers. If on the contrary it is left to force itself on, human nature must shudder at the prospect held up. We should in vain look for an example in the Spanish deportation or deletion of the Moors. This precedent would fall far short of our case.

I considered 4 of these bills, passed or reported, as forming a system by which every fibre would be eradicated of antient or future aristocracy; and a foundation laid for a government truly republican. The repeal of the laws of entail would prevent the accumulation and perpetuation of wealth in select families, and preserve the soil of the country from being daily more & more absorbed in Mortmain. The abolition of primogeniture, and equal partition of inheritances removed the feudal and unnatural distinctions which made one member of every family rich, and all the rest poor, substituting equal partition, the best of all Agrarian laws. The restoration of the rights of conscience relieved the people from taxation for the support of a religion not theirs; for the establishment was truly of the religion of the rich, the dissenting sects being entirely composed of the less wealthy people; and these, by the bill for a general education, would be qualified to understand their rights, to maintain them, and to exercise with intelligence their parts in self-government: and all this would be effected without the violation of a single natural right of any one individual citizen. To these too might be added, as a further security, the introduction of the trial by jury, into the Chancery courts, which have already ingulfed and continue to ingulf, so great a proportion of the jurisdiction over our property. . . .

B. Bill 51, A Bill concerning Slaves. *Enacted by the General Assembly in 1785, except for portion in brackets.*

Be it enacted by the General Assembly, that no person shall, henceforth be slaves within this commonwealth, except such as were so on the first day of this present session of assembly, and the descendants of the females of them.

Negroes and mulattoes which shall hereafter be brought into this commonwealth and kept therein one whole year, together, or so long at different times as shall amount to one year, shall be free. [But if they shall not depart the commonwealth within one year thereafter they shall be out of the protection of the laws.

Those which shall come into this commonwealth of their own accord shall be out of the protection of the laws; save only such as being seafaring persons and navigating vessels hither, shall not leave the same while here more than twenty four hours together.

It shall not be lawful for any person to emancipate a slave but by deed executed, proved and recorded as is required by law in the case of a conveyance of goods and chattels, on consideration not deemed valuable in law, or by last will and testament, and with the free consent of such slave, expressed in presence of the court of the county wherein he resides: And if such slave, so emancipated, shall not within one year thereafter, depart the commonwealth, he shall be out of the protection of the laws. All conditions, restrictions and limitations annexed to any act of emancipation shall be void from the time such emancipation is to take place.

If any white woman shall have a child by a negro or mulatto, she and her child shall depart the commonwealth within one year thereafter. If they fail so to do, the woman shall be out of the protection of the laws, and the child shall be bound out by the Aldermen of the county, in like manner as poor orphans are by law directed to be, and within one year after its term of service expired shall depart the commonwealth, or on failure so to do, shall be out of the protection of the laws.

Where any of the persons before described shall be disabled from departing the commonwealth by grievous sickness, the protection of the law shall be continued to him until such disability be removed: And if the county shall in the mean time, incur any expence in taking care of him, as of other county poor, the Aldermen shall be intitled to recover the same from his former master, if he had one, his heirs, executors and administrators.]

No negro or mulatto shall be a witness except in pleas of the commonwealth against negroes or mulattoes, or in civil pleas wherein negroes or mulattoes alone shall be parties.

No slave shall go from the tenements of his master, or other person with whom he lives, without a pass, or some letter or token whereby it may appear that he is proceeding by authority from his master, employer, or overseer: If he does, it shall be lawful for any person to apprehend and carry him before a Justice of the Peace, to be by his order punished with stripes, or not, in his discretion.

No slave shall keep any arms whatever, nor pass, unless with written orders from his master or employer, or in his company, with arms from one place to another. Arms in possession of a slave contrary to this prohibition shall be forfeited to him who will seize them.

Riots, routs, unlawful assemblies, trespasses and seditious speeches by a negro or mulatto shall be punished with stripes at the discretion of a Justice of the Peace; and he who will may apprehend and carry him before such Justice.

C. Bill 54, A Bill Declaring What Persons Shall be Deemed Mulattoes.
Enacted by the General Assembly in 1785.

Be it enacted by the General Assembly, that every person, of whose grandfathers or grandmothers any one is, or shall have been, a negro, although all his other progenitors, except that descending from the negro, shall have been white persons, shall be deemed a mulatto; and so every person, who shall have one fourth part or more of negro blood, shall, in like manner be deemed a mulatto.

D. Bill 55, A Bill Declaring Who Shall Be Deemed Citizens of this Commonwealth. *Enacted by General Assembly in June 1779.*

SECTION I. Be it enacted by the General Assembly, that all white persons born within the territory of this commonwealth and all who have resided therein two years next before the passing of this act, and all who shall hereafter migrate into the same; and shall before any court of record give satisfactory proof by their own oath or affirmation, that they intend to reside therein, and moreover shall give assurance of fidelity to the commonwealth; and all infants wheresoever born, whose father, if living, or otherwise, whose mother was, a citizen at the time of their birth, or who migrate hither, their father, if living, or otherwise their mother becoming a citizen, or who migrate hither without father or mother, shall be deemed citizens of this commonwealth, until they relinquish that character in manner as herein after expressed: And all others not being citizens of any the United States of America, shall be deemed aliens. The clerk of the court shall enter such oath of record, and give the person taking the same a certificate thereof, for which he shall receive the fee of one dollar. And in order to preserve to the citizens of this commonwealth, that natural right, which all men have of relinquishing the country, in which birth, or other accident may have thrown them, and, seeking subsistance and happiness wheresoever they may be able, or may hope to find them: And to declare unequivocally what circumstances shall be deemed evidence of an intention in any citizen to exercise that right, it is enacted and declared, that whensoever any citizen of this commonwealth, shall by word of mouth in the presence of the court of the county, wherein he resides, or of the General Court, or by deed in writing, under his hand and seal, executed in the presence of three witnesses, and by them proved in either of the said courts, openly declare to the same court, that he relinquishes the character of a citizen, and shall depart the commonwealth; or whensoever he shall without such declaration depart the commonwealth and enter into the service of any other state, not in enmity with this, or any other of the United States of America, or do any act whereby he shall become a subject or citizen of such state, such person shall be considered as having exercised his natural right of expatriating himself, and shall be deemed no citizen of this commonwealth from the time of his departure. The free white inhabitants of every of the states, parties to the American confederation, paupers, vagabonds and fugitives from justice excepted, shall be intitled to all rights, privileges, and immunities of free citizens in this commonwealth, and shall have free egress, and regress, to and from the same, and shall enjoy therein, all the privileges of trade, and commerce, subject to the same duties, impositions and restrictions as the citizens of this commonwealth. And if any person guilty of, or charged with treason, felony, or other high misdemeanor, in any of the said states, shall flee from justice and be found in this commonwealth, he shall, upon demand of the Governor, or Executive power of the state, from which he fled, be delivered up to be removed to the state having jurisdiction of his offence. Where any person holding property, within this commonwealth, shall be attainted within any of the said states, parties to the said confederation, of any of those crimes, which by the laws of this commonwealth shall be punishable by forfeiture of such property, the said property shall be disposed of in the same manner as it would have been if the owner thereof had been attainted of the like crime in this commonwealth.

E. Bill 64, A Bill for Proportioning Crimes and Punishments in Cases Heretofore Capital. *Never passed by the General Assembly.*

SECTION I. Whereas it frequently happens that wicked and dissolute men, resigning themselves to the dominion of inordinate passions, commit violations on the lives, liberties, and property of others, and the secure enjoyment of these having principally induced men to enter into society, government would be defective in its principal purpose, were it not to restrain such criminal acts by inflicting due punishments on those who perpetrate them; but it appears at the same time equally deducible from the purposes of society, that a member thereof, committing an inferior injury, does not wholly forfeit the protection of his fellow citizens, but after suffering a punishment in proportion to his offence, is entitled to their protection from all greater pain, so that it becomes a duty in the Legislature to arrange in a proper scale the crimes which it may be necessary for them to repress, and to adjust thereto a corresponding gradation of punishments. And whereas the reformation of offenders, though an object worthy the attention of the laws, is not effected at all by capital punishments which exterminate instead of reforming, and should be the last melancholy resource against those whose existence is become inconsistent with the safety of their fellow citizens; which also weaken the State by cutting off so many, who, if reformed, might be restored sound members to society, who, even under a course of correction, might be rendered useful in various labours for the public, and would be, living, and long-continued spectacles to deter others from committing the like offences. And forasmuch as the experience of all ages and countries hath shewn, that cruel and sanguinary laws defeat their own purpose, by engaging the benevolence of mankind to withhold prosecutions, to smother testimony, or to listen to it with bias; and by producing in many instances a total dispensation and impunity under the names of pardon and privilege of clergy; when, if the punishment were only proportioned to the injury, men would feel it their inclination, as well as their duty, to see the laws observed; and the power of dispensation, so dangerous and mischievous, which produces crimes by holding up a hope of impunity, might totally be abolished, so that men while contemplating to perpetrate a crime would see their punishment ensuing as necessarily as effects follow their causes; for rendering crimes and punishments, therefore, more proportionate to each other. . . .

F. Bill 79, A Bill for the More General Diffusion of Knowledge. *Never passed by General Assembly.*

SECTION I. Whereas it appeareth that however certain forms of government are better calculated than others to protect individuals in the free exercise of their natural rights, and are at the same time themselves better guarded against degeneracy, yet experience hath shewn, that even under the best forms, those entrusted with power have, in time, and by slow operations, perverted it into tyranny; and it is believed that the most effectual means of preventing this would be, to illuminate, as far as practicable, the minds of the people at large, and more especially to give them knowledge of those facts, which history exhibiteth, that, possessed thereby of the experience of other ages and countries, they may be enabled to know ambition under all its shapes, and prompt to exert their natural powers to defeat its purposes; And whereas it is generally true that the people will be happiest whose laws are best, and are best administered, and that laws will be wisely formed, and honestly administered, in proportion as those who form and administer them are wise and honest; whence it becomes expedient for promoting the publick happiness that those persons, whom nature hath endowed with genius and virtue, should be rendered by liberal education worthy to receive, and able to guard the sacred deposit of the rights and liberties of their fellow citizens, and that they should be called to that charge without regard to wealth, birth or other accidental condition or circumstance; but the indigence of the greater number disabling them from so educating, at their own expence, those of their children whom nature hath fitly formed and disposed to become useful instruments for the public, it is better that such should be sought for and educated at the common expence of all, than that the happiness of all should be confided to the weak or wicked. . . .

G. Bill 82, A Bill for Establishing Religious Freedom. *Enacted by the General Assembly in 1785.*

SECTION I. Well aware that the opinions and belief of men depend not on their own will, but follow involuntarily the evidence proposed to their minds; that Almighty God hath created the mind free, and manifested his supreme will that free it shall remain by making it altogether insusceptible of restraint; that all attempts to influence it by temporal punishments, or burthens, or by civil incapacitations, tend only to beget habits of hypocrisy and meanness, and are a departure from the plan of the holy author of our religion, who being lord both of body and mind, yet chose not to propagate it by coercions on either, as was in his Almighty power to do, but to extend it by its influence on reason alone; that the impious presumption of legislators and rulers, civil as well as ecclesiastical, who, being themselves but fallible and uninspired men, have assumed dominion over the faith of others, setting up their own opinions and modes of thinking as the only true and infallible, and as such endeavoring to impose them on others, hath established and maintained false religions over the greatest part of the world and through all time: That to compel a man to furnish contributions of money for the propagation of opinions which he disbelieves and abhors, is sinful and tyrannical; that even the forcing him to support this or that teacher of his own religious persuasion, is depriving him of the comfortable liberty of giving his contributions to the particular pastor whose morals he would make his pattern, and whose powers he feels most persuasive to righteousness; and is withdrawing from the ministry those temporary rewards, which proceeding from an approbation of their personal conduct, are an additional incitement to earnest and unremitting labours for the instruction of mankind; that our civil rights have no dependance on our religious opinions, any more than our opinions in physics or geometry; that therefore the proscribing any citizen as unworthy the pub-

lic confidence by laying upon him an incapacity of being called to offices
of trust and emolument, unless he profess or renounce this or that religious opinion, is depriving him injuriously of those privileges and advantages to which, in common with his fellow citizens, he has a natural right;
that it tends also to corrupt the principles of that very religion it is meant
to encourage, by bribing, with a monopoly of worldly honours and emoluments, those who will externally profess and conform to it; that though
indeed these are criminal who do not withstand such temptation, yet neither are those innocent who lay the bait in their way; that the opinions of
men are not the object of civil government, nor under its jurisdiction; that
to suffer the civil magistrate to intrude his powers into the field of opinion
and to restrain the profession or propagation of principles on supposition
of their ill tendency is a dangerous falacy, which at once destroys all religious liberty, because he being of course judge of that tendency will make
his opinions the rule of judgment, and approve or condemn the sentiments of others only as they shall square with or differ from his own; that
it is time enough for the rightful purposes of civil government for its officers to interfere when principles break out into overt acts against peace
and good order; and finally, that truth is great and will prevail if left to herself; that she is the proper and sufficient antagonist to error, and has nothing to fear from the conflict unless by human interposition disarmed of
her natural weapons, free argument and debate; errors ceasing to be dangerous when it is permitted freely to contradict them.

SECT. II. WE the General Assembly of Virginia do enact that no man
shall be compelled to frequent or support any religious worship, place, or
ministry whatsoever, nor shall be enforced, restrained, molested, or burthened in his body or goods, nor shall otherwise suffer, on account of his
religious opinions or belief; but that all men shall be free to profess, and
by argument to maintain, their opinions in matters of religion, and that
the same shall in no wise diminish, enlarge, or affect their civil capacities.

SECT. III. AND though we well know that this Assembly, elected by the
people for the ordinary purposes of legislation only, have no power to
restrain the acts of succeeding Assemblies, constituted with powers equal
to our own, and that therefore to declare this act irrevocable would be of
no effect in law; yet we are free to declare, and do declare, that the rights
hereby asserted are of the natural rights of mankind, and that if any act
shall be hereafter passed to repeal the present or to narrow its operation,
such act will be an infringement of natural right.

7. To James Monroe, Monticello, 20 May 1782. *James Monroe (1758–
1831) served with distinction in the Continental Army, subsequently studied law
with TJ and was elected to the House of Delegates. At the time of this letter, TJ
was in retirement at Monticello, still bitter about charges that he had failed to exercise effective leadership during the last weeks of his governorship in 1781, when
British forces led by Benedict Arnold met with little resistance. Though the Virginia
assembly exonerated him of these charges, they continued to cause him embarrassment in later years. TJ's gubenatorial travails did not deter his Albemarle neighbors
from electing him to the House in the spring 1782 elections. TJ's refusal to serve,*

reinforced by the poor state of wife Martha's health, inspired unfriendly comments in Richmond, the state's capital since 1780.

It gives me pleasure that your county has been wise enough to enlist your talents into their service. I am much obliged by the kind wishes you express of seeing me also in Richmond, and am always mortified when anything is expected from me which I cannot fulfill, & more especially if it relate to the public service. Before I ventured to declare to my countrymen my determination to retire from public employment, I examined well my heart to know whether it were thoroughly cured of every principle of political ambition, whether no lurking particle remained which might leave me uneasy when reduced within the limits of mere private life. I became satisfied that every fibre of that passion was thoroughly eradicated. I examined also in other views my right to withdraw. I considered that I had been thirteen years engaged in public service, that during that time I had so totally abandoned all attention to my private affairs as to permit them to run into great disorder and ruin, that I had now a family advanced to years which require my attention & instruction, that to these were added the hopeful offspring of a deceased friend whose memory must be forever dear to me who have no other reliance for being rendered useful to themselves & their country, that by a constant sacrifice of time, labour, loss, parental & family duties, I had been so far from gaining the affection of my countrymen, which was the only reward I ever asked or could have felt, that I had even lost the small estimation before possessed. That however I might have comforted myself under the disapprobation of the well-meaning but uninformed people yet that of their representatives was a shock on which had not calculated: that this indeed had been followed by an exculpatory declaration. But in the meantime I had been suspected & suspended in the eyes of the world without the least hint then or afterwards made public which might restrain them from supposing that I stood arraigned for treason of the heart and not merely weakness of the head; and I felt that these injuries, for such they have been since acknowledged had inflicted a wound on my spirit which will only be cured by the all-healing grave. If reason & inclination unite in justifying my retirement, the laws of my country are equally in favor of it. Whether the state may command the political services of all it's members to an indefinite extent, or if these be among the rights never wholly ceded to the public power, is a question which I do not find expressly decided in England. Obiter dictums on the subject I have indeed met with, but the complexion of the times in which these have dropped would generally answer them, besides that this species of authority is not acknowledged in our profession. In this country however since the present government has been established the point has been settled by uniform, pointed & multiplied precedents. Offices of every kind, and given by every power, have been daily & hourly declined & resigned from the declaration of independance to this moment. The genl assembly has accepted these without discrimination of office, and without ever questioning them in point of right. If a difference between the office of a delegate & any other could ever have been supposed, yet in the case of Mr. Thompson Mason who declined the office of delegate & was permitted so to do by the house that supposition has been proved to be groundless. But indeed no such distinction of offices can be admitted. Reason and the opinions of the lawyers putting all on a footing as to this question and so giving to the delegate the aid of all the precedents of the refusal of other offices. The law then does not warrant the assumption of such a power by the state over it's members. For if it does where is that law? nor yet does reason, for tho' I will admit that this does subject every individual if called on to an equal tour of political duty yet it can never go so far as to submit to it his whole existence. If we are made in some degree for others, yet in a greater are we made for ourselves. It were contrary to feeling & indeed ridiculous to suppose that a man had less right in himself than one of his neighbors or indeed all of them put together. This would be slavery & not that liberty which the bill of rights has made inviolable and for the preservation of which our government has been charged. Nothing could so completely divest us of that liberty as the establishment of the opinion that the state has a perpetual right to the services of all it's members. This to men of certain ways of thinking would be to annihilate the blessing of existence; to contradict the giver of life who gave it for happiness & not for wretchedness; and certainly to such it were better that they had never been born. However with these may think public service & private misery inseparably linked together, I have not the vanity to count myself among those whom the state would think worth oppressing with *perpetual* service, have received a sufficient memento to the contrary. I am persuaded that having hitherto dedicated to them the whole of the active & useful part of my life I shall be permitted to pass the rest in mental quiet. I hope too that I did not mistake the modes any more than the matter of right when I preferred a simple act of renunciation to the taking sanctuary under those disqualifications provided by the law for other purposes indeed, but which afford asylum also for rest to the wearied. I dare say you did not expect by the few words you dropped on the right of renunciation to expose yourself to the fatigue of so long a letter, but I wished you to see that if I had done wrong I had been betrayed by a semblance of right at least. . . .

8. To François Jean de Chastellux, Ampthill, 26 November 1782.
François Jean de Chastellux, an officer in Rochambeau's army and a member of the French Academy, visited Monticello in the spring of 1782. His Voyages in North-America, *first published in Paris in 1786, included a flattering depiction of TJ and his mountaintop home. When TJ accepted Congress's appointment to join the U.S. delegation at the Paris peace talks, he hoped to make the Atlantic crossing with his new friend. His sailing was delayed for various reasons, however, and Congress eventually postponed his departure until July 1784. After TJ's arrival in the French capital, he and Chastellux resumed their friendship.*

[*Your letter*] found me a little emerging from the stupor of mind which had rendered me as dead to the world as she [*TJ's wife Martha, who dies in September*] was whose loss occasioned it. Your letter recalled to my memory that there were persons still living of much value to me. If you should have thought me remiss in not testifying to you sooner how deeply I had been impressed with your worth in the little time I had the happiness of being with you you will I am sure ascribe it to it's true cause the state of dreadful suspense in which I had been kept all the summer & the catastrophe which closed it. Before that event my scheme of life had been determined. I had folded myself in the arms of retirement, and rested all prospects of future happiness on domestic & literary objects. A single event wiped away all my plans and left me a blank which I had not the spirits to fill up. In this state of mind an appointment from Congress found me, requiring me to cross the Atlantic. And that temptation might be added to duty I was informed at the same time from his Excy the Chevalier de Luzerne that a vessel of force would be sailing about the middle of Dec. in which you would be passing to France. I accepted the appointment and my only object now is so to hasten over those obstacles which would retard my departure as to be ready to join you in your voyage, fondly measuring your affections by my own & presuming your consent. It is not certain that by any exertion I can be in Philadelphia by the middle of December. The contrary is most probable. But hoping it will not be much later and counting on those procrastinations which usually attend the departure of vessels of size I have hopes of being with you in time. This will give me full leisure to learn the result of your observations on the natural bridge, to communicate to you my answers to the queries of Monsr de Marbois, to receive edification from you on these and on other subjects of science, considering chess too as a matter of science. . . .

CHAPTER TWO

Notes on the State of Virginia

Sometime in mid-1780 François Marbois, secretary to the French legation at Philadelphia, circulated a set of queries to leading figures throughout the United States, seeking comprehensive information on the population, manners, institutions, resources, and history of all the members of the far-flung American union. Marbois gave the queries for Virginia to Congressman Joseph Jones, the uncle of Jefferson's protégé James Monroe, and Jones passed them on to Governor Jefferson. There was probably no one better equipped in the state to provide such an encyclopedic account of its circumstances and prospects, and none of the recipients of the queries in the other states produced anything comparable.

After British forces withdrew from Virginia in October 1780, and before Benedict Arnold launched his nearly disastrous invasion at the very end of the year, Jefferson eagerly turned to his task. For the next six months the beleaguered governor put aside the manuscript, resuming his labors after his retirement from office in June. Forwarding a completed draft to Marbois in December 1781, he soon undertook substantial revisions. During his brief tenure at the Confederation Congress in 1783 and 1784, he gathered additional materials, some supplied by friendly readers of his manuscript draft. Deterred from its immediate issue by the high costs of publishing in Philadelphia, Jefferson took the manuscript with him to France in July 1784. An anonymous French edition of only two hundred copies intended for private distribution was brought out in May 1785. Concern about the possibility of an unauthorized translation eventually led Jefferson to arrange the first English language edition of *The Notes on the State of Virginia* by English bookseller John Stockdale in 1787. This is the edition from which the excerpts below were taken.

Responding to Marbois' queries according to his own sense of their logical order, answering some at great length and others in cursory fashion, Jefferson begins in responses to the first five queries with a description of the state's "Boundaries" and physical geography. Next comes in number VI an exhaustive inventory of "Productions Mineral, Vegetable and Animal." Toward the end of this discussion, containing his famous challenge to the thesis of the great French naturalist Georges Louis Leclerc, the Comte de Buffon, that animal species degenerated in the New World, Jefferson first considers the indigenous people of Virginia. After treating Virginia's "Climate" in VII, he comprehensively reviews Virginia's population and history, commenting in VIII on immigration and giving in IX data on military manpower and on Indians in XI.

Jefferson's attention then shifts to political and constitutional questions. His extended discussion of the state's "Constitution" in XIII rehearses some of the serious misgivings he had always had about that document, misgivings that were undoubtedly exacerbated by his experiences as governor. "Laws," an equally long response in XIV to the next query, includes some of the most fascinating and controversial material in the entire manuscript, most notably the famous treatment of race and slavery. Juxtaposing the rule of law for white Virginians to the despotic, lawless enslavement of Afro-Virginians prefigures a tension that carries through much of the rest of the *Notes*.

Jefferson's account of the state's institutions continues in subsequent discussions of "Colleges, Buildings, and Roads" in XV and "Religion" in XVII. In XVIII, his brief account of "Manners," Jefferson returns to the institution of slavery, this time emphasizing its demoralizing effects on the master class. "Manufactures," numbered XIX, also considers moral threats to the health of the commonwealth. Virginia should leave its "work-shops . . . in Europe," Jefferson insists, so avoiding the kind of servile dependency that advanced manufactures and a degraded working population entail. This discussion leads in turn to linked essays in political economy, including in XX a review of export statistics and in XXII an account of "Public Revenue and Expences." Number XXIII, the final response of the *Notes*, offers a comprehensive list of "Histories, Memorials and State Papers" and serves as a guide to further reading and documentary support for the commonwealth's political pretensions, among these the claim to the boundaries described at the beginning of the book.

Though an accomplished writer, Jefferson was always reluctant to publish under his own name. This characteristic reticence was reinforced in the case of the *Notes* by his anxiety that Virginians at home would object to his critical treatment of their constitution and his even more devastating commentary on slavery. Enlightened European readers, undoubtedly seeing in these criticisms the promise of yet further reform, would associate the state's institutional and moral development with its tremendous potential for economic development. But Jefferson's wariness about his countrymen's response (at first he proposed to circulate the *Notes* only among the presumably enlightened students at William and Mary) suggested that the republican millennium he envisioned might be indefinitely postponed.

As Jefferson's only published book, the *Notes on Virginia* has attracted extraordinary attention from scholars (see the Introduction). It is an invaluable source for students of Jefferson's thought, providing the most sustained treatment in all his writings of many important issues, notably race and slavery. Coming at a moment when Jefferson's career radically shifted focus, from the republican reform of Virginia's institutions to the promotion of the new nation's interests and image during his years of diplomacy in Paris, the *Notes* illuminates Jefferson's hopes and fears for the ultimate outcome of the American Revolution.

* * * * * * * * *

1. From Query II, Rivers.

The *Missisipi* will be one of the principal channels of future commerce for the country westward of the Alleghaney. From the mouth of this river to where it receives the Ohio, is 1000 miles by water, but only 500 by land, passing through the Chickasaw country. From the mouth of the Ohio to that of the Missouri, is 230 miles by water, and 140 by land. From thence to the mouth of the Illinois river, is about 25 miles. The Missisipi, below the mouth of the Missouri, is always muddy, and abounding with sand bars, which frequently change their places. However, it carries 15 feet water to the mouth of the Ohio, to which place it is from one and a half to two miles wide, and thence to Kaskaskia from one mile to a mile and a quarter wide. Its current is so rapid, that it never can be stemmed by the force of the wind alone, acting on sails. Any vessel, however, navigated with oars, may come up at any time, and receive much aid from the wind. A batteau passes from the mouth of Ohio to the mouth of Missisipi in three weeks, and is from two to three months getting up again. During its floods, which are periodical as those of the Nile, the largest vessels may pass down it, if their steerage can be ensured. These floods begin in April, and the river returns into its banks early in August. The inundation extends further on the western than eastern side, covering the lands in some places for 50 miles from its banks. Above the mouth of the Missouri, it becomes much such a river as the Ohio, like it clear, and gentle in its current, not quite so wide, the period of its floods nearly the same, but not rising to so great a height. . . .

The country watered by the Missisipi and its eastern branches, constitutes five-eighths of the United States, two of which five-eighths are occupied by the Ohio and its waters: the residuary streams which run into the Gulph of Mexico, the Atlantic, and the St. Laurence water, the remaining three-eighths.

Before we quit the subject of the western waters, we will take a view of their principal connections with the Atlantic. These are three; the Hudson's river, the Patowmac, and the Missisipi itself. Down the last will pass all heavy commodities. But the navigation through the Gulph of Mexico is so dangerous, and that up the Missisipi so difficult and tedious, that it is thought probable that European merchandize will not return through that channel. It is most likely that flour, timber, and other heavy articles will be floated on rafts, which will themselves be an article for sale as well as their loading, the navigators returning by land or in light batteaux. There will therefore be a competition between the Hudson and Patowmac rivers for the residue of the commerce of all the country westward of Lake Erié, on the waters of the lakes, of the Ohio, and upper parts of the Missisipi. To go to New-York, that part of the trade which comes from the lakes or their waters must first be brought into Lake Erié. Between Lake Superior and its waters and Huron are the rapids of St. Mary, which will permit boats to pass, but not larger vessels. Lakes Huron and Michigan afford communication with Lake Erié by vessels of 8 feet draught. That part of the trade which comes from the waters of the Missisipi must pass from them through some portage into the waters of the lakes. The portage from the Illinois river into a water of Michigan is of one mile only. From the Wabash, Miami, Muskingum, or Alleghaney, are portages into the waters of Lake Erié, of from one to fifteen miles. When the commodities are brought into, and have passed through Lake Erié, there is between that and

Ontario an interruption by the falls of Niagara, where the portage is of 8 miles; and between Ontario and the Hudson's river are portages at the falls of Onondago, a little above Oswego, of a quarter of a mile; from Wood creek to the Mohawks river two miles; at the little falls of the Mohawks river half a mile, and from Schenectady to Albany 16 miles. Besides the increase of expence occasioned by frequent change of carriage, there is an increased risk of pillage produced by committing merchandize to a greater number of hands successively. The Patowmac offers itself under the following circumstances. For the trade of the lakes and their waters westward of Lake Erié, when it shall have entered that lake, it must coast along its southern shore, on account of the number and excellence of its harbours, the northern, though shortest, having few harbours, and these unsafe. Having reached Cayahoga, to proceed on to New-York it will have 825 miles and five portages: whereas it is but 425 miles to Alexandria, its emporium on the Patowmac, if it turns into the Cayahoga, and passes through that, Bigbeaver, Ohio, Yohoganey, (or Monongalia and Cheat) and Patowmac, and there are but two portages; the first of which between Cayahoga and Beaver may be removed by uniting the sources of these waters, which are lakes in the neighbourhood of each other, and in a champaign country; the other from the waters of Ohio to Patowmac will be from 15 to 40 miles, according to the trouble which shall be taken to approach the two navigations. For the trade of the Ohio, or that which shall come into it from its own waters or the Missisipi, it is nearer through the Patowmac to Alexandria than to New-York by 580 miles, and it is interrupted by one portage only. There is another circumstance of difference too. The lakes themselves never freeze, but the communications between them freeze, and the Hudson's river is itself shut up by the ice three months in the year; whereas the channel to the Chesapeak leads directly into a warmer climate. The southern parts of it very rarely freeze at all, and whenever the northern do, it is so near the sources of the rivers, that the frequent floods to which they are there liable break up the ice immediately, so that vessels may pass through the whole winter, subject only to accidental and short delays. Add to all this, that in case of a war with our neighbours the Anglo-Americans or the Indians, the route to New-York becomes a frontier through almost its whole length, and all commerce through it ceases from that moment.—But the channel to New-York is already known to practice; whereas the upper waters of the Ohio and the Patowmac, and the great falls of the latter, are yet to be cleared of their fixed obstructions.

2. From Query IV, Mountains.

The passage of the Patowmac through the Blue ridge is one of the most stupendous scenes in nature. You stand on a very high point of land. On your right comes up the Shenandoah, having ranged along the foot of the mountain an hundred miles to seek a vent. On your left approaches the Patowmac, in quest of a passage also. In the moment of their junction they rush together against the mountain, rend it asunder, and pass off to the sea. The first glance of this scene hurries our senses into the opinion, that this earth has been created in time, that the mountains were formed first, that the rivers began to flow afterwards, that in this place particularly they have been dammed up by the Blue ridge of mountains, and have formed an ocean which filled the whole valley; that continuing to rise they have at length broken over at this spot, and have torn the mountain down from its summit to its base. The piles of rock on each hand, but particularly on the Shenandoah, the evident marks of their disrupture and avulsion from their beds by the most powerful agents of nature, corroborate the impression. But the distant finishing which nature has given to the picture is of a very different character. It is a true contrast to the fore-ground. It is as placid and delightful, as that is wild and tremendous. For the mountain being cloven asunder, she presents to your eye, through the cleft, a small catch of smooth blue horizon, at an infinite distance in the plain country, inviting you, as it were, from the riot and tumult roaring around, to pass through the breach and participate of the calm below. Here the eye ultimately composes itself; and that way too the road happens actually to lead. You cross the Patowmac above the junction, pass along its side through the base of the mountain for three miles, its terrible precipices hanging in fragments over you, and within about 20 miles reach Frederic town and the fine country round that. This scene is worth a voyage across the Atlantic. Yet here, as in the neighbourhood of the natural bridge, are people who have passed their lives within half a dozen miles, and have never been to survey these monuments of a war between rivers and mountains, which must have shaken the earth itself to its center.—The height of our mountains has not yet been estimated with any degree of exactness. The Alleghaney being the great ridge which divides the waters of the Atlantic from those of the Missisipi, its summit is doubtless more elevated above the ocean than that of any other mountain. But its relative height, compared with the base on which it stands, is not so great as that of some others, the country rising behind the successive ridges like the steps of stairs. The mountains of the Blue ridge, and of these the Peaks of Otter, are thought to be of a greater height, measured from their base, than any others in our country, and perhaps in North America. From data, which may found a tolerable conjecture, we suppose the highest peak to be about 4000 feet perpendicular, which is not a fifth part of the height of the mountains of South America, nor one third of the height which would be necessary in our latitude to preserve ice in the open air unmelted through the year. The ridge of mountains next beyond the Blue ridge, called by us the North mountain, is of the greatest extent; for which reason they were named by the Indians the Endless mountains.

3. From Query V, Cascades.

The Natural bridge, the most sublime of Nature's works, though not comprehended under the present head, must not be pretermitted. It is on the ascent of a hill, which seems to have been cloven through its length by some great convulsion. The fissure, just at the bridge, is, by some admeasurements, 270 feet deep, by others only 205. It is about 45 feet wide at the bottom, and 90 feet at the top; this of course determines the length of the bridge, and its height from the water. Its breadth in the middle, is about

60 feet, but more at the ends, and the thickness of the mass at the summit of the arch, about 40 feet. A part of this thickness is constituted by a coat of earth, which gives growth to many large trees. The residue, with the hill on both sides, is one solid rock of lime-stone. The arch approaches the Semi-elliptical form; but the larger axis of the ellipsis, which would be the cord of the arch, is many times longer than the transverse. Though the sides of this bridge are provided in some parts with a parapet of fixed rocks, yet few men have resolution to walk to them and look over into the abyss. You involuntarily fall on your hands and feet, creep to the parapet and peep over it. Looking down from this height about a minute, gave me a violent head ach. If the view from the top be painful and intolerable, that from below is delightful in an equal extreme. It is impossible for the emotions arising from the sublime, to be felt beyond what they are here: so beautiful an arch, so elevated, so light, and springing as it were up to heaven, the rapture of the spectator is really indescribable! The fissure continuing narrow, deep, and straight for a considerable distance above and below the bridge, opens a short but very pleasing view of the North mountain on one side, and Blue ridge on the other, at the distance each of them of about five miles. This bridge is in the county of Rock bridge, to which it has given name, and affords a public and commodious passage over a valley, which cannot be crossed elsewhere for a considerable distance. The stream passing under it is called Cedar creek. It is a water of James river, and sufficient in the driest seasons to turn a grist-mill, though its fountain is not more than two miles above.

4. From Query VI, Productions Mineral, Vegetable and Animal.

The opinion advanced by the Count de Buffon, is 1. That the animals common both to the old and new world, are smaller in the latter. 2. That those peculiar to the new, are on a smaller scale. 3. That those which have been domesticated in both, have degenerated in America: and 4. That on the whole it exhibits fewer species. And the reason he thinks is, that the heats of America are less; that more waters are spread over its surface by nature, and fewer of these drained off by the hand of man. In other words, that heat is friendly, and *moisture* adverse to the production and devel{}opement of large quadrupeds. I will not meet this hypothesis on its first doubtful ground, whether the climate of America be comparatively more humid? Because we are not furnished with observations sufficient to decide this question. And though, till it be decided, we are as free to deny, as others are to affirm the fact, yet for a moment let it be supposed. The hypothesis, after this supposition, proceeds to another; that *moisture* is unfriendly to animal growth. The truth of this is inscrutable to us by reasonings a priori. Nature has hidden from us her modus agendi. Our only appeal on such questions is to experience; and I think that experience is against the supposition. It is by the assistance of *heat* and *moisture* that vegetables are elaborated from the elements of earth, air, water, and fire. We accordingly see the more humid climates produce the greater quantity of vegetables. Vegetables are mediately or immediately the food of every animal: and in proportion to the quantity of food, we see animals not only multiplied in their numbers, but improved in their bulk, as far as the laws of their nature will admit. . . . Let us take two portions of the earth, Europe and America for instance, sufficiently extensive to give operation to general causes; let us consider the circumstances peculiar to each, and observe their effect on animal nature. America, running through the torrid as well as temperate zone, has more heat, collectively taken, than Europe. But Europe, according to our hypothesis, is the dryest. They are equally adapted then to animal productions; each being endowed with one of those causes which befriend animal growth, and with one which opposes it. . . . [*TJ proceeds to demonstrate, in a series of tables, that American animals are at least equal to their European counterparts.*]

Hitherto I have considered this hypothesis as applied to brute animals only, and not in its extension to the man of America, whether aboriginal or transplanted. It is the opinion of Mons. de Buffon that the former furnishes no exception to it: "Although the savage of the new world is about the same height as man in our world, this does not suffice for him to constitute an exception to the general fact that all living nature has become smaller on that continent. The savage is feeble, and has small organs of generation; he has neither hair nor beard, and no ardor for his female. . . ." An afflicting picture indeed, which, for the honor of human nature, I am glad to believe has no original. Of the Indian of South America I know nothing; for I would not honor with the appellation of knowledge, what I derive from the fables published of them. These I believe to be just as true as the fables of Aesop. This belief is founded on what I have seen of man, white, red, and black, and what has been written of him by authors, enlightened themselves, and writing amidst an enlightened people. The Indian of North America being more within our reach, I can speak of him somewhat from my own knowledge, but more from the information of others better acquainted with him, and on whose truth and judgment I can rely. From these sources I am able to say, in contradiction to this representation, that he is neither more defective in ardor, nor more impotent with his female, than the white reduced to the same diet and exercise: that he is brave, when an enterprize depends on bravery; education with him making the point of honor consist in the destruction of an enemy by stratagem, and in the preservation of his own person free from injury; or perhaps this is nature; while it is education which teaches us to honor force more than finesse: that he will defend himself against an host of enemies, always chusing to be killed, rather than to surrender, though it be to the whites, who he knows will treat him well: that in other situations also he meets death with more deliberation, and endures tortures with a firmness unknown almost to religious enthusiasm with us: that he is affectionate to his children, careful of them, and indulgent in the extreme: that his affections comprehend his other connections, weakening, as with us, from circle to circle, as they recede from the center: that his friendships are strong and faithful to the uttermost extremity: that his sensibility is keen, even the warriors weeping most bitterly on the loss of their children, though in general they endeavour to appear superior to human events: that his vivacity and activity of mind is equal to ours in the same situation; hence his eagerness for hunting, and for games of chance. The women are submitted to unjust drudgery. This I believe is the case with every barbarous people. With such, force is law. The stronger sex therefore imposes on the weaker. It is civilization alone which replaces women in the enjoyment of their natural equality. That first teaches us to subdue the selfish passions, and to respect those rights in others which we value in ourselves. Were we in equal barbarism, our females would be equal drudges. The man with them is less strong than with us, but their woman stronger than ours; and both for the same obvious reason; because our man and their woman is habituated to labour, and formed by it. With both races the sex which is indulged with ease is least athletic. An Indian man is small in the hand and wrist for the same reason for which a sailor is large and strong in the arms and shoulders, and a porter in the legs and thighs.—They raise fewer children than we do. The causes of this are to be found, not in a difference of nature, but of circumstance. The women very frequently attending the men in their parties of war and of hunting, child-bearing becomes extremely inconvenient to them. It is said, therefore, that they have learnt the practice of procuring abortion by the use of some vegetable; and that it even extends to prevent conception for a considerable time after. During these parties they are exposed to numerous hazards, to excessive exertions, to the greatest extremities of hunger. Even at their homes the nation depends for food, through a certain part of every year, on the gleanings of the forest: that is, they experience a famine once in every year. With all animals, if the female be badly fed, or not fed at all, her young perish: and if both male and female be reduced to like want, generation becomes less active, less productive. To the obstacles then of want and hazard, which nature has opposed to the multiplication of wild animals, for the purpose of restraining their numbers within certain bounds, those of labour and of voluntary abortion are added with the Indian. No wonder then if they multiply less than we do. Where food is regularly supplied, a single farm will shew more of cattle, than a whole country of forests can of buffaloes. The same Indian women, when married to white traders, who feed them and their children plentifully and regularly, who exempt them from excessive drudgery, who keep them stationary and unexposed to accident, produce and raise as many children as the white women. Instances are known, under these circumstances, of their rearing a dozen children. An inhuman practice once prevailed in this country of making slaves of the Indians. It is a fact well known with us, that the Indian women so enslaved produced and raised as numerous families as either the whites or blacks among whom they lived.—It has been said, that Indians have less hair than the whites, except on the head. But this is a fact of which fair proof can scarcely be had. With them it is disgraceful to be hairy on the body. They say it likens them to hogs. They therefore pluck the hair as fast as it appears. But the traders who marry their women, and prevail on them to discontinue this practice, say, that nature is the same with them as with the whites. Nor, if the fact be true, is the consequence necessary which has been drawn from it. Negroes have notoriously less hair than the whites; yet they are more ardent. But if cold and moisture be the agents of nature for diminishing the races of animals, how comes she all at once to suspend their operation as to the physical man of the new world, whom the Count acknowledges to be "about the same size as the man of our hemisphere," and to let loose their influence on his moral faculties? How has this "combination of the elements and other physical causes, so contrary to the enlargement of animal nature in this new world, these obstacles to the developement and formation of great germs," been arrested and suspended, so as to permit the human body to acquire its just dimensions, and by what inconceivable process has their action been directed on his mind alone? To judge of the truth of this, to form a just estimate of their genius and mental powers, more facts are wanting, and great allowance to be made for those circumstances of their situation which call for a display of particular talents only. This done, we shall probably find that they are formed in mind as well as in body, on the same module with the "Homo sapiens Europaeus." The principles of their society forbidding all compulsion, they are to be led to duty and to enterprize by personal influence and persuasion. Hence eloquence in council, bravery and address in war, become the foundations of all consequence with them. To these acquirements all their faculties are directed. Of their bravery and address in war we have multiplied proofs, because we have been the subjects on which they were exercised. Of their eminence in oratory we have fewer examples, because it is displayed chiefly in their own councils. Some, however, we have of very superior lustre. I may challenge the whole orations of Demosthenes and Cicero, and of any more eminent orator, if Europe has furnished more eminent, to produce a single passage, superior to the speech of Logan, a Mingo chief, to Lord Dunmore, when governor of this state. And, as a testimony of their talents in this line, I beg leave to introduce it, first stating the incidents necessary for understanding it. In the spring of the year 1774, a robbery and murder were committed on an inhabitant of the frontiers of Virginia, by two Indians of the Shawanee tribe. The neighbouring whites, according to their custom, undertook to punish this outrage in a summary way. Col. Cresap, a man infamous for the many murders he had committed on those much-injured people, collected a party, and proceeded down the Kanhaway in quest of vengeance. Unfortunately a canoe of women and children, with one man only, was seen coming from the opposite shore, unarmed, and unsuspecting an hostile attack from the whites. Cresap and his party concealed themselves on the bank of the river, and the moment the canoe reached the shore, singled out their objects, and, at one fire, killed every person in it. This happened to be the family of Logan, who had long been distinguished as a friend of the whites. This unworthy return provoked his vengeance. He accordingly signalized himself in the war which ensued. In the autumn of the same year, a decisive battle was fought at the mouth of the Great Kanhaway, between the collected forces of the Shawanees, Mingoes, and Delawares, and a detachment of the Virginia militia. The Indians were defeated, and sued for peace. Logan however disdained to be seen among the suppliants. But, lest the sincerity of a treaty should be distrusted, from which so distinguished a chief absented himself, he sent by a messenger the following speech to be delivered to Lord Dunmore.

"I appeal to any white man to say, if ever he entered Logan's cabin hungry, and he gave him not meat; if ever he came cold and naked, and he clothed him not. During the course of the last long and bloody war, Logan remained idle in his cabin, an advocate for peace. Such was my love for the whites, that my countrymen pointed as they passed, and said, 'Logan is the friend of white men.' I had even thought to have lived with you, but for the injuries of one man. Col. Cresap, the last spring, in cold blood, and unprovoked, murdered all the relations of Logan, not sparing even my women and children. There runs not a drop of my blood in the veins of any living creature. This called on me for revenge. I have sought it: I have killed many: I have fully glutted my vengeance. For my country, I rejoice at the beams of peace. But do not harbour a thought that mine is the joy of fear. Logan never felt fear. He will not turn on his heel to save his life. Who is there to mourn for Logan?—Not one. "

Before we condemn the Indians of this continent as wanting genius, we must consider that letters have not yet been introduced among them. Were we to compare them in their present state with the Europeans North of the Alps, when the Roman arms and arts first crossed those mountains, the comparison would be unequal, because, at that time, those parts of Europe were swarming with numbers; because numbers produce emulation, and multiply the chances of improvement, and one improvement begets another. Yet I may safely ask, How many good poets, how many able mathematicians, how many great inventors in arts or sciences, had Europe North of the Alps then produced? And it was sixteen centuries after this before a Newton could be formed. I do not mean to deny, that there are varieties in the race of man, distinguished by their powers both of body and mind. I believe there are, as I see to be the case in the races of other animals. I only mean to suggest a doubt, whether the bulk and faculties of animals depend on the side of the Atlantic on which their food happens to grow, or which furnishes the elements of which they are compounded? Whether nature has enlisted herself as a Cis or Trans-Atlantic partisan? I am induced to suspect, there has been more eloquence than sound reasoning displayed in support of this theory; that it is one of those cases where the judgment has been seduced by a glowing pen: and whilst I render every tribute of honor and esteem to the celebrated Zoologist, who has added, and is still adding, so many precious things to the treasures of science, I must doubt whether in this instance he has not cherished error also, by lending her for a moment his vivid imagination and bewitching language.

So far the Count de Buffon has carried this new theory of the tendency of nature to belittle her productions on this side the Atlantic. Its application to the race of whites, transplanted from Europe, remained for the Abbé Raynal. "One must be astonished (he says) that America has not yet produced one good poet, one able mathematician, one man of genius in a single art or a single science." "America has not yet produced one good poet." When we shall have existed as a people as long as the Greeks did before they produced a Homer, the Romans a Virgil, the French a Racine and Voltaire, the English a Shakespeare and Milton, should this reproach be still true, we will enquire from what unfriendly causes it has proceeded, that the other countries of Europe and quarters of the earth shall not have inscribed any name in the roll of poets. But neither has America produced "one able mathematician, one man of genius in a single art or a single science." In war we have produced a Washington, whose memory will be adored while liberty shall have votaries, whose name will triumph over time, and will in future ages assume its just station among the most celebrated worthies of the world, when that wretched philosophy shall be forgotten which would have arranged him among the degeneracies of nature. In physics we have produced a Franklin, than whom no one of the present age has made more important discoveries, nor has enriched philosophy with more, or more ingenious solutions of the phænomena of nature. We have supposed Mr. Rittenhouse second to no astronomer living: that in genius he must be the first, because he is self-taught. As an artist he has exhibited as great a proof of mechanical genius as the world has ever produced. He has not indeed made a world; but he has by imitation approached nearer its Maker than any man who has lived from the creation to this day. As in philosophy and war, so in government, in oratory, in painting, in the plastic art, we might shew that America, though but a child of yesterday, has already given hopeful proofs of genius, as well of the nobler kinds, which arouse the best feelings of man, which call him into action, which substantiate his freedom, and conduct him to happiness, as of the subordinate, which serve to amuse him only. We therefore suppose, that this reproach is as unjust as it is unkind; and that, of the geniuses which adorn the present age, America contributes its full share. For comparing it with those countries, where genius is most cultivated, where are the most excellent models for art, and scaffoldings for the attainment of science, as France and England for instance, we calculate thus. The United States contain three millions of inhabitants; France twenty millions; and the British islands ten. We produce a Washington, a Franklin, a Rittenhouse. France then should have half a dozen in each of these lines, and Great-Britain half that number, equally eminent. It may be true, that France has: we are but just becoming acquainted with her, and our acquaintance so far gives us high ideas of the genius of her inhabitants. It would be injuring too many of them to name particularly a Voltaire, a Buffon, the constellation of Encyclopedists, the Abbé Raynal himself, &c. &c. We therefore have reason to believe she can produce her full quota of genius. The present war having so long cut off all communication with Great-Britain, we are not able to make a fair estimate of the state of science in that country. The spirit in which she wages war is the only sample before our eyes, and that does not seem the legitimate offspring either of science or of civilization. The sun of her glory is fast descending to the horizon. Her philosophy has crossed the Channel, her freedom the Atlantic, and herself seems passing to that awful dissolution, whose issue is not given human foresight to scan.

5. From Query VIII, Population.

During the infancy of the colony, while numbers were small, wars, importations, and other accidental circumstances render the progression fluctuating and irregular. By the year 1654, however, it becomes tolerably uniform, importations having in a great measure ceased from the dissolution of the company, and the inhabitants become too numerous to be sensibly affected by Indian wars. Beginning at that period, therefore, we find that from thence to the year 1772, our tythes [*free males above 16 years of age, and slaves above that age of both sexes*] had increased from 7209 to 153,000. The whole term being of 118 years, yields a duplication once in every 27¼ years. The intermediate enumerations taken in 1700, 1748, and 1759, furnish proofs of the uniformity of this progression. Should this rate of increase continue, we shall have between six and seven millions of inhabitants within 95 years. If we suppose our country to be bounded, at some future day, by the meridian of the mouth of the Great Kanhaway, (within which it has been before conjectured, are 64,491 square miles) there will then be 100 inhabitants for every square mile, which is nearly the state of population in the British islands.

Here I will beg leave to propose a doubt. The present desire of America is to produce rapid population by as great importations of foreigners as possible. But is this founded in good policy? The advantage proposed is the multiplication of numbers. Now let us suppose (for example only) that, in this state, we could double our numbers in one year by the importation of foreigners; and this is a greater accession than the most sanguine advocate for emigration has a right to expect. Then I say, beginning with a double stock, we shall attain any given degree of population only 27 years and 3 months sooner than if we proceed on our single stock. If we propose four millions and a half as a competent population for this state, we should be 54½ years attaining it, could we at once double our numbers; and 81¾ years, if we rely on natural propagation, as may be seen by the following table.

	Proceeding on our present stock	Proceeding on a double stock
1781	564,614	1,135,228
1808 ¼	1,135,228	2,270,456
1835 ½	2,270,456	4,540,912
1862 ¾	4,540,912	

In the first column are stated periods of 27¼ years; in the second are our numbers, at each period, as they will be if we proceed on our actual stock; and in the third are what they would be, at the same periods, were we to set out from the double of our present stock. Proceeding on our present stock, I have taken the term of four millions and a half of inhabitants for example's sake only. Yet I am persuaded it is a greater number than the country spoken of, considering how much inarrable land it contains, can clothe and feed, without a material change in the quality of their diet. But are there no inconveniences to be thrown into the scale against the advantage expected from a multiplication of numbers by the importation of foreigners? It is for the happiness of those united in society to harmonize as much as possible in matters which they must of necessity transact together. Civil government being the sole object of forming societies, its administration must be conducted by common consent. Every species of government has its specific principles. Ours perhaps are more peculiar than those of any other in the universe. It is a composition of the freest principles of the English constitution, with others derived from natural right and natural reason. To these nothing can be more opposed than the maxims of absolute monarchies. Yet, from such, we are to expect the greatest number of emigrants. They will bring with them the principles of the governments they leave, imbibed in their early youth; or, if able to throw them off, it will be in exchange for an unbounded licentiousness, passing, as is usual, from one extreme to another. It would be a miracle were they to stop precisely at the point of temperate liberty. These principles, with their language, they will transmit to their children. In proportion to their numbers, they will share with us the legislation. They will infuse into it their spirit, warp and bias its direction, and render it a heterogeneous, incoherent, distracted mass. I may appeal to experience, during the present contest, for a verification of these conjectures. But, if they be not certain in event, are they not possible, are they not probable? Is it not safer to wait with patience 27 years and three months longer, for the attainment of any degree of population desired, or expected? May not our government be more homogeneous, more peaceable, more durable? Suppose 20 millions of republican Americans thrown all of a sudden into France, what would be the condition of that kingdom? If it would be more turbulent, less happy, less strong, we may believe that the addition of half a million of foreigners to our present numbers would produce a similar effect here. If they come of themselves, they are entitled to all the rights of citizenship: but I doubt the expediency of inviting them by extraordinary encouragements. I mean not that these doubts should be extended to the importation of useful artificers. The policy of that measure depends on very different considerations. Spare no expence in obtaining them. They will after a while go to the plough and the hoe; but, in the mean time, they will teach us something we do not know. It is not so in agriculture. The indifferent state of that among us does not proceed from a want of knowledge merely; it is from our having such quantities of land to waste as we please. In Europe the object is to make the most of their land, labour being abundant: here it is to make the most of our labour, land being abundant.

It will be proper to explain how the numbers for the year 1782 have been obtained; as it was not from a perfect census of the inhabitants. It will at the same time develope the proportion between the free inhabitants and slaves. The following return of taxable articles for that year was given in.

53,289	free males above 21 years of age.
211,698	slaves of all ages and sexes.
23,766	not distinguished in the returns, but said to be titheable slaves.
195,439	horses.
609,734	cattle.
5,126	wheels of riding-carriages.
191	taverns.

There were no returns from the 8 counties of Lincoln, Jefferson, Fayette, Monongalia, Yohogania, Ohio, Northampton, and York. To find the number of slaves which should have been returned instead of the 23,766 titheables, we must mention that some observations on a former census had given reason to believe that the numbers above and below 16 years of age were equal. The double of this number, therefore, to wit, 47,532 must be added to 211,698, which will give us 259,230 slaves of all ages and sexes. To find the number of free inhabitants, we must repeat the observation, that those above and below 16 are nearly equal. But as the number 53,289 omits the males between 16 and 21, we must supply them from conjecture. On a former experiment it had appeared that about one-third of our militia, that is, of the males between 16 and 50, were unmarried. Knowing how early marriage takes place here, we shall not be far wrong in supposing that the unmarried part of our militia are those between 16 and 21. If there be young men who do not marry till after 21, there are as many who marry before that age. But as the men above 50 were not included in the militia, we will suppose the unmarried, or those between 16 and 21, to be one-fourth of the whole number above 16, then we have the following calculation:

53,289	free males above 21 years of age.
17,763	free males between 16 and 21.
71,052	free males under 16.
142,104	free females of all ages.
284,208	free inhabitants of all ages.
259,230	slaves of all ages.

543,438   inhabitants, exclusive of the 8 counties from which were no returns. In these 8 counties in the years 1779 and 1780 were 3,161 militia. Say then,

3,161	free males above the age of 16.
3,161	ditto under 16.
6,322	free females.

12,644   free inhabitants in these 8 counties. To find the number of slaves, say, as 284,208 to 259,230, so is 12,644 to 11,532. Adding the third of these numbers to the first, and the fourth to the second, we have,

296,852	free inhabitants.
270,762	slaves.

567,614   inhabitants of every age, sex, and condition. But 296,852, the number of free inhabitants, are to 270,762, the number of slaves, nearly as 11 to 10. Under the mild treatment our slaves experience, and their wholesome, though coarse, food, this blot in our country increases as fast, or faster, than the whites. During the regal government, we had at one time obtained a law, which imposed such a duty on the importation of slaves, as amounted nearly to a prohibition, when one inconsiderate assembly, placed under a peculiarity of circumstance, repealed the law. This repeal met a joyful sanction from the then sovereign, and no devices, no expedients, which could ever after be attempted by subsequent assemblies, and they seldom met without attempting them, could succeed in getting the royal assent to a renewal of the duty. In the very first session held under the republican government, the assembly passed a law for the perpetual prohibition of the importation of slaves. This will in some measure stop the increase of this great political and moral evil, while the minds of our citizens may be ripening for a complete emancipation of human nature.

6. From Query XIII, Constitution.

This constitution [*the Virginia Constitution of 1776*] was formed when we were new and unexperienced in the science of government. It was the first too which was formed in the whole United States. No wonder then that time and trial have discovered very capital defects in it.

1. The majority of the men in the state, who pay and fight for its support, are unrepresented in the legislature, the roll of freeholders intitled to vote, not including generally the half of those on the roll of the militia, or of the tax-gatherers.

2. Among those who share the representation, the shares are very unequal. Thus the county of Warwick, with only one hundred fighting men, has an equal representation with the county of Loudon, which has 1746. So that every man in Warwick has as much influence in the government as 17 men in Loudon. But lest it should be thought that an equal interspersion of small among large counties, through the whole state, may prevent any danger of injury to particular parts of it, we will divide it into districts, and shew the proportions of land, of fighting men, and of representation in each.

	square miles	fighting men	delegates	senators
Between the sea-coast and } falls of the rivers	11,205	19,012	71	12
Between the falls of the rivers and } the Blue ridge of mountains	18,759	18,288	46	8
Between the Blue ridge and } the Alleghaney	11,911	7,673	16	2
Between the Alleghaney and Ohio	79,650	4,458	16	2
Total ———————————	121,525	49,971	149	24

An inspection of this table will supply the place of commentaries on it. It will appear at once that nineteen thousand men, living below the falls of the rivers, possess half the senate, and want four members only of possessing a majority of the house of delegates; a want more than supplied by the vicinity of their situation to the seat of government, and of course the greater degree of convenience and punctuality with which their members may and will attend in the legislature. These nineteen thousand, therefore, living in one part of the country, give law to upwards of thirty thousand, living in another, and appoint all their chief officers executive and judiciary. From the difference of their situation and circumstances, their interests will often be very different.

3. The senate is, by its constitution, too homogeneous with the house of delegates. Being chosen by the same electors, at the same time, and out of the same subjects, the choice falls of course on men of the same description. The purpose of establishing different houses of legislation is to introduce the influence of different interests or different principles. Thus in Great-Britain it is said their constitution relies on the house of commons for honesty, and the lords for wisdom; which would be a rational reliance if honesty were to be bought with money, and if wisdom were hereditary. In some of the American states the delegates and senators are so chosen, as that the first represent the persons, and the second the property of the state. But with us, wealth and wisdom have equal chance for admission into both houses. We do not therefore derive from the separation of our legislature into two houses, those benefits which a proper complication of principles is capable of producing, and those which alone can compensate the evils which may be produced by their dissensions.

4. All the powers of government, legislative, executive, and judiciary, result to the legislative body. The concentrating these in the same hands is precisely the definition of despotic government. It will be no alleviation that these powers will be exercised by a plurality of hands, and not by a single one. 173 despots would surely be as oppressive as one. Let those who doubt it turn their eyes on the republic of Venice. As little will it avail us that they are chosen by ourselves. An elective despotism was not the government we fought for; but one which should not only be founded on free principles, but in which the powers of government should be so divided and balanced among several bodies of magistracy, as that no one could transcend their legal limits, without being effectually checked and restrained by the others. For this reason that convention, which passed the ordinance of government, laid its foundation on this basis, that the legislative, executive and judiciary departments should be separate and distinct, so that no person should exercise the powers of more than one of them at the same time. But no barrier was provided between these several powers. The judiciary and executive members were left dependant on the legislative, for their subsistence in office, and some of them for their continuance in it. If therefore the legislature assumes executive and judiciary powers, no opposition is likely to be made; nor, if made, can it be effectual; because in that case they may put their proceedings into the form of an act of assembly, which will render them obligatory on the other branches. They have accordingly, in many instances, decided rights which should have been left to judiciary controversy: and the direction of the executive, during the whole time of their session, is becoming habitual and familiar. And this is done with no ill intention. The views of the present members are perfectly upright. When they are led out of their regular province, it is by art in others, and inadvertence in themselves. And this will probably be the case for some time to come. But it will not be a very long time.

Mankind soon learn to make interested uses of every right and power which they possess, or may assume. The public money and public liberty, intended to have been deposited with three branches of magistracy, but found inadvertently to be in the hands of one only, will soon be discovered to be sources of wealth and dominion to those who hold them; distinguished too by this tempting circumstance, that they are the instrument, as well as the object of acquisition. With money we will get men, said Caesar, and with men we will get money. Nor should our assembly be deluded by the integrity of their own purposes, and conclude that these unlimited powers will never be abused, because themselves are not disposed to abuse them. They should look forward to a time, and that not a distant one, when corruption in this, as in the country from which we derive our origin, will have seized the heads of government, and be spread by them through the body of the people; when they will purchase the voices of the people, and make them pay the price. Human nature is the same on every side of the Atlantic, and will be alike influenced by the same causes. The time to guard against corruption and tyranny, is before they shall have gotten hold on us. It is better to keep the wolf out of the fold, than to trust to drawing his teeth and talons after he shall have entered. To render these considerations the more cogent, we must observe in addition,

5. That the ordinary legislature may alter the constitution itself. On the discontinuance of assemblies, it became necessary to substitute in their place some other body, competent to the ordinary business of government, and to the calling forth the powers of the state for the maintenance of our opposition to Great-Britain. Conventions were therefore introduced, consisting of two delegates from each county, meeting together and forming one house, on the plan of the former house of Burgesses, to whose places they succeeded. These were at first chosen anew for every particular session. But in March 1775, they recommended to the people to chuse a convention, which should continue in office a year. This was done accordingly in April 1775, and in the July following that convention passed an ordinance for the election of delegates in the month of April annually. It is well known, that in July 1775, a separation from Great-Britain and establishment of Republican government had never yet entered into any person's mind. A convention therefore, chosen under that ordinance, cannot be said to have been chosen for purposes which certainly did not exist in the minds of those who passed it. Under this ordinance, at the annual election in April 1776, a convetion for the year was chosen. Independance, and the establishment of a new form of government, were not even yet the objects of the people at large. One extract from the pamphlet called Common Sense had appeared in the Virginia papers in February, and copies of the pamphlet itself had got into a few hands. But the idea had not been opened to the mass of the people in April, much less can it be said that they had made up their minds in its favor. So that the electors of April 1776, no more than the legislators of July 1775, not thinking of independance and a permanent republic, could not mean to vest in these delegates powers of establishing them, or any authorities other than those of the ordinary legislature. So far as a temporary organization of government was necessary to render our opposition energetic, so far their organization

was valid. But they received in their creation no powers but what were given to every legislature before and since. They could not therefore pass an act transcendant to the powers of other legislatures. If the present assembly pass any act, and declare it shall be irrevocable by subsequent assemblies, the declaration is merely void, and the act repealable, as other acts are. So far, and no farther authorized, they organized the government by the ordinance entitled a Constitution or Form of government. It pretends to no higher authority than the other ordinances of the same session; it does not say, that it shall be perpetual; that it shall be unalterable by other legislatures; that it shall be transcendant above the powers of those, who they knew would have equal power with themselves. Not only the silence of the instrument is a proof they thought it would be alterable, but their own practice also: for this very convention, meeting as a House of Delegates in General Assembly with the new Senate in the autumn of that year, passed acts of assembly in contradiction to their ordinance of government; and every assembly from that time to this has done the same. I am safe therefore in the position, that the constitution itself is alterable by the ordinary legislature. Though this opinion seems founded on the first elements of common sense, yet is the contrary maintained by some persons. 1. Because, say they, the conventions were vested with every power necessary to make effectual opposition to Great-Britain. But to complete this argument, they must go on, and say further, that effectual opposition could not be made to Great-Britain, without establishing a form of government perpetual and unalterable by the legislature; which is not true. An opposition which at some time or other was to come to an end, could not need a perpetual institution to carry it on: and a government, amendable as its defects should be discovered, was as likely to make effectual resistance, as one which should be unalterably wrong. Besides, the assemblies were as much vested with all powers requisite for resistance as the conventions were. If therefore these powers included that of modelling the form of government in the one case, they did so in the other. The assemblies then as well as the conventions may model the government; that is, they may alter the ordinance of government. 2. They urge, that if the convention had meant that this instrument should be alterable, as their other ordinances were, they would have called it an ordinance: but they have called it a *constitution,* which *by force of the term* means "an act above the power of the ordinary legislature." I answer that *constitutio, constitutum, statutum, lex,* are convertible terms. "A *constitution* is called that which is made by the ruler. An *ordinance,* that which is rewritten by emperors or ordained. A *statute* is called the same as law." *Constitution* and *statute* were originally terms of the civil law, and from thence introduced by Ecclesiastics into the English law. Thus in the statute 25 Hen. 8. c. 19. § 1. *"Constitutions* and *ordinances"* are used as synonimous. The term *constitution* has many other significations in physics and in politics; but in Jurisprudence, whenever it is applied to any act of the legislature, it invariably means a statute, law, or ordinance, which is the present case. No inference then of a different meaning can be drawn from the adoption of this title: on the contrary, we might conclude, that, by their affixing to it a term synonimous with ordinance, or statute, they meant it to be an ordinance or statute. But of what consequence is their meaning, where their power is denied? If they meant to do more than they had power to do, did this give them power? It is not the name, but the authority which renders an act obligatory. Lord Coke says, "an article of the statute 11 R. 2. c. 5. that no person should attempt to revoke any ordinance then made, is repealed, for that such restraint is against the jurisdiction and power of the parliament." 4. inst. 42. and again, "though divers parliaments have attempted to restrain subsequent parliaments, yet could they never effect it; for the latter parliament hath ever power to abrogate, suspend, qualify, explain, or make void the former in the whole or in any part thereof, notwithstanding any words of restraint, prohibition, or penalty, in the former: for it is a maxim in the laws of the parliament, *"because subsequent laws nullify earlier laws which are contrary."* 4. inst. 43. — To get rid of the magic supposed to be in the word constitution, let us translate it into its definition as given by those who think it above the power of the law; and let us suppose the convention instead of saying, "We, the ordinary legislature, establish a *constitution,*" had said, "We, the ordinary legislature, establish an act *above the power of the ordinary legislature.*" Does not this expose the absurdity of the attempt? 3. But, say they, the people have acquiesced, and this has given it an authority superior to the laws. It is true, that the people did not rebel against it: and was that a time for the people to rise in rebellion? Should a prudent acquiescence, at a critical time, be construed into a confirmation of every illegal thing done during that period? Besides, why should they rebel? At an annual election, they had chosen delegates for the year, to exercise the ordinary powers of legislation, and to manage the great contest in which they were engaged. These delegates thought the contest would be best managed by an organized government. They therefore, among others, passed an ordinance of government. They did not presume to call it perpetual and unalterable. They well knew they had no power to make it so; that our choice of them had been for no such purpose, and at a time when we could have no such purpose in contemplation. Had an unalterable form of government been meditated, perhaps we should have chosen a different set of people. There was no cause then for the people to rise in rebellion. But to what dangerous lengths will this argument lead? Did the acquiescence of the colonies under the various acts of power exercised by Great-Britain in our infant state, confirm these acts, and so far invest them with the authority of the people as to render them unalterable, and our present resistance wrong? On every unauthoritative exercise of power by the legislature, must the people rise in rebellion, or their silence be construed into a surrender of that power to them? If so, how many rebellions should we have had already? One certainly for every session of assembly. The other states in the Union have been of opinion, that to render a form of government unalterable by ordinary acts of assembly, the people must delegate persons with special powers. They have accordingly chosen special conventions to form and fix their governments. The individuals then who maintain the contrary opinion in this country, should have the modesty to suppose it possible that they may be wrong and the rest of America right. But if there be only a possibility of their being wrong, if only a plausible doubt remains of the validity of the ordinance of government, is it not better to remove that doubt, by placing it on a bottom which none will dispute? If they be right, we shall only have the unnecessary trouble of meeting once in convention. If they be wrong, they expose us to the hazard of having no fundamental rights at all. True it is, this is no time for deliberating on forms of government. While an enemy is within our bowels, the first object is to expel him. But when this shall be done, when peace shall be established, and leisure given us for intrenching within good forms, the rights for which we have bled, let no man be found indolent enough to decline a little more trouble for placing them beyond the reach of question. If any thing more be requisite to produce a conviction of the expediency of calling a convention, at a proper season, to fix our form of government, let it be the reflection,

6. That the assembly exercises a power of determining the Quorum of their own body which may legislate for us. After the establishment of the new form they adhered to the *Law of the makority*, founded in common law as well as common right. It is the natural law of every assembly of men, whose numbers are not fixed by any other law. They continued for some time to require the presence of a majority of their whole number, to pass an act. But the British parliament fixes its own quorum: our former assemblies fixed their own quorum: and one precedent in favour of power is stronger than an hundred against it. The house of delegates therefore have lately voted that, during the present dangerous invasion, forty members shall be a house to proceed to business. They have been moved to this by the fear of not being able to collect a house. But this danger could not authorize them to call that a house which was none: and if they may fix it at one number, they may at another, till it loses its fundamental character of being a representative body. As this vote expires with the present invasion, it is probable the former rule will be permitted to revive: because at present no ill is meant. The power however of fixing their own quorum has been avowed, and a precedent set. From forty it may be reduced to four, and from four to one: from a house to a committee, from a committee to a chairman or speaker, and thus an oligarchy or monarchy be substituted under forms supposed to be regular. "All bad examples are derived from good ones; but when power comes to the ignorant or the less good, the new example is transferred from the worthy and fit to the unworthy and unfit." When therefore it is considered, that there is no legal obstacle to the assumption by the assembly of all the powers legislative, executive, and judiciary, and that these may come to the hands of the smallest rag of delegation, surely the people will say, and their representatives, while yet they have honest representatives, will advise them to say, that they will not acknowledge as laws any acts not considered and assented to by the major part of their delegates.

In enumerating the defects of the constitution, it would be wrong to count among them what is only the error of particular persons. In December 1776, our circumstances being much distressed, it was proposed in the house of delegates to create a *dictator*, invested with every power legislative, executive and judiciary, civil and military, of life and of death, over our persons and over our properties: and in June 1781, again under calamity, the same proposition was repeated, and wanted a few votes only of being passed.—One who entered into this contest from a pure love of liberty, and a sense of injured rights, who determined to make every sacrifice, and to meet every danger, for the re-establishment of those rights on a firm basis, who did not mean to expend his blood and substance for the wretched purpose of changing this master for that, but to place the powers of governing him in a plurality of hands of his own choice, so that the corrupt will of no one man might in future oppress him, must stand confounded and dismayed when he is told, that a considerable portion of that plurality had meditated the surrender of them into a single hand, and, in lieu of a limited monarch, to deliver him over to a despotic one! How must we find his efforts and sacrifices abused and baffled, if he may still by a single vote be laid prostrate at the feet of one man! In God's name, from whence have they derived this power? Is it from our ancient laws? None such can be produced. Is it from any principle in our new constitution, expressed or implied? Every lineament of that expressed or implied, is in full opposition to it. Its fundamental principle is, that the state shall be governed as a commonwealth. It provides a republican organization, proscribes under the name of prerogative the exercise of all powers undefined by the laws; places on this basis the whole system of our laws; and, by consolidating them together, chuses that they shall be left to stand or fall together, never providing for any circumstances, nor admitting that such could arise, wherein either should be suspended, no, not for a moment. Our antient laws expressly declare, that those who are but delegates themselves shall not delegate to others powers which require judgment and integrity in their exercise. —Or was this proposition moved on a supposed right in the movers of abandoning their posts in a moment of distress? The same laws forbid the abandonment of that post, even on ordinary occasions; and much more a transfer of their powers into other hands and other forms, without consulting the people. They never admit the idea that these, like sheep or cattle, may be given from hand to hand without an appeal to their own will.—Was it from the necessity of the case? Necessities which dissolve a government, do not convey its authority to an oligarchy or a monarchy. They throw back, into the hands of the people, the powers they had delegated, and leave them as individuals to shift for themselves. A leader may offer, but not impose himself, nor be imposed on them. Much less can their necks be submitted to his sword, their breath be held at his will or caprice. The necessity which should operate these tremendous effects should at least be palpable and irresistible. Yet in both instances, where it was feared, or pretended with us, it was belied by the event. It was belied too by the preceding experience of our sister states, several of whom had grappled through greater difficulties without abandoning their forms of government. When the proposition was first made, Massachusets had found even the government of committees sufficient to carry them through an invasion. But we at the time of that proposition were under no invasion. When the second was made, there had been added to this example those of Rhode-Island, New-York, New-Jersey, and Pennsylvania, in all of which the republican form had been found equal to the task of carrying them through the severest trials. In this state alone did there exist so little virtue, that fear was to be fixed in the hearts of the people, and to become the motive of their exertions and the principle of their government? The very thought alone was treason against the people; was treason against mankind in general; as rivetting for ever the chains which bow down their necks, by giving to their oppressors a proof, which they would have trumpeted through the universe, of the imbecility of republican government, in times of pressing danger, to shield them from harm. Those who assume the right of giving away the reins of government in any case, must be sure that the herd, whom they hand on to the rods and hatchet of the dictator, will lay their necks on the block when he shall nod to them. But if our assemblies supposed such a resignation in the people, I hope they mistook their character. I am of opinion, that the government, instead of being braced and invigorated for greater exertions under their difficulties, would have been thrown back upon the bungling machinery of county committees for administration, till a convention could have been called, and its wheels again set into regular motion. What a cruel moment was this for creating such an embarrassment, for putting to the proof the attachment of our countrymen to republican government! Those who meant well, of the advocates for this measure, (and most of them meant well, for I know them personally, had been their fellow-labourers in the common cause, and had often proved the purity of their principles), had been seduced in their judgment by the example of an ancient republic, whose constitution and circumstances were fundamentally different. They had sought this precedent in the history of Rome, where alone it was to be found, and where at length too it had proved fatal. They had taken it from a republic, rent by the most bitter factions and tumults, where the government was of a heavy-handed unfeeling aristocracy, over a people ferocious, and rendered desperate by poverty and wretchedness; tumults which could not be allayed under the most trying circumstances, but by the omnipotent hand of a single despot. Their constitution therefore allowed a temporary tyrant to be erected, under the name of a Dictator; and that temporary tyrant, after a few examples, became perpetual. They misapplied this precedent to a people, mild in their dispositions, patient under their trial, united for the public liberty, and affectionate to their leaders. But if from the constitution of the Roman government there resulted to their Senate a power of submitting all their rights to the will of one man, does it follow, that the assembly of Virginia have the same authority? What clause in our constitution has substituted that of Rome, by way of residuary provision, for all cases not otherwise provided for? Or if they may step ad libitum into any other form of government for precedents to rule us by, for what oppression may not a precedent be found in this world of the bellum omnium in omnia? —Searching for the foundations of this proposition, I can find none which may pretend a colour of right or reason, but the defect before developed, that there being no barrier between the legislative, executive, and judiciary departments, the legislature may seize the whole: that having seized it, and possessing a right to fix their own quorum, they may reduce that quorum to one, whom they may call a chairman, speaker, dictator, or by any other name they please.—Our situation is indeed perilous, and I hope my countrymen will be sensible of it, and will apply, at a proper season, the proper remedy; which is a convention to fix the constitution, to amend its defects, to bind up the several branches of government by certain laws, which when they transgress their acts shall become nullities; to render unnecessary an appeal to the people, or in other words a rebellion, on every infraction of their rights, on the peril that their acquiescence shall be construed into an intention to surrender those rights.

7. From Query XIV, Laws.

Many of the laws which were in force during the monarchy being relative merely to that form of government, or inculcating principles inconsistent with republicanism, the first assembly which met after the establishment of the commonwealth appointed a committee to revise the whole code, to reduce it into proper form and volume, and report it to the assembly. This work has been executed by three gentlemen, and reported; but probably will not be taken up till a restoration of peace shall leave to the legislature leisure to go through such a work.

[*Among the measures considered by the Committee of Revisors was one "to emancipate all slaves born after passing the act."*] The bill reported by the revisors does not itself contain this proposition; but an amendment containing it was prepared, to be offered to the legislature whenever the bill should be taken up, and further directing, that they should continue with their parents to a certain age, then be brought up, at the public expence, to tillage, arts or sciences, according to their geniusses, till the females should be eighteen, and the males twenty-one years of age, when they should be colonized to such place as the circumstances of the time should render most proper, sending them out with arms, implements of houshold and of the handicraft arts, feeds, pairs of the useful domestic animals, &c. to declare them a free and independant people, and extend to them our alliance and protection, till they shall have acquired strength; and to send vessels at the same time to other parts of the world for an equal number of white inhabitants; to induce whom to migrate hither, proper encouragements were to be proposed. It will probably be asked, Why not retain and incorporate the blacks into the state, and thus save the expence of supplying, by importation of white settlers, the vacancies they will leave? Deep rooted prejudices entertained by the whites; ten thousand recollections, by the blacks, of the injuries they have sustained; new provocations; the real distinctions which nature has made; and many other circumstances, will divide us into parties, and produce convulsions which will probably never end but in the extermination of the one or the other race.—To these objections, which are political, may be added others, which are physical and moral. The first difference which strikes us is that of colour. Whether the black of the negro resides in the reticular membrane between the skin and scarf-skin, or in the scarf-skin itself; whether it proceeds from the colour of the blood, the colour of the bile, or from that of some other secretion, the difference is fixed in nature, and is as real as if its seat and cause were better known to us. And is this difference of no importance? Is it not the foundation of a greater or less share of beauty in the two races? Are not the fine mixtures of red and white, the expressions of every passion by greater or less suffusions of colour in the one, preferable to that eternal monotony, which reigns in the countenances, that immoveable veil of black which covers all the emotions of the other race? Add to these, flowing hair, a more elegant symmetry of form, their own judgment in favour of the whites, declared by their preference of them, as uniformly as is the preference of the Oranootan for the black women over those of his own species. The circumstance of superior beauty, is thought worthy attention in the propagation of our horses, dogs, and other domestic animals; why not in that of man? Besides those of colour, figure, and hair, there are other physical distinctions proving a difference of race. They have less hair on the face and body. They secrete less by the kidnies, and more by the glands of the skin, which gives them a very strong and disagreeable odour. This greater degree of transpiration renders them more tolerant of heat, and less so of cold, than the whites. Perhaps too a difference of structure in the pulmonary apparatus, which a late ingenious experimentalist has discovered to be the principal regulator of animal heat, may have disabled them from extricating, in the act of inspiration, so much of that fluid from the outer air, or obliged them in expiration, to part with more of it. They seem to require less sleep. A black, after hard labour through the day, will be induced by the slightest amusements to sit up till midnight, or later, though knowing he must be out with the first dawn of the morning. They are at least as brave, and more adventuresome. But this may perhaps proceed from a want of forethought, which prevents their seeing a danger till it be present. When present, they do not go through it with more coolness or steadiness than the whites. They are more ardent after their female: but love seems with them to be more an eager desire, than a tender delicate mixture of sentiment and sensation. Their griefs are transient. Those numberless afflictions, which render it doubtful whether heaven has given life to us in mercy or in wrath, are less felt, and sooner forgotten with them. In general, their existence appears to participate more of sensation than reflection. To this must be ascribed their disposition to sleep when abstracted from their diversions, and unemployed in labour. An animal whose body is at rest, and who does not reflect, must be disposed to sleep of course. Comparing them by their faculties of memory, reason, and imagination, it appears to me, that in memory they are equal to the whites; in reason much inferior, as I think one could scarcely be found capable of tracing and comprehending the investigations of Euclid; and that in imagination they are dull, tasteless, and anomalous. It would be unfair to follow them to Africa for this investigation. We will consider them here, on the same stage with the whites, and where the facts are not apocryphal on which a judgment is to be formed. It will be right to make great allowances for the difference of condition, of education, of conversation, of the sphere in which they move. Many millions of them have been brought to, and born in America. Most of them indeed have been confined to tillage, to their own homes, and their own society: yet many have been so situated, that they might have availed themselves of the conversation of their masters; many have been brought up to the handicraft arts, and from that circumstance have always been associated with the whites. Some have been liberally educated, and all have lived in countries where the arts and sciences are cultivated to a considerable degree, and have had before their eyes samples of the best works from abroad. The Indians, with no advantages of this kind, will often carve figures on their pipes not destitute of design and merit. They will crayon out an animal, a plant, or a country, so as to prove the existence of a germ in their minds which only wants cultivation. They astonish you with strokes of the most sublime oratory; such as prove their reason and sentiment strong, their imagination glowing and elevated. But never yet could I find that a black had uttered a thought above the level of plain narration; never see even an elementary trait of painting or sculpture. In music they are more generally gifted than the whites with accurate ears for tune and time, and they have been found capable of imagining a small catch.[1] Misery is often the parent of the most affecting touches in poetry. —Among the blacks is misery enough, God knows, but no poetry. Love is the peculiar oestrum of the poet. Their love is ardent, but it kindles the senses only, not the imagination. Religion indeed has produced a Phyllis Whately; but it could not produce a poet. The compositions published under her name are below the dignity of criticism. The heroes of the Dunciad are to her, as Hercules to the author of that poem. Ignatius Sancho has approached nearer to merit in composition; yet his letters do more honour to the heart than the head. They breathe the purest effusions of friendship and general philanthropy, and shew how great a degree of the latter may be compounded with strong religious zeal. He is often happy in the turn of his compliments, and his stile is easy and familiar, except when he affects a Shandean fabrication of words. But his imagination is wild and extravagant, escapes incessantly from every restraint of reason and taste, and, in the course of its vagaries, leaves a tract of thought as incoherent and eccentric, as is the course of a meteor through the sky. His subjects should often have led him to a process of sober reasoning: yet we find him always substituting sentiment for demonstration. Upon the whole, though we admit him to the first place among those of his own colour who have presented themselves to the public judgment, yet when we compare him with the writers of the race among whom he lived, and particularly with the epistolary class, in which he has taken his own stand, we are compelled to enroll him at the bottom of the column. This criticism supposes the letters published under his name to be genuine, and to have received amendment from no other hand; points which would not be of easy investigation. The improvement of the blacks in body and mind, in the first instance of their mixture with the whites, has been observed by every one, and proves that their inferiority is not the effect merely of their condition of life. We know that among the Romans, about the Augustan age especially, the condition of their slaves was much more deplorable than that of the blacks on the continent of America. The two sexes were confined in separate apartments, because to raise a child cost the master more than to buy one. Cato, for a very

---

1. The instrument proper to them is the Banjar, which they brought hither from Africa, and which is the original of the guitar, its chords being precisely the four lower chords of the guitar. Whether they will be equal to the composition of a more extensive run of melody, or of complicated harmony, is yet to be proved [*TJ's note*].

restricted indulgence to his slaves in this particular, took from them a certain price. But in this country the slaves multiply as fast as the free inhabitants. Their situation and manners place the commerce between the two sexes almost without restraint. —The same Cato, on a principle of œconomy, always sold his sick and superannuated slaves. He gives it as a standing precept to a master visiting his farm, to sell his old oxen, old waggons, old tools, old and diseased servants, and every thing else become useless. . . . The American slaves cannot enumerate this among the injuries and insults they receive. It was the common practice to expose in the island of Aesculapius, in the Tyber, diseased slaves, whose cure was like to become tedious. The Emperor Claudius, by an edict, gave freedom to such of them as should recover, and first declared, that if any person chose to kill rather than to expose them, it should be deemed homicide. The exposing them is a crime of which no instance has existed with us; and were it to be followed by death, it would be punished capitally. We are told of a certain Vedius Pollio, who, in the presence of Augustus, would have given a slave as food to his fish, for having broken a glass. With the Romans, the regular method of taking the evidence of their slaves was under torture. Here it has been thought better never to resort to their evidence. When a master was murdered, all his slaves, in the same house, or within hearing, were condemned to death. Here punishment falls on the guilty only, and as precise proof is required against him as against a freeman. Yet notwithstanding these and other discouraging circumstances among the Romans, their slaves were often their rarest artists. They excelled too in science, insomuch as to be usually employed as tutors to their master's children. Epictetus, Terence, and Phaedrus, were slaves. But they were of the race of whites. It is not their condition then, but nature, which has produced the distinction. —Whether further observation will or will not verify the conjecture, that nature has been less bountiful to them in the endowments of the head, I believe that in those of the heart she will be found to have done them justice. That disposition to theft with which they have been branded, must be ascribed to their situation, and not to any depravity of the moral sense. The man, in whose favour no laws of property exist, probably feels himself less bound to respect those made in favour of others. When arguing for ourselves, we lay it down as a fundamental, that laws, to be just, must give a reciprocation of right: that, without this, they are mere arbitrary rules of conduct, founded in force, and not in conscience: and it is a problem which give to the master to solve, whether the religious precepts against the violation of property were not framed for him as well as his slave? And whether the slave may not as justifiably take a little from one, who has taken all from him, as he may slay one who would slay him? That a change in the relations in which a man is placed should change his ideas of moral right and wrong, is neither new, nor peculiar to the colour of the blacks. Homer tells us it was so 2600 years ago. . . .

> Jove fix'd it certain, that whatever day
> Makes man a slave, takes half his worth away.

But the slaves of which Homer speaks were whites. Notwithstanding these considerations which must weaken their respect for the laws of property, we find among them numerous instances of the most rigid integrity, and as many as among their better instructed masters, of benevolence, gratitude, and unshaken fidelity. —The opinion, that they are inferior in the faculties of reason and imagination, must be hazarded with great diffidence. To justify a general conclusion, requires many observations, even where the subject may be submitted to the Anatomical knife, to Optical glasses, to analysis by fire, or by solvents. How much more then where it is a faculty, not a substance, we are examining; where it eludes the research of all the senses; where the conditions of its existence are various and variously combined; where the effects of those which are present or absent bid defiance to calculation; let me add too, as a circumstance of great tenderness, where our conclusion would degrade a whole race of men from the rank in the scale of beings which their Creator may perhaps have given them. To our reproach it must be said, that though for a century and a half we have had under our eyes the races of black and of red men, they have never yet been viewed by us as subjects of natural history. I advance it therefore as a suspicion only, that the blacks, whether originally a distinct race, or made distinct by time and circumstances, are inferior to the whites in the endowments both of body and mind. It is not against experience to suppose, that different species of the same genus, or varieties of the same species, may possess different qualifications. Will not a lover of natural history then, one who views the gradations in all the races of animals with the eye of philosophy, excuse an effort to keep those in the department of man as distinct as nature has formed them? This unfortunate difference of colour, and perhaps of faculty, is a powerful obstacle to the emancipation of these people. Many of their advocates, while they wish to vindicate the liberty of human nature, are anxious also to preserve its dignity and beauty. Some of these, embarrassed by the question "What further is to be done with them?" join themselves in opposition with those who are actuated by sordid avarice only. Among the Romans emancipation required but one effort. The slave, when made free, might mix with, without staining the blood of his master. But with us a second is necessary, unknown to history. When freed, he is to be removed beyond the reach of mixture.

8. Query XVII, Religion.

The first settlers in this country were emigrants from England, of the English church, just at a point of time when it was flushed with complete victory over the religious of all other persuasions. Possessed, as they became, of the powers of making, administering, and executing the laws, they shewed equal intolerance in this country with their Presbyterian brethren, who had emigrated to the northern government. The poor Quakers were flying from persecution in England. They cast their eyes on these new countries as asylums of civil and religious freedom; but they found them free only for the reigning sect. Several acts of the Virginia assembly of 1659, 1662, and 1693, had made it penal in parents to refuse to have their children baptized; had prohibited the unlawful assembling of Quakers; had made it penal for any master of a vessel to bring a Quaker into the state; had ordered those already here, and such as should come thereafter, to be imprisoned till they should abjure the country; provided a milder punishment for their first and second return, but death for their third; had inhibited all persons from suffering their meetings in or near their houses, entertaining them individually, or disposing of books which supported their tenets. If no capital execution took place here, as did in New-England, it was not owing to the moderation of the church, or spirit of the legislature, as may be inferred from the law itself; but to historical circumstances which have not been handed down to us. The Anglicans retained full possession of the country about a century. Other opinions began then to creep in, and the great care of the government to support their own church, having begotten an equal degree of indolence in its clergy, two-thirds of the people had become dissenters at the commencement of the present revolution. The laws indeed were still oppressive on them, but the spirit of the one party had subsided into moderation, and of the other had risen to a degree of determination which commanded respect.

The present state of our laws on the subject of religion is this. The convention of May 1776, in their declaration of rights, declared it to be a truth, and a natural right, that the exercise of religion should be free; but when they proceeded to form on that declaration the ordinance of government, instead of taking up every principle declared in the bill of rights, and guarding it by legislative sanction, they passed over that which asserted our religious rights, leaving them as they found them. The same convention, however, when they met as a member of the general assembly in October 1776, repealed all acts of parliament which had rendered criminal the maintaining any opinions in matters of religion, the forbearing to repair to church, and the exercising any mode of worship; and suspended the laws giving salaries to the clergy, which suspension was made perpetual in October 1779. Statutory oppressions in religion being thus wiped away, we remain at present under those only imposed by the common law, or by our own acts of assembly. At the common law, heresy was a capital offence, punishable by burning. Its definition was left to the ecclesiastical judges, before whom the conviction was, till the statute of the 1 El. c. 1. circumscribed it, by declaring, that nothing should be deemed heresy, but what had been so determined by authority of the canonical scriptures, or by one of the four first general councils, or by some other council having for the grounds of their declaration the express and plain words of the scriptures. Heresy, thus circumscribed, being an offence at the common law, our act of assembly of October 1777, c. 17. gives cognizance of it to the general court, by declaring, that the jurisdiction of that court shall be general in all matters at the common law. The execution is by the writ De haeretico comburendo [*for burning a heretic*]. By our own act of assembly of 1705, c. 30, if a person brought up in the Christian religion denies the being of a God, or the Trinity, or asserts there are more Gods than one, or denies the Christian religion to be true, or the scriptures to be of divine authority, he is punishable on the first offence by incapacity to hold any office or employment ecclesiastical, civil, or military; on the second by disability to sue, to take any gift or legacy, to be guardian, executor, or administrator, and by three years imprisonment, without bail. A father's right to the custody of his own children being founded in law on his right of guardianship, this being taken away, they may of course be severed from him, and put, by the authority of a court, into more orthodox hands. This is a summary view of that religious slavery, under which a people have been willing to remain, who have lavished their lives and fortunes for the establishment of their civil freedom. The error seems not sufficiently eradicated, that the operations of the mind, as well as the acts of the body, are subject to the coercion of the laws. But our rulers can have authority over such natural rights only as we have submitted to them. The rights of conscience we never submitted, we could not submit. We are answerable for them to our God. The legitimate powers of government extend to such acts only as are injurious to others. But it does me no injury for my neighbour to say there are twenty gods, or no god. It neither picks my pocket nor breaks my leg. If it be said, his testimony in a court of justice cannot be relied on, reject it then, and be the stigma on him. Constraint may make him worse by making him a hypocrite, but it will never make him a truer man. It may fix him obstinately in his errors, but will not cure them. Reason and free enquiry are the only effectual agents against error. Give a loose to them, they will support the true religion, by bringing every false one to their tribunal, to the test of their investigation. They are the natural enemies of error, and of error only. Had not the Roman government permitted free enquiry, Christianity could never have been introduced. Had not free enquiry been indulged, at the aera of the reformation, the corruptions of Christianity could not have been purged away. If it be restrained now, the present corruptions will be protected, and new ones encouraged. Was the government to prescribe to us our medicine and diet, our bodies would be in such keeping as our souls are now. Thus in France the emetic was once forbidden as a medicine, and the potatoe as an article of food. Government is just as infallible too when it fixes systems in physics. Galileo was sent to the inquisition for affirming that the earth was a sphere: the government had declared it to be as flat as a trencher, and Galileo was obliged to abjure his error. This error however at length prevailed, the earth became a globe, and Descartes declared it was whirled round its axis by a vortex. The government in which he lived was wise enough to see that this was no question of civil jurisdiction, or we should all have been involved by authority in vortices. In fact, the vortices have been exploded, and the Newtonian principle of gravitation is now more firmly established, on the basis of reason, than it would be were the government to step in, and to make it an article of necessary faith. Reason and experiment have been indulged, and error has fled before them. It is error alone which needs the support of government. Truth can stand by itself. Subject opinion to coercion: whom will you make your inquisitors? Fallible men; men governed by bad passions, by private as well as public reasons. And why subject it to coercion? To produce uniformity. But is uniformity of opinion desireable? No more than of face and stature. Introduce the bed of Procrustes then, and as there is danger that the large men may beat the small, make us all of a size, by lopping the former and stretching the latter. Difference of opinion is advantageous in religion. The several sects perform the office of a Censor morum over each other. Is uniformity attainable? Millions of innocent men, women, and children, since the introduction of Christianity, have been burnt, tortured, fined, imprisoned; yet we have not advanced one inch towards uniformity. What has been the effect of coercion? To make one half the world fools, and the other half hypocrites. To support roguery and error all over the earth. Let us reflect that it is inhabited by a thousand millions of people. That these profess probably a thousand different systems of religion. That ours is but one of that thousand. That if there be but one right, and ours that one, we should wish to see the 999 wandering sects gathered into the fold of truth. But against such a majority we cannot effect this by force. Reason and persuasion are the only practicable instruments. To make way for these, free enquiry must be indulged; and how can we wish others to indulge it while we refuse it ourselves. But every state, says an inquisitor, has established some religion. No two, say I, have established the same. Is this a proof of the infallibility of establishments? Our sister states of Pennsylvania and New York, however, have long subsisted without any establishment at all. The experiment was new and doubtful when they made it. It has answered beyond conception. They flourish infinitely. Religion is well supported; of various kinds, indeed, but all good enough; all sufficient to preserve peace and order: or if a sect arises, whose tenets would subvert morals, good sense has fair play, and reasons and laughs it out of doors, without suffering the state to be troubled with it. They do not hang more malefactors than we do. They are not more disturbed with religious dissensions. On the contrary, their harmony is unparalleled, and can be ascribed to nothing but their unbounded tolerance, because there is no other circumstance in which they differ from every nation on earth. They have made the happy discovery, that the way to silence religious disputes, is to take no notice of them. Let us too give this experiment fair play, and get rid, while we may, of those tyrannical laws. It is true, we are as yet secured against them by the spirit of the times. I doubt whether the people of this country would suffer an execution for heresy, or a three years imprisonment for not comprehending the mysteries of the Trinity. But is the spirit of the people an infallible, a permanent reliance? Is it government? Is this the kind of protection we receive in return for the rights we give up? Besides, the spirit of the times may alter, will alter. Our rulers will become corrupt, our people careless. A single zealot may commence persecutor, and better men be his victims. It can never be too often repeated, that the time for fixing every essential right on a legal basis is while our rulers are honest, and ourselves united. From the conclusion of this war we shall be going down hill. It will not then be necessary to resort every moment to the people for support. They will be forgotten, therefore, and their rights disregarded. They will forget themselves, but in the sole faculty of making money, and will never think of uniting to effect a due respect for their rights. The shackles, therefore, which shall not be knocked off at the conclusion of this war, will remain on us long, will be made heavier and heavier, till our rights shall revive or expire in a convulsion.

9. Query XVIII, Manners.

It is difficult to determine on the standard by which the manners of a nation may be tried, whether *catholic,* or *particular.* It is more difficult for a native to bring to that standard the manners of his own nation, familiarized to him by habit. There must doubtless be an unhappy influence on the manners of our people produced by the existence of slavery among us. The whole commerce between master and slave is a perpetual exercise of the most boisterous passions, the most unremitting despotism on the one part, and degrading submissions on the other. Our children see this, and learn to imitate it; for man is an imitative animal. This quality is the germ of all education in him. From his cradle to his grave he is learning to do what he sees others do. If a parent could find no motive either in his philanthropy or his self-love, for restraining the intemperance of passion towards his slave, it should always be a sufficient one that his child is present. But generally it is not sufficient. The parent storms, the child looks on, catches the lineaments of wrath, puts on the same airs in the circle of smaller slaves, gives a loose to his worst of passions, and thus nursed, educated, and daily exercised in tyranny, cannot but be stamped by it with odious peculiarities. The man must be a prodigy who can retain his manners and morals undepraved by such circumstances. And with what execration should the statesman be loaded, who permitting one half the citizens thus to trample on the rights of the other, transforms those into despots, and these into enemies, destroys the morals of the one part, and the amor patriae of the other. For if a slave can have a country in this world, it must be any other in preference to that in which he is born to live and labour for another: in which he must lock up the faculties of his nature, contribute as far as depends on his individual endeavours to the evanishment of the human race, or entail his own miserable condition on the endless generations proceeding from him. With the morals of the people, their industry also is destroyed. For in a warm climate, no man will labour for himself who can make another labour for him. This is so true, that of the proprietors of slaves a very small proportion indeed are ever seen to labour. And can the liberties of a nation be thought secure when we have removed their only firm basis, a conviction in the minds of the people that these liberties are of the gift of God? That they are not to be violated but with his wrath? Indeed I tremble for my country when reflect that God is just: that his justice cannot sleep for ever: that considering numbers, nature and natural means only, a revolution of the wheel of fortune, an exchange of situation, is among possible events: that it may become probable by supernatural interference! The Almighty has no attribute which can take side with us in such a contest. —But it is impossible to be temperate and to pursue this subject through the various considerations of policy, of morals, of history natural and civil. We must be contented to hope they will force their way into every one's mind. I think a change already perceptible, since the origin of the present revolution. The spirit of the master is abating, that of the slave rising from the dust, his condition mollifying, the way I hope preparing, under the auspices of heaven, for a total emancipation, and that this is disposed, in the order of events, to be with the consent of the masters, rather than by their extirpation.

10. Query XIX, Manufactures.

We never had an interior trade of any importance. Our exterior commerce has suffered very much from the beginning of the present contest.

During this time we have manufactured within our families the most necessary articles of cloathing. Those of cotton will bear some comparison with the same kinds of manufacture in Europe; but those of wool, flax and hemp are very coarse, unsightly, and unpleasant: and such is our attachment to agriculture, and such our preference for foreign manufactures, that be it wise or unwise, our people will certainly return as soon as they can, to the raising raw materials, and exchanging them for finer manufactures than they are able to execute themselves.

The political œconomists of Europe have established it as a principle that every state should endeavour to manufacture for itself: and this principle, like many others, we transfer to America, without calculating the difference of circumstance which should often produce a difference of result. In Europe the lands are either cultivated, or locked up against the cultivator. Manufacture must therefore be resorted to of necessity not of choice, to support the surplus of their people. But we have an immensity of land courting the industry of the husbandman. Is it best then that all our citizens should be employed in its improvement, or that one half should be called off from that to exercise manufactures and handicraft arts for the other? Those who labour in the earth are the chosen people of God, if ever he had a chosen people, whose breasts he has made his peculiar deposit for substantial and genuine virtue. It is the focus in which he keeps alive that sacred fire, which otherwise might escape from the face of the earth. Corruption of morals in the mass of cultivators is a phænomenon of which no age nor nation has furnished an example. It is the mark set on those, who not looking up to heaven, to their own soil and industry, as does the husbandman, for their subsistance, depend for it on the casualties and caprice of customers. Dependance begets subservience and venality, suffocates the germ of virtue, and prepares fit tools for the designs of ambition. This, the natural progress and consequence of the arts, has sometimes perhaps been retarded by accidental circumstances: but, generally speaking, the proportion which the aggregate of the other classes of citizens bears in any state to that of its husbandmen, is the proportion of its unsound to its healthy parts, and is a good-enough barometer whereby to measure its degree of corruption. While we have land to labour then, let us never wish to see our citizens occupied at a work-bench, or twirling a distaff. Carpenters, masons, smiths, are wanting in husbandry: but, for the general operations of manufacture, let our work-shops remain in Europe. It is better to carry provisions and materials to workmen there, than bring them to the provisions and materials, and with them their manners and principles. The loss by the transportation of commodities across the Atlantic will be made up in happiness and permanence of government. The mobs of great cities add just so much to the support of pure government, as sores do to the strength of the human body. It is the manners and spirit of a people which preserve a republic in vigour. A degeneracy in these is a canker which soon eats to the heart of its laws and constitution.

11. From Query XXII, Public Revenue and Expences.

To this estimate of our abilities, let me add a word as to the application of them, if, when cleared of the present contest, and of the debts with which that will charge us, we come to measure force hereafter with any European power. Such events are devoutly to be deprecated. Young as we are, and with such a country before us to fill with people and with happiness, we should point in that direction the whole generative force of nature, wasting none of it in efforts of mutual destruction. It should be our endeavour to cultivate the peace and friendship of every nation, even of that which has injured us most, when we shall have carried our point against her. Our interest will be to throw open the doors of commerce, and to knock off all its shackles, giving perfect freedom to all persons for the vent of whatever they may chuse to bring into our ports, and asking the same in theirs. Never was so much false arithmetic employed on any subject, as that which has been employed to persuade nations that it is their interest to go to war. Were the money which it has cost to gain, at the close of a long war, a little town, or a little territory, the right to cut wood here, or to catch fish there, expended in improving what they already possess, in making roads, opening rivers, building ports, improving the arts, and finding employment for their idle poor, it would render them much stronger, much wealthier and happier. This I hope will be our wisdom. And, perhaps, to remove as much as possible the occasions of making war, it might be better for us to abandon the ocean altogether, that being the element whereon we shall be principally exposed to jostle with other nations: to leave to others to bring what we shall want, and to carry what we can spare. This would make us invulnerable to Europe, by offering none of our property to their prize, and would turn all our citizens to the cultivation of the earth; and, I repeat it again, cultivators of the earth are the most virtuous and independant citizens. It might be time enough to seek employment for them at sea, when the land no longer offers it. But the actual habits of our countrymen attach them to commerce. They will exercise it for themselves. Wars then must sometimes be our lot; and all the wise can do, will be to avoid that half of them which would be produced by our own follies, and our own acts of injustice; and to make for the other half the best preparations we can. Of what nature should these be? A land army would be useless for offence, and not the best nor safest instrument of defence. For either of these purposes, the sea is the field on which we should meet an European enemy. On that element it is necessary we should possess some power. To aim at such a navy as the greater nations of Europe possess, would be a foolish and wicked waste of the energies of our countrymen. It would be to pull on our own heads that load of military expence, which makes the European labourer go supperless to bed, and moistens his bread with the sweat of his brows. It will be enough if we enable ourselves to prevent insults from those nations of Europe which are weak on the sea, because circumstances exist, which render even the stronger ones weak as to us. Providence has placed their richest and most defenceless possessions at our door; has obliged their most precious commerce to pass as it were in review before us. To protect this, or to assail us, a small part only of their naval force will ever be risqued across the Atlantic. The dangers to which the elements expose them here are too well known, and the greater dangers to which they would be exposed at home, were any general calamity to involve their whole fleet. They can attack us by detachment only; and it will suffice to make ourselves equal to what they may detach. Even a smaller force than they may detach will be rendered equal or superior by the quickness with which any check may be repaired with us, while losses with them will be irreparable till too late. A small naval force then is sufficient for us, and a small one is necessary. What this should be, I will not undertake to say. I will only say, it should by no means be so great as we are able to make it. Suppose the million of dollars, or 300,000 pounds, which Virginia could annually spare without distress, to be applied to the creating a navy. A single year's contribution would build, equip, man, and send to sea a force which should carry 300 guns. The rest of the confederacy, exerting themselves in the same proportion, would equip in the same time 1500 guns more. So that one year's contributions would set up a navy of 1800 guns. The British ships of the line average 76 guns; their frigates 38. 1800 guns then would form a fleet of 30 ships, 18 of which might be of the line, and 12 frigates. Allowing 8 men, the British average, for every gun, their annual expence, including subsistence, cloathing, pay, and ordinary repairs, would be about 1280 dollars for every gun, or 2,304,000 dollars for the whole. I state this only as one year's possible exertion, without deciding whether more or less than a year's exertion should be thus applied.

The value of our lands and slaves, taken conjunctly, doubles in about twenty years. This arises from the multiplication of our slaves, from the extension of culture, and increased demand for lands. The amount of what may be raised will of course rise in the same proportion.

CHAPTER THREE

New World and Old World

Before sailing from Boston in July 1784 to assume the duties of American minister in Paris, Jefferson represented Virginia in Congress for a few eventful months. The major problem before the Confederation government was the organization and development of the new national domain in the Northwest Territory that came into existence when Virginia ceded its claims to the region in March 1784. Jefferson had already given much thought to the problem of the formation of new states, including in his proposed draft of the Virginia State Constitution of 1776 a provision for their creation. As a leading advocate of the long-delayed Virginia cession, he was well prepared to take the lead in drafting congressional ordinances for western government and land sales (document 3).

Jefferson's brief tenure in the Confederation Congress had given him a good sense of the weaknesses of an arrangement that had no effective controls over fractious member states. This concern deepened over his years in Paris, even while he sought to assure friendly correspondents such as the English radical Richard Price that the republican experiment would succeed (document 4). Jefferson had not arrived in time to participate in the Paris peace negotiations, completed in 1783, and he quickly found that the United States was not in a strong position to negotiate further treaty agreements with France and other European powers that would promote American commercial and political interests. He also discovered that his predecessor, Benjamin Franklin, who had been lionized by Parisian polite society, would be a very hard act to follow. Jefferson was always somewhat awkward in public settings and, though a master of the written language, not a fluent French speaker.

Yet while frustrated in diplomacy, Jefferson put the time to intellectual advantage. His official inactivity provided ample scope for the studious Jefferson to pursue his intellectual interests and to cultivate friendships within the great Enlightenment "republic of letters." Distance from his native country gave him perspectives that would have a profound effect on the rest of his career. The opening phases of the French Revolution, from Jefferson's view the ultimate tribute to the revolutionary achievement of the Americans, were particularly exhilarating for him, giving rise to some of his most radical political ideas (see document 17). The leisure he had to explore Europe and its institutions, to observe the inner workings of the old regime, enabled him to clarify—and reveal to us—some of his fundamental principles. For Jefferson, as so many of the documents collected below reveal, a great moral and political division separated the old world from the new: for all its charms, the "vaunted scene of Europe" revealed the enormous human costs of despotic rule and popular ignorance. Jefferson was convinced that the American Revolution constituted a great leap forward for mankind as a whole: one day, Europe would catch up.

Jefferson found irresistible the opportunity to hold forth on the new nation's moral superiority. But this did not stop him from savoring the delights of refined and civilized life in the great European metropolis. New scenes and sensations enabled the grieving widower to explore dormant aspects in his own emotional life. His passionate, possibly sexual relationship with the artist Maria Cosway was only one of many close, sentimentally satisfying friendships he made with European women and men. At this time, Jefferson also probably initiated a long-term sexual relationship with his slave Sally Hemings, the half-sister of his deceased wife Martha.

Jefferson was still in Europe while his friend James Madison and his colleagues were crafting a proposal for a stronger federal government in America. Jefferson's responses to the plan (see documents 14–16) are particularly interesting and significant, for his interpretation of the new constitutional system would be critical for his subsequent roles in President Washington's cabinet and then in the leadership of the antiadministration Republican opposition. If Jefferson recovered his emotional equilibrium during his protracted European interludes, reaffirming and strengthening his most fundamental ideological commitments also prepared him for a career of intense partisan political activity.

* * * * * * * * * *

1. To Edmund Randolph, Baltimore, 15 February 1783. *In December 1782, Edmund Randolph (1753–1813), the patriot son of the loyalist John Randolph, resigned his seat in the Confederation Congress, returning to Virginia to become attorney general, the position his father had held under the Crown. TJ had recently seen a set of resolutions by the Virginia House of Delegates, adopted in December 1782, justifying the confiscation of loyalist property on the basis of the commonwealth's "natural right to frame a new social compact" excluding its enemies. TJ feared that refractory state legislatures would subvert any durable peace settlement with Britain and threaten the survival of the union. The "Vermonteers" had set a bad example for radical elements in other states by proclaiming their independence of New York in 1777 in defiance of existing jurisdictional and property rights.*

You will be surprised to hear I am still in America. The vessel, in which Ct. Rochambeau and Chast[el]lux went, having been destined for Cadix it was thought more adviseable for me to take my passage in the Romulus which was to sail within a few days. . . . In the mean time things are changing appearance. I received last night a copy of the k's speech announcing that preliminaries are agreed between us and them, to be in force on the conclusion of the war with France, that the negotiations with the other powers are considerably advanced, insomuch that he hopes a speedy pacification. I have therefore written to Mr. Livingston that he may submit to Congress a suggestion of the small likelihood there is of my arriving at the scene of negociation in time for any new communications I carry to make impressions on the definitive treaty, to weigh this chance against the certain expence and to say whether they think it more eligible or not for me to discontinue my voiage. Within a week I shall probably get an answer, and within the same space after your receiving this I think it probable you will see me at Richmond, as I shall take that route home to pick up my little family in that neighborhood. The king seems to part with us with a sigh; he makes it his earnest and humble prayer to Almighty god that Great Britain may experience no evils on so important a dismemberment of the empire, and that we may not find in experience as she had done how necessary *Monarchy* is for the preservation of constitutional liberty. He prays them to turn their attention to their extensive Asiatic possessions and seems to consider these as succeeding to our places. There is much lying and some puffing in the speech.

I hear with very great pleasure thro' Mr. Madison that you have a thought of qualifying yourself for a seat in the legislature. Indeed I hear it with as much pleasure as I have seen with depression of spirit the very low state to which that body has been reduced. I am satisfied there is in it much good intention, but little knowlege of the science to which they are called. I only fear you will find the unremitting drudgery, to which any one man must be exposed who undertakes to stem the torrent, will be too much for any degree of perseverance. I sincerely wish you may undertake and persevere in it. I hope you will be joined e'er long by Madison and Short. I observe the assembly in it's last session led into a declaration of a doctrine of the most mischeivous tendency. The object of the paper I allude to was the excluding the return of refugees and insisting on the escheat of their property; a very tempting bait indeed, and which would dispose them not to be nice in the preliminary reasoning which was to lead to it. This matter stands on it's best ground when urged on the reasonableness of a mutual risk in all contests, on the superior dangers we encountered, and the inequality of our conditions if we staked every thing and they nothing. But not content with this they go on to talk of the dissolution of the social contract on a revolution of government, and much other little stuff by which I collect their meaning to have been that on changing the doctrine against which the other states and Virginia most especially has been strenuously contending. The Vermonteers insist that on the demolition of the regal government all the municipal laws became abrogated, and of course those which had constituted any particular tract of country into one state, that any portion of what had been an integral state had then a right to assume a separate existence, and to govern themselves: and I have no doubt that their next declarations will cite that of the Virginia assembly which is the first authority they have ever had it in their power to cite. For my part, if the term social contract is to be forced from theoretical into practical use, I shall apply it to all the laws obligatory on the state, and which may be considered as contracts to which all the individuals are parties. And that whenever it becomes necessary to amend any of these, whether they respect the mode of administering the government or the transmission or regulation of private property, or any other branch of the laws, that any of these may be amended without affecting the residue. If you and I have a contract of six articles and agree to amend two of them, this does not dissolve the remaining four. The former laws had fixed the mode of transmitting the executive powers from one hand to another, the mode of appointing the judges, the mode of making alterations in the laws. These modes were found prejudicial to the state and it became necessary to change the laws which had fixed them. Why should this abrogate another law which had said that on the death of a father his eldest son shall inherit his lands? I find also the pride of independence taking deep and dangerous hold on the hearts of individual states. I know no danger so dreadful and so probable as that of internal contests. And I know no remedy so likely to prevent it as the strengthening the band which connects us. We have substituted a Congress of deputies from every state to perform this task: but we have done nothing which would enable them to enforce their decisions. What will be the case? They will not be enforced. The states will go to war with each other in defiance of Congress; one will call in France to her assistance; another Gr. Britain, and so we shall have all the wars of Europe brought to our own doors. Can any man be so puffed up with his little portion of sovereignty as to prefer this calamitous accompaniment to the parting with a little of his sovereign right and placing it in a council from all the states, who being chosen by himself annually, removeable at will, subject in a private capacity to every act of power he does in a public one, cannot possibly do him an injury, or if he does will be hauled for it? It is very important to unlearn the lessons we have learnt under our former government, to discard the maxims which were the bulwark of that, but would be the ruin of the one we have erected. I feel great comfort on the prospect of getting yourself and two or three others into the legislature. My "humble and earnest prayer to Almighty god" will be that you may bring into fashion principles suited to the form of government we have adopted, and not of that we have rejected, that you will first lay your shoulders to the strengthening the band of our confederacy and averting those cruel evils to which it's present weakness will expose us, and that you will see the necessity of doing this instantly before we forget the advantages of union, or acquire a degree of ill-temper against each other which will daily increase the obstacles to that good work.

2. To Martha Jefferson, Annapolis, 28 November 1783. *When TJ joined Congress, then sitting in the capital of Maryland, he left his elder daughter Martha ("Patsy") in Philadelphia under the care of Mrs. Thomas Hopkinson. Mrs. Hopkinson was the widowed mother of Francis Hopkinson, TJ's friend and cosigner of the Declaration of Independence. At this time young Martha, born in September 1772, was eleven years old.*

After four days journey I arrived here without any accident and in as good health as when I left Philadelphia. The conviction that you would be more improved in the situation I have placed you than if still with me, has solaced me on my parting with you, which my love for you has rendered a difficult thing. The acquirements which I hope you will make under the tutors I have provided for you will render you more worthy of my love, and if they cannot increase it they will prevent it's diminution. Consider the good lady who has taken you under her roof, who has undertaken to see that you perform all your exercises, and to admonish you in all those wanderings from what is right or what is clever to which your inexperience would expose you, consider her I say as your mother, as the only person to whom, since the loss with which heaven has been pleased to afflict you, you can now look up; and that her displeasure or disapprobation on any occasion will be an immense misfortune which should you be so unhappy as to incur by any unguarded act, think no concession too much to regain her good will. With respect to the distribution of your time the following is what I should approve.

from 8. to 10 o'clock practise music.
from 10. to 1. dance one day and draw another
from 1. to 2. draw on the day you dance, and write a letter the next day.
from 3. to 4. read French.
from 4. to 5. exercise yourself in music.
from 5. till bedtime read English, write &c.

Communicate this plan to Mrs. Hopkinson and if she approves of it pursue it. As long as Mrs. Trist remains in Philadelphia cultivate her affections. She has been a valuable friend to you and her good sense and good heart make her valued by all who know her and by nobody on earth more than by me. Expect you will write to me by every post. Inform me what books you read, what tunes you learn, and inclose me your best copy of every lesson in drawing. Write also one letter every week either to your aunt Eppes, your aunt Skipwith, your aunt Carr, or the little lady from whom I now inclose a letter, and always put the letter you so write under cover to me. Take care that you never spell a word wrong. Always before you write a word consider how it is spelt, and if you do not remember it, turn to a dictionary. It produces great praise to a lady to spell well. I have placed my happiness on seeing you good and accomplished, and no distress which this world can now bring on me could equal that of your disappointing my hopes. If you love me then, strive to be good under every situation and to all living creatures, and to acquire those accomplishments which I have put in your power, and which will go far towards ensuring you the warmest love of your affectionate father,

P. S. Keep my letters and read them at times that you may always have present in your mind those things which will endear you to me.

3. Report of Committee on Government for Western Territory, 1 March 1784. *Anticipating the cession of Virginia's vast domain north and west of the Ohio River, Congress named a committee, chaired by TJ and including David Howell of Rhode Island and Jeremiah Townley Chase of Maryland, to prepare a plan of government for the new national domain. The committee reported on*

1 March, the same day Congress finally accepted the Virginia cession; its plan, drafted by TJ, was endorsed by Congress on 23 April, though the ban on slavery after 1800 was excised. Though the Government Ordinance of 1784 was never implemented, its basic principle—the equality of new western states—was adapted by Congress in the Northwest Ordinance of 13 July 1787. TJ was also influential in drafting the first ordinance for selling lands of 30 April 1784, which first proposed the plan for the rectangular survey of federal lands that was subsequently incorporated in Congress's Land Ordinance of 20 May 1785.

The committee appointed to prepare a plan for the temporary Government of the Western territory have agreed to the following resolutions:

Resolved that the territory ceded or to be ceded by Individual States to the United States whensoever the same shall have been purchased of the Indian Inhabitants & offered for sale by the U. S. shall be formed into distinct States bounded in the following manner as nearly as such cessions will admit, that is to say; Northwardly & Southwardly by parallels of latitude so that each state shall comprehend from South to North two degrees of latitude beginning to count from the completion of thirty-one degrees North of the equator, but any territory Northwardly of the 47th. degree shall make part of the state—below, and Eastwardly & Westwardly they shall be bounded, those on the Mississippi by that river on one side and the meridian of the lowest point of the rapids of Ohio on the other; and those adjoining on the East by the same meridian on their Western side, and on their eastern by the meridian of the Western cape of the mouth of the Great Kanhaway. And the territory eastward of this last meridian between the Ohio, Lake Erie & Pennsylvania shall be one state.

That the settlers within the territory so to be purchased & offered for sale shall, either on their own petition, or on the order of Congress, receive authority from them, with appointments of time and place for their free males of full age to meet together for the purpose of establishing a temporary government, to adopt the constitution & laws of any one of these states, so that such laws nevertheless shall be subject to alteration by their ordinary legislature, and to erect, subject to a like alteration counties or townships for the election of members for their legislature.

That such temporary government shall only continue in force in any state until it shall have acquired 20,000 free inhabitants, when, giving due proof thereof to Congress, they shall receive from them authority with appointments of time and place to call a Convention of representatives to establish a permanent Constitution & Government for themselves.

Provided that both the temporary & permanent Governments be established on these principles as their basis. 1, That they shall forever remain a part of the United States of America. 2, That in their persons, property & territory, they shall be subject to the Government of the United States in Congress assembled and to the articles of confederation in all those cases in which the original states shall be so subject. 3, That they shall be subject to pay a part of the federal debts contracted or to be contracted to be apportioned on them by Congress, according to the same common rule and measure by which apportionments thereof shall be made on the other states. 4, That their respective Governments shall be in republican forms, and shall admit no person to be a citizen, who holds any hereditary title. 5, That after the year 1800 of the Christian æra, there shall be neither slavery nor involuntary servitude in any of the said states, otherwise than in punishment of crimes, whereof the party shall have been duly convicted to have been personally guilty.

That whenever any of the said states shall have, of free inhabitants as many as shall then be in any one the least numerous of the thirteen original states, such state shall be admitted by it's delegates into the Congress of the United States, on an equal footing with the said original states: After which the assent of two thirds of the United States in Congress assembled shall be requisite in all those cases, wherein by the Confederation the assent of nine States is now required. Provided the consent of nine states to such admission may be obtained according to the eleventh of the Articles of Confederation. Until such admission by their delegates into Congress, any of the said states, after the establishment of their temporary Government, shall have authority to keep a sitting Member in Congress, with a right of debating, but not of voting.

That the territory Northward of the 45th. degree, that is to say of the completion of 45° from the Equator & extending to the Lake of the Woods, shall be called SYLVANIA:

That of the territory under the 45th. & 44th. degrees that which lies Westward of Lake Michigan shall be called MICHIGANIA, and that which is Eastward thereof within the peninsula formed by the lakes & waters of Michigan, Huron, St. Clair and Erie, shall be called CHERRONESUS, and shall include any part of the peninsula which may extend above the 45th degree.

Of the territory under the 43d & 42d degrees, that to the Westward thro' which the Assenisipi or Rock river runs shall be called ASSENISIPIA, and that to the Eastward in which are the fountains of the Muskingum, the two Miamis of Ohio, the Wabash, the Illinois, the Miami of the lake and Sandusky rivers, shall be called METROPOTAMIA.

Of the territory which lies under the 41st. & 40th. degrees the Western, thro which the river Illinois runs, shall be called ILLINOIA; that next adjoining to the Eastward SARATOGA, and that between this last & Pennsylvania & extending from the Ohio to Lake Erie shall be called WASHINGTON.

Of the territory which lies under the 39th. & 38th. degrees to which shall be added so much of the point of land within the fork of the Ohio & Missisipi as lies under the 37th. degree, that to the Westward within & adjacent to which are the confluences of the rivers Wabash, Shawanee, Tanisse, Ohio, Illinois, Missisipi & Missouri, shall be called POLYPOTAMIA, and that to the Eastward farther up the Ohio otherwise called the PELISIPI shall be called PELISIPIA.

That the preceding articles shall be formed into a charter of Compact, shall be duly executed by the President of the U. S. in Congress assembled under his hand and the seal of the United States, shall be promulgated, and shall stand as fundamental constitutions between the thirteen original

States, & those now newly described unalterable but by the joint consent of the U. S. in Congress assembled and of the particular state within which such alteration is proposed to be made.

4. To Richard Price, Paris, 1 February 1785. *Richard Price (1723–1791) was an eminent Welsh philosopher, dissenting minister, and friend of the new American nation. His widely circulated* Observations on the Importance of the American Revolution, *published in 1784, expressed grave concerns about the ability of Congress ("the federal head") to resist centrifugal tendencies that would subvert the union and jeopardize American independence.*

The copy of your Observations on the American Revolution which you were so kind as to direct to me came duly to hand, and I should sooner have acknowledged the receipt of it but that I awaited a private conveiance for my letter, having experienced much delay and uncertainty in the posts between this place and London. I have read it with very great pleasure, as have done many others to whom I have communicated it. The spirit which it breathes is as affectionate as the observations themselves are wise and just. I have no doubt it will be reprinted in America and produce much good there. The want of power in the federal head was early perceived, and foreseen to be the flaw in our constitution which might endanger its destruction. I have the pleasure to inform you that when I left America in July the people were becoming universally sensible of this, and a spirit to enlarge the powers of Congress was becoming general. Letters and other information recently received shew that this has continued to increase, and that they are likely to remedy this evil effectually. The happiness of governments like ours, wherein the people are truly the mainspring, is that they are never to be despaired of. When an evil becomes so glaring as to strike them generally, they arrouse themselves, and it is redressed. He only is then the popular man and can get into office who shews the best dispositions to reform the evil. This truth was obvious on several occasions during the late war, and this character in our governments saved us. Calamity was our best physician. Since the peace it was observed that some nations of Europe, counting on the weakness of Congress and the little probability of a union in measure among the States, were proposing to grasp at unequal advantages in our commerce. The people are become sensible of this, and you may be assured that this evil will be immediately redressed, and redressed radically. I doubt still whether in this moment they will enlarge those powers in Congress which are necessary to keep the peace among the States. I think it possible that this may be suffered to lie till some two States commit hostilities on each other, but in that moment the hand of the union will be lifted up and interposed, and the people will themselves demand a general concession to Congress of means to prevent similar mischeifs. Our motto is truly "nil desperandum." The apprehensions you express of danger from the want of powers in Congress, led me to note to you this character in our governments, which, since the retreat behind the Delaware, and the capture of Charlestown, has kept my mind in perfect quiet as to the ultimate fate of our union; and I am sure, from the spirit which breathes thro your book, that whatever promises permanence to that will be a comfort to your mind.

5. To François Jean de Chastellux, Paris, 7 June 1785. *On his arrival in Paris TJ resumed his friendship with Chastellux (see Chapter 1, document 8). The first edition of TJ's* Notes *had been published in May; in this letter, TJ elaborates on his response to the Comte de Buffon's "degeneracy thesis" in Query VI (Chapter 2, document 4).*

I . . . thank you . . . sincerely, for the partiality with which you receive the copy of the Notes on my country. As I can answer for the facts therein reported on my own observation, and have admitted none on the report of others, which were not supported by evidence sufficient to command my own assent, I am not afraid that you should make any extracts you please for the Journal de Physique, which come within their plan of publication. The strictures on slavery and on the constitution of Virginia, are not of that kind, and they are the parts which I do not wish to have made public, at least, till I know whether their publication would do most harm or good. It is possible, that in my own country, these strictures might produce an irritation, which would indispose the people towards the two great objects I have in view; that is, the emancipation of their slaves, and the settlement of their constitution on a firmer and more permanent basis. If I learn from thence, that they will not produce that effect, I have printed and reserved just copies enough to be able to give one to every young man at the College. It is to them I look, to the rising generation, and not to the one now in power, for these great reformations. . . .

I will beg leave to say here a few words on the general question of the degeneracy of animals in America. 1. As to the degeneracy of the man of Europe transplanted to America, it is no part of Monsieur de Buffon's system. He goes, indeed, within one step of it, but he stops there. The Abbé Raynal alone has taken that step. Your knowledge of America enables you to judge this question, to say, whether the lower class of people in America, are less informed and less susceptible of information, than the lower class in Europe: and whether those in America, who have received such an education as that country can give, are less improved by it than Europeans of the same degree of education. 2. As to the aboriginal man of America, I know of no respectable evidence on which the opinion of his inferiority of genius has been founded, but that of Don Ulloa. As to Robertson, he never was in America, he relates nothing on his own knowledge, he is a compiler only of the relations of others, and a mere translator of the opinions of Monsieur de Buffon. I should as soon, therefore, add the translators of Robertson to the witnesses of this fact, as himself. Paw, the beginner of this charge, was a compiler from the works of others; and of the most unlucky description; for he seems to have read the writings of travellers, only to collect and republish their lies. It is really remarkable, that in three volumes 12mo, of small print, it is scarcely possible to find one truth, and yet, that the author should be able to produce authority for every fact he states, as he says he can. Don Ulloa's testimony is of the most respectable. He wrote of what he saw, but he saw the Indian of South America only, and that, after he had passed through ten generations of slavery. It is very unfair, from this sample, to judge of the natural genius of this race of men; and after supposing that Don Ulloa had not sufficiently calculated the allowance which should be made for this circumstance, we do him no injury in considering the picture he draws of the present Indians of South America, as no picture of what their ancestors were, three hundred years ago. It is in North America we are to seek their original character. And I am safe in affirming, that the proofs of genius given by the Indians of North America, place them on a level with whites in the same uncultivated state. The North of Europe furnishes subjects enough for comparison with them, and for a proof of their equality. I have seen some thousands myself, and conversed much with them, and have found in them a masculine, sound understanding. I have had much information from men who had lived among them, and whose veracity and good sense were so far known to me, as to establish a reliance on their information. They have all agreed in bearing witness in favor of the genius of this people. As to their bodily strength, their manners rendering it disgraceful to labor, those muscles employed in labor will be weaker with them, than with the European laborer; but those which are exerted in the chase, and those faculties which are employed in the tracing an enemy or a wild beast, in contriving ambuscades for him, and in carrying them through their execution, are much stronger than with us, because they are more exercised. I believe the Indian, then, to be, in body and mind, equal to the white man. I have supposed the black man, in his present state, might not be so; but it would be hazardous to affirm, that, equally cultivated for a few generations, he would not become so. 3. As to the inferiority of the other animals of America, without more facts, I can add nothing to what I have said in my Notes.

As to the theory of Monsieur de Buffon, that heat is friendly, and moisture adverse to the production of large animals, I am lately furnished with a fact by Dr. Franklin, which proves the air of London and of Paris to be more humid than that of Philadelphia, and so creates a suspicion that the opinion of the superior humidity of America may, perhaps, have been too hastily adopted. And supposing that fact admitted, I think the physical reasonings urged to show, that in a moist country animals must be small, and that in a hot one they must be large, are not built on the basis of experiment. These questions, however, cannot be decided, ultimately, at this day. More facts must be collected, and more time flow off, before the world will be ripe for decision. In the mean time, doubt is wisdom.

6. To Peter Carr, Paris, 19 August 1785. *Peter Carr (1770–1815) was TJ's nephew, the son of his younger sister Martha and his childhood friend Dabney Carr. When Dabney Carr died in 1773, TJ became the guardian of Peter and his brother Samuel; the Carrs lived at Monticello for an indefinite period before TJ's departure for Europe. While TJ was abroad, James Madison assumed responsibility* *for young Peter, though TJ continued to take a close interest in his charge's moral and intellectual progress.*

I am much mortified to hear that you have lost so much time; and that when you arrived in Williamsburg, you were not at all advanced from what you were when you left Monticello. Time now begins to be precious to you. Every day you lose, will retard a day your entrance on that public stage whereon you may begin to be useful to yourself. However, the way to repair the loss is to improve the future time. I trust, that with your dispositions, even the acquisition of science is a pleasing employment. I can assure you, that the possession of it is, what (next to an honest heart) will above all things render you dear to your friends, and give you fame and promotion in your own country. When your mind shall be well improved with science, nothing will be necessary to place you in the highest points of view, but to pursue the interests of your country, the interests of your friends, and your own interests also, with the purest integrity, the most chaste honor. The defect of these virtues can never be made up by all the other acquirements of body and mind. Make these then your first object. Give up money, give up fame, give up science, give the earth itself and all it contains, rather than do an immoral act. And never suppose, that in any possible situation, or under any circumstances, it is best for you to do a dishonorable thing, however slightly so it may appear to you. Whenever you are to do a thing, though it can never be known but to yourself, ask yourself how you would act were all the world looking at you, and act accordingly. Encourage all your virtuous dispositions, and exercise them whenever an opportunity arises; being assured that they will gain strength by exercise, as a limb of the body does, and that exercise will make them habitual. From the practice of the purest virtue, you may be assured you will derive the most sublime comforts in every moment of life, and in the moment of death. If ever you find yourself environed with difficulties and perplexing circumstances, out of which you are at a loss how to extricate yourself, do what is right, and be assured that that will extricate you the best out of the worst situations. Though you cannot see, when you take one step, what will be the next, yet follow truth, justice, and plain dealing, and never fear their leading you out of the labyrinth, in the easiest manner possible. The knot which you thought a Gordian one, will untie itself before you. Nothing is so mistaken as the supposition, that a person is to extricate himself from a difficulty, by intrigue, by chicanery, by dissimulation, by trimming, by an untruth, by an injustice. This increases the difficulties ten fold; and those who pursue these methods, get themselves so involved at length, that they can turn no way but their infamy becomes more exposed. It is of great importance to set a resolution, not to be shaken, never to tell an untruth. There is no vice so mean, so pitiful, so contemptible; and he who permits himself to tell a lie once, finds it much easier to do it a second and third time, till at length it becomes habitual; he tells lies without attending to it, and truths without the world's believing him. This falsehood of the tongue leads to that of the heart, and in time depraves all its good dispositions.

An honest heart being the first blessing, a knowing head is the second. It is time for you now to begin to be choice in your reading; to begin to pursue a regular course in it; and not to suffer yourself to be turned to the right or left by reading any thing out of that course. I have long ago digested a plan for you, suited to the circumstances in which you will be placed. This I will detail to you, from time to time, as you advance. For the present, I advise you to begin a course of antient history, reading every thing in the original and not in translations. First read Goldsmith's history of Greece. This will give you a digested view of that field. Then take up antient history in the detail, reading the following books, in the following order: Herodotus, Thucydides, Xenophontis Hellenica, Xenophontis Anabasis, Arrian, Quintus Curtius, Diodorus Siculus, Justin. This shall form the first stage of your historical reading, and is all I need mention to you now. The next, will be of Roman history. Livy, Sullust, Caesar, Cicero's epistles, Suetonius, Tacitus, Gibbon. From that, we will come down to modern history. In Greek and Latin poetry, you have read or will read at school, Virgil, Terence, Horace, Anacreon, Theocritus, Homer, Euripides, Sophocles. Read also Milton's Paradise Lost, Shakspeare, Ossian, Pope's and Swift's works, in order to form your style in your own language. In morality, read Epictetus, Xenophontis Memorabilia, Plato's Socratic dialogues, Cicero's philosophies, Antoninus, and Seneca. In order to assure a certain progress in this reading, consider what hours you have free from the school and the exercises of the school. Give about two of them, every day, to exercise; for health must not be sacrificed to learning. A strong body makes the mind strong. As to the species of exercise, I advise the gun. While this gives a moderate exercise to the body, it gives boldness, enterprise, and independence to the mind. Games played with the ball, and others of that nature, are too violent for the body, and stamp no character on the mind. Let your gun therefore be the constant companion of your walks. Never think of taking a book with you. The object of walking is to relax the mind. You should therefore not permit yourself even to think while you walk; but divert your attention by the objects surrounding you. Walking is the best possible exercise. Habituate yourself to walk very far. The Europeans value themselves on having subdued the horse to the uses of man; but doubt whether we have not lost more than we have gained, by the use of this animal. No one has occasioned so much, the degeneracy of the human body. An Indian goes on foot nearly as far in a day, for a long journey, as an enfeebled white does on his horse; and he will tire the best horses. There is no habit you will value so much as that of walking far without fatigue, would advise you to take your exercise in the afternoon: not because it is the best time for exercise, for certainly it is not; but because it is the best time to spare from your studies; and habit will soon reconcile it to health, and render it nearly as useful as if you gave to that the more precious hours of the day. A little walk of half an hour, in the morning, when you first rise, is advisable also. It shakes off sleep, and produces other good effects in the animal economy. Rise at a fixed and an early hour, and go to bed at a fixed and early hour also. Sitting up late at night is injurious to the health, and not useful to the mind. Having ascribed proper hours to exercise, divide what remain, (I mean of your vacant hours) into three portions. Give the principal to History, the other two, which should be shorter, to Philosophy and Poetry. Write to me once every month or two, and let me know the progress you make. Tell me in what manner you employ every hour in the day. The plan I have proposed for you is adapted to your present situation only. When that is changed, I shall propose a corresponding change of plan. I have ordered the following books to be sent to you *[list omitted]*. . . . You are now, I expect, learning French. You must push this; because the books which will be put into your hands when you advance into Mathematics, Natural philosophy, Natural history, &c. will be mostly French, these sciences being better treated by the French than the English writers. Our future connection with Spain renders that the most necessary of the modern languages, after the French. When you become a public man, you may have occasion for it, and the circumstance of your possessing that language, may give you a preference over other candidates. I have nothing further to add for the present, but husband well your time, cherish your instructors, strive to make every body your friend. . . .

7. To John Jay, Paris, 23 August 1785. *John Jay (1745–1829) was Congress's secretary of foreign affairs during the entire period of TJ's sojourn in Paris. A leading statesman and jurist in his home state of New York, Jay had previously served as president of Congress and minister to Spain. Along with his routine diplomatic dispatches, TJ forwarded "private" letters to Jay in which he developed broader themes in his political philosophy. Here he refers to "Manufactures," the subject of a famous Query in his recently published* Notes on Virginia *(see Chapter 2, document 10).*

I shall sometimes ask your permission to write you letters, not official but private. The present is of this kind, and is occasioned by the question proposed in yours of June 14. "whether it would be useful to us to carry all our own productions, or none?" Were we perfectly free to decide this question, I should reason as follows. We have now lands enough to employ an infinite number of people in their cultivation. Cultivators of the earth are the most valuable citizens. They are the most vigorous, the most independant, the most virtuous, & they are tied to their country & wedded to it's liberty & interests by the most lasting bonds. As long therefore as they can find employment in this line, I would not convert them into mariners, artisans or anything else. But our citizens will find employment in this line till their numbers, & of course their productions, become too great for the demand both internal & foreign. This is not the case as yet, & probably will not be for a considerable time. As soon as it is, the surplus of hands must be turned to something else. I should then perhaps wish to turn them to the sea in preference to manufactures, because comparing the characters of the two classes I find the former the most valuable citizens. I consider the class of artificers as the panders of vice & the instruments by which the liberties of a country are generally overturned. However we are not free to decide this question on principles of theory only. Our people are decided in the opinion that it is necessary for us to take a share in the occupation of the ocean, & their established habits induce them to require that the sea be kept open to them, and that that line of policy be pursued which will render the use of that element as great as possible to them. I think it a duty in those entrusted with the administration of their affairs to conform themselves to the decided choice of their constituents: and that therefore we should in every instance preserve an equality of right to them in the transportation of commodities, in the right of fishing, & in the other uses of the sea. But what will be the consequence? Frequent wars without a doubt. Their property will be violated on the sea, & in foreign ports, their persons will be insulted, imprisoned &c. for pretended debts, contracts, crimes, contraband, &c., &c. These insults must be resented, even if we had no feelings, yet to prevent their eternal repetition, or in other words, our commerce on the ocean & in other countries must be paid for by frequent war. The justest dispositions possible in ourselves will not secure us against it. It would be necessary that all other nations were just also. Justice indeed on our part will save us from those wars which would have been produced by a contrary disposition. But to prevent those produced by the wrongs of other nations? By putting ourselves in a condition to punish them. Weakness provokes insult & injury, while a condition to punish it often prevents it. This reasoning leads to the necessity of some naval force, that being the only weapon with which we can reach an enemy. I think it to our interest to punish the first insult; because an insult unpunished is the parent of many others. We are not at this moment in a condition to do it, but we should put ourselves into it as soon as possible. If a war with England should take place, it seems to me that the first thing necessary would be a resolution to abandon the carrying trade because we cannot protect it. Foreign nations must in that case be invited to bring us what we want & to take our productions in their own bottoms. This alone could prevent the loss of those productions to us & the acquisition of them to our enemy. Our seamen might be employed in depredations on their trade. But how dreadfully we shall suffer on our coasts, if we have no force on the water, former experience has taught us. Indeed I look forward with horror to the very possible case of war with an European power, & think there is no protection against them but from the possession of some force on the sea. Our vicinity to their West India possessions & to the fisheries is a bridle which a small naval force on our part would hold in the mouths of the most powerful of these countries. I hope our land office will rid us of our debts, & that our first attention then will be to the beginning a naval force of some sort. This alone can countenance our people as carriers on the water, & I suppose them to be determined to continue such.

8. To Charles Bellini, Paris, 30 September 1785. *A native of Florence, Charles (Carlo) Bellini (1735–1804) arrived in Virginia in 1774. For a few years Bellini was TJ's neighbor in Albemarle County; on TJ's recommendation, he was named translator for the state government in 1778. TJ was also instrumental in Bellini's subsequent appointment as Professor of Modern Languages at the College of William and Mary following its reorganization in 1779.*

Behold me at length on the vaunted scene of Europe! It is not necessary for your information, that I should enter into details concerning it. But you are, perhaps, curious to know how this new scene has struck a savage of the mountains of America. Not advantageously, I assure you. I find the general fate of humanity here, most deplorable. The truth of Voltaire's observation, offers itself perpetually, that every man here must be either the hammer or the anvil. It is a true picture of that country to which they say we shall pass hereafter, and where we are to see God and his angels in splendor, and crowds of the damned trampled under their feet. While the great mass of the people are thus suffering under physical and moral oppression, I have endeavored to examine more nearly the condition of the great, to appreciate the true value of the circumstances in their situation, which dazzle the bulk of spectators, and, especially, to compare it with that degree of happiness which is enjoyed in America, by every class of people. Intrigues of love occupy the younger, and those of ambition, the elder part of the great. Conjugal love having no existence among them, domestic happiness, of which that is the basis, is utterly unknown. In lieu of this, are substituted pursuits which nourish and invigorate all our bad passions, and which offer only moments of ecstacy, amidst days and months of restlessness and torment. Much, very much inferior, this, to the tranquil, permanent felicity with which domestic society in America, blesses most of its inhabitants; leaving them to follow steadily those pursuits which health and reason approve, and rendering truly delicious the intervals of those pursuits.

In science, the mass of the people is two centuries behind ours; their literati, half a dozen years before us. Books, really good, acquire just reputation in that time, and so become known to us, and communicate to us all their advances in knowledge. Is not this delay compensated, by our being placed out of the reach of that swarm of nonsensical publications, which issues daily from a thousand presses, and perishes almost in issuing? With respect to what are termed polite manners, without sacrificing too much the sincerity of language, I would wish my countrymen to adopt just so much of European politeness, as to be ready to make all those little sacrifices of self, which really render European manners amiable, and relieve society from the disagreeable scenes to which rudeness often subjects it. Here, it seems that a man might pass a life without encountering a single rudeness. In the pleasures of the table they are far before us, because, with good taste they unite temperance. They do not terminate the most sociable meals by transforming themselves into brutes. I have never yet seen a man drunk in France, even among the lowest of the people. Were I to proceed to tell you how much I enjoy their architecture, sculpture, painting, music, I should want words. It is in these arts they shine. The last of them, particularly, is an enjoyment, the deprivation of which with us, cannot be calculated. I am almost ready to say, it is the only thing which from my heart I envy them, and which, in spite of all the authority of the Decalogue, I do covet. But I am running on in an estimate of things infinitely better known to you than to me, and which will only serve to convince you, that I have brought with me all the prejudices of country, habit and age. But whatever I may allow to be charged to me as prejudice, in every other instance, I have one sentiment at least, founded in reality: it is that of the perfect esteem which your merit and that of Mrs. Bellini have produced, and which will for ever enable me to assure you of *[my]* . . . sincere regard.

9. To G. K. van Hogendorp, Paris, 13 October 1785. *A young Dutch aristocrat, Gijbert Karel, Count van Hogendorp, had recently toured the United States, where he met TJ in Annapolis in the spring of 1784. Always critical of America's republican experiment, the royalist van Hogendorp aligned himself with the Prince of Orange—and his British and Prussian patrons—in 1786, which brought the termination of his brief but warmly cordial correspondence with TJ.*

What you are pleased to say on the subject of my Notes is more than they deserve. The condition in which you first saw them would prove to you how hastily they had been originally written; as you may remember the numerous insertions had made in them from time to time, when I could find a moment for turning to them from other occupations. I have never yet seen Monsr. de Buffon. He has been in the country all the summer. I sent him a copy of the book, & have only heard his sentiments on one particular of it, that of the identity of the Mammoth & Elephant. As to this he retains his opinion that they are the same. If you had formed any considerable expectations from our Revised code of laws you will be much disappointed. It contains not more than three or four laws which could strike the attention of the foreigner. Had it been a digest of all our laws, it would not have been comprehensible or instructive but to a native. But it is still less so, as it digests only the British statutes & our own acts of assembly, which are but a supplementary part of our law. The great basis of it is anterior to the date of the Magna charta, which is the oldest statute extant. The only merit of this work is that it may remove from our book shelves about twenty folio volumes of our statutes, retaining all the parts of them which either their own merit or the established system of laws required.

You ask me what are those operations of the British nation which are likely to befriend us, and how they will produce this effect? The British government as you may naturally suppose have it much at heart to reconcile their nation to the loss of America. This is essential to the repose, perhaps even to the safety of the King & his ministers. The most effectual engines for this purpose are the public papers. You know well that that government always kept a kind of standing army of news writers who without any regard to truth, or to what should be like truth, invented & put into the papers whatever might serve the minister. This suffices with the mass of the people who have no means of distinguishing the false from the true paragraphs of a newspaper. When forced to acknolege our independance they were forced to redouble their efforts to keep the nation quiet. Instead of a few of the papers formerly engaged, they now engaged every one. No paper therefore comes out without a dose of paragraphs against America. These are calculated for a secondary purpose also, that of preventing the emigrations of their people to America. They dwell very much on American bankruptcies. To explain these would require a long detail, but would shew you that nine tenths of these bankruptcies are truly English bankruptcies in no wise chargeable on America. However they have produced effects the most desirable of all others for us. They have destroyed our credit & thus checked our disposition to luxury; & forcing our merchants to buy no more than they have ready money to pay for, they force them to go to those markets where that ready money will buy most. Thus you see they check our luxury, they force us to connect ourselves with all the world, & they prevent foreign emigrations to our country all of which I consider as advantageous to us. They are doing us another good turn. They attempt without disguise to possess themselves of the carriage of our produce, & to prohibit our own vessels from participating of it. This has raised a general indignation in America. The states see however that their constitutions have provided no means of counteracting it. They are therefore beginning to invest Congress with the absolute power of regulating their commerce, only reserving all revenue arising from it to the state in which it is levied. This will consolidate our federal building very much, and for this we shall be indebted to the British.

You ask what I think on the expediency of encouraging our states to be commercial? Were I to indulge my own theory, should wish them to practise neither commerce nor navigation, but to stand with respect to Europe precisely on the footing of China. We should thus avoid wars, and all our citizens would be husbandmen. Whenever indeed our numbers should so increase as that our produce would overstock the markets of those nations who should come to seek it, the farmers must either employ the surplus of their time in manufactures, or the surplus of our hands must be employed in manufactures, or in navigation. But that day would, I think be distant, and we should long keep our workmen in Europe, while Europe should be drawing rough materials & even subsistence from America. But this is theory only, & a theory which the servants of America are not at liberty to follow. Our people have a decided taste for navigation & commerce. They take this from their mother country: & their servants are in duty bound to calculate all their measures on this datum: we wish to do it by throwing open all the doors of commerce & knocking off its shackles. But as this cannot be done for others, unless they will do it for us, & there is no great probability that Europe will do this, I suppose we shall be obliged to adopt a system which may shackle them in our ports as they do us in theirs.

With respect to the sale of our lands, that cannot begin till a considerable portion shall have been surveyed. They cannot begin to survey till the fall of the leaf of this year, nor to sell probably till the ensuing spring. So that it will be yet a twelve-month before we shall be able to judge of the efficacy of our land office to sink our national debt. It is made a fundamental that the proceeds shall be solely & sacredly applied as a sinking fund to discharge the capital only of the debt. It is true that the tobaccos of Virginia go almost entirely to England. The reason is that they owe a great debt there which they are paying as fast as they can.

10. To Maria Cosway, Paris, 12 October 1786. *Perhaps the most famous letter TJ ever wrote, this dialogue between "Head" and "Heart" was addressed to the Englishwoman Maria Hadfield Cosway, a beautiful twenty-seven-year-old artist who was married to the miniaturist Richard Cosway, a notorious rake and libertine. Historians have long debated whether the passionate correspondence between TJ and*

Cosway was the result of a sexual relationship or a substitute for one. In any event, this famous dialogue discloses TJ's strong feelings on many other matters close to him.

Having performed the last sad office of handing you into your carriage at the pavillon de St. Denis, and seen the wheels get actually into motion, I turned on my heel & walked, more dead than alive, to the opposite door, where my own was awaiting me. Mr. Danquerville was missing. He was sought for, found, & dragged down stairs. We were crammed into the carriage, like recruits for the Bastille, & not having soul enough to give orders to the coachman, he presumed Paris our destination, & drove off. After a considerable interval, silence was broke with a "Je suis vraiment afflige du depart de ces bons gens." This was a signal for a mutual confession of distress. We began immediately to talk of Mr. & Mrs. Cosway, of their goodness, their talents, their amiability; & tho we spoke of nothing else, we seemed hardly to have entered into matter when the coachman announced the rue St. Denis, & that we were opposite Mr. Danquerville's. He insisted on descending there & traversing a short passage to his lodgings. I was carried home. Seated by my fireside, solitary & sad, the following dialogue took place between my Head & my Heart:

Head. Well, friend, you seem to be in a pretty trim.

Heart. I am indeed the most wretched of all earthly beings. Overwhelmed with grief, every fibre of my frame distended beyond its natural powers to bear, I would willingly meet whatever catastrophe should leave me no more to feel or to fear.

Head. These are the eternal consequences of your warmth & precipitation. This is one of the scrapes into which you are ever leading us. You confess your follies indeed; but still you hug & cherish them; & no reformation can be hoped, where there is no repentance.

Heart. Oh, my friend! this is no moment to upbraid my foibles. I am rent into fragments by the force of my grief! If you have any balm, pour it into my wounds; if none, do not harrow them by new torments. Spare me in this awful moment! At any other I will attend with patience to your admonitions.

Head. On the contrary I never found that the moment of triumph with you was the moment of attention to my admonitions. While suffering under your follies, you may perhaps be made sensible of them, but, the paroxysm over, you fancy it can never return. Harsh therefore as the medicine may be, it is my office to administer it. You will be pleased to remember that when our friend Trumbull used to be telling us of the merits & talents of these good people, I never ceased whispering to you that we had no occasion for new acquaintance; that the greater their merits & talents, the more dangerous their friendship to our tranquillity, because the regret at parting would be greater.

Heart. Accordingly, Sir, this acquaintance was not the consequence of my doings. It was one of your projects which threw us in the way of it. It was you, remember, & not I, who desired the meeting at Legrand & Molinos. I never trouble myself with domes nor arches. The Halle aux bleds might have rotted down before I should have gone to see it. But you, for-sooth, who are eternally getting us to sleep with your diagrams & crotch-ets, must go & examine this wonderful piece of architecture. And when you had seen it, oh! it was the most superb thing on earth! What you had seen there was worth all you had yet seen in Paris! I thought so too. But I meant it of the lady & gentleman to whom we had been presented; & not of a parcel of sticks & chips put together in pens. You then, Sir, & not I, have been the cause of the present distress.

Head. It would have been happy for you if my diagrams & crotchets had gotten you to sleep on that day, as you are pleased to say they eternally do. My visit to Legrand & Molinos had public utility for it's object. A market is to be built in Richmond. What a commodious plan is that of Legrand & Molinos; especially if we put on it the noble dome of the Halle aux bleds. If such a bridge as they shewed us can be thrown across the Schuylkill at Philadelphia, the floating bridges taken up & the navigation of that river opened, what a copious resource will be added, of wood & provisions, to warm & feed the poor of that city? While I was occupied with these objects, you were dilating with your new acquaintances, & contriving how to prevent a separation from them. Every soul of you had an engagement for the day. Yet all these were to be sacrificed, that you might dine together. Lying messengers were to be despatched into every quarter of the city, with apologies for your breach of engagement. You particularly had the effron-tery to send word to the Dutchess Danville that, on the moment we were setting out to dine with her, despatches came to hand which required immediate attention. You wanted me to invent a more ingenious excuse; but I knew you were getting into a scrape, & I would have nothing to do with it. Well, after dinner to St. Cloud, from St. Cloud to Ruggieri's, from Ruggieri to Krumfoltz, & if the day had been as long as a Lapland summer day, you would still have contrived means among you to have filled it.

Heart. Oh! my dear friend, how you have revived me by recalling to my mind the transactions of that day! How well remember them all, & that when I came home at night & looked back to the morning, it seemed to have been a month agone. Go on then, like a kind comforter & paint to me the day we went to St. Germains. How beautiful was every object! the Port de Reuilly, the hills along the Seine, the rainbows of the machine of Marly, the terrace of St. Germains, the chateaux, the gardens, the statues of Marly, the pavillon of Lucienne. Recollect too Madrid, Bagatelle, the King's garden, the Dessert. How grand the idea excited by the remains of such a column! The spiral staircase too was beautiful. Every moment was filled with something agreeable. The wheels of time moved on with a rapidity of which those of our carriage gave but a faint idea. And yet in the evening when one took a retrospect of the day, what a mass of happiness had we travelled over! Retrace all those scenes to me, my good companion, & I will forgive the unkindness with which you were chiding me. The day we went to St. Germains was a little too warm, I think; was it not?

Head. Thou art the most incorrigible of all the beings that ever sinned! I reminded you of the follies of the first day, intending to deduce from thence some useful lessons for you, but instead of listening to these, you kindle at the recollection, you retrace the whole series with a fondness which shews you want nothing but the opportunity to act it over again. I often told you during its course that you were imprudently engaging your affections under circumstances that must have cost you a great deal of pain: that the persons indeed were of the greatest merit, possessing good sense, good humour, honest hearts, honest manners, & eminence in a lovely art; that the lady had moreover qualities & accomplishments, belonging to her sex, which might form a chapter apart for her: such as music, modesty, beauty, & that softness of disposition which is the ornament of her sex & charm of ours, but that all these considerations would increase the pang of separation: that their stay here was to be short: that you rack our whole system when you are parted from those you love, complaining that such a separation is worse than death, inasmuch as this ends our sufferings, whereas that only begins them: & that the separation would in this instance be the more severe as you would probably never see them again.

Heart. But they told me they would come back again the next year.

Head. But in the meantime see what you suffer: & their return too depends on so many circumstances that if you had a grain of prudence you would not count upon it. Upon the whole it is improbable & therefore you should abandon the idea of ever seeing them again.

Heart. May heaven abandon me if I do!

Head. Very well. Suppose then they come back. They are to stay two months, & when these are expired, what is to follow? Perhaps you flatter yourself they may come to America?

Heart. God only knows what is to happen. I see nothing impossible in that supposition. And I see things wonderfully contrived sometimes to make us happy. Where could they find such objects as in America for the exercise of their enchanting art? especially the lady, who paints landscapes so inimitably. She wants only subjects worthy of immortality to render her pencil immortal. The Falling Spring, the Cascade of Niagara, the Passage of the Potowmac through the Blue Mountains, the Natural bridge. It is worth a voyage across the Atlantic to see these objects; much more to paint, and make them, & thereby ourselves, known to all ages. And our own dear Monticello, where has nature spread so rich a mantle under the eye? mountains, forests, rocks, rivers. With what majesty do we there ride above the storms! How sublime to look down into the workhouse of nature, to see her clouds, hail, snow, rain, thunder, all fabricated at our feet! and the glorious sun when rising as if out of a distant water, just gilding the tops of the mountains, & giving life to all nature! I hope in God no circumstance may ever make either seek an asylum from grief! With what sincere sympathy I would open every cell of my composition to receive the effusion of their woes! I would pour my tears into their wounds: & if a drop of balm could be found on the top of the Cordilleras, or at the remotest sources of the Missouri, I would go thither myself to seek & to bring it. Deeply practised in the school of affliction, the human heart knows no joy which I have not lost, no sorrow of which I have not drunk! Fortune can present no grief of unknown form to me! Who then can so softly bind up the wound of another as he who has felt the same wound himself? But Heaven forbid they should ever know a sorrow! Let us turn over another leaf, for this has distracted me.

Head. Well. Let us put this possibility to trial then on another point. When you consider the character which is given of our country by the lying newspapers of London, & their credulous copyers in other countries; when you reflect that all Europe is made to believe we are a lawless banditti, in a state of absolute anarchy, cutting one another's throats, & plundering without distinction, how can you expect that any reasonable creature would venture among us?

Heart. But you & I know that all this is false: that there is not a country on earth where there is greater tranquillity, where the laws are milder, or better obeyed: where every one is more attentive to his own business, or meddles less with that of others: where strangers are better received, more hospitably treated, & with a more sacred respect.

Head. True, you & I know this, but your friends do not know it.

Heart. But they are sensible people who think for themselves. They will ask of impartial foreigners who have been among us, whether they saw or heard on the spot any instances of anarchy. They will judge too that a people occupied as we are in opening rivers, digging navigable canals, making roads, building public schools, establishing academies, erecting busts & statues to our great men, protecting religious freedom, abolishing sanguinary punishments, reforming & improving our laws in general, they will judge I say for themselves whether these are not the occupations of a people at their ease, whether this is not better evidence of our true state than a London newspaper, hired to lie, & from which no truth can ever be extracted but by reversing everything it says.

Head. I did not begin this lecture my friend with a view to learn from you what America is doing. Let us return then to our point. I wished to make you sensible how imprudent it is to place your affections, without reserve, on objects you must so soon lose, & whose loss when it comes must cost you such severe pangs. Remember the last night. You knew your friends were to leave Paris to-day. This was enough to throw you into agonies. All night you tossed us from one side of the bed to the other. No sleep, no rest. The poor crippled wrist too, never left one moment in the same position, now up, now down, now here, now there; was it to be wondered at if it's pains returned? The Surgeon then was to be called, & to be rated as an ignoramus because he could not divine the cause of this extraordinary change. In fine, my friend, you must mend your manners. This is not a world to live at random in as you do. To avoid those eternal distresses, to which you are forever exposing us, you must learn to look forward before you take a step which may interest our peace. Everything in this world is a matter of calculation. Advance then with caution, the balance in your hand. Put into one scale the pleasures which any object may offer; but put fairly into the other the pains which are to follow, & see which preponderates. The making an acquaintance is not a matter of indifference. When a new one is proposed to you, view it all round. Consider what advantages it presents, & to what inconveniences it may expose you. Do not bite at the bait of pleasure till you know there is no hook beneath it. The art of life is the art of avoiding pain: & he is the best pilot who steers clearest of the rocks & shoals with which he is beset. Pleasure is always before us; but misfortune is at our side: while running after that, this arrests us. The most effectual means of being secure against pain is to retire within ourselves, & to suffice for our own happiness. Those, which depend on ourselves, are the only pleasures a wise man will count on: for nothing is ours which another may deprive us of. Hence the inestimable value of intellectual pleasures. Even in our power, always leading us to something new, never cloying, we ride serene & sublime above the concerns of this mortal world, contemplating truth & nature, matter & motion, the laws which bind up their existence, & that eternal being who made & bound them up by those laws. Let this be our employ. Leave the bustle & tumult of society to those who have not talents to occupy themselves without them. Friendship is but another name for an alliance with the follies & the misfortunes of others. Our own share of miseries is sufficient: why enter then as volunteers into those of another? Is there so little gall poured into our cup that we must needs help to drink that of our neighbor? A friend dies or leaves us: we feel as if a limb was cut off. He is sick: we must watch over him, & participate of his pains. His fortune is shipwrecked; ours must be laid under contribution. He loses a child, a parent, or a partner: we must mourn the loss as if it were our own.

Heart. And what more sublime delight than to mingle tears with one whom the hand of heaven hath smitten! to watch over the bed of sickness, & to beguile it's tedious & it's painful moments! to share our bread with one to whom misfortune has left none! This world abounds indeed with misery: to lighten it's burthen we must divide it with one another. But let us now try the virtues of your mathematical balance, & as you have put into one scale the burthen of friendship, let me put it's comforts into the other. When languishing then under disease, how grateful is the solace of our friends! how are we penetrated with their assiduities & attentions! how much are we supported by their encouragements & kind offices! When heaven has taken from us some object of our love, how sweet is it to have a bosom whereon to recline our heads, & into which we may pour the torrent of our tears! Grief, with such a comfort, is almost a luxury! In a life where we are perpetually exposed to want & accident, yours is a wonderful proposition, to insulate ourselves, to retire from all aid, & to wrap ourselves in the mantle of self-sufficiency! For assuredly nobody will care for him who cares for nobody. But friendship is precious, not only in the shade but in the sunshine of life; & thanks to a benevolent arrangement of things, the greater part of life is sunshine. I will recur for proof to the days we have lately passed. On these indeed the sun shone brightly. How gay did the face of nature appear! Hills, valleys, chateaux, gardens, rivers, every object wore it's liveliest hue! Whence did they borrow it? From the presence of our charming companion. They were pleasing, because she seemed pleased. Alone, the scene would have been dull & insipid: the participation of it with her gave it relish. Let the gloomy monk, sequestered from the world, seek unsocial pleasures in the bottom of his cell! Let the sublimated philosopher grasp visionary happiness while pursuing phantoms dressed in the garb of truth! Their supreme wisdom is supreme folly; & they mistake for happiness the mere absence of pain. Had they ever felt the solid pleasure of one generous spasm of the heart, they would ex-change for it all the frigid speculations of their lives, which you have been vaunting in such elevated terms. Believe me then my friend, that that is a miserable arithmetic which could estimate friendship at nothing, or at less than nothing. Respect for you has induced me to enter into this discussion, & to hear principles uttered which I detest & abjure. Respect for myself now obliges me to recall you into the proper limits of your office. When nature assigned us the same habitation, she gave us over it a divided empire. To you she allotted the field of science; to me that of morals. When the circle is to be squared, or the orbit of a comet to be traced; when the arch of greatest strength, or the solid of least resistance is to be inves-tigated, take up the problem; it is yours; nature has given me no cog-nizance of it. In like manner, in denying to you the feelings of sympathy, of benevolence, of gratitude, of justice, of love, of friendship, she has excluded you from their controul. To these she has adapted the mecha-nism of the heart. Morals were too essential to the happiness of man to be risked on the incertain combinations of the head. She laid their founda-tion therefore in sentiment, not in science. That she gave to all, as neces-sary to all: this to a few only, as sufficing with a few. I know indeed that you pretend authority to the sovereign controul of our conduct in all its parts: & a respect for your grave saws & maxims, a desire to do what is right, has sometimes induced me to conform to your counsels. A few facts however which I can readily recall to your memory, will suffice to prove to you that nature has not organized you for our moral direction. When the poor wea-ried souldier whom we overtook at Chickahomony with his pack on his back, begged us to let him get up behind our chariot, you began to calcu-late that the road was full of souldiers, & that if all should be taken up our horses would fail in their journey. We drove on therefore. But soon becom-ing sensible you had made me do wrong, that tho we cannot relieve all the distressed we should relieve as many as we can, I turned about to take up the souldier; but he had entered a bye path, & was no more to be found; & from that moment to this I could never find him out to ask his forgive-ness. Again, when the poor woman came to ask a charity in Philadelphia, you whispered that she looked like a drunkard, & that half a dollar was enough to give her for the ale-house. Those who want the dispositions to give, easily find reasons why they ought not to give. When I sought her out afterwards, & did what I should have done at first, you know that she employed the money immediately towards placing her child at school. If our country, when pressed with wrongs at the point of the bayonet, had been governed by it's heads instead of it's hearts, where should we have been now? Hanging on a gallows as high as Haman's. You began to calcu-late & to compare wealth and numbers: we threw up a few pulsations of our warmest blood; we supplied enthusiasm against wealth and numbers; we put our existence to the hazard when the hazard seemed against us, and we saved our country: justifying at the same time the ways of Provi-dence, whose precept is to do always what is right, and leave the issue to him. In short, my friend, as far as my recollection serves me, I do not know that I ever did a good thing on your suggestion, or a dirty one without it. I do forever then disclaim your interference in my province. Fill papers as you please with triangles & squares: try how many ways you can hang & combine them together. I shall never envy nor controul your sublime delights. But leave me to decide when & where friendships are to be contracted. You say contract them at random. So you said the woman at Philadelphia was a drunkard. I receive no one into my esteem till I know they are worthy of it. Wealth, title, office, are no recommendations to my friendship. On the contrary great good qualities are requisite to make amends for their having wealth, title, & office. You confess that in the present case I could not have made a worthier choice. You only object that I was so soon to lose them. We are not immortal ourselves, my friend; how can we expect our enjoyments to be so? We have no rose without it's thorn; no pleasure without alloy. It is the law of our existence; & we must acquiesce. It is the condition annexed to all our pleasures, not by us who receive, but by him who gives them. True, this condition is pressing cruelly on me at this moment. I feel more fit for death than life. But when I look back on the pleasures of which it is the consequence, I am conscious they were worth the price I am paying. Notwithstanding your endeavours too to damp my hopes, I comfort myself with expectations of their promised return. Hope is sweeter than despair, & they were too good to mean to deceive me. In the summer, said the gentleman; but in the spring, said the lady: & should love her forever, were it only for that! Know then, my friend, that I have taken these good people into my bosom; that have lodged them in the warmest cell I could find: that I love them, & will continue to love them through life: that if fortune should dispose them on one side the globe, & me on the other, my affections shall pervade it's whole mass to reach them. Knowing then my determination, attempt not to disturb it. If you can at any time furnish matter for their amusement, it will be the office of a good neighbor to do it. I will in like manner seize any occasion which may offer to do the like good turn for you with Condorcet, Rittenhouse, Madison, La Cretelle, or any other of those worthy sons of science whom you so justly prize.

I thought this a favorable proposition whereon to rest the issue of the dialogue. So I put an end to it by calling for my night-cap. Methinks I hear you wish to heaven I had called a little sooner, & so spared you the ennui of such a sermon. I did not interrupt them sooner because I was in a mood for hearing sermons. You too were the subject; & on such a thesis I never think the theme long; not even if I am to write it, and that slowly & awkwardly, as now, with the left hand. But that you may not be discouraged from a correspondence which begins so formidably, I will promise you on my honour that my future letters shall be of a reasonable length. I will even agree to express but half my esteem for you, for fear of cloying you with too full a dose. But, on your part, no curtailing. If your letters are as long as the bible, they will appear short to me. Only let them be brimful of affection. I shall read them with the dispositions with which Arlequin, in Les deux billets spelt the words "je t'aime," and wished that the whole alphabet had entered into their composition. We have had incessant rains since your departure. These make me fear for your health, as well as that you had an uncomfortable journey. The same cause has prevented me from being able to give you any account of your friends here. This voyage to Fontainebleau will probably send the Count de Moustier & the Marquise de Brehan to America. Danquerville promised to visit me, but has not done it as yet. De la Tude comes sometimes to take family soup with me, & entertains me with anecdotes of his five & thirty years imprisonment. How fertile is the mind of man which can make the Bastile & Dungeon of Vincennes yield interesting anecdotes! You know this was for making four verses on Mme de Pompadour. But I think you told me you did not know the verses. They were these: "*Sans esprit, sans sentiment, Sans etre belle, ni neuve, En France on peut avoir le premier amant: Pompadour en est l' epreuve.*" I have read the memoir of his three escapes. As to myself my health is good, except my wrist which mends slowly, & my mind which mends not at all, but broods constantly over your departure. The lateness of the season obliges me to decline my journey into the south of France. Present me in the most friendly terms to Mr. Cosway, & receive me into your own recollection with a partiality & a warmth, proportioned, not to my own poor merit, but to the sentiments of sincere affection & esteem with which I have the honour to be, my dear Madam, your most obedient humble servant.

11. To the Marquis de Lafayette, Nice, 11 April 1787. *Gilbert du Motier de Lafayette (1757–1834) volunteered for the American war effort in 1777, becoming the protégé of General George Washington and the cherished friend of numerous other Revolutionary leaders. TJ and Lafayette became close during TJ's Paris years, when Lafayette was a prominent friend of the United States and a leading light in the emerging French Revolutionary movement.*

I am constantly roving about, to see what I have never seen before, and shall never see again. In the great cities, I go to see what travellers think alone worthy of being seen; but I make a job of it, and generally gulp it all down in a day. On the other hand, I am never satiated with rambling through the fields and farms, examining the culture and cultivators, with a degree of curiosity which makes some take me to be a fool, and others to be much wiser than I am. I have been pleased to find among the people a less degree of physical misery than I had expected. They are generally well clothed, and have a plenty of food, not animal indeed, but vegetable, which is as wholesome. Perhaps they are over worked, the excess of the rent required by the landlord, obliging them to too many hours of labor in order to produce that, and where-with to feed and clothe themselves. The soil of Champagne and Burgundy I have found more universally good than I had expected, and as I could not help making a comparison with England, I found that comparison more unfavorable to the latter than is generally admitted. The soil, the climate, and the productions are superior to those of England, and the husbandry as good, except in one point; that of manure. In England, long leases for twenty-one years, or three lives, to wit, that of the farmer, his wife, and son, renewed by the son as soon as he comes to the possession, for his own life, his wife's and eldest child's, and so on, render the farms there almost hereditary, make it worth the farmer's while to manure the lands highly, and give the landlord an opportunity of occasionally making his rent keep pace with the improved state of the lands. Here the leases are either during pleasure, or for three, six, or nine years, which does not give the farmer time to repay himself for the expensive operation of well manuring, and therefore, he manures ill, or not at all. I suppose, that could the practice of leasing for three lives be introduced in the whole kingdom, it would, within the term of your life, increase agricultural productions fifty per cent; or were any one proprietor to do it with his own lands, it would increase his rents fifty per cent, in the course of twenty-five years. But am told the laws do not permit it. The laws then, in this particular, are unwise and unjust, and ought to give that permission. In the southern provinces, where the soil is poor, the climate hot and dry, and there are few animals, they would learn the art, found so precious in England, of making vegetable manure, and thus improving these provinces in the article in which nature has been least kind to them. Indeed, these provinces afford a singular spectacle. Calculating on the poverty of their soil, and their climate by its latitude only, they should have been the poorest in France. On the contrary, they are the richest, from one fortuitous circumstance. Spurs or ramifications of high mountains, making down from the Alps, and as it were, reticulating these provinces, give to the vallies the protection of a particular inclosure to each, and the benefit of a general stagnation of the northern winds produced by the whole of them, and thus countervail the advantage of several degrees of latitude. From the first olive fields of Pierrelatte, to the orangeries of Hieres, has been continued rapture to me. I have often wished for you. I think you have not made this journey. It is a pleasure you have to come, and an improvement to be added to the many you have already made. It will be a great comfort to you, to know, from your own inspection, the condition of all the provinces of your own country, and it will be interesting to them at some future day, to be known to you. This is, perhaps, the only moment of your life in which you can acquire that knowledge. And to do it most effectually, you must be absolutely incognito, you must ferret the people out of their hovels as I have done, look into their kettles, eat their bread, loll on their beds under pretence of resting yourself, but in fact to find if they are soft. You will feel a sublime pleasure in the course of this investigation, and a sublimer one hereafter, when you shall be able to apply your knowledge to the softening of their beds, or the throwing a morsel of meat into their kettle of vegetables.

12. To Martha Jefferson, 21 May 1787. *Martha, now fourteen years old, had accompanied TJ to Paris in 1784, where she studied at an exclusive convent school. Her younger sister Maria, TJ's only other surviving child after daughter Lucy's death the previous autumn, would join the family in July.*

I write to you, my dear Patsy, from the Canal of Languedoc, on which I am at present sailing, as I have been for a week past, cloudless skies above, limpid waters below, and find on each hand a row of nightingales in full chorus. This delightful bird had given me a rich treat before at the fountain of Vaucluse. After visiting the tomb of Laura at Avignon, I went to see this fountain, a noble one of itself, and rendered for ever famous by the songs of Petrarch who lived near it. I arrived there somewhat fatigued, and sat down by the fountain to repose myself. It gushes, of the size of a river, from a secluded valley of the mountain, the ruins of Petrarch's chateau being perched on a rock 200 feet perpendicular above. To add to the enchantment of the scene, every tree and bush was filled with nightingales in full song. I think you told me you had not yet noticed this bird. As you have trees in the garden of the convent, there must be nightingales in them, and this is the season of their song. Endeavor my dear, to make yourself acquainted with the music of this bird, that when you return to your own country you may be able to estimate it's merit in comparison with that of the mocking bird. The latter has the advantage of singing thro' a great part of the year, whereas the nightingale sings but about 5 or 6 weeks in the spring, and a still shorter term and with a more feeble voice in the fall. I expect to be at Paris about the middle of next month. By that time we may begin to expect our dear Polly. It will be a circumstance of inexpressible comfort to me to have you both with me once more. The object most interesting to me for the residue of my life, will be to see you both developing daily those principles of virtue and goodness which will make you valuable to others and happy in yourselves, and acquiring those talents and that degree of science which will guard you at all times against ennui, the most dangerous poison of life. A mind always employed is always happy. This is the true secret, the grand recipe for felicity. The idle are the only wretched. In a world which furnishes so many emploiments which are useful, and so many which are amusing, it is our own fault if we ever know what ennui is, or if we are ever driven to the miserable resource of gaming, which corrupts our dispositions, and teaches us a habit of hostility against all mankind. We are now entering the port of Toulouse, where I quit my bark; and of course must conclude my letter. Be good and be industrious, and you will be what I shall most love in the world.

13. To Peter Carr, Paris, 10 August 1787. *TJ was "very happy" to hear that nephew Peter had "been so fortunate as to attract" the "notice & good will" of TJ's mentor George Wythe in Williamsburg (see document 6 above).*

I am sure you will find this to have been one of the most fortunate events of your life, as I have ever been sensible it was of mine. I inclose you a sketch of the sciences to which I would wish you to apply in such order as Mr. Wythe shall advise; I mention also the books in them worth your reading, which submit to his correction. Many of these are among your father's books, which you should have brought to you. As I do not recollect those of them not in his library, you must write to me for them, making out a catalogue of such as you think you shall have occasion for in 18 months from the date of your letter, & consulting Mr. Wythe on the subject. To this sketch I will add a few particular observations.

1. Italian. I fear the learning this language will confound your French and Spanish. Being all of them degenerated dialects of the Latin, they are apt to mix in conversation. have never seen a person speaking the three languages who did not mix them. It is a delightful language, but late events having rendered the Spanish more useful, lay it aside to prosecute that.

2. Spanish. Bestow great attention on this, & endeavor to acquire an accurate knowlege of it. Our future connections with Spain & Spanish America will render that language a valuable acquisition. The antient history of a great part of America, too, is written in that language. I send you a dictionary.

3. Moral philosophy. I think it lost time to attend lectures in this branch. He who made us would have been a pitiful bungler if he had made the rules of our moral conduct a matter of science. For one man of science, there are thousands who are not. What would have become of them? Man was destined for society. His morality therefore was to be formed to this object. He was endowed with a sense of right & wrong merely relative to this. This sense is as much a part of his nature as the sense of hearing, seeing, feeling; it is the true foundation of morality. . . . The moral sense, or conscience, is as much a part of man as his leg or arm. It is given to all human beings in a stronger or weaker degree, as force of members is given them in a greater or less degree. It may be strengthened by exercise, as may any particular limb of the body. This sense is submitted indeed in some degree to the guidance of reason; but it is a small stock which is required for this: even a less one than what we call common sense. State a moral case to a ploughman & a professor. The former will decide it as well, & often better than the latter, because he has not been led astray by artificial rules. In this branch therefore read good books because they will encourage as well as direct your feelings. The writings of Sterne particularly form the best course of morality that ever was written. Besides these read the books mentioned in the enclosed paper; and above all things lose no occasion of exercising your dispositions to be grateful, to be generous, to be charitable, to be humane, to be true, just, firm, orderly, courageous &c. Consider every act of this kind as an exercise which will strengthen your moral faculties, & increase your worth.

4. Religion. Your reason is now mature enough to examine this object. In the first place divest yourself of all bias in favour of novelty & singularity of opinion. Indulge them in any other subject rather than that of religion. It is too important, & the consequences of error may be too serious. On the other hand shake off all the fears & servile prejudices under which weak minds are servilely crouched. Fix reason firmly in her seat, and call to her tribunal every fact, every opinion. Question with boldness even the existence of a god; because, if there be one, he must more approve of the homage of reason, than that of blindfolded fear. You will naturally examine first the religion of your own country. Read the bible then, as you would read Livy or Tacitus. The facts which are within the ordinary course of nature you will believe on the authority of the writer, as you do those of the same kind in Livy & Tacitus. The testimony of the writer weighs in their favor in one scale, and their not being against the laws of nature does not weigh against them. But those facts in the bible which contradict the laws

of nature, must be examined with more care, and under a variety of faces. Here you must recur to the pretensions of the writer to inspiration from god. Examine upon what evidence his pretensions are founded, and whether that evidence is so strong as that its falsehood would be more improbable than a change in the laws of nature in the case he relates. For example in the book of Joshua we are told the sun stood still several hours. Were we to read that fact in Livy or Tacitus we should class it with their showers of blood, speaking of statues, beasts, &c. But it is said that the writer of that book was inspired. Examine therefore candidly what evidence there is of his having been inspired. The pretension is entitled to your inquiry, because millions believe it. On the other hand you are astronomer enough to know how contrary it is to the law of nature that a body revolving on its axis as the earth does, should have stopped, should not by that sudden stoppage have prostrated animals, trees, buildings, and should after a certain time have resumed its revolution, & that without a second general prostration. Is this arrest of the earth's motion, or the evidence which affirms it, most within the law of probabilities? You will next read the new testament. It is the history of a personage called Jesus. Keep in your eye the opposite pretensions 1. of those who say he was begotten by god, born of a virgin, suspended & reversed the laws of nature at will, & ascended bodily into heaven: and 2. of those who say he was a man of illegitimate birth, of a benevolent heart, enthusiastic mind, who set out without pretensions to divinity, ended in believing them, & was punished capitally for sedition by being gibbeted according to the Roman law which punished the first commission of that offence by whipping, & the second by exile or death. . . . These questions are examined in the books I have mentioned under the head of religion, & several others. They will assist you in your inquiries, but keep your reason firmly on the watch in reading them all. Do not be frightened from this inquiry by any fear of it's consequences. If it ends in a belief that there is no god, you will find incitements to virtue in the comfort & pleasantness you feel in it's exercise, and the love of others which it will procure you. If you find reason to believe there is a god, a consciousness that you are acting under his eye, & that he approves you, will be a vast additional incitement; if that there be a future state, the hope of a happy existence in that increases the appetite to deserve it; if that Jesus was also a god, you will be comforted by a belief of his aid and love. In fine, I repeat that you must lay aside all prejudice on both sides, & neither believe nor reject anything because any other persons, or description of persons have rejected or believed it. Your own reason is the only oracle given you by heaven, and you are answerable not for the rightness but uprightness of the decision. I forgot to observe when speaking of the new testament that you should read all the histories of Christ, as well of those whom a council of ecclesiastics have decided for us to be Pseudo-evangelists, as those they named Evangelists. Because these Pseudo-evangelists pretended to inspiration as much as the others, and you are to judge their pretensions by your own reason, & not by the reason of those ecclesiastics. Most of these are lost. There are some however still extant, collected by Fabricius which I will endeavor to get & send you. 5. Travelling. This makes men wiser, but less happy. When men of sober age travel, they gather knolege which they may apply usefully for their country, but they are subject ever after to recollections mixed with regret, their affections are weakened by being extended over more objects, & they learn new habits which cannot be gratified when they return home. Young men who travel are exposed to all these inconveniences in a higher degree, to others still more serious, and do not acquire that wisdom for which a previous foundation is requisite by repeated & just observations at home. The glare of pomp & pleasure is analogous to the motion of their blood, it absorbs all their affection & attention, they are torn from it as from the only good in this world, and return to their home as to a place of exile & condemnation. Their eyes are for ever turned back to the object they have lost, & it's recollection poisons the residue of their lives. Their first & most delicate passions are hackneyed on unworthy objects here, & they carry home only the dregs, insufficient to make themselves or anybody else happy. Add to this that a habit of idleness, an inability to apply themselves to business is acquired & renders them useless to themselves & their country. These observations are founded in experience. There is no place where your pursuit of knolege will be so little obstructed by foreign objects as in your own country, nor any wherein the virtues of the heart will be less exposed to be weakened. Be good, be learned, & be industrous, & you will not want the aid of travelling to render you precious to your country, dear to your friends, happy within yourself. Repeat my advice to take a great deal of exercise, & on foot. Health is the first requisite after morality. Write to me often & be assured of the interest I take in your success, as well as of the warmth of those sentiments of attachment with which I am, dear Peter, your affectionate friend.

P. S. Let me know your age in your next letter. Your cousins here are well & desire to be remembered to you.

14. From Jefferson's Autobiography, Written 6 January–29 July 1821.
In his old age TJ reviewed the crisis of the American Confederation government that had led to the movement for a new federal Constitution. TJ's ambivalent response to the proposed plan, drafted at Philadelphia in the summer of 1787 under the leadership of his friend and colleague James Madison, reflected both the concerns of a diplomat with the new nation's obvious weakness and vulnerability in its foreign relations and his wariness about dangerous concentrations of power. By the time he wrote his autobiography, TJ's long experience in Republican partisanship made domestic threats to liberty seem more compelling.

Our first essay in America to establish a federative government had fallen, on trial, very short of it's object. During the war of Independance, while the pressure of an external enemy hooped us together, and their enterprises kept us necessarily on the alert, the spirit of the people, excited by danger, was a supplement to the Confederation, and urged them to zealous exertions, whether claimed by that instrument, or not. But when peace and safety were restored, and every man became engaged in useful and profitable occupation, less attention was paid to the calls of Congress.

The fundamental defect of the Confederation was that Congress was not authorized to act immediately on the people, & by it's own officers. Their power was only requisitory, and these requisitions were addressed to the several legislatures, to be by them carried into execution, without other coercion than the moral principle of duty. This allowed in fact a negative to every legislature, on every measure proposed by Congress; a negative so frequently exercised in practice as to benumb the action of the federal government, and to render it inefficient in it's general objects, & more especially in pecuniary and foreign concerns. The want too of a separation of the legislative, executive, & judiciary functions worked disadvantageously in practice. Yet this state of things afforded a happy augury of the future march of our confederacy, when it was seen that the good sense and good dispositions of the people, as soon as they perceived the incompetence of their first compact, instead of leaving it's correction to insurrection and civil war, agreed with one voice to elect deputies to a general convention, who should peaceably meet and agree on such a constitution as "would ensure peace, justice, liberty, the common defence & general welfare."

This Convention met at Philadelphia on the 25th. of May '87. It sate with closed doors and kept all it's proceedings secret, until it's dissolution on the 17th. of September, when the results of their labors were published all together. I received a copy early in November, and read and contemplated it's provisions with great satisfaction. As not a member of the Convention however, nor probably a single citizen of the Union, had approved it in all it's parts, so I too found articles which I thought objectionable. The absence of express declarations ensuring freedom of religion, freedom of the press, freedom of the person under the uninterrupted protection of the Habeas corpus, & trial by jury in civil as well as in criminal cases excited my jealousy; and the re-eligibility of the President for life, I quite disapproved. I expressed freely in letters to my friends, and most particularly to Mr. Madison & General Washington, my approbations and objections. How the good should be secured, and the ill brought to rights was the difficulty. To refer it back to a new Convention might endanger the loss of the whole. My first idea was that the 9. states first acting should accept it unconditionally, and thus secure what in it was good, and that the 4. last should accept on the previous condition that certain amendments should be agreed to, but a better course was devised of accepting the whole and trusting that the good sense & honest intentions of our citizens would make the alterations which should be deemed necessary. Accordingly all accepted, 6. without objection, and 7. with recommendations of specified amendments. Those respecting the press, religion, & juries, with several others, of great value, were accordingly made; but the Habeas corpus was left to the discretion of Congress, and the amendment against the reeligibility of the President was not proposed by that body. My fears of that feature were founded on the importance of the office, on the fierce contentions it might excite among ourselves, if continuable for life, and the dangers of interference either with money or arms, by foreign nations, to whom the choice of an American President might become interesting. Examples of this abounded in history; in the case of the Roman emperors for instance, of the Popes while of any significance, of the German emperors, the Kings of Poland, & the Deys of Barbary. I had observed too in the feudal History, and in the recent instance particularly of the Stadtholder of Holland, how easily offices or tenures for life slide into inheritances. My wish therefore was that the President should be elected for 7. years & be ineligible afterwards. This term thought sufficient to enable him, with the concurrence of the legislature, to carry thro' & establish any system of improvement he should propose for the general good. But the practice adopted I think is better allowing his continuance for 8. years with a liability to be dropped at half way of the term, making that a period of probation. That his continuance should be restrained to 7. years was the opinion of the Convention at an early stage of it's session, when it voted that term by a majority of 8. against 2. and by a simple majority that he should be ineligible a second time. This opinion &c. was confirmed by the house so late as July 26. referred to the committee of detail, reported favorably by them, and changed to the present form by final vote on the last day but one only of their session. Of this change three states expressed their disapprobation, N. York by recommending an amendment that the President should not be eligible a third time, and Virginia and N. Carolina that he should not be capable of serving more than 8. in any term of 16. years. And altho' this amendment has not been made in form, yet practice seems to have established it. The example of 4 Presidents voluntarily retiring at the end of their 8th year, & the progress of public opinion that the principle is salutary, have given ,it in practice the force of precedent & usage; insomuch that should a President consent to be a candidate for a 3d. election, I trust he would be rejected on this demonstration of ambitious views.

But there was another amendment of which none of us thought at the time and in the omission of which lurks the germ that is to destroy this happy combination of National powers in the General government for matters of National concern, and independent powers in the states for what concerns the states severally. In England it was a great point gained at the Revolution, that the commissions of the judges, which had hitherto been during pleasure, should thenceforth be made during good behavior. A Judiciary dependent on the will of the King had proved itself the most oppressive of all tools in the hands of that Magistrate. Nothing then could be more salutary than a change there to the tenure of good behavior; and the question of good behavior left to the vote of a simple majority in the two houses of parliament. Before the revolution we were all good English Whigs, cordial in their free principles, and in their jealousies of their executive Magistrate. These jealousies are very apparent in all our state constitutions; and, in the general government in this instance, we have gone even beyond the English caution, by requiring a vote of two thirds in one of the Houses for removing a judge; a vote so impossible where any defence is made, before men of ordinary prejudices & passions, that our judges are effectually independent of the nation. But this ought not to be. I would not indeed make them dependant on the Executive authority, as they formerly were in England; but I deem it indispensable to the continuance of this government that they should be submitted to some practical & impartial controul: and that this, to be imparted, must be compounded of a mixture of state and federal authorities. It is not enough that honest men are appointed judges. All know the influence of interest on the mind of man, and how unconsciously his judgment is warped by that influence. To this bias add that of the esprit de corps, of their peculiar maxim and creed that "it is the office of a good judge to enlarge his jurisdiction," and the absence of responsibility, and how can we expect impartial decision between the General government, of which they are themselves so eminent a part, and an individual state from which they have nothing to hope or fear. We have seen too that, contrary to all correct example, they are in the habit of going out of the question before them, to throw an anchor ahead and grapple further hold for future advances of power. They are then in fact the corps of sappers & miners, steadily working to undermine the independant rights of the States, & to consolidate all power in the hands of that government in which they have so important a freehold estate. But it is not by the consolidation, or concentration of powers, but by their distribution, that good government is effected. Were not this great country already divided into states, that division must be made, that each might do for itself what concerns itself directly, and what it can so much better do than a distant authority. Every state again is divided into counties, each to take care of what lies within it's local bounds; each county again into townships or wards, to manage minuter details; and every ward into farms, to be governed each by it's individual proprietor. Were we directed from Washington when to sow, & when to reap, we should soon want bread. It is by this partition of cares, descending in gradation from general to particular, that the mass of human affairs may be best managed for the good and prosperity of all. I repeat that I do not charge the judges with wilful and ill-intentioned error; but honest error must be arrested where it's toleration leads to public ruin. As, for the safety of society, we commit honest maniacs to Bedlam, so judges should be withdrawn from their bench, whose erroneous biases are leading us to dissolution. It may indeed injure them in fame or in fortune; but it saves the republic, which is the first and supreme law.

15. To William S. Smith, Paris, 13 November 1787. *Colonel William Stephens Smith (1755–1816), a revolutionary war veteran who served on General Lafayette' staff in 1780–1781, was secretary of the American Legation at London under his father-in-law John Adams.*

I do not know whether it is to yourself or Mr. Adams I am to give my thanks for the copy of the new constitution. I beg leave through you to place them where due. It will be yet three weeks before I shall receive them from America. There are very good articles in it: & very bad. I do not know which preponderate. What we have lately read in the history of Holland, in the chapter on the Stadtholder, would have sufficed to set me against a chief magistrate eligible for a long duration, if I had ever been disposed towards one: & what we have always read of the elections of Polish kings should have forever excluded the idea of one continuable for life. Wonderful is the effect of impudent & persevering lying. The British ministry have so long hired their gazetteers to repeat and model into every form lies about our being in anarchy, that the world has at length believed them, the English nation has believed them, the ministers themselves have come to believe them, & what is more wonderful, we have believed them ourselves. Yet where does this anarchy exist? Where did it ever exist, except in the single instance of Massachusetts? And can history produce an instance of rebellion so honourably conducted? I say nothing of it's motives. They were founded in ignorance, not wickedness. God forbid we should ever be 20 years without such a rebellion. The people cannot be all, & always, well informed. The part which is wrong will be discontented in proportion to the importance of the facts they misconceive. If they remain quiet under such misconceptions it is a lethargy, the forerunner of death to the public liberty. We have had 13. states independent 11. years. There has been one rebellion. That comes to one rebellion in a century & a half for each state. What country before ever existed a century & half without a rebellion? & what country can preserve it's liberties if their rulers are not warned from time to time that their people preserve the spirit of resistance? Let them take arms. The remedy is to set them right as to facts, pardon & pacify them. What signify a few lives lost in a century or two? The tree of liberty must be refreshed from time to time with the blood of patriots & tyrants. It is it's natural manure. Our Convention has been too much impressed by the insurrection of Massachusetts: and in the spur of the moment they are setting up a kite to keep the hen-yard in order. I hope in God this article will be rectified before the new constitution is accepted.—You ask me if any thing transpires here on the subject of S. America? Not a word. I know that there are combustible materials there, and that they wait the torch only. But this country probably will join the extinguishers.

16. To James Madison, Paris, 20 December 1787. *James Madison (1751–1836) had been TJ's close friend and political ally for almost a decade, serving on the Virginia Council of State when TJ was governor and subsequently as congressman from 1780 to 1783 and from 1784 to 1786 as a member of the Virginia House of Delegates; Madison took the leading role in the movement for a new federal Constitution, which TJ discusses here.*

The season admitting only of operations in the Cabinet, and these being in a great measure secret, I have little to fill a letter. I will therefore make up the deficiency by adding a few words on the Constitution proposed by our Convention. I like much the general idea of framing a government which should go on of itself peaceably, without needing continual recurrence to the state legislatures. I like the organization of the government into Legislative, Judiciary & Executive. I like the power given the Legislature to levy taxes, and for that reason solely approve of the greater house being chosen by the people directly. For tho' I think a house chosen by them will be very illy qualified to legislate for the Union, for foreign nations &c. yet this evil does not weigh against the good of preserving inviolate the fundamental principle that the people are not to be taxed but by representatives chosen immediately by themselves. I am captivated by the compromise of the opposite claims of the great & little states, of the latter to equal, and the former to proportional influence. I am much pleased too with the substitution of the method of voting by persons, instead of that of voting by states: and I like the negative given to the Executive with a third of either house, though I should have liked it better had the Judiciary been associated for that purpose, or invested with a similar and separate power. There are other good things of less moment. I will now add what I do not like. First the omission of a bill of rights providing clearly & without the aid of sophisms for freedom of religion, freedom of the press, protection against standing armies, restriction against monopolies, the eternal & unremitting force of the habeas corpus laws, and trials by jury in all matters of fact triable by the laws of the land & not by the law of nations. To say, as Mr. Wilson does that a bill of rights was not necessary because all is reserved in the case of the general government which is not given, while in the particular ones all is given which is not reserved, might do for the audience to whom it was addressed, but is surely a gratis dictum, opposed by strong inferences from the body of the instrument, as well as from the omission of the clause of our present confederation which had declared that in express terms. It was a hard conclusion to say because there has been no uniformity among the states as to the cases triable by jury, because some have been so incautious as to abandon this mode of trial, therefore the more prudent states shall be reduced to the same level of calamity. It would have been much more just & wise to have concluded the other way that as most of the states had judiciously preserved this palladium, those who had wandered should be brought back to it, and to have established general right instead of general wrong. Let me add that a bill of rights is what the people are entitled to against every government on earth, general or particular, & what no just government should refuse, or rest on inferences. The second feature I dislike, and greatly dislike, is the abandonment in every instance of the necessity of rotation in office, and most particularly in the case of the President. Experience concurs with reason in concluding that the first magistrate will always be re-elected if the Constitution permits it. He is then an officer for life. This once observed, it becomes of so much consequence to certain nations to have a friend or a foe at the head of our affairs that they will interfere with money & with arms. A Galloman or an Angloman will be supported by the nation he befriends. If once elected, and at a second or third election out voted by one or two votes, he will pretend false votes, foul play, hold possession of the reins of government, be supported by the States voting for him, especially if they are the central ones lying in a compact body themselves & separating their opponents: and they will be aided by one nation of Europe, while the majority are aided by another. The election of a President of America some years hence will be much more interesting to certain nations of Europe than ever the election of a king of Poland was. Reflect on all the instances in history antient & modern, of elective monarchies, and say if they do not give foundation for my fears. The Roman emperors, the popes, while they were of any importance, the German emperors till they became hereditary in practice, the kings of Poland, the Deys of the Ottoman dependances. It may be said that if elections are to be attended with these disorders, the seldomer they are renewed the better. But experience shews that the only way to prevent disorder is to render them uninteresting by frequent changes. An incapacity to be elected a second time would have been the only effectual preventative. The power of removing him every fourth year by the vote of the people is a power which will not be exercised. The king of Poland is removeable every day by the Diet, yet he is never removed.—Smaller objections are the Appeal in fact as well as law, and the binding all persons Legislative Executive & Judiciary by oath to maintain that constitution. I do not pretend to decide what would be the best method of procuring the establishment of the manifold good things in this constitution, and of getting rid of the bad. Whether by adopting it in hopes of future amendment, or, after it has been duly weighed & canvassed by the people, after seeing the parts they generally dislike, & those they generally approve, to say to them 'We see now what you wish. Send together your deputies again, let them frame a constitution for you omitting what you have condemned, & establishing the powers you approve. Even these will be a great addition to the energy of your government.' —At all events I hope you will not be discouraged from other trials, if the present one should fail of its full effect. —I have thus told you freely what I like & dislike: merely as a matter of curiosity, for I know your own judgment has been formed on all these points after having heard everything which could be urged on them. I own I am not a friend to a very energetic government. It is always oppressive. The late rebellion in Massachusetts has given more alarm than I think it should have done. Calculate that one rebellion in 13 states in the course of 11 years, is but one for each state in a century & a half. No country should be so long without one. Nor will any degree of power in the hands of government prevent insurrections. France, with all it's despotism, and two or three hundred thousand men always in arms has had three insurrections in the three years I have been here in every one of which greater numbers were engaged than in Massachusetts & a great deal more blood was spilt. In Turkey, which Montesquieu supposes more despotic, insurrections are the events of every day. In England, where the hand of power is lighter than here, but heavier than with us they happen every half dozen years. Compare again the ferocious depredations of their insurgents with the order, the moderation & the almost self extinguishment of ours.— After all, it is my principle that the will of the majority should always prevail. If they approve the proposed Convention in all it's parts, I shall concur in it chearfully, in hopes that they will amend it whenever they shall find it work wrong. I think our governments will remain virtuous for many centuries; as long as they are chiefly agricultural; and this will be as long as there shall be vacant lands in any part of America. When they get piled upon one another in large cities, as in Europe, they will become corrupt as in Europe. Above all things I hope the education of the common people will be attended to; convinced that on their good sense we may rely with the most security for the preservation of a due degree of liberty.

17. To James Madison, Paris, 6 September 1789. *This essay on the generational problem is one of the most important statements of TJ's political philosophy (see the discussion in the Introduction). TJ's radical ideas about generational sovereignty reflected the heady atmosphere in Paris at the onset of the French Revolution.*

They met with a chilly response from Madison, the "father" of a new federal Constitution designed to secure political stability—and prevent further revolutionary turmoil—in the United States.

The question Whether one generation of men has a right to bind another, seems never to have been started either on this or our side of the water. Yet it is a question of such consequences as not only to merit decision, but place also, among the fundamental principles of every government. The course of reflection in which we are immersed here on the elementary principles of society has presented this question to my mind; and that no such obligation can be transmitted I think very capable of proof. I set out on this ground which I suppose to be self evident, "*that the earth belongs in usufruct to the living*," that the dead have neither powers nor rights over it. The portion occupied by an individual ceases to be his when himself ceases to be, and reverts to the society. If the society has formed no rules for the appropriation of its lands in severalty, it will be taken by the first occupants. These will generally be the wife and children of the decedent. If they have formed rules of appropriation, those rules may give it to the wife and children, or to some one of them, or to the legatee of the deceased. So they may give it to his creditor. But the child, the legatee or creditor takes it, not by any natural right, but by a law of the society of which they are members, and to which they are subject. Then no man can by *natural right* oblige the lands he occupied, or the persons who succeed him in that occupation, to the paiment of debts contracted by him. For if he could, he might during his own life, eat up the usufruct of the lands for several generations to come, and then the lands would belong to the dead, and not to the living, which would be reverse of our principle. What is true of every member of the society individually, is true of them all collectively, since the rights of the whole can be no more than the sum of the rights of individuals. To keep our ideas clear when applying them to a multitude, let us suppose a whole generation of men to be born on the same day, to attain mature age on the same day, and to die on the same day, leaving a succeeding generation in the moment of attaining their mature age all together. Let the ripe age be supposed of 21. years, and their period of life 34. years more, that being the average term given by the bills of mortality to persons who have already attained 21. years of age. Each successive generation would, in this way, come on and go off the stage at a fixed moment, as individuals do now. Then I say the earth belongs to each of these generations during it's course, fully, and in their own right. The 2d. generation receives it clear of the debts and incumbrances of the 1st., the 3d. of the 2d. and so on. For if the 1st. could charge it with a debt, then the earth would belong to the dead and not the living generation. Then no generation can contract debts greater than may be paid during the course of it's own existence. At 21. years of age they may bind themselves and their lands for 34. years to come: at 22. for 33: at 23 for 32. and at 54 for one year only; because these are the terms of life which remain to them at those respective epochs. But a material difference must be noted between the succession of an individual and that of a whole generation. Individuals are parts only of a society, subject to the laws of a whole. These laws may appropriate the portion of land occupied by a decedent to his creditor rather than to any other, or to his child, on condition he satisfies his creditor. But when a whole generation, that is, the whole society dies, as in the case we have supposed, and another generation or society succeeds, this forms a whole, and there is no superior who can give their territory to a third society, who may have lent money to their predecessors beyond their faculty of paying.

What is true of a generation all arriving to self-government on the same day, and dying all on the same day, is true of those on a constant course of decay and renewal, with this only difference. A generation coming in and going out entire, as in the first case, would have a right in the 1st year of their self dominion to contract a debt for 33. years, in the 10th. for 24. in the 20th. for 14. in the 30th. for 4. whereas generations changing daily, by daily deaths and births, have one constant term beginning at the date of their contract, and ending when a majority of those of full age at that date shall be dead. The length of that term may be estimated from the tables of mortality, corrected by the circumstances of climate, occupation &c. peculiar to the country of the contractors. Take, for instance, the table of M. de Buffon wherein he states that 23,994 deaths, and the ages at which they happened. Suppose a society in which 23,994 persons are born every year and live to the ages stated in this table. The conditions of that society will be as follows. 1st. it will consist constantly of 617,703 persons of all ages. 2dly. of those living at any one instant of time, one half will be dead in 24. years 8. months. 3dly. 10,675 will arrive every year at the age of 21. years complete. 4thly. it will constantly have 348,417 persons of all ages above 21. years. 5ly. and the half of those of 21. years and upwards living at any one instant of time will be dead in 18. years 8. months, or say 19. years as the nearest integral number. Then 19. years is the term beyond which neither the representatives of a nation, nor even the whole nation itself assembled, can validly extend a debt.

To render this conclusion palpable by example, suppose that Louis XIV. and XV. had contracted debts in the name of the French nation to the amount of 10.000 milliards of livres and that the whole had been contracted in Genoa. The interest of this sum would be 500 milliards, which is said to be the whole rent-roll, or nett proceeds of the territory of France. Must the present generation of men have retired from the territory in which nature produced them, and ceded it to the Genoese creditors? No. They have the same rights over the soil on which they were produced, as the preceding generations had. They derive these rights not from their predecessors, but from nature. They then and their soil are by nature clear of the debts of their predecessors. Again suppose Louis XV. and his contemporary generation had said to the money lenders of Genoa, give us money that we may eat, drink, and be merry in our day; and on condition you will demand no interest till the end of 19. years, you shall then forever after receive an annual interest of 12.5 per cent. The money is lent on these conditions, is divided among the living, eaten, drank, and squandered. Would the present generation be obliged to apply the produce of the earth and of their labour to replace their dissipations? Not at all.

I suppose that the received opinion, that the public debts of one generation devolve on the next, has been suggested by our seeing habitually in private life that he who succeeds to lands is required to pay the debts of his ancestor or testator, without considering that this requisition is municipal only, not moral, flowing from the will of the society which has found it convenient to appropriate the lands become vacant by the death of their occupant on the condition of a paiment of his debts; but that between society and society, or generation and generation there is no municipal obligation, no umpire but the law of nature. We seem not to have perceived that, by the law of nature, one generation is to another as one independant nation to another.

The interest of the national debt of France being in fact but a two thousandth part of it's rent-roll, the paiment of it is practicable enough; and so becomes a question merely of honor or expediency. But with respect to future debts; would it not be wise and just for that nation to declare in the constitution they are forming that neither the legislature, nor the nation itself can validly contract more debt, than they may pay within their own age, or within the term of 19. years? And that all future contracts shall be deemed void as to what shall remain unpaid at the end of 19. years from their date? This would put the lenders, and the borrowers also, on their guard. By reducing too the faculty of borrowing within its natural limits, it would bridle the spirit of war, to which too free a course has been procured by the inattention of money lenders to this law of nature, that succeeding generations are not responsible for the preceding.

On similar ground it may be proved that no society can make a perpetual constitution, or even a perpetual law. The earth belongs always to the living generation. They may manage it then, and what proceeds from it, as they please, during their usufruct. They are masters too of their own persons, and consequently may govern them as they please. But persons and property make the sum of the objects of government. The constitution and the laws of their predecessors extinguished them, in their natural course, with those whose will gave them being. This could preserve that being till it ceased to be itself, and no longer. Every constitution, then, and every law, naturally expires at the end of 19. years. If it be enforced longer, it is an act of force and not of right.

It may be said that the succeeding generation exercising in fact the power of repeal, this leaves them as free as if the constitution or law had been expressly limited to 19. years only. In the first place, this objection admits the right, in proposing an equivalent. But the power of repeal is not an equivalent. It might be indeed if every form of government were so perfectly contrived that the will of the majority could always be obtained fairly and without impediment. But this is true of no form. The people cannot assemble themselves; their representation is unequal and vicious. Various checks are opposed to every legislative proposition. Factions get possession of the public councils. Bribery corrupts them. Personal interests lead them astray from the general interests of their constituents; and other impediments arise so as to prove to every practical man that a law of limited duration is much more manageable than one which needs a repeal.

This principle that the earth belongs to the living and not to the dead is of very extensive application and consequences in every country, and most especially in France. It enters into the resolution of the questions Whether the nation may change the descent of lands holden in tail? Whether they may change the appropriation of lands given antiently to the church, to hospitals, colleges, orders of chivalry, and otherwise in perpetuity? whether they may abolish the charges and privileges attached on lands, including the whole catalogue ecclesiastical and feudal? it goes to hereditary offices, authorities and jurisdictions; to hereditary orders, distinctions and appellations; to perpetual monopolies in commerce, the arts or sciences; with a long train of et ceteras: and it renders the question of reimbursement a question of generosity and not of right. In all these cases the legislature of the day could authorize such appropriations and establishments for their own time, but no longer; and the present holders, even where they or their ancestors have purchased, are in the case of bona fide purchasers of what the seller had no right to convey.

Turn this subject in your mind, my Dear Sir, and particularly as to the power of contracting debts, and develope it with that perspicuity and cogent logic which is so peculiarly yours. Your station in the councils of our country gives you an opportunity of producing it to public consideration, of forcing it into discussion. At first blush it may be rallied as a theoretical speculation; but examination will prove it to be solid and salutary. It would furnish matter for a fine preamble to our first law for appropriating the public revenue; and it will exclude, at the threshold of our new government the contagious and ruinous errors of this quarter of the globe, which have armed despots with means not sanctioned by nature for binding in chains their fellow-men. We have already given, in example one effectual check to the Dog of war, by transferring the power of letting him loose from the executive to the Legislative body, from those who are to spend to those who are to pay. I should be pleased to see this second obstacle held out by us also in the first instance. No nation can make a declaration against the validity of long-contracted debts so disinterestedly as we, since we do not owe a shilling which may not be paid with ease principal and interest, within the time of our own lives. Establish the principle also in the new law to be passed for protecting copy rights and new inventions, by securing the exclusive right for 19. instead of 14. years. Besides familiarising us to this term. It will be an instance the more of our taking reason for our guide instead of English precedents, the habit of which fetters us, with all the political herecies of a nation, equally remarkable for it's encitement from some errors, as long slumbering under others.

CHAPTER FOUR

Jeffersonian Republicanism

When Jefferson sailed from France in October 1789, he hoped to attend to personal business in Virginia—most urgently, to sort out his tangled financial affairs—before returning to his post in Paris. But an invitation awaited him from George Washington to join the new President's cabinet as secretary of state. The reluctant Jefferson finally decided in February to accept his offer, and in late March joined the new government in New York.

Jefferson had every reason to believe that he would take the lead in formulating Washington's first administration. Because the new government presumably would earn more respect from foreign powers than its predecessor, Jefferson could follow through on diplomatic initiatives that had eluded him during his Paris years. But well before Jefferson's arrival his cabinet colleague, Treasury Secretary Alexander Hamilton, had already set the tone for the administration. Hamilton's Report on the Public Credit, delivered to Congress on 14 January, outlined a bold financial policy for servicing federal and state revolutionary war debts. The need for assuring a steady flow of revenue, primarily through import duties on Anglo-American trade, dictated a conciliatory commercial policy toward Britain that most severely curtailed the new nation's—and Jefferson's—diplomatic options. Implementation of Hamilton's financial plan, including the establishment of a national bank (document 1), depended on an expansive definition of the federal government's powers under the new federal Constitution. For the emerging "Republican" opposition, the resulting consolidation of authority threatened to obliterate the state governments and to transform the federal government into an American version of the British imperial regime that the Revolution had overthrown (document 15). The British character of the new administration, the foreign policy tilt toward Britain, and the dominating presence of Hamilton himself made the nonpartisan Jefferson into a party leader in spite of himself.

Jefferson's self-exculpatory letter to Washington in September 1792 (document 3) makes evident his estrangement from the administration and the discomfort he suffered as he encouraged James Madison and other like-minded congressmen to obstruct Hamilton's policy initiatives. Refusing to make peace with his adversary and so restore harmony to the cabinet, Jefferson launched into a wide-ranging diatribe against Hamilton's political character. His certainty of the righteousness of his own position was reinforced by events in Europe, where the expanding conflict between republican France and the counterrevolutionary "conspiracy of kings" revealed to him the identical battle line between progressive and reactionary forces that seemed to be unfolding in America (see documents 2 and 4).

Jefferson's political principles took their mature form during the great struggles over foreign policy divisions between Anglophile Federalists and Francophile Republicans. But his affinity for France also led to political embarrassments that tarnished the Republican cause and sustained the Federalists in power through the 1790s. The pattern was set when Citizen Edmond Genet, minister from the French Republic, made a sensational tour across the country in 1793, distributing military commissions and rousing popular support for the French cause in defiance of Washington's Neutrality Proclamation of 22 April 1793. Federalists could link Republicanism with challenges to legitimate, constituted authority, a charge that would continue to resonate after Jefferson withdrew from the cabinet at the end of 1793, notably when western farmers resisted the excise on whiskey (document 7) or the Kentucky and Virginia legislatures challenged the constitutionality of federal laws (document 12).

Jefferson's retirement to Monticello was brief. As the runner-up to John Adams in the 1796 presidential contest, he became Vice President, finding himself yet once again in the position of partisan opponent of the administration he ostensibly served. Adams and the Federalists prospered as Federalist diplomatic successes preempted the threat of war with Britain and opened the Mississippi to the nation's commerce, both fostering a booming economy. Meanwhile, French anger at John Jay's "English Treaty" led to a rapid deterioration in Franco-American relations, and French depredations on American shipping that led to an undeclared war. During this quasi-war, which lasted from 1798 to 1800, the Republican partiality toward France was a tremendous liability (document 11). The Republican challenge was to sever the French connection and adopt a plausibly neutral stance; then, as Jefferson counseled his allies, Republicans should bide their time, waiting for the "reign of witches" to subside as Federalist warmongers overplayed their hand (document 10). If the quasi-war ever became full-blown, peace-loving Americans averse to taxation would recover their senses; if the administration launched a sustained assault on its domestic enemies, liberty-loving republicans would remember why they had fought the Revolution in the first place.

Jefferson's counsels of patience betrayed mounting desperation: for the time being, the Republicans could do little more than wait. The recourse to the state legislatures was counterproductive: if Kentucky and Virginia followed through on their disunionist threats they would find themselves standing alone. Yet in the Republicans' darkest hour, Federalists divided among themselves over appropriate preparations for war and, finally and fatally, over Adams's ultimately successful peace negotiation with France, leading to the Convention of 1800. As the threat of war diminished, Federalists were hard-pressed to justify the war against domestic dissidents that they had launched under the aegis of the Alien and Sedition Acts of 1798.

* * * * * * * * * *

1. Opinion on the Constitutionality of a National Bank, 15 February 1791. *On 13 December 1790, Secretary of the Treasury Alexander Hamilton submitted to Congress his proposal to charter the Bank of the United States. President George Washington then solicited the opinions of cabinet members on the constitutionality of the measure. Controversy over the Bank, the centerpiece of Hamilton's financial plan, inaugurated the divisions in the cabinet and in Congress that would give rise to the first party system. TJ's report, arguing that the charter would exceed Congress's constitutional powers, set forth the central positions of the emerging Republican opposition. Reassured by Hamilton's favorable opinion of 23 February on the Bank's constitutionality, Washington on 25 February signed the charter bill.*

The bill for establishing a National Bank undertakes among other things: —

1. the subscribers into a corporation.

2. To enable them in their corporate capacities to receive grants of land; and so far is against the laws of Mortmain. Though the Constitution controls the laws of Mortmain so far as to permit Congress itself to hold land for certain purposes, yet not so far as to permit them to communicate a similar right to other corporate bodies.

3. To make alien subscribers capable of holding lands; and so far is against the laws of Alienage.

4. To transmit these lands, on the death of a proprietor, to a certain line of successors; and so far changes the course of Descents.

5. To put the lands out of the reach of forfeiture or escheat; and so far is against the laws of Forfeiture and Escheat.

6. To transmit personal chattels to successors in a certain line; and so far is against the laws of Distribution.

7. To give them the sole and exclusive right of banking under the national authority; and so far is against the laws of Monopoly.

8. To communicate to them a power to make laws paramount to the laws of the States: for so they must be construed, to protect the institution from the control of the State legislatures; and so, probably, they will be construed.

I consider the foundation of the Constitution as laid on this ground: That "all powers not delegated to the United States, by the Constitution, nor prohibited by it to the States, are reserved to the States or to the people." [XIIth amendment.] To take a single step beyond the boundaries thus specially drawn around the powers of Congress, is to take possession of a boundless field of power, no longer susceptible of any definition.

The incorporation of a bank, and the powers assumed by this bill, have not, in my opinion, been delegated to the United States, by the Constitution.

I. They are not among the powers specially enumerated: for these are: 1st. A power to lay taxes for the purpose of paying the debts of the United States; but no debt is paid by this bill, nor any tax laid. Were it a bill to raise money, its origination in the Senate would condemn it by the Constitution.

2d. "To borrow money." But this bill neither borrows money nor ensures the borrowing it. The proprietors of the bank will be just as free as any other money holders, to lend or not to lend their money to the public. The operation proposed in the bill, first, to lend them two millions, and then to borrow them back again, cannot change the nature of the latter act, which will still be a payment, and not a loan, call it by what name you please.

3. To "regulate commerce with foreign nations, and among the States, and with the Indian tribes." To erect a bank, and to regulate commerce, are very different acts. He who erects a bank, creates a subject of commerce in its bills; so does he who makes a bushel of wheat, or digs a dollar out of the mines; yet neither of these persons regulates commerce thereby. To make a thing which may be bought and sold, is not to prescribe regulations for buying and selling. Besides, if this was an exercise of the power of regulating commerce, it would be void, as extending as much to the internal commerce of every State, as to its external. For the power given to Congress by the Constitution does not extend to the internal regulation of the commerce of a State, (that is to say of the commerce between citizen and citizen,) which remain exclusively with its own legislature; but to its external commerce only, that is to say, its commerce with another State, or with foreign nations, or with the Indian tribes. Accordingly the bill does not propose the measure as a regulation of trade, but as "productive of considerable advantages to trade." Still less are these powers covered by any other of the special enumerations.

II. Nor are they within either of the general phrases, which are the two following: —

1. To lay taxes to provide for the general welfare of the United States, that is to say, "to lay taxes for *the purpose* of providing for the general welfare." For the laying of taxes is the *power*, and the general welfare the *purpose* for which the power is to be exercised. They are not to lay taxes *ad libitum for any purpose they please*, but only *to pay the debts or provide for the welfare of the Union*. In like manner, they are not *to do anything they please* to provide for the general welfare, but only to *lay taxes* for that purpose. To consider the latter phrase, not as describing the purpose of the first, but as giving a distinct and independent power to do any act they please, which might be for the good of the Union, would render all the preceding and subsequent enumerations of power completely useless.

It would reduce the whole instrument to a single phrase, that of instituting a Congress with power to do whatever would be for the good of the United States; and, as they would be the sole judges of the good or evil, it would be also a power to do whatever evil they please.

It is an established rule of construction where a phrase will bear either of two meanings, to give it that which will allow some meaning to the other parts of the instrument, and not that which would render all the others useless. Certainly no such universal power was meant to be given them. It was intended to lace them up straitly within the enumerated powers, and those without which, as means, these powers could not be carried into effect. It is known that the very power now proposed *as a means* was rejected as *an end* by the Convention which formed the Constitution. A proposition was made to them to authorize Congress to open canals, and an amendatory one to empower them to incorporate. But the whole was rejected, and one of the reasons for rejection urged in debate was, that then they would have a power to erect a bank, which would render the great cities, where there were prejudices and jealousies on the subject, adverse to the reception of the Constitution.

2. The second general phrase is, "to make all laws *necessary* and proper for carrying into execution the enumerated powers." But they can all be carried into execution without a bank. A bank therefore is not *necessary,* and consequently not authorized by this phrase.

It has been urged that a bank will give great facility or convenience in the collection of taxes. Suppose this were true: yet the Constitution allows only the means which are *"necessary,"* not those which are merely "convenient" for effecting the enumerated powers. If such a latitude of construction be allowed to this phrase as to give any non-enumerated power, it will go to every one, for there is not one which ingenuity may not torture into a *convenience* in some instance *or other,* to *some one* of so long a list of enumerated powers. It would swallow up all the delegated powers, and reduce the whole to one power, as before observed. Therefore it was that the Constitution restrained them to the *necessary* means, that is to say, to those means without which the grant of power would be nugatory.

But let us examine this convenience and see what it is. The report on this subject, page 3, states the only *general* convenience to be, the preventing the transportation and re-transportation of money between the States and the treasury, (for I pass over the increase of circulating medium, ascribed to it as a want, and which, according to my ideas of paper money, is clearly a demerit.) Every State will have to pay a sum of tax money into the treasury; and the treasury will have to pay, in every State, a part of the interest on the public debt, and salaries to the officers of government resident in that State. In most of the States there will still be a surplus of tax money to come up to the seat of government for the officers residing there. The payments of interest and salary in each State may be made by treasury orders on the State collector. This will take up the greater part of the money he has collected in his State, and consequently prevent the great mass of it from being drawn out of the State. If there be a balance of commerce in favor of that State against the one in which the government resides, the surplus of taxes will be remitted by the bills of exchange drawn for that commercial balance. And so it must be if there was a bank. But if there be no balance of commerce, either direct or circuitous, all the banks in the world could not bring up the surplus of taxes but in the form of money. Treasury orders then, and bills of exchange may prevent the displacement of the main mass of the money collected, without the aid of any bank; and where these fail, it cannot be prevented even with that aid.

Perhaps, indeed, bank bills may be a more *convenient* vehicle than treasury orders. But a little *difference* in the degree of *convenience,* cannot constitute the necessity which the constitution makes the ground for assuming any non-enumerated power.

Besides; the existing banks will, without a doubt, enter into arrangements for lending their agency, and the more favorable, as there will be a competition among them for it; whereas the bill delivers us up bound to the national bank, who are free to refuse all arrangement, but on their own terms, and the public not free, on such refusal, to employ any other bank. That of Philadelphia, I believe, now does this business, by their post-notes, which, by an arrangement with the treasury, are paid by any State collector to whom they are presented. This expedient alone suffices to prevent the existence of that *necessity* which may justify the assumption of a non-enumerated power as a means for carrying into effect an enumerated one. The thing may be done, and has been done, and well done, without this assumption; therefore, it does not stand on that degree of *necessity* which can honestly justify it.

It may be said that a bank whose bills would have a currency all over the States, would be more convenient than one whose currency is limited to a single State. So it would be still more convenient that there should be a bank, whose bills should have a currency all over the world. But it does not follow from this superior conveniency, that there exists anywhere a power to establish such a bank; or that the world may not go on very well without it.

Can it be thought that the Constitution intended that for a shade or two of *convenience*, more or less, Congress should be authorised to break down the most ancient and fundamental laws of the several States; such as those against Mortmain, the laws of Alienage, the rules of descent, the acts of distribution, the laws of escheat and forfeiture, the laws of monopoly? Nothing but a necessity invincible by any other means, can justify such a prostitution of laws, which constitute the pillars of our whole system of jurisprudence. Will Congress be too straight-laced to carry the constitution into honest effect, unless they may pass over the foundation-laws of the State government for the slightest convenience of theirs?

The negative of the President is the shield provided by the constitution to protect against the invasions of the legislature: 1. The right of the Executive. 2. Of the Judiciary. 3. Of the States and State legislatures. The present is the case of a right remaining exclusively with the States, and consequently one of those intended by the Constitution to be placed under its protection.

It must be added, however, that unless the President's mind on a view of everything which is urged for and against this bill, is tolerably clear that it is unauthorised by the Constitution; if the pro and the con hang so even as to balance his judgment, a just respect for the wisdom of the legislature would naturally decide the balance in favor of their opinion. It is chiefly for cases where they are clearly misled by error, ambition, or interest, that the Constitution has placed a check in the negative of the President.

2. To the Marquis de Lafayette, Philadelphia, 16 June 1792. *TJ linked the Anglophile Federalist administration party in America with the "conspiracy of the kings" against the French Revolution in Europe. When TJ wrote, the moderate constitutionalist Lafayette (1757–1834) had already resigned in October 1791 his command of the Parisian National Guard and lost favor with the increasingly radical Jacobin leadership.*

Behold you, then, my dear friend, at the head of a great army, establishing the liberties of your country against a foreign enemy. May heaven favor your cause, and make you the channel thro' which it may pour it's favors. While you are exterminating the monster aristocracy, & pulling out the teeth & fangs of it's associate monarchy, a contrary tendency is discovered in some here. A sect has shewn itself among us, who declare they espoused our new constitution, not as a good & sufficient thing itself, but only as a step to an English constitution, the only thing good & sufficient in itself, in their eye. It is happy for us that these are preachers without followers, and that our people are firm & constant in their republican purity. You will wonder to be told that it is from the Eastward chiefly that these champions for a king, lords & commons come. They get some important associates from New York, and are puffed off by a tribe of Agioteurs which have been hatched in a bed of corruption made up after the model of their beloved England. Too many of these stock jobbers & king-jobbers have come into our legislature, or rather too many of our legislature have become stock jobbers & king-jobbers. However the voice of the people is beginning to make itself heard, and will probably cleanse their seats at the ensuing election. —The machinations of our old enemies are such as to keep us still at bay with our Indian neighbors. —What are you doing for your colonies? They will be lost if not more effectually succoured. Indeed no future efforts you can make will ever be able to reduce the blacks. All that can be done in my opinion will be to compound with them as has been done formerly in Jamaica. We have been less zealous in aiding them, lest your government should feel any jealousy on our account. But in truth we as sincerely wish their restoration, and their connection with you, as you do yourselves. We are satisfied that neither your justice nor their distresses will ever again permit their being forced to seek at dear & distant markets those first necessaries of life which they may have at cheaper markets placed by nature at their door, & formed by her for their support. . . .

3. To President George Washington, Monticello, 9 September 1792.
Hoping to heal the growing breach within his own cabinet, President Washington appealed to Hamilton and Jefferson to put an end to the "internal dissentions . . . harrowing and tearing our vitals." The specific controversy here concerned TJ's sponsorship of the poet Philip Freneau (1752–1832) as editor of the anti-administration National Gazette. *TJ offered Freneau a sinecure as translator in the State Department in order to establish the new paper that, TJ hoped, would counter the pernicious influence of John Fenno's* Gazette of the United States, *supportive of the administration. TJ's anger at Hamilton, a frequent contributor to Fenno's columns, reflected mounting frustration over a series of political defeats, including the infamous bargain of July 1790 in which Jefferson and his allies agreed to Hamilton's proposal that the federal government assume responsibility for the states' revolutionary war debts in exchange for siting the new national capital on the Potomac: "of all the errors of my political life," TJ writes below, "this has occasioned me the deepest regret." Washington hoped to make peace in his cabinet so that he could retire at the end of his first term; TJ responded by proposing his own early retirement.*

I now take the liberty of proceeding to that part of your letter wherein you notice the internal dissentions which have taken place within our government, & their disagreeable effect on it's movements. That such dis-

sentions have taken place is certain, & even among those who are nearest
to you in the administration. To no one have they given deeper concern
than myself: to no one equal mortification at being myself a part of them.
Tho' I take to myself no more than my share of the general observations
of your letter, yet I am so desirous ever that you should know the whole
truth, & believe no more than the truth, that I am glad to seize every occasion of developing to you whatever I do or think relative to the government; & shall therefore ask permission to be more lengthy now than the
occasion particularly calls for, or could otherwise perhaps justify.

When I embarked in the government, it was with a determination to
intermeddle not at all with the legislature, & as little as possible with my
co-departments. The first and only instance of variance from the former
part of my resolution, I was duped into by the Secretary of the Treasury
and made a tool for forwarding his schemes, not then sufficiently understood by me; and of all the errors of my political life, this has occasioned
me the deepest regret. It has ever been my purpose to explain this to you,
when, from being actors on the scene, we shall have become uninterested
spectators only. The second part of my resolution has been religiously
observed with the war department; & as to that of the Treasury, has never
been farther swerved from than by the mere enunciation of my sentiments
in conversation, and chiefly among those who, expressing the same sentiments, drew mine from me. If it has been supposed that have ever in-
trigued among the members of the legislatures to defeat the plans of the
Secretary of the Treasury, it is contrary to all truth. As I never had the
desire to influence the members, so neither had I any other means than
my friendships, which I valued too highly to risk by usurpations on their
freedom of judgment, & the conscientious pursuit of their own sense of
duty. That I have utterly, in my private conversations, disapproved of the
system of the Secretary of the treasury, acknolege & avow: and this was not
merely a speculative difference. His system flowed from principles adverse
to liberty, & was calculated to undermine and demolish the republic, by
creating an influence of his department over the members of the legislature. I saw this influence actually produced, & it's first fruits to be the
establishment of the great outlines of his project by the votes of the very
persons who, having swallowed his bait were laying themselves out to profit
by his plans: & that had these persons withdrawn, as those interested in a
question ever should, the vote of the disinterested majority was clearly the
reverse of what they made it. These were no longer the votes then of the
representatives of the people, but of deserters from the rights & interests
of the people: & it was impossible to consider their decisions, which had
nothing in view but to enrich themselves, as the measures of the fair majority, which ought always to be respected.—If what was actually doing begat
uneasiness in those who wished for virtuous government, what was further
proposed was not less threatening to the friends of the Constitution. For,
in a Report on the subject of manufactures (still to be acted on) it was
expressly assumed that the general government has a right to exercise all
powers which may be for the *general welfare,* that is to say, all the legitimate
powers of government: since no government has a legitimate right to do
what is not for the welfare of the governed. There was indeed a sham-

limitation of the universality of this power *to cases where money is to be employed.* But about what is it that money cannot be employed? Thus the object of these plans taken together is to draw all the powers of government into the hands of the general legislature, to establish means for corrupting a sufficient corps in that legislature to divide the honest votes & preponderate, by their own, the scale which suited, & to have that corps under the command of the Secretary of the Treasury for the purpose of subverting step by step the principles of the constitution, which he has so often declared to be a thing of nothing which must be changed. Such views might have justified something more than mere expressions of dissent, beyond which, nevertheless, I never went. —Has abstinence from the department committed to me been equally observed by him? To say nothing of other interferences equally known, in the case of the two nations with which we have the most intimate connections, France & England, my system was to give some satisfactory distinctions to the former, of little cost to us, in return for the solid advantages yielded us by them; & to have met the English with some restrictions which might induce them to abate their severities against our commerce. I have always supposed this coincided with your sentiments. Yet the Secretary of the treasury, by his cabals with members of the legislature, & by high-toned declamation on other occasions, has forced down his own system, which was exactly the reverse. He undertook, of his own authority, the conferences with the ministers of those two nations, & was, on every consultation, provided with some report of a conversation with the one or the other of them, adapted to his views. These views, thus made to prevail, their execution fell of course to me; & I can safely appeal to you, who have seen all my letters & proceedings, whether I have not carried them into execution as sincerely as if they had been my own, tho' I ever considered them as inconsistent with the honor & interest of our country. That they have been inconsistent with our interest is but too fatally proved by the stab to our navigation given by the French. —So that if the question be By whose fault is it that Colo Hamilton & myself have not drawn together? the answer will depend on that to two other questions; whose principles of administration best justify, by their purity, conscientious adherence? and which of us has, notwithstanding, stepped farthest into the controul of the department of the other?

To this justification of opinions, expressed in the way of conversation, against the views of Colo Hamilton, I beg leave to add some notice of his late charges against me in Fenno's gazette; for neither the stile, matter, nor venom of the pieces alluded to can leave a doubt of their author. Spelling my name & character at full length to the public, while he conceals his own under the signature of "an American" he charges me 1. With having written letters from Europe to my friends to oppose the present constitution while depending. 2. With a desire of not paying the public debt. 3. With setting up a paper to decry & slander the government. 1. The first charge is most false. No man in the U. S. I suppose, approved of every title in the constitution: no one, I believe approved more of it than I did: and more of it was certainly disproved by my accuser than by me, and of it's parts most vitally republican. Of this the few letters I wrote on the subject (not half a dozen I believe) will be a proof: & for my own satisfaction

& justification, I must tax you with the reading of them when I return to where they are. You will there see that my objection to the constitution was that it wanted a bill of rights securing freedom of religion, freedom of the press, freedom from standing armies, trial by jury, & a constant Habeas corpus act. Colo Hamilton's was that it wanted a king and house of lords. The sense of America has approved my objection & added the bill of rights, not the king and lords. I also thought a longer term of service, insusceptible of renewal, would have made a President more independant. My country has thought otherwise, & I have acquiesced implicitly. He wishes the general government should have power to make laws binding the states in all cases whatsoever. Our country has thought otherwise: has he acquiesced? Notwithstanding my wish for a bill of rights, my letters strongly urged the adoption of the constitution, by nine states at least, to secure the good it contained. I at first thought that the best method of securing the bill of rights would be for four states to hold off till such a bill should be agreed to. But the moment I saw Mr. Hancock's proposition to pass the constitution as it stood, and give perpetual instructions to the representatives of every state to insist on a bill of rights, I acknoleged the superiority of his plan, & advocated universal adoption. 2. The second charge is equally untrue. My whole correspondence while in France, & every word, letter, & act on the subject since my return, prove that no man is more ardently intent to see the public debt soon & sacredly paid off than I am. This exactly marks the difference between Colo Hamilton's views & mine, that would wish the debt paid tomorrow; he wishes it never to be paid, but always to be a thing where with to corrupt & manage the legislature. 3. I have never enquired what number of sons, relations & friends of Senators, representatives, printers or other useful partisans Colo Hamilton has provided for among the hundred clerks of his department, the thousand excisemen, custom-house officers, loan officers &c. &c. &c. appointed by him, or at his nod, and spread over the Union; nor could ever have imagined that the man who has the shuffling of millions backwards & forwards from paper into money & money into paper, from Europe to America, & America to Europe, the dealing out of Treasury-secrets among his friends in what time & measure he pleases, and who never slips an occasion of making friends with his means, that such an one I say would have brought forward a charge against me for having appointed the poet Freneau translating clerk to my office, with a salary of 250. dollars a year. That fact stands thus. While the government was at New York I was applied to on behalf of Freneau to know if there was any place within my department to which he could be appointed. I answered there were but four clerkships, all of which I found full, and continued without any change. When we removed to Philadelphia, Mr. Pintard the translating clerk, did not chuse to remove with us. His office then became vacant. I was again applied to there for Freneau, & had no hesitation to promise the clerkship for him. I cannot recollect whether it was at the same time, or afterwards, that I was told he had a thought of setting up a newspaper there. But whether then, or afterwards, I considered it as a circumstance of some value, as it might enable me to do, what had long wished to have done, that is, to have the material parts of the Leyden gazette brought under your eye & that of the public, in order to possess yourself & them of a juster view of the affairs of Europe than could be obtained from any other public source. This I had ineffectually attempted through the press of Mr. Fenno while in New York, selecting & translating passages myself at first then having it done by Mr. Pintard the translating clerk, but they found their way too slowly into Mr. Fenno's papers. Mr. Bache essayed it for me in Philadelphia, but his being a daily paper, did not circulate sufficiently in the other states. He even tried, at my request, the plan of a weekly paper of recapitulation from his daily paper, in hopes that that might go into the other states, but in this too we failed. Freneau, as translating clerk, & the printer of a periodical paper likely to circulate thro' the states (uniting in one person the parts of Pintard & Fenno) revived my hopes that the thing could at length be effected. On the establishment of his paper therefore, I furnished him with the Leyden gazettes, with an expression of my wish that he could always translate & publish the material intelligence they contained; & have continued to furnish them from time to time, as regularly as I received them. But as to any other direction or indication of my wish how his press should be conducted, what sort of intelligence he should give, what essays encourage, I can protest in the presence of heaven, that I never did by myself or any other, directly or indirectly, say a syllable, nor attempt any kind of influence. I can further protest, in the same awful presence, that I never did by myself or any other, directly or indirectly, write, dictate or procure any one sentence or sentiment to be inserted *in his, or any other gazette*, to which my name was not affixed or that of my office. —I surely need not except here a thing so foreign to the present subject as a little paragraph about our Algerine captives, which I put once into Fenno's paper. —Freneau's proposition to publish a paper, having been about the time that the writings of Publicola, & the discourses on Davila had a good deal excited the public attention, I took for granted from Freneau's character, which had been marked as that of a good whig, that he would give free place to pieces written against the aristocratical & monarchical principles these papers had inculcated. This having been in my mind, it is likely enough may have expressed it in conversation with others; tho' I do not recollect that I did. To Freneau I think I could not, because I had still seen him but once, & that was at a public table, at breakfast, at Mrs. Elsworth's, as I passed thro' New York the last year. And I can safely declare that my expectations looked only to the chastisement of the aristocratical & monarchical writers, & not to any criticisms on the proceedings of government: Colo Hamilton can see no motive for any appointment but that of making a convenient partizan. But you Sir, who have received from me recommendations of a Rittenhouse, Barlow, Paine, will believe that talents & science are sufficient motives with me in appointments to which they are fitted: & that Freneau, as a man of genius, might find a preference in my eye to be a translating clerk, & make good title to the little aids I could give him as the editor of a gazette, by procuring subscriptions to his paper, as I did some, before it appeared, & as I have with pleasure done for the labours of other men of genius. I hold it to be one of the distinguishing excellencies of elective over hereditary succesions, that the talents, which nature has provided in sufficient proportion, should be selected by the society for the government of their affairs, rather than that this should be transmitted through the loins of knaves & fools passing from the debauches of the table to those of the bed. Colo Hamilton, alias "Plain facts," says that Freneau's salary began before he resided in Philadelphia. I do not know what quibble he may have in reserve on the word "residence." He may mean to include under that idea the removal of his family; for I believe he removed, himself, before his family did, to Philadelphia. But no act of mine gave commencement to his salary before he so far took up his abode in Philadelphia as to be sufficiently in readiness for the duties of the office. As to the merits or demerits of his paper, they certainly concern me not. He & Fenno are rivals for the public favor. The one courts them by flattery, the other by censure, & I believe it will be admitted that the one has been as servile, as the other severe. But is not the dignity, & even decency of government committed, when one of it's principal ministers enlists himself as an anonymous writer or paragraphist for either the one or the other of them? —No government ought to be without censors: & where the press is free, no one ever will. If virtuous, it need not fear the fair operation of attack & defence. Nature has given to man no other means of sifting out the truth either in religion, law, or politics. I think it as honorable to the government neither to know, nor notice, it's sycophants or censors, as it would be undignified & criminal to pamper the former & persecute the latter. —So much for the past. A word now of the future.

When I came into this office, it was with a resolution to retire from it as soon as I could with decency. It pretty early appeared to me that the proper moment would be the first of those epochs at which the constitution seems to have contemplated a periodical change or renewal of the public servants. In this was confirmed by your resolution respecting the same period; from which however I am happy in hoping you have departed. I look to that period with the longing of a wave-worn mariner, who has at length the land in view, & shall count the days & hours which still lie between me & it. In the meanwhile my main object will be to wind up the business of my office avoiding as much as possible all new enterprize. With the affairs of the legislature, as I never did intermeddle, so I certainly shall not now begin. I am more desirous to predispose everything for the repose to which I am withdrawing, than expose it to be disturbed by newspaper contests. If these however cannot be avoided altogether, yet a regard for your quiet will be a sufficient motive for my deferring it till I become merely a private citizen, when the propriety or impropriety of what I may say or do may fall on myself alone. I may then too avoid the charge of misapplying that time which now belonging to those who employ me, should be wholly devoted to their service. If my own justification, or the interests of the republic shall require it, I reserve to myself the right of then appealing to my country, subscribing my name to whatever I write, & using with freedom & truth the facts & names necessary to place the cause in it's just form before that tribunal. To a thorough disregard of the honors & emoluments of office I join as great a value for the esteem of my countrymen,

& conscious of having merited it by an integrity which cannot be re-
proached, & by an enthusiastic devotion to their rights & liberty, I will not
suffer my retirement to be clouded by the slanders of a man whose history,
from the moment at which history can stoop to notice him, is a tissue of
machinations against the liberty of the country which has not only received
and given him bread, but heaped it's honors on his head. —Still however
I repeat the hope that it will not be necessary to make such an appeal.
Though little known to the people of America, I believe that, as far as I am
known, it is not as an enemy to the republic, nor an intriguer against it,
nor a waster of it's revenue, nor prostitutor of it to the purposes of corruption, as the American represents me; and I confide that yourself are
satisfied that, as to dissensions in the newspapers, not a syllable of them
has ever proceeded from me; & that no cabals or intrigues of mine have
produced those in the legislature, & I hope I may promise, both to you &
myself, that none will receive aliment from me during the short space I
have to remain in office, which will find ample employment in closing the
present business of the department.

4. To William Short, Philadelphia, 3 January 1793. *William Short
(1759–1849), TJ's secretary when he was the American minister in Paris, served as
chargé d'affaires after TJ's return to the United States. Short, a graduate in 1779 of
the College of William and Mary, had become TJ's protégé as a young man in Virginia: as TJ wrote in 1789, Short "is to me . . . as an adoptive son." This letter,
counseling a more favorable stance toward the increasingly radical Jacobin leadership of the French Revolution, is one of the most controversial in all of TJ's correspondence.*

The tone of your letters had for some time given me pain, on account
of the extreme warmth with which they censured the proceedings of the
Jacobins of France. I considered that sect as the same with the Republican
patriots, & the Feuillants as the Monarchical patriots, well known in the
early part of the revolution, & but little distant in their views, both having
in object the establishment of a free constitution, & differing only on the
question whether their chief Executive should be hereditary or not. The
Jacobins (as since called) yielded to the Feuillants & tried the experiment
of retaining their hereditary Executive. The experiment failed completely,
and would have brought on the reestablishment of despotism had it been
pursued. The Jacobins saw this, and that the expunging that officer was of
absolute necessity. And the Nation was with them in opinion, for however
they might have been formerly for the constitution framed by the first
assembly, they were come over from their hope in it, and were now generally Jacobins. In the struggle which was necessary, many guilty persons fell
without the forms of trial, and with them some innocent. These I deplore
as much as any body, & shall deplore some of them to the day of my death.
But I deplore them as I should have done had they fallen in battle. It was
necessary to use the arm of the people, a machine not quite so blind as
balls and bombs, but blind to a certain degree. A few of their cordial

friends met at their hands the fate of enemies. But time and truth will rescue & embalm their memories, while their posterity will be enjoying that very liberty for which they would never have hesitated to offer up their lives. The liberty of the whole earth was depending on the issue of the contest, and was ever such a prize won with so little innocent blood? My own affections have been deeply wounded by some of the martyrs to this cause, but rather than it should have failed, I would have seen half the earth desolated. Were there but an Adam & an Eve left in every country, & left free, it would be better than as it now is. have expressed to you my sentiments, because they are really those of 99. in an hundred of our citizens. The universal feasts, and rejoicings which have lately been had on account of the successes of the French shewed the genuine effusions of their hearts. You have been wounded by the sufferings of your friends, and have by this circumstance been hurried into a temper of mind which would be extremely disrelished if known to your countrymen. The *reserve of the President of the United States* had never permitted me to discover the light in which he viewed it, and as I was more anxious that you should satisfy him than me, I had still avoided explanations with you on the subject. But [*one of your letters*] induced him to break silence and to notice the extreme acrimony of your expressions. He added that he had been informed the sentiments you expressed in your conversations were equally offensive to our allies, & that you should consider yourself as the representative of your country and that what you say might be imputed to your constituents. He desired me therefore to write to you on this subject. He added that he considered *France as the sheet anchor of this country and its friendship as a first object.* There are in the U. S. some characters of opposite principles; some of them are high in office, others possessing great wealth, and all of them hostile to France and fondly looking to England as the staff of their hope. These I named to you on a former occasion. Their prospects have certainly not brightened. Excepting them, this country is entirely republican, friends to the constitution, anxious to preserve it and to have it administered according to it's own republican principles. The little party above mentioned have espoused it only as a stepping stone to monarchy, and have endeavored to approximate it to that in it's administration in order to render it's final transition more easy. The successes of republicanism in France have given the coup de grace to their prospects, and I hope to their projects. —I have developed to you faithfully the sentiments of your country, that you may govern yourself accordingly. I know your republicanism to be pure, and that it is no decay of that which has embittered you against it's votaries in France, but too great a sensibility at the partial evil which it's object has been accomplished there. I have written to you in the stile to which I have been always accustomed with you, and which perhaps it is time I should lay aside. But while old men are sensible enough of their own advance in years, they do not sufficiently recollect it in those whom they have seen young. In writing too the last private letter which will probably be written under present circumstances, in contemplating that your correspondence will shortly be turned over to I know not but certainly to some one not in the habit of considering your interests with the same fostering anxieties I do, I have presented things without reserve, satisfied you will ascribe what I have said to it's true motive, use it for your own best interest, and in that fulfil completely what I had in view.

5. To Angelica Church, Germantown, 27 November 1793. *TJ met Angelica Schuyler Church, daughter of Revolutionary General and statesman Philip Schuyler and sister-in-law of TJ's political rival Alexander Hamilton, in Paris in 1787. The wife of John Barker Church, an Englishman, she was one of several married women TJ befriended during these years; others included Maria Cosway and Marguerite-Victoire de Corny, both mentioned below. Lafayette was now a political prisoner in France.*

I have received, my good friend, your kind letter of August 19th, with the extract from that of Lafayette, for whom my heart has been constantly bleeding. The influence of the United States has been put into action, as far as it could be either with decency or effect. But I fear that distance and difference of principle give little hold to General Washington on the jailers of Lafayette. However, his friends may be assured that our zeal has not been inactive. Your letter gives me the first information that our dear friend Madame de Corny has been, as to her fortune among the victims of the times. Sad times, indeed! and much lamented victim! I know no country where the remains of a fortune could place her so much at her ease as this, and where public esteem is so attached to worth, regardless of wealth; but our manners, and the state of our society here, are so different from those to which her habits have been formed, that she would lose more perhaps in that scale. And Madame Cosway in a convent! I knew that to much goodness of heart she joined enthusiasm and religion; but I thought that very enthusiasm would have prevented her from shutting up her adoration of the God of the universe within the walls of a cloister; that she would rather have sought the *mountain-top*. How happy should I be that it were *mine* that you, she, and Madame de Corny would seek. You say, indeed, that you are coming to America, but I know that means New York. In the meantime I am going to Virginia. I have at length become able to fix that to the beginning of the new year. I am then to be liberated from the hated occupations of politics, and to remain in the bosom of my family, my farm, and my books. I have my house to build, my fields to farm, and to watch for the happiness of those who labor for mine. I have one daughter married to a man of science, sense, virtue, and competence; in whom indeed I have nothing more to wish. They live with me. If the other shall be as fortunate, in due process of time I shall imagine myself as blessed as the most blessed of the patriarchs. Nothing could then withdraw my thoughts a moment from home but the recollection of my friends abroad. I often put the question, whether yourself and Kitty will ever come to see your friends at Monticello? but it is my affection and not my experience of things which has leave to answer, and I am determined to believe the answer, because in that belief I find I sleep sounder, and wake more cheerful.

6. From the Report on the Privileges and Restrictions on the Commerce of the United States in Foreign Countries, 16 December 1793. *TJ submitted this report to the House of Representatives just two weeks before resigning from his position of secretary of state. Since 1791, when the British government refused to negotiate a commercial treaty with the Americans, TJ had been developing the arguments set forth in this excerpt. His long-cherished hope was that the United States could dismantle remaining mercantilist restrictions on trade through commercial treaties ("friendly arrangements") or by imposing "countervailing" restrictions on powers—like Britain—that refused to negotiate favorable terms. Mounting British depredations on American shipping, justified by the British government's expansive definition of its rights under its navigation acts, offered a favorable opportunity for the aggressive response through trade sanctions that TJ and his allies had been agitating for years. The Republican majority in the recently elected House promised a warm reception to TJ's proposed reorientation of American foreign policy. By this time, the split over foreign policy was the leading cause of party divisions, Federalists favoring Britain and Jeffersonian Republicans tilting toward France.*

. . . Such being the restrictions on the commerce and navigation of the United States; the question is, in what way they may best be removed, modified or counteracted?

As to commerce, two methods occur. 1. By friendly arrangements with the several nations with whom these restrictions exist; Or, 2. By the separate act of our own legislatures for countervailing their effects.

There can be no doubt but that of these two, friendly arrangements is the most eligible. Instead of embarrassing commerce under piles of regulating laws, duties, and prohibitions, could it be relieved from all its shackles in all parts of the world, could every country be employed in producing that which nature has best fitted it to produce, and each be free to exchange with others mutual surplusses for mutual wants, the greatest mass possible would then be produced of those things which contribute to human life and human happiness; the numbers of mankind would be increased, and their condition bettered.

Would even a single nation begin with the United States this system of free commerce, it would be advisable to begin it with that nation; since it is one by one only that it can be extended to all. Where the circumstances of either party render it expedient to levy a revenue, by way of impost, on commerce, its freedom might be modified, in that particular, by mutual and equivalent measures, preserving it entire in all others.

Some nations, not yet ripe for free commerce in all its extent, might still be willing to mollify its restrictions and regulations for us, in proportion to the advantages which an intercourse with us might offer. Particularly they may concur with us in reciprocating the duties to be levied on each side, or in compensating any excess of duty by equivalent advantages of another nature. Our commerce is certainly of a character to entitle it to favor in most countries. The commodities we offer are either necessaries of life, or materials for manufacture, or convenient subjects of revenue; and we take in exchange, either manufactures, when they have received the last finish of art and industry, or mere luxuries. Such customers may reasonably expect welcome and friendly treatment at every market. Customers, too, whose demands, increasing with their wealth and population, must very shortly give full employment to the whole industry of any nation whatever, in any line of supply they may get into the habit of calling for from it.

But should any nation, contrary to our wishes, suppose it may better find its advantage by continuing its system of prohibitions, duties and regulations, it behooves us to protect our citizens, their commerce and navigation, by counter prohibitions, duties and regulations, also. Free commerce and navigation are not to be given in exchange for restrictions and vexations; nor are they likely to produce a relaxation of them.

Our navigation involves still higher considerations. As a branch of industry, it is valuable, but as a resource of defence, essential.

Its value, as a branch of industry, is enhanced by the dependence of so many other branches on it. In times of general peace it multiplies competitors for employment in transportation, and so keeps that at its proper level; and in times of war, that is to say, when those nations who may be our principal carriers, shall be at war with each other, if we have not within ourselves the means of transportation, our produce must be exported in belligerent vessels, at the increased expense of war-freight and insurance, and the articles which will not bear that, must perish on our hands.

But it is as a resource of defence that our navigation will admit neither negligence nor forbearance. The position and circumstances of the United States leave them nothing to fear on their land-board, and nothing to desire beyond their present rights. But on their seaboard, they are open to injury, and they have there, too, a commerce which must be protected. This can only be done by possessing a respectable body of citizen-seamen, and of artists and establishments in readiness for ship-building.

Were the ocean, which is the common property of all, open to the industry of all, so that every person and vessel should be free to take employment wherever it could be found, the United States would certainly not set the example of appropriating to themselves, exclusively, any portion of the common stock of occupation. They would rely on the enterprise and activity of their citizens for a due participation of the benefits of the seafaring business, and for keeping the marine class of citizens equal to their object. But if particular nations grasp at undue shares, and, more especially, if they seize on the means of the United States, to convert them into aliment for their own strength, and withdraw them entirely from the support of those to whom they belong, defensive and protecting measures become necessary on the part of the nation whose marine resources are thus invaded; or it will be disarmed of its defence; its productions will lie at the mercy of the nation which has possessed itself exclusively of the means of carrying them, and its politics may be influenced by those who command its commerce. The carriage of our own commodities, if once established in another channel, cannot be resumed in the moment we may desire. If we lose the seamen and artists whom it now occupies, we lose the present means of marine defence, and time will be requisite to raise up others, when disgrace or losses shall bring home to our feelings the error of having abandoned them. The materials for maintaining our due share of navigation, are ours in abundance. And, as to the mode of using them, we have only to adopt the principles of those who put us on the defensive, or others equivalent and better fitted to our circumstances.

The following principles, being founded in reciprocity, appear perfectly just, and to offer no cause of complaint to any nation:

1. Where a nation imposes high duties on our productions, or prohibits them altogether, it may be proper for us to do the same by theirs; first burdening or excluding those productions which they bring here, in competition with our own of the same kind; selecting next, such manufactures as we take from them in greatest quantity, and which, at the same time, we could the soonest furnish to ourselves, or obtain from other countries; imposing on them duties lighter at first, but heavier and heavier afterwards, as other channels of supply open. Such duties having the effect of indirect encouragement to domestic manufactures of the same kind, may induce the manufacturer to come himself into these States, where cheaper subsistence, equal laws, and a vent of his wares, free of duty, may ensure him the highest profits from his skill and industry. And here, it would be in the power of the State governments to co-operate essentially, by opening the resources of encouragement which are under their control, extending them liberally to artists in those particular branches of manufacture for which their soil, climate, population and other circumstances have matured them, and fostering the precious efforts and progress of *household* manufacture, by some patronage suited to the nature of its objects, guided by the local informations they possess, and guarded against abuse by their presence and attentions. The oppressions on our agriculture, in foreign ports, would thus be made the occasion of relieving it from a dependence on the councils and conduct of others, and of promoting arts, manufactures and population at home.

2. Where a nation refuses permission to our merchants and factors to reside within certain parts of their dominions, we may, if it should be thought expedient, refuse residence to theirs in any and every part of ours, or modify their transactions.

3. Where a nation refuses to receive in our vessels any productions but our own, we may refuse to receive, in theirs, any but their own productions. The first and second clauses of the bill reported by the committee, are well formed to effect this object.

4. Where a nation refuses to consider any vessel as ours which has not been built within our territories, we should refuse to consider as theirs, any vessel not built within their territories.

5. Where a nation refuses to our vessels the carriage even of our own productions, to certain countries under their domination, we might refuse to theirs of every description, the carriage of the same productions to the same countries. But as justice and good neighborhood would dictate that those who have no part in imposing the restriction on us, should not be the victims of measures adopted to defeat its effect, it may be proper to confine the restrictions to vessels owned or navigated by any subjects of the same dominant power, other than the inhabitants of the country to which the said productions are to be carried. And to prevent all inconvenience to the said inhabitants, and to our own, by too sudden a check on the

means of transportation, we may continue to admit the vessels marked for future exclusion, on an advanced tonnage, and for such length of time only, as may be supposed necessary to provide against that inconvenience.

The establishment of some of these principles by Great Britain, alone, has already lost to us in our commerce with that country and its possessions, between eight and nine hundred vessels of near 40,000 tons burden, according to statements from official materials, in which they have confidence. This involves a proportional loss of seamen, shipwrights, and shipbuilding, and is too serious a loss to admit forbearance of some effectual remedy.

It is true we must expect some inconvenience in practice from the establishment of discriminating duties. But in this, as in so many other cases, we are left to choose between two evils. These inconveniences are nothing when weighed against the loss of wealth and loss of force, which will follow our perseverance in the plan of indiscrimination. When once it shall be perceived that we are either in the system or in the habit of giving equal advantages to those who extinguish our commerce and navigation by duties and prohibitions, as to those who treat both with liberality and justice, liberality and justice will be converted by all into duties and prohibitions. It is not to the moderation and justice of others we are to trust for fair and equal access to market with our productions, or for our due share in the transportation of them; but to our own means of independence, and the firm will to use them. Nor do the inconveniences of discrimination merit consideration. Not one of the nations before mentioned, perhaps not a commercial nation on earth, is without them. In our case one distinction alone will suffice: that is to say, between nations who favor our productions and navigation, and those who do not favor them. One set of moderate duties, say the present duties, for the first, and a fixed advance on these as to some articles, and prohibitions as to others, for the last.

Still, it must be repeated that friendly arrangements are preferable with all who will come into them; and that we should carry into such arrangements all the liberality and spirit of accommodation which the nature of the case will admit.

France has, of her own accord, proposed negotiations for improving, by a new treaty on fair and equal principles, the commercial relations of the two countries. But her internal disturbances have hitherto prevented the prosecution of them to effect, though we have had repeated assurances of a continuance of the disposition.

Proposals of friendly arrangement have been made on our part, by the present government, to that of Great Britain, as the message states; but, being already on as good a footing in law, and a better in fact, than the most favored nation, they have not, as yet, discovered any disposition to have it meddled with.

We have no reason to conclude that friendly arrangements would be declined by the other nations, with whom we have such commercial intercourse as may render them important. In the meanwhile, it would rest with the wisdom of Congress to determine whether, as to those nations, they will not surcease *ex parte* regulations, on the reasonable presumption that they will concur in doing whatever justice and moderation dictate should be done.

7. To James Madison, Monticello, 28 December 1794. *In August and September 1794 President Washington issued proclamations ordering the suppression of the Whiskey Rebellion in western Pennsylvania. The rebellion reflected the discontent of backcountry distillers with federal efforts to collect an excise on whiskey; for Alexander Hamilton, who marched west with an expeditionary force to suppress the rebels, the federal government's ability to levy excises and other internal taxes was crucial to its long-term survival. In its response to Washington's Annual Message of 19 November 1794, explaining the successful measures he had taken against the rebels, the Federalist Senate castigated "certain self-created societies" for fomenting opposition to government. The reference was to the Democratic-Republican societies that had been so energetic in mobilizing popular support for the Republican cause.*

The denunciation of the democratic societies is one of the extraordinary acts of boldness of which we have seen so many from the fraction of monocrats. It is wonderful indeed, that the President should have permitted himself to be the organ of such an attack on the freedom of discussion, the freedom of writing, printing & publishing. It must be a matter of rare curiosity to get at the modifications of these rights proposed by them, and to see what line their ingenuity would draw between democratical societies, whose avowed object is the nourishment of the republican principles of our constitution, and the society of the Cincinnati, *a self-created* one, carving out for itself hereditary distinctions, lowering over our Constitution eternally, meeting together in all parts of the Union, periodically, with closed doors, accumulating a capital in their separate treasury, corresponding secretly & regularly, & of which society the very persons denouncing the democrats are themselves the fathers, founders, & high officers. Their sight must be perfectly dazzled by the glittering of crowns & coronets, not to see the extravagance of the proposition to suppress the friends of general freedom, while those who wish to confine that freedom to the few, are permitted to go on in their principles & practices. I here put out of sight the persons whose misbehavior has been taken advantage of to slander the friends of popular rights; and I am happy to observe, that as far as the circle of my observation & information extends, everybody has lost sight of them, and views the abstract attempt on their natural & constitutional rights in all it's nakedness. I have never heard, or heard of, a single expression or opinion which did not condemn it as an inexcusable aggression. And with respect to the transactions against the excise law, it appears to me that you are all swept away in the torrent of governmental opinions, or that we do not know what these transactions have been. We know of none which, according to the definitions of the law, have been anything more than riotous. There was indeed a meeting to consult about a separation. But to consult on a question does not amount to a determination of that question in the affirmative, still less to the acting on such a determination; but we shall see, I suppose, what the court lawyers, & courtly judges, & would-be ambassadors will make of it. The excise law is an infernal one. The first error was to admit it by the Constitution; the 2d., to act on that admission; the 3d & last will be, to make it the instrument of dismembering the Union, & setting us all afloat to chuse which part of it we will adhere to. The information of our militia, returned from the Westward, is uniform, that tho the people there let them pass quietly, they were objects of their laughter, not of their fear; that 1000 men could have cut off their whole force in a thousand places of the Alleganey; that their detestation of the excise law is universal, and has now associated to it a detestation of the government; & that separation which perhaps was a very distant & problematical event, is now near, & certain, & determined in the mind of every man. I expected to have seen some justification of arming one part of the society against another; of declaring a civil war the moment before the meeting of that body which has the sole right of declaring war; of being so patient of the kicks & scoffs of our enemies, & rising at a feather against our friends; of adding a million to the public debt & deriding us with recommendations to pay it if we can &c., &c. But the part of the speech which was to be taken as a justification of the armament, reminded me of parson Saunders' demonstration why minus into minus make plus. After a parcel of shreds of stuff from Aesop's fables, and Tom Thumb, he jumps all at once into his Ergo, minus multiplied into minus make plus. Just so the 15,000 men enter after the fables, in the speech. —However, the time is coming when we shall fetch up the leeway of our vessel. The changes in your house, I see, are going on for the better, and even the Augean herd over your heads are slowly purging off their impurities. Hold on then, my dear friend, that we may not shipwreck in the meanwhile. I do not see, in the minds of those with whom I converse, a greater affliction than the fear of your retirement; but this must not be, unless to a more splendid & a more efficacious post. There I should rejoice to see you; I hope I may say, I shall rejoice to see you. I have long had much in my mind to say to you on that subject. But double delicacies have kept me silent. I ought perhaps to say, while I would not give up my own retirement for the empire of the universe, how I can justify wishing one whose happiness I have so much at heart as yours, to take the front of the battle which is fighting for my security. This would be easy enough to be done, but not at the heel of a lengthy epistle.

8. To Jean Nicolas Démeunier, Monticello, 29 April 1795. *In 1786 Jean Nicolas Démeunier (1751–1814), a friend from TJ's Paris years, had asked TJ about American slavery. As editor of the* Encyclopédie méthodique, *Démeunier had sought TJ's comments on his book-length entry on the United States. The Brissotine or Girondist faction had been driven from power by more radical elements in the Jacobin coalition in mid-1793.*

Being myself a warm zealot for the attainment & enjoiment by all mankind of as much liberty, as each may exercise without injury to the equal liberty of his fellow citizens, I have lamented that in France the endeavours to obtain this should have been attended with the effusion of so much blood. I was intimate with the leading characters of the year 1789.

So I was with those of the Brissotine party who succeeded them: & have always been persuaded that their views were upright. Those who have followed have been less known to me: but I have been willing to hope that they also meant the establishment of a free government in their country, excepting perhaps the party which has lately been suppressed. The government of those now at the head of affairs appears to hold out many indications of good sense, moderation & virtue; & I cannot but presume from their character as well as your own that you would find a perfect safety in the bosom of your own country. I think it fortunate for the United States to have become the asylum for so many virtuous patriots of different denominations: but their circumstances, with which you were so well acquainted before, enabled them to be but a bare asylum, & to offer nothing for them but an entire freedom to use their own means & faculties as they please. There is no such thing in this country as what would be called wealth in Europe. The richest are but a little at ease, & obliged to pay the most rigorous attention to their affairs to keep them together. I do not mean to speak here of the Beaujons of America. For we have some of these tho' happily they are but ephemeral. Our public oeconomy also is such as to offer drudgery and subsistence only to those entrusted with its administration, a wise & necessary precaution against the degeneracy of the public servants. In our private pursuits it is a great advantage that every honest employment is deemed honorable. I am myself a nail-maker. On returning home after an absence of ten years, I found my farms so much deranged that I saw evidently they would be a burden to me instead of a support till I could regenerate them; & consequently that it was necessary for me to find some other resource in the meantime. I thought for awhile of taking up the manufacture of pot-ash, which requires but small advances of money. I concluded at length however to begin a manufacture of nails, which needs little or no capital, & I now employ a dozen little boys from 10. to 16. years of age, overlooking all the details of their business myself & drawing from it a profit on which can get along till I can put my farms into a course of yielding profit. My new trade of nail-making is to me in this country what an additional title of nobility or the ensigns of a new order are in Europe. In the commercial line, the grocers business is that which requires the least capital in this country. The grocer generally obtains a credit of three months, & sells for ready money so as to be able to make his paiments & obtain a new supply. But I think I have observed that your countrymen who have been obliged to work out their own fortunes here, have succeeded best with a small farm. Labour indeed is dear here, but rents are low & on the whole a reasonable profit & comfortable subsistence results. It is at the same time the most tranquil, healthy, & independent.

9. To Philip Mazzei, Monticello, 24 April 1796. *Philip Mazzei (1730–1816) came to Virginia from Italy in 1773 and settled for a time in Albemarle County. Returning to Europe permanently in 1785, Mazzei was a leading advocate of liberal causes. This letter, first published in a Florentine newspaper and then in the Paris* Moniteur, *caused a scandal in the United States when it was reprinted here in May 1797. At a time when American public opinion was warming toward*

Britain and relations with France were rapidly deteriorating, Vice President Jefferson stood revealed as a rabidly partisan Anglophobe.

I enclosed in two of [*my letters to you*] some seeds of the squash as you desired. Send me in return some seeds of the winter vetch, I mean that kind which is sewn in autumn & stands thro the cold of winter, furnishing a crop of green fodder in March. Put a few seeds in every letter you may write to me. In England only the spring vetch can be had. Pray fail not in this. I have it greatly at heart.

The aspect of our politics has wonderfully changed since you left us. In place of that noble love of liberty, & republican government which carried us triumphantly thro' the war, an Anglican monarchical, & aristocratical party has sprung up, whose avowed object is to draw over us the substance, as they have already done the forms, of the British government. The main body of our citizens, however, remain true to their republican principles; the whole landed interest is republican, and so is a great mass of talents. Against us are the Executive, the Judiciary, two out of three branches of the legislature, all the officers of the government, all who want to be officers, all timid men who prefer the calm of despotism to the boisterous sea of liberty, British merchants & Americans trading on British capitals, speculators & holders in the banks & public funds, a contrivance invented for the purposes of corruption, & for assimilating us in all things to the rotten as well as the sound parts of the British model. It would give you a fever were I to name to you the apostates who have gone over to these heresies, men who were Samsons in the field & Solomons in the council, but who have had their heads shorn by the harlot England. In short, we are likely to preserve the liberty we have obtained only by unremitting labors & perils. But we shall preserve them; and our mass of weight & wealth on the good side is so great, as to leave no danger that force will ever be attempted against us. We have only to awake and snap the Lilliputian cords with which they have been entangling us during the first sleep which succeeded our labors. . . . I begin to feel the effects of age. My health has suddenly broke down, with symptoms which give me to believe I shall not have much to encounter of the *tedium vitae.*

10. To John Taylor, Philadelphia, 4 June 1798. *John Taylor of Caroline (1754–1824), Revolutionary War veteran, lawyer, and agricultural reformer, served as senator from Virginia from October 1792 until his resignation in May 1794. In a series of important pamphlets beginning with* An Examination of the Late Proceedings in Congress, *published in 1793, the arch-Republican Taylor developed an ideologically rigorous critique of Federalism. In this letter, TJ seeks to temper his alienated colleague's disunionist tendencies during the "reign of witches."*

I promised you, long ago, a description of a mould board. I now send it; it is a press copy & therefore dim. It will be less so by putting a sheet of white paper behind the one you are reading. I would recommend to you first to have a model made of about 3 i. to the foot, or 1/4 the real dimensions, and to have two blocks, the 1st of which, after taking out the pyramidal piece & sawing it crosswise above & below, should be preserved in that form to instruct workmen in making the large & real one. The 2^d block may be carried through all the operations, so as to present the form of the mould board complete. If I had an opportunity of sending you a model I would do it. It has been greatly approved here, as it has been before by some very good judges at my house, where I have used it for 5 years with entire approbation.

Mr. New shewed me your letter on the subject of the patent, which gave me an opportunity of observing what you said as to the effect with you of public proceedings, and that it was not unusual now to estimate the separate mass of Virginia and N. Carolina with a view to their separate existence. It is true that we are compleatly under the saddle of Massachusets & Connecticut, and that they ride us very hard, cruelly insulting our feelings as well as exhausting our strength and substance. Their natural friends, the three other eastern States, join them from a sort of family pride, and they have the art to divide certain other parts of the Union so as to make use of them to govern the whole. This is not new. It is the old practice of despots to use a part of the people to keep the rest in order, and those who have once got an ascendency and possessed themselves of all the resources of the nation, their revenues and offices, have immense means for retaining their advantages. But our present situation is not a natural one. The body of our countrymen is substantially republican through every part of the Union. It was the irresistable influence & popularity of Genl Washington, played off by the cunning of Hamilton, which turned the government over to anti-republican hands, or turned the republican members, chosen by the people, into anti-republicans. He delivered it over to his successor in this state, and very untoward events, since improved with great artifice, have produced on the public mind the impression we see; but still, repeat it, this is not the natural state. Time alone would bring round an order of things more correspondent to the sentiments of our constituents; but are there not events impending which will do it within a few months? The invasion of England, the public and authentic avowal of sentiments hostile to the leading principles of our Constitution, the prospect of a war in which we shall stand alone, land-tax, stamp-tax, increase of public debt, &c. Be this as it may, in every free & deliberating society there must, from the nature of man, be opposite parties & violent dissensions & discords; and one of these, for the most part, must prevail over the other for a longer or shorter time. Perhaps this party division is necessary to induce each to watch & delate to the people the proceedings of the other. But if on a temporary superiority of the one party, the other is to resort to a scission of the Union, no federal government can ever exist. If to rid ourselves of the present rule of Massachusets & Connecticut we break the Union, will the evil stop there? Suppose the N. England States alone cut off, will our natures be changed? are we not men still to the south of that, & with all the passions of men? Immediately we shall see a Pennsylvania & a Virginia party arise in the residuary confederacy, and the public mind will be distracted with the same party spirit. What a game, too, will the one party have in their hands by eternally threatening the other that unless they do so & so, they will join their Northern neighbors. If we reduce our Union to Virginia

& N. Carolina, immediately the conflict will be established between the representatives of these two States, and they will end by breaking into their simple units. Seeing, therefore, that an association of men who will not quarrel with one another is a thing which never yet existed, from the greatest confederacy of nations down to a town meeting or a vestry, seeing that we must have somebody to quarrel with, I had rather keep our New England associates for that purpose than to see our bickerings transferred to others. They are circumscribed within such narrow limits, & their population so full, that their numbers will ever be the minority, and they are marked, like the Jews, with such a peculiarity of character as to constitute from that circumstance the natural division of our parties. A little patience, and we shall see the reign of witches pass over, their spells dissolve, and the people, recovering their true sight, restore their government to it's true principles. It is true that in the mean time we are suffering deeply in spirit, and incurring the horrors of a war & long oppressions of enormous public debt. But who can say what would be the evils of a scission, and when & where they would end? Better keep together as we are, hawl off from Europe as soon as we can, & from all attachments to any portions of it. And if we feel their power just sufficiently to hoop us together, it will be the happiest situation in which we can exist. If the game runs sometimes against us at home we must have patience till luck turns, & then we shall have an opportunity of winning back the *principles* we have lost, for this is a game where principles are the stake. Better luck, therefore, to us all; and health, happiness, & friendly salutations to yourself. Adieu.

P. S. It is hardly necessary to caution you to let nothing of mine get before the public. A single sentence, got hold of by the Porcupines, will suffice to abuse & persecute me in their papers for months.

11. To Samuel Smith, Monticello, 22 August 1798. *Samuel Smith (1752–1839) of Maryland was a Republican member of Congress from 1793 to 1803. The failure of American commissioners to head off impending conflict with France in the notorious XYZ affair that stretched from October 1797 to January 1798 constituted an enormous setback for Francophile Republicans; TJ vainly hoped that Elbridge Gerry, the only commissioner who remained in France, would be able to save the day by negotiating a last minute peace with Charles Maurice de Talleyrand-Périgord, the French foreign minister. The publication of the XYZ dispatches in April and the undeclared naval war with France from July 1798 to 1800 brought John Adams' Federalist administration unprecedented public support. Partisanship was also fueled by scandal. TJ begins by assuring Smith that he had taken no direct role in the recent revelation of Alexander Hamilton's adulterous affair with Maria Reynolds and her husband's subsequent blackmailing of Hamilton.*

Your favor of Aug 4 came to hand by our last post, together with the "extract of a letter from a gentleman of Philadelphia, dated July 10," cut from a newspaper stating some facts which respect me. I shall notice these facts. The writer says that "the day after the last despatches were communicated to Congress, Bache, Leib, &c. , and a Dr. Reynolds were closeted with me." If the receipt of visits in my public room, the door continuing free to every one who should call at the same time, may be called closeting, then it is true that was closeted with every person who visited me; in no other sense is it true as to any person. I sometimes received visits from Mr. Bache & Dr. Leib. I received them always with pleasure, because they are men of abilities, and of principles the most friendly to liberty & our present form of government. Mr. Bache has another claim on my respect, as being the grandson of Dr. Franklin, the greatest man & ornament of the age and country in which he lived. Whether I was visited by Mr. Bache or Dr. Leib the day after the communication referred to, I do not remember. I know that all my motions at Philadelphia, here, and everywhere, are watched & recorded. Some of these spies, therefore, may remember better than I do, the dates of these visits. If they say these two gentlemen visited me on the day after the communications, as their trade proves their accuracy, I shall not contradict them, tho' I affirm that I do not recollect it. However, as to Dr. Reynolds I can be more particular, because never saw him but once, which was on an introductory visit he was so kind as to pay me. This, I well remember, was before the communication alluded to, & that during the short conversation had with him, not one word was said on the subject of any of the communications. Not that I should not have spoken freely on their subject to Dr. Reynolds, as I should also have done to the letter writer, or to any other person who should have introduced the subject. I know my own principles to be pure, & therefore am not ashamed of them. On the contrary, I wish them known, & therefore willingly express them to every one. They are the same I have acted on from the year 1775 to this day, and are the same, I am sure, with those of the great body of the American people. I only wish the real principles of those who censure mine were also known. But warring against those of the people, the delusion of the people is necessary to the dominant party. see the extent to which that delusion has been already carried, and I see there is no length to which it may not be pushed by a party in possession of the revenues & the legal authorities of the U S, for a short time indeed, but yet long enough to admit much particular mischief. There is no event, therefore, however atrocious, which may not be expected. I have contemplated every event which the Maratists of the day can perpetrate, and am prepared to meet every one in such a way, as shall not be derogatory either to the public liberty or my own personal honor. The letter writer says, I am "for peace; but it is only with France." He has told half the truth. He would have told the whole, if he had added England. I am for peace with both countries. I know that both of them have given, & are daily giving, sufficient cause of war; that in defiance of the laws of nations, they are every day trampling on the rights of all the neutral powers, whenever they can thereby do the least injury, either to the other. But, as I view a peace between France & England the ensuing winter to be certain, I have thought it would have been better for us to continue to bear from France through the present summer, what we have been bearing both from her & England these four years, and still continue to bear from England, and to have required indemnification in the hour of peace, when I verily believe it would have been yielded by both. This seems to be the plan of the other neutral nations; and whether this, or the commencing war on one of them, as we have done, would have been wisest, time & events must decide. But am quite at a loss on what ground the letter writer can question the opinion, that France had no intention of making war on us, & was willing to treat with Mr. Gerry, when we have this from Taleyrand's letter, and from the written and verbal information of our envoys. It is true then, that, as with England, we might of right have chosen either peace or war, & have chosen peace, and prudently in my opinion, so with France, we might also of right have chosen either peace or war, & we have chosen war. Whether the choice may be a popular one in the other States, I know not. Here it certainly is not; & I have no doubt the whole American people will rally ere long to the same sentiment, & rejudge those who, at present, think they have all judgment in their own hands.

These observations will show you, how far the imputations in the paragraph sent me approach the truth. Yet they are not intended for a newspaper. At a very early period of my life, I determined never to put a sentence into any newspaper. I have religiously adhered to the resolution through my life, and have great reason to be contented with it. Were I to undertake to answer the calumnies of the newspapers, it would be more than all my own time, & that of 20. aids could effect. For while should be answering one, twenty new ones would be invented. have thought it better to trust to the justice of my countrymen, that they would judge me by what they *see* of my conduct on the stage where they have placed me, & what they know of me *before* the epoch since which a particular party has supposed it might answer some view of theirs to vilify me in the public eye. Some, I know, will not reflect how apocryphal is the testimony of enemies so palpably betraying the views with which they give it. But this is an injury to which duty requires every one to submit whom the public think proper to call inn to it's councils. thank you, my dear Sir, for the interest you have taken for me on this occasion. Though I have made up my mind not to suffer calumny to disturb my tranquillity, yet I retain all my sensibilities for the approbation of the good & just. That is, indeed, the chief consolations for the hatred of so many, who, without the least personal knowledge, & on the sacred evidence of Porcupine & Fenno alone, cover me with their implacable hatred. The only return I will ever make them, will be to do them all the good I can, in spite of their teeth.

12. Draft of the Kentucky Resolutions, October 1798. *Driven to desperate measures by the Federalists' complete control of the federal government, Jefferson and his Republican colleagues sought to mobilize popular opposition at the state level. The administration's controversial Alien Act, adopted in June 1798, and Sedition Act of July were designed to destroy Republicanism by extending the period of naturalization from five to fourteen years, by authorizing the President to remove aliens (who gravitated to the Republicans), and by giving federal courts the power to punish and suppress Republican editors making "any false, scandalous, and malicious writing" against the administration. TJ's draft Resolutions, printed* *below, revised at James Madison's suggestion to exclude the portentous reference to "nullification," were submitted to the Kentucky Legislature by TJ's friend and partisan ally John Breckinridge and approved on 16 and 22 November; their authorship remained a secret. Together with Madison's more moderate Virginia Resolutions, adopted by the Virginia legislature on 24 December, the Kentucky Resolutions set forth what Republicans would subsequently celebrate as "The Principles of '98." The immediate response was, however, not encouraging; the legislatures of other states either ignored or denounced Jefferson's and Madison's interpretation of the federal compact.*

1. *Resolved,* That the several States composing the United States of America, are not united on the principle of unlimited submission to their General Government; but that, by a compact under the style and title of a Constitution for the United States, and of amendments thereto, they constituted a General Government for special purposes,—delegated to that government certain definite powers, reserving, each State to itself, the residuary mass of right to their own self-government; and that whensoever the General Government assumes undelegated powers, its acts are unauthoritative, void, and of no force; that to this compact each State acceded as a State, and is an integral party, its co-States forming, as to itself, the other party: that the government created by this compact was not made the exclusive or final judge of the extent of the powers delegated to itself; since that would have made its discretion, and not the Constitution, the measure of its powers; but that, as in all other cases of compact among powers having no common judge, each party has an equal right to judge for itself, as well of infractions as of the mode and measure of redress.

2. *Resolved,* That the Constitution of the United States, having delegated to Congress a power to punish treason, counterfeiting the securities and current coin of the United States, piracies, and felonies committed on the high seas, and offences against the law of nations, and no other crimes whatsoever; and it being true as a general principle, and one of the amendments to the Constitution having also declared, that "the powers not delegated to the United States by the Constitution, nor prohibited by it to the States, are reserved to the States respectively, or to the people," therefore the act of Congress, passed on the 14th day of July, 1798, and intituled "An Act in addition to the act intituled An Act for the punishment of certain crimes against the United States," as also the act passed by them on the — day of June, 1798, intituled "An Act to punish frauds committed on the bank of the United States," (and all their other acts which assume to create, define, or punish crimes, other than those so enumerated in the Constitution,) are altogether void, and of no force; and that the power to create, define, and punish such other crimes is reserved, and, of right, appertains solely and exclusively to the respective States, each within its own territory.

3. *Resolved,* That it is true as a general principle, and is also expressly declared by one of the amendments to the Constitution, that "the powers not delegated to the United States by the Constitution, nor prohibited by it to the States, are reserved to the States respectively, or to the people;" and that no power over the freedom of religion, freedom of speech, or freedom of the press being delegated to the United States by the Consti-

tution, nor prohibited by it to the States, all lawful powers respecting the same did of right remain, and were reserved to the States or the people: that thus was manifested their determination to retain to themselves the right of judging how far the licentiousness of speech and of the press may be abridged without lessening their useful freedom, and how far those abuses which cannot be separated from their use should be tolerated, rather than the use be destroyed. And thus also they guarded against all abridgment by the United States of the freedom of religious opinions and exercises, and retained to themselves the right of protecting the same, as this State, by a law passed on the general demand of its citizens, had already protected them from all human restraint or interference. And that in addition to this general principle and express declaration, another and more special provision has been made by one of the amendments to the Constitution, which expressly declares, that "Congress shall make no law respecting an establishment of religion, or prohibiting the free exercise thereof, or abridging the freedom of speech or of the press:" thereby guarding in the same sentence, and under the same words, the freedom of religion, of speech, and of the press: insomuch, that whatever violated either, throws down the sanctuary which covers the others, and that libels, falsehood, and defamation, equally with heresy and false religion, are withheld from the cognizance of federal tribunals. That, therefore, the act of Congress of the United States, passed on the 14th day of July, 1798, intituled "An Act in addition to the act intituled An Act for the punishment of certain crimes against the United States," which does abridge the freedom of the press, is not law, but is altogether void, and of no force.

4. *Resolved,* That alien friends are under the jurisdiction and protection of the laws of the State wherein they are: that no power over them has been delegated to the United States, nor prohibited to the individual States, distinct from their power over citizens. And it being true as a general principle, and one of the amendments to the Constitution having also declared, that "the powers not delegated to the United States by the Constitution, nor prohibited by it to the States, are reserved to the States respectively, or to the people," the act of the Congress of the United States, passed on the — day of July, 1798, intituled "An Act concerning aliens," which assumes powers over alien friends, not delegated by the Constitution, is not law, but is altogether void, and of no force.

5. *Resolved,* That in addition to the general principle, as well as the express declaration, that powers not delegated are reserved, another and more special provision, inserted in the Constitution from abundant caution, has declared that "the migration or importation of such persons as any of the States now existing shall think proper to admit, shall not be prohibited by the Congress prior to the year 1808;" that this commonwealth does admit the migration of alien friends, described as the subject of the said act concerning aliens: that a provision against prohibiting their migration, is a provision against all acts equivalent thereto, or it would be nugatory: that to remove them when migrated, is equivalent to a prohibition of their migration, and is, therefore, contrary to the said provision of the Constitution, and void.

6. *Resolved,* That the imprisonment of a person under the protection of the laws of this commonwealth, on his failure to obey the simple order

of the President to depart out of the United States, as is undertaken by said act intituled "An Act concerning aliens," is contrary to the Constitution, one amendment to which has provided that "no person shall be deprived of liberty without due process of law;" and that another having provided that "in all criminal prosecutions the accused shall enjoy the right to public trial by an impartial jury, to be informed of the nature and cause of the accusation, to be confronted with the witnesses against him, to have compulsory process for obtaining witnesses in his favor, and to have the assistance of counsel for his defence," the same act, undertaking to authorize the President to remove a person out of the United States, who is under the protection of the law, on his own suspicion, without accusation, without jury, without public trial, without confrontation of the witnesses against him, without hearing witnesses in his favor, without defence, without counsel, is contrary to the provision also of the Constitution, is therefore not law, but utterly void, and of no force: that transferring the power of judging any person, who is under the protection of the laws, from the courts to the President of the United States, as is undertaken by the same act concerning aliens, is against the article of the Constitution which provides that "the judicial power of the United States shall be vested in courts, the judges of which shall hold their offices during good behavior;" and that the said act is void for that reason also. And it is further to be noted, that this transfer of judiciary power is to that magistrate of the General Government who already possesses all the Executive, and a negative on all legislative powers.

7. *Resolved*, That the construction applied by the General Government (as is evidenced by sundry of their proceedings) to those parts of the Constitution of the United States which delegate to Congress a power "to lay and collect taxes, duties, imports, and excises, to pay the debts, and provide for the common defence and general welfare of the United States," and "to make all laws which shall be necessary and proper for carrying into execution the powers vested by the Constitution in the government of the United States, or in any department or officer thereof," goes to the destruction of all limits prescribed to their power by the Constitution: that words meant by the instrument to be subsidiary only to the execution of limited powers, ought not to be so construed as themselves to give unlimited powers, nor a part to be so taken as to destroy the whole residue of that instrument: that the proceedings of the General Government under color of these articles, will be a fit and necessary subject of revisal and correction, at a time of greater tranquillity, while those specified in the preceding resolutions call for immediate redress.

8th. *Resolved*, That a committee of conference and correspondence be appointed, who shall have in charge to communicate the preceding resolutions to the legislatures of the several States; to assure them that this commonwealth continues in the same esteem of their friendship and union which it has manifested from that moment at which a common danger first suggested a common union: that it considers union, for specified national purposes, and particularly to those specified in their late federal compact, to be friendly to the peace, happiness and prosperity of all the States: that faithful to that compact, according to the plain intent and meaning in which it was understood and acceded to by the several parties, it is sincerely anxious for its preservation: that it does also believe, that to take from the States all the powers of self-government and transfer them to a general and consolidated government, without regard to the special delegations and reservations solemnly agreed to in that compact, is not for the peace, happiness or prosperity of these States; and that therefore this commonwealth is determined, as it doubts not its co-States are, to submit to undelegated, and consequently unlimited powers in no man, or body of men on earth: that in cases of an abuse of the delegated powers, the members of the General Government, being chosen by the people, a change by the people would be the constitutional remedy; but, where powers are assumed which have not been delegated, a nullification of the act is the rightful remedy: that every State has a natural right in cases not within the compact, (casus non foederis,) to nullify of their own authority all assumptions of power by others within their limits: that without this right, they would be under the dominion, absolute and unlimited, of whosoever might exercise this right of judgment for them: that nevertheless, this commonwealth, from motives of regard and respect for its co-States, has wished to communicate with them on the subject: that with them alone it is proper to communicate, they alone being parties to the compact, and solely authorized to judge in the last resort of the powers exercised under it, Congress being not a party, but merely the creature of the compact, and subject as to its assumptions of power to the final judgment of those by whom, and for whose use itself and its powers were all created and modified: that if the acts before specified should stand, these conclusions would flow from them; that the General Government may place any act they think proper on the list of crimes, and punish it themselves whether enumerated or not enumerated by the Constitution as cognizable by them: that they may transfer its cognizance to the President, or any other person, who may himself be the accuser, counsel, judge and jury, whose suspicions may be the evidence, his order the sentence, his officer the executioner, and his breast the sole record of the transaction: that a very numerous and valuable description of the inhabitants of these States being, by this precedent, reduced, as outlaws, to the absolute dominion of one man, and the barrier of the Constitution thus swept away from us all, no rampart now remains against the passions and the powers of a majority in Congress to protect from a like exportation, or other more grievous punishment, the minority of the same body, the legislatures, judges, governors, and counsellors of the States, nor their other peaceable inhabitants, who may venture to reclaim the constitutional rights and liberties of the States and people, or who for other causes, good or bad, may be obnoxious to the views, or marked by the suspicions of the President, or be thought dangerous to his or their election, or other interests, public or personal: that the friendless alien has indeed been selected as the safest subject of a first experiment; but the citizen will soon follow, or rather, has already followed, for already has a sedition act marked him as its prey: that these and successive acts of the same character, unless arrested at the threshold, necessarily drive these States into revolution and blood, and will furnish new calumnies against republican government, and new pretexts for those who wish it to be believed that man cannot be governed but by a rod of iron: that it would be a dangerous delusion were a confidence in the men of our choice to silence our fears for the safety of our rights: that confidence is everywhere the parent of despotism—free government is founded in jealousy, and not in confidence; it is jealousy and not confidence which prescribes limited constitutions, to bind down those whom we are obliged to trust with power: that our Constitution has accordingly fixed the limits to which, and no further, our confidence may go; and let the honest advocate of confidence read the alien and sedition acts, and say if the Constitution has not been wise in fixing limits to the government it created, and whether we should be wise in destroying those limits. Let him say what the government is, if it be not a tyranny, which the men of our choice have conferred on our President, and the President of our choice has assented to, and accepted over the friendly strangers to whom the mild spirit of our country and its laws have pledged hospitality and protection: that the men of our choice have more respected the bare suspicions of the President, than the solid right of innocence, the claims of justification, the sacred force of truth, and the forms and substance of law and justice. In questions of power, then, let no more be heard of confidence in man, but bind him down from mischief by the chains of the Constitution. That this commonwealth does therefore call on its co-States for an expression of their sentiments on the acts concerning aliens, and for the punishment of certain crimes herein before specified, plainly declaring whether these acts are or are not authorized by the federal compact. And it doubts not that their sense will be so announced as to prove their attachment unaltered to limited government, whether general or particular. And that the rights and liberties of their co-States will be exposed to no dangers by remaining embarked in a common bottom with their own. That they will concur with this commonwealth in considering the said acts as so palpably against the Constitution as to amount to an undisguised declaration that that compact is not meant to be the measure of the powers of the General Government, but that it will proceed in the exercise over these States, of all powers whatsoever: that they will view this as seizing the rights of the States, and consolidating them in the hands of the General Government, with a power assumed to bind the States, not merely as the cases made federal, (casus foederis,) but in all cases whatsoever, by laws made, not with their consent, but by others against their consent: that this would be to surrender the form of government we have chosen, and live under one deriving its powers from its own will, and not from our authority; and that the co-States, recurring to their natural right in cases not made federal, will concur in declaring these acts void, and of no force, and will each take measures of its own for providing that neither these acts, nor any others of the General Government not plainly and intentionally authorized by the Constitution, shall be exercised within their respective territories.

9th. *Resolved,* That the said committee be authorized to communicate by writing or personal conferences, at any times or places whatever, with any person or person who may be appointed by any one or more co-States to correspond or confer with them; and that they lay their proceedings before the next session of Assembly.

13. To Elbridge Gerry, Philadelphia, 26 January 1799. *Elbridge Gerry of Massachusetts (1744–1814) had been a member of the Continental Congress, a del-*

egate to the Constitutional Convention in Philadelphia, and an Anti-Federalist representative to the first two federal congresses, which together met from 1789 to 1793. An old-fashioned revolutionary republican who prized his independence from party affiliation, Gerry as a peace commissioner nonetheless became a hero for Jeffersonian Republicans when he stayed on in France in 1798 after his Federalist colleagues John Marshall and Charles Cotesworth Pinckney returned to the United States (see document 11). This extraordinary letter, one of the most elaborate professions of political faith in all of TJ's writings, was designed to recruit an influential New Englander to TJ's cause and thus counter the charge that Republicanism was a sectional, not a truly national, political movement.

Our very long intimacy as fellow-laborers in the same cause, the recent expressions of mutual confidence which had preceded your mission, the interesting course which that had taken, & particularly & personally as it regarded yourself, made me anxious to hear from you on your return. I was the more so too, as I had myself during the whole of your absence, as well as since your return, been a constant butt for every shaft of calumny which malice & falsehood could form, & the presses, public speakers, or private letters disseminate. One of these, too, was of a nature to touch yourself; as if, wanting confidence in your efforts, I had been capable of usurping powers committed to you, & authorizing negociations private & collateral to yours. The real truth is, that though Dr Logan, the pretended missionary, about 4. or 5. days before he sailed for Hamburgh, told me he was going there, & thence to Paris, & asked & received from me a certificate of his citizenship, character, & circumstances of life, merely as a protection, should he be molested on his journey, in the present turbulent & suspicious state of Europe, yet I had been led to consider his object as relative to his private affairs; and tho', from an intimacy of some standing, he knew well my wishes for peace and my political sentiments in general, he nevertheless received then no particular declaration of them, no authority to communicate them to any mortal, nor to speak to any one in my name, or in anybody's name, on that, or on any other subject whatever; nor did I write by him a scrip of a pen to any person whatever. This he has himself honestly & publicly declared since his return; & from his well-known character & every other circumstance, every candid man must perceive that his enterprise was dictated by his own enthusiasm, without consultation or communication with any one; that he acted in Paris on his own ground, & made his own way. Yet to give some color to his proceedings, which might implicate the republicans in general, & myself particularly, they have not been ashamed to bring forward a suppositious paper, drawn by one of their own party in the name of Logan, and falsely pretended to have been presented by him to the government of France; counting that the bare mention of my name therein, would connect that in the eye of the public with this transaction. In confutation of these and all future calumnies, by way of anticipation, I shall make to you a profession of my political faith; in confidence that you will consider every future imputation on me of a contrary complexion, as bearing on its front the mark of falsehood & calumny.

I do then, with sincere zeal, wish an inviolable preservation of our present federal constitution, according to the true sense in which it was adopted by the States, that in which it was advocated by it's friends, & not that which it's enemies apprehended, who therefore became it's enemies; and I am opposed to the monarchising it's features by the forms of it's administration, with a view to conciliate a first transition to a President & Senate for life, & from that to a hereditary tenure of these offices, & thus to worm out the elective principle. I am for preserving to the States the powers not yielded by them to the Union, & to the legislature of the Union it's constitutional share in the division of powers; and I am not for transferring all the powers of the States to the general government, & all those of that government to the Executive branch. I am for a government rigorously frugal & simple, applying all the possible savings of the public revenue to the discharge of the national debt; and not for a multiplication of officers & salaries merely to make partisans, & for increasing, by every device, the public debt, on the principle of it's being a public blessing. I am for relying, for internal defence, on our militia solely, till actual invasion, and for such a naval force only as may protect our coasts and harbors from such depredations as we have experienced; and not for a standing army in time of peace, which may overawe the public sentiment; nor for a navy, which, by it's own expenses and the eternal wars in which it will implicate us, will grind us with public burthens, & sink us under them. I am for free commerce with all nations; political connection with none; & little or no diplomatic establishment. And I am not for linking ourselves by new treaties with the quarrels of Europe; entering that field of slaughter to preserve their balance, or joining in the confederacy of kings to war against the principles of liberty. I am for freedom of religion, & against all maneuvres to bring about a legal ascendancy of one sect over another: for freedom of the press, & against all violations of the constitution to silence by force & not by reason the complaints or criticisms, just or unjust, of our citizens against the conduct of their agents. And I am for encouraging the progress of science in all it's branches; and not for raising a hue and cry against the sacred name of philosophy; for awing the human mind by stories of raw-head & bloody bones to a distrust of its own vision, & to repose implicitly on that of others; to go backwards instead of forwards to look for improvement; to believe that government, religion, morality, & every other science were in the highest perfection in ages of the darkest ignorance, and that nothing can ever be devised more perfect than what was established by our forefathers. To these I will add, that I was a sincere well-wisher to the success of the French revolution, and still wish it may end in the establishment of a free & well-ordered republic; but I have not been insensible under the atrocious depredations they have committed on our commerce. The first object of my heart is my own country. In that is embarked my family, my fortune, & my own existence. I have not one farthing of interest, nor one fibre of attachment out of it, nor a single motive of preference of any one nation to another, but in proportion as they are more or less friendly to us. But though deeply feeling the injuries of France, I did not think war the surest means of redressing them. I did believe, that a mission sincerely disposed to preserve peace, would obtain for us a peaceable & honorable settlement & retribution; and I appeal to you to say, whether this might not have been obtained, if either of your colleagues had been of the same sentiment with yourself.

These, my friend, are my principles; they are unquestionably the principles of the great body of our fellow citizens, and I know there is not one of them which is not yours also. In truth, we never differed but on one ground, the funding system; and as, from the moment of it's being adopted by the constituted authorities, I became religiously principled in the sacred discharge of it to the uttermost farthing, we are united now even on that single ground of difference.

I turn now to your inquiries. The enclosed paper will answer one of them. But you also ask for such political information as may be possessed by me, & interesting to yourself in regard to your embassy. As a proof of my entire confidence in you, I shall give it fully & candidly. When Pinckney, Marshall, and Dana, were nominated to settle our differences with France, it was suspected by many, from what was understood of their dispositions, that their mission would not result in a settlement of differences, but would produce circumstances tending to widen the breach, and to provoke our citizens to consent to a war with that nation, & union with England. Dana's resignation & your appointment gave the first gleam of hope of a peaceable issue to the mission. For it was believed that you were sincerely disposed to accommodation; & it was not long after your arrival there, before symptoms were observed of that difference of views which had been suspected to exist. In the meantime, however, the aspect of our government towards the French republic had become so ardent, that the people of America generally took the alarm. To the southward, their apprehensions were early excited. In the Eastern States also, they at length began to break out. Meetings were held in many of your towns, & addresses to the government agreed on in opposition to war. The example was spreading like a wildfire. Other meetings were called in other places, & a general concurrence of sentiment against the apparent inclinations of the government was imminent; when, most critically for the government, the despatches of Octr 22, prepared by your colleague Marshall, with a view to their being made public, dropped into their laps. It was truly a God-send to them, & they made the most of it. Many thousands of copies were printed & dispersed gratis, at the public expence; & the zealots for war co-operated so heartily, that there were instances of single individuals who printed & dispersed 10. or 12,000 copies at their own expence. The odiousness of the corruption supposed in those papers excited a general & high indignation among the people. Unexperienced in such maneuvres, they did not permit themselves even to suspect that the turpitude of private swindlers might mingle itself unobserved, & give it's own hue to the communications of the French government, of whose participation there was neither proof nor probability. It served, however, for a time, the purpose intended. The people, in many places, gave a loose to the expressions of their warm indignation, & of their honest preference of war to dishonor. The fever was long & successfully kept up, and in the meantime, war measures as ardently crowded. Still, however, as it was known that your colleagues were coming away, and yourself to stay, though disclaiming a separate power to conclude a treaty, it was hoped by the lovers of peace, that a project of treaty would have been prepared, ad referendum, on principles which would have satisfied our citizens, & overawed any bias of the government towards a different policy. But the expedition of the Sophia, and, as was supposed, the suggestions of the person charged with your despatches, & his probable misrepresentations of the real wishes of the American people, prevented these hopes. They had then only to look forward to your return for such information, either through the Executive, or from yourself, as might present to our view the other side of the medal. The despatches of Oct 22, 97, had presented one face. That information, to a certain degree, is now received, & the public will see from your correspondence with Taleyrand, that France, as you testify, "was sincere and anxious to obtain a reconciliation, not wishing us to break the British treaty, but only to give her equivalent stipulations; and in general was disposed to a liberal treaty." And they will judge whether mr. Pickering's report shews an inflexible determination to believe no declarations the French government can make, nor any opinion which you, judging on the spot & from actual view, can give of their sincerity, and to meet their designs of peace with operations of war. The alien & sedition acts have already operated in the South as powerful sedatives of the X. Y. Z. inflammation. In your quarter, where violations of principle are either less regarded or more concealed, the direct tax is likely to have the same effect, & to excite inquiries into the object of the enormous expences & taxes we are bringing on. And your information supervening, that we might have a liberal accommodation if we would, there can be little doubt of the reproduction of that general movement, by the despatches of Oct. 22. And tho' small checks & stops, like Logan's pretended embassy, may be thrown in the way from time to time, & may a little retard it's motion, yet the tide is already turned, and will sweep before it all the feeble obstacles of art. The unquestionable republicanism of the American mind will break through the mist under which it has been clouded, and will oblige it's agents to reform the principles & practices of their administration.

You suppose that you have been abused by both parties. As far as has come to my knowledge, you are misinformed. I have never seen or heard a sentence of blame uttered against you by the republicans; unless we were so to construe their wishes that you had more boldly co-operated in a project of a treaty, and would more explicitly state, whether there was in your colleages that flexibility, which persons earnest after peace would have practised? Whether, on the contrary, their demeanor was not cold, reserved, and distant, at least, if not backward? And whether, if they had yielded to those informal conferences which Taleyrand seems to have courted, the liberal accommodation you suppose might not have been effected, even with their agency? Your fellow-citizens think they have a right to full information, in a case of such great concern to them. It is their sweat which is to earn all the expences of the war, and their blood which is to flow in expiation of the causes of it. It may be in your power to save them from these miseries by full communications and unrestrained details, postponing motives of delicacy to those of duty. It rests for you to come forward independently; to take your stand on the high ground of your own character; to disregard calumny, and to be borne above it on the shoulders of your grateful fellow citizens; or to sink into the humble oblivion, to which the Federalists (self-called) have secretly condemned you;

and even to be happy if they will indulge you with oblivion, while they have beamed on your colleagues meridian splendor. Pardon me, my dear Sir, if my expressions are strong. My feelings are so much more so, that it is with difficulty reduce them even to the tone I use. If you doubt the dispositions towards you, look into the papers, on both sides, for the toasts which were given throughout the States on the 4th of July. You will there see whose hearts were with you, and whose were ulcerated against you. Indeed, as soon as it was known that you had consented to stay in Paris, there was no measure observed in the execrations of the war party. They openly wished you might be guillotined, or sent to Cayenne, or anything else. And these expressions were finally stifled from a principle of policy only, & to prevent you from being urged to a justification of yourself. From this principle alone proceed the silence and cold respect they observe towards you. Still, they cannot prevent at times the flames bursting from under the embers, as mr. Pickering's letters, report, & conversations testify, as well as the indecent expressions respecting you, indulged by some of them in the debate on these despatches. These sufficiently show that you are never more to be honored or trusted by them, and that they await to crush you for ever, only till they can do it without danger to themselves.

When I sat down to answer your letter, but two courses presented themselves, either to say nothing or everything; for half confidences are not in my character. I could not hesitate which was due to you. I have unbosomed myself fully; & it will certainly be highly gratifying if I receive like confidence from you. For even if we differ in principle more than I believe we do, you & I know too well the texture of the human mind, & the slipperiness of human reason, to consider differences of opinion otherwise than differences of form or feature. Integrity of views more than their soundness, is the basis of esteem. I shall follow your direction in conveying this by a private hand; tho' know not as yet when one worthy of confidence will occur. And my trust in you leaves me without a fear that this letter, meant as a confidential communication of my impressions, will ever go out of your hand, or be suffered in anywise to commit my name. Indeed, besides the accidents which might happen to it even under your care, considering the accident of death to which you are liable, I think it safest to pray you, after reading it as often as you please, to destroy at least the 2d & 3d leaves. The 1st contains principles only, which I fear not to avow; but the 2d & 3d contain facts stated for your information, and which, though sacredly conformable to my firm belief, yet would be galling to some, & expose me to illiberal attacks. I therefore repeat my prayer to burn the 2d & 3d leaves. And did we ever expect to see the day, when, breathing nothing but sentiments of love to our country & it's freedom & happiness, our correspondence must be as secret as if we were hatching it's destruction! Adieu, my friend, and accept my sincere & affectionate salutations. I need not add my signature.

14. To William Green Munford, Monticello, 18 June 1799. *William Green Munford was probably from Charles City County and a student at the College of William and Mary.*

I am among those who think well of the human character generally. I consider man as formed for society, and endowed by nature with those dispositions which fit him for society. I believe also, with Condorcet, as mentioned in your letter, that his mind is perfectible to a degree of which we cannot as yet form any conception. It is impossible for a man who takes a survey of what is already known, not to see what an immensity in every branch of science yet remains to be discovered, & that too of articles to which our faculties seem adequate. In geometry & calculation we know a great deal. Yet there are some desiderata. In anatomy great progress has been made; but much is still to be acquired. In natural history we possess knowlege; but we want a great deal. In chemistry we are not yet sure of the first elements. Our natural philosophy is in a very infantine state; perhaps for great advances in it, a further progress in chemistry is necessary. Surgery is well advanced; but prodigiously short of what may be. The state of medecine is worse than that of total ignorance. Could we divest ourselves of every thing we suppose we know in it, we should start from a higher ground & with fairer prospects. From Hippocrates to Brown we have had nothing but a succession of hypothetical systems each having it's day of vogue, like the fashions & fancies of caps & gowns, & yielding in turn to the next caprice. Yet the human frame, which is to be the subject of suffering & torture under these learned modes, does not change. We have a few medecines, as the bark, opium, mercury, which in a few well defined diseases are of unquestionable virtue: but the residuary list of the materia medica, long as it is, contains but the charlataneries of the art; and of the diseases of doubtful form, physicians have ever had a false knowlege, worse than ignorance. Yet surely the list of unequivocal diseases & remedies is capable of enlargement; and it is still more certain that in the other branches of science, great fields are yet to be explored to which our faculties are equal, & that to an extent of which we cannot fix the limits. I join you therefore in branding as cowardly the idea that the human mind is incapable of further advances. This is precisely the doctrine which the present despots of the earth are inculcating, & their friends here re-echoing; & applying especially to religion & politics; 'that it is not probable that any thing better will be discovered than what was known to our fathers.' We are to look backwards then & not forwards for the improvement of science, & to find it amidst feudal barbarisms and the fires of Spital-fields. But thank heaven the American mind is already too much opened, to listen to these impostures; and while the art of printing is left to us, science can never be retrograde; what is once acquired of real knowlege can never be lost. To preserve the freedom of the human mind then & freedom of the press, every spirit should be ready to devote itself to martyrdom; for as long as we may think as we will, & speak as we think, the condition of man will proceed in improvement. The generation which is going off the stage has deserved well of mankind for the struggles it has made, & for having arrested that course of despotism which had overwhelmed the world for thousands & thousands of years. If there seems to be danger that the ground they have gained will be lost again, that danger comes from the generation your cotemporary. But that the enthusiasm which characterises youth should lift its parricide hands against freedom & science, would be such a monstrous phænomenon as I cannot place among possible things in this age & this country. Your college at least has shewn itself incapable of it; and if the youth of any other place have seemed to rally under other banners it has been from delusions which they will soon dissipate.

15. To Edmund Randolph, Monticello, 18 August 1799. *For TJ and fellow Republicans, the quarrel with Federalism ultimately focused on constitutional interpretation. The gravest danger of all, TJ here tells Edmund Randolph (1753–1813), was that federal courts would assume a common law jurisdiction that could cover all legal questions and thereby subvert the undelegated authority of the sovereign states. Randolph, in 1794 and 1795 successor to TJ as secretary of state, was an able lawyer with Republican sympathies, now in private practice in Richmond.*

Of all the doctrines which have ever been broached by the federal government, the novel one, of the common law being in force & cognizable as an existing law in their courts, is to me the most formidable. All their other assumptions of un-given powers have been in the detail. The bank law, the treaty doctrine, the sedition act, alien act, the undertaking to change the state laws of evidence in the state courts by certain parts of the stamp act, &c., &c., have been solitary, unconsequential, timid things, in comparison with the audacious, barefaced and sweeping pretension to a system of law for the U S, without the adoption of their legislature, and so infinitively beyond their power to adopt. If this assumption be yielded to, the state courts may be shut up, as there will then be nothing to hinder citizens of the same state suing each other in the federal courts in every case, as on a bond for instance, because the common law obliges payment of it, & the common law they say is their law. I am happy you have taken up the subject; & I have carefully perused & considered the notes you enclosed, and find but a single paragraph which I do not approve. It is that wherein (page 2.) you say, that laws being emanations from the legislative department, &, when once enacted, continuing in force from a presumption that their will so continues, that that presumption fails & the laws of course fall, on the destruction of that legislative department. I do not think this is the true bottom on which laws & the administering them rest. The whole body of the nation is the sovereign legislative, judiciary and executive power for itself. The inconvenience of meeting to exercise these powers in person, and their inaptitude to exercise them, induce them to appoint special organs to declare their legislative will, to judge & to execute it. It is the will of the nation which makes the law obligatory; it is their will which creates or annihilates the organ which is to declare & announce it. They may do it by a single person, as an Emperor of Russia, (constituting his declarations evidence of their will,) or by a few persons, as the Aristocracy of Venice, or by a complication of councils, as in our former regal government, or our present republican one. The law being law because it is the will of the nation, is not changed by their changing the organ through which they chuse to announce their future will; no more than the acts have done by one attorney lose their obligation by my changing or discontinuing that attorney. This doctrine has been, in a certain degree sanctioned by the federal executive. For it is precisely that on which the continuance of obligation from our treaty with France was established, and the doctrine was particularly developed in a letter to Gouverneur Morris, written with the approbation of President Washington and his cabinet. Mercer once prevailed on the Virginia Assembly to declare a different doctrine in some resolutions. These met universal disapprobation in this, as well as the other States, and if mistake not, a subsequent Assembly did something to do away the authority of their former unguarded resolutions. In this case, as in all others, the true principle will be quite as effectual to establish the just deductions, for before the revolution, the nation of Virginia had, by the organs they then thought proper to constitute, established a system of laws, which they divided into three denominations of 1, common law; 2, statute law; 3, Chancery: or if you please, into two only, of 1, common law; 2, Chancery. When, by the declaration of Independence, they chose to abolish their former organs of declaring their will, the acts of will already formally & constitutionally declared, remained untouched. For the nation was not dissolved, was not annihilated; it's will, therefore, remained in full vigor; and on the establishing the new organs, first of a convention, & afterwards a more complicated legislature, the old acts of national will continued in force, until the nation should, by its new organs, declare it's will changed. The common law, therefore, which was not in force when we landed here, nor till we had formed ourselves into a nation, and had manifested by the organs we constituted that the common law was to be our law, continued to be our law, because the nation continued in being, & because though it changed the organs for the future declarations of its will, yet it did not change its former declarations that the common law was it's law. Apply these principles to the present case. Before the revolution there existed no such nation as the U S; they then first associated as a nation, but for special purposes only. They had all their laws to make, as Virginia had on her first establishment as a nation. But they did not, as Virginia had done, proceed to adopt a whole system of laws ready made to their hand. As their association as a nation was only for special purposes, to wit, for the management of their concerns with one another & with foreign nations, and the states composing the association chose to give it powers for those purposes & no others, they could not adopt any general system, because it would have embraced objects on which this association had no right to form or declare a will. It was not the organ for declaring a national will in these cases. In the cases confided to them, they were free to declare the will of the nation, the law; but till it was declared there could be no law. So that the common law did not become, ipso facto, law on the new association; it could only become so by a positive adoption, & so far only as they were authorized to adopt.

I think it will be of great importance, when you come to the proper part, to portray at full length the consequences of this new doctrine, that the common law is the law of the U S, & that their courts have, of course, jurisdiction co-extensive with that law, that is to say, general over all cases & persons. But, great heavens! Who could have conceived in 1789 that within ten years we should have to combat such windmills.

CHAPTER FIVE

The Revolution of 1800

Jefferson hailed his ascension to the presidency as a return to the revolutionary principles of 1776. The experience of opposition party leader in the dark days of Federalist rule had not taught him to accept the legitimacy of party competition: aristocratic High Federalists were, in his mind, not merely a mistaken factor within a republican polity but an enemy to republican self-government itself. Jefferson's understanding of partisan conflict in the 1790s as a clash of fundamentally opposed philosophies and systems was reinforced by the global struggle between revolutionary republicanism and monarchical reaction that had been initiated by the French Revolution. In the presidential election of 1800 Jefferson and Aaron Burr received the same number of votes in the electoral college. This went against the intention of the Republicans. They saw Burr as an ally but wanted him to get fewer votes than Jefferson, which according to the constitutional arrangement at that time would have made him Jefferson's Vice President. Not until the Twelfth Amendment of 1904 would the Constitution provide that the electoral college distinguish its presidential from its vice-presidential vote. The election was deadlocked, and as the Constitution dictated it went to the House of Representatives, controlled by Federalists, that had been elected in 1798 and was not scheduled to give way to the newly chosen House until early the next year. Rumors spread that embittered Federalists meant to steal the presidential election from the people who had clearly won it. For the presidency, a Federalist caucus decided to support Burr, who though a Republican was thought to be possibly more compliant than Jefferson to the Federalist view. But the plan could not muster the votes of a sufficient number of states: the Constitution declared that in cases in which presidential elections went to the House the representatives of a particular state would together wield a single vote. After thirty-six ballots, a few important Federalists relented, perhaps recognizing that their defiance of the popular will—Republican voters in 1800 believed they were voting for Jefferson—would precipitate a genuine constitutional crisis and jeopardize the survival of the union. Some Federalists, including Jefferson's nemesis Alexander Hamilton, were also persuaded that Jefferson would not tamper with the basic structure of the federal regime and that Federalist interests would be best served by graceful acquiescence in his election.

How revolutionary was the event that histories have described as the Revolution of 1800? Jefferson's Inaugural Address (document 1) provided an ambiguous answer. Asserting that the Republicans' "federal and republican principles" would henceforth be the standard of patriotic American-ism, Jefferson invited his erstwhile opponents to recant their heresies and join the new national consensus. He believed that fortunes had shifted, irrevocably: the new Republican administration would not have to resort to the kind of repressive measures that Federalists had so eagerly and fool-ishly embraced in 1798. He projected a moderate and conciliatory pos-ture: under the able administration of Treasury Secretary Albert Gallatin, Hamilton's financial system remained intact, but would no longer serve as the engine of consolidation; internal taxes were repealed and import revenues were used for paying down the national debt from $83,000,000 to $57,000,000 by 1809. Nor were Federalists driven en masse from ap-pointive offices in the federal bureaucracy. In making appointments, of course, Jefferson was attentive to the needs of Republican loyalists. Repub-lican animosity toward Federalist judges led to repeal of the Judiciary Act of 1801, which had expanded the federal court system for the purpose of adding to the number of Federalist judges before Jefferson's administra-tion replaced a lot of his enemies. Republicans also had to prosecute par-ticularly obnoxious incumbents such as John Pickering of New Hampshire, convicted and removed in March 1804, and Samuel Chase of Maryland, acquitted in March 1805. Jefferson's revolution did not result in wholesale purges of political enemies. But Federalists learned to play by the new rules; and many, finding Jefferson much less dangerous to the established order than their own campaign rhetoric had led them to fear, were drawn into the Republican ranks.

The success of the Republican revolution was measured not by any vio-lence of retaliation against the Federalists, but by growing majorities in both houses of Congress and by Jefferson's landslide reelection in 1804. As the nation grew more Republican, it expanded in size: the administra-tion's greatest coup, the Louisiana Purchase of 1803, doubled the extent of the national territory and removed the danger of a destabilizing French presence in the Mississippi Valley (document 5). When Jefferson delivered his Second Inaugural Address in March 1805 (document 8), the new na-tion's prospects could not have been more favorable. Yet the vulnerability of Jefferson's achievement would soon become apparent. American peace and prosperity were dependent on maintaining neutrality toward the Na-poleonic wars that were engulfing the Atlantic world. The European war opened up extraordinary new market opportunities to American pro-ducers and shippers, but it also put commerce at grave risk: when their own vital interests were at stake, France and Britain showed little respect for neutral rights. Jefferson found that threats of commercial sanctions against the belligerents, culminating in the ill-fated embargo stretching from 1807 to 1809, were ineffective, even counterproductive. By the end of his presidency, the possibility of war with one power or the other seemed increasingly strong (document 13).

American foreign policy had been inextricably fixed to sectional ten-sions and centrifugal tendencies in the American federal union. Aaron Burr's western "conspiracy" of 1806 illuminates these connections. Jeffer-son was convinced that his former Vice President was guilty of treason against the United States, but it was by no means clear that Burr had contemplated disunion, a filibuster into Spanish territory, or a combination of the two. Jefferson's relentless pursuit of Burr, culminating in the adventurer's trial for treason (he was acquitted), revealed how anxious the President was about the very survival of the union (documents 11 and 12).

As opposition to Jefferson's foreign and domestic policies grew, his old enemies gained new life. Meanwhile, Republicans divided among themselves, Old Republican purists aligning against moderates who leaned too much toward Federalist heresies (document 10). These divisions, originating late in Jefferson's first term, became more pronounced as Republicans looked toward the presidential succession. Insurgent Old Republicans rallied around James Monroe, moderates around James Madison, Jefferson's secretary of state and heir apparent. Some Republicans thought that the only hope for the survival of the party and the union was that Jefferson agree to serve a third term. But by 1809, Jefferson at sixty-five, suffering through one of the worst phases of his political career, longed to return to private life.

* * * * * * * * * *

1. First Inaugural Address, 4 March 1801. *TJ's address was delivered in the Senate chamber, the only completed portion of the United States Capitol in the new federal city, the seat of government first occupied by Jefferson's predecessor John Adams in the previous November. Few of his listeners could hear the soft-spoken TJ in the crowded chamber. But the text of his redress, widely reprinted across the country, was warmly received by readers.*

FRIENDS AND FELLOW-CITIZENS,

Called upon to undertake the duties of the first executive office of our country, I avail myself of the presence of that portion of my fellow-citizens which is here assembled to express my grateful thanks for the favor with which they have been pleased to look toward me, to declare a sincere consciousness that the task is above my talents, and that I approach it with those anxious and awful presentiments which the greatness of the charge and the weakness of my powers so justly inspire. A rising nation, spread over a wide and fruitful land, traversing all the seas with the rich productions of their industry, engaged in commerce with nations who feel power and forget right, advancing rapidly to destinies beyond the reach of mortal eye—when I contemplate these transcendent objects, and see the honor, the happiness, and the hopes of this beloved country committed to the issue and the auspices of this day, I shrink from the contemplation, and humble myself before the magnitude of the undertaking. Utterly, indeed, should I despair did not the presence of many whom I here see remind me that in the other high authorities provided by our Constitution I shall find resources of wisdom, of virtue, and of zeal on which to rely under all difficulties. To you, then, gentlemen, who are charged with the sovereign functions of legislation, and to those associated with you, I look with encouragement for that guidance and support which may enable us to steer with safety the vessel in which we are all embarked amidst the conflicting elements of a troubled world.

During the contest of opinion through which we have passed the animation of discussions and of exertions has sometimes worn an aspect which might impose on strangers unused to think freely and to speak and to write what they think; but this being now decided by the voice of the nation, announced according to the rules of the Constitution, all will, of course, arrange themselves under the will of the law, and unite in common efforts for the common good. All, too, will bear in mind this sacred principle, that though the will of the majority is in all cases to prevail, that will to be rightful must be reasonable; that the minority possess their equal rights, which equal law must protect, and to violate would be oppression. Let us, then, fellow-citizens, unite with one heart and one mind. Let us restore to social intercourse that harmony and affection without which liberty and even life itself are but dreary things. And let us reflect that, having banished from our land that religious intolerance under which mankind so long bled and suffered, we have yet gained little if we countenance a political intolerance as despotic, as wicked, and capable of as bitter and bloody persecutions. During the throes and convulsions of the ancient world, during the agonizing spasms of infuriated man, seeking through blood and slaughter his long-lost liberty, it was not wonderful that the agitation of the billows should reach even this distant and peaceful shore; that this should be more felt and feared by some and less by others, and should divide opinions as to measures of safety. But every difference of opinion is not a difference of principle. We have called by different names brethren of the same principle. We are all republicans, we are all federalists. If there be any among us who would wish to dissolve this Union or to change its republican form, let them stand undisturbed as monuments of the safety with which error of opinion may be tolerated where reason is left free to combat it. I know, indeed, that some honest men fear that a republican government can not be strong, that this Government is not strong enough; but would the honest patriot, in the full tide of successful experiment, abandon a government which has so far kept us free and firm on the theoretic and visionary fear that this Government, the world's best hope, may by possibility want energy to preserve itself? I trust not. I believe this, on the contrary, the strongest Government on earth. I believe it the only one where every man, at the call of the law, would fly to the standard of the law, and would meet invasions of the public order as his own personal concern. Sometimes it is said that man can not be trusted with the government of himself. Can he, then, be trusted with the government of others? Or have we found angels in the forms of kings to govern him? Let history answer this question.

Let us, then, with courage and confidence pursue our own Federal and Republican principles, our attachment to union and representative government. Kindly separated by nature and a wide ocean from the exterminating havoc of one quarter of the globe; too high-minded to endure the degradations of the others; possessing a chosen country, with room enough for our descendants to the thousandth and thousandth generation; entertaining a due sense of our equal right to the use of our own faculties, to the acquisitions of our own industry, to honor and confidence from our fellow-citizens, resulting not from birth, but from our actions and their sense of them; enlightened by a benign religion, professed, indeed, and practiced in various forms, yet all of them inculcating honesty, truth, temperance, gratitude, and the love of man; acknowledging and adoring an overruling Providence, which by all its dispensations proves that it delights in the happiness of man here and his greater happiness hereafter—with all these blessings, what more is necessary to make us a happy and a prosperous people? Still one thing more, fellow-citizens—a wise and frugal Government, which shall restrain men from injuring one another, shall leave them otherwise free to regulate their own pursuits of industry and improvement, and shall not take from the mouth of labor the bread it has earned. This is the sum of good government, and this is necessary to close the circle of our felicities.

About to enter, fellow-citizens, on the exercise of duties which comprehend everything dear and valuable to you, it is proper you should understand what I deem the essential principles of our Government, and consequently those which ought to shape its Administration. I will compress them within the narrowest compass they will bear, stating the general principle, but not all its limitations. Equal and exact justice to all men, of whatever state or persuasion, religious or political; peace, commerce, and honest friendship with all nations, entangling alliances with none; the support of the State governments in all their rights, as the most competent administrations for our domestic concerns and the surest bulwarks against antirepublican tendencies; the preservation of the General Government in its whole constitutional vigor, as the sheet anchor of our peace at home and safety abroad; a jealous care of the right of election by the people—a mild and safe corrective of abuses which are lopped by the sword of revolution where peaceable remedies are unprovided; absolute acquiescence in the decisions of the majority, the vital principle of republics, from which is no appeal but to force, the vital principle and immediate parent of despotism; a well-disciplined militia, our best reliance in peace and for the first moments of war till regulars may relieve them; the supremacy of the civil over the military authority; economy in the public expense, that labor may be lightly burthened; the honest payment of our debts and sacred preservation of the public faith; encouragement of agriculture, and of commerce as its handmaid; the diffusion of information and arraignment of all abuses at the bar of the public reason; freedom of religion; freedom of the press, and freedom of person under the protection of the habeas corpus, and trial by juries impartially selected. These principles form the bright constellation which has gone before us and guided our steps through an age of revolution and reformation. The wisdom of our sages and blood of our heroes have been devoted to their attainment. They should be the creed of our political faith, the text of civic instruction, the touchstone by which to try the services of those we trust; and should we wander from them in moments of error or of alarm, let us hasten to retrace our steps and to regain the road which alone leads to peace, liberty, and safety.

I repair, then, fellow-citizens, to the post you have assigned me. With experience enough in subordinate offices to have seen the difficulties of this the greatest of all, I have learnt to expect that it will rarely fall to the lot of imperfect man to retire from this station with the reputation and the favor which bring him into it. Without pretensions to that high confidence you reposed in our first and greatest revolutionary character, whose pre-eminent services had entitled him to the first place in his country's love and destined for him the fairest page in the volume of faithful history, I ask so much confidence only as may give firmness and effect to the legal administration of your affairs. I shall often go wrong through defect of judgment. When right, I shall often be thought wrong by those whose posi-tions will not command a view of the whole ground. I ask your indulgence for my own errors, which will never be intentional, and your support against the errors of others, who may condemn what they would not if seen in all its parts. The approbation implied by your suffrage is a great conso-lation to me for the past, and my future solicitude will be to retain the good opinion of those who have bestowed it in advance, to conciliate that of others by doing them all the good in my power, and to be instrumental to the happiness and freedom of all.

Relying, then, on the patronage of your good will, I advance with obe-dience to the work, ready to retire from it whenever you become sensible how much better choice it is in your power to make. And may that Infinite Power which rules the destinies of the universe lead our councils to what is best, and give them a favorable issue for your peace and prosperity.

2. To Dr. Joseph Priestley, Washington, 21 March 1801. *Dr. Joseph Priestley (1733–1804), the English chemist and Unitarian theologian, emigrated to Northumberland, Pennsylvania in 1794. A friend of the French Revolution, Priest-ley suffered persecution during the period of anti-Jacobin reaction in Britain. TJ was a great admirer of Priestley's philosophical and political writings.*

I learnt some time ago that you were in Philadelphia, but that it was only for a fortnight; & supposed you were gone. It was not till yesterday I received information that you were still there, had been very ill, but were on the recovery. I sincerely rejoice that you are so. Yours is one of the few lives precious to mankind, & for the continuance of which every thinking man is solicitous. Bigots may be an exception. What an effort, my dear Sir, of bigotry in Politics & Religion have we gone through! The barbarians really flattered themselves they should be able to bring back the times of Vandalism, when ignorance put everything into the hands of power & priestcraft. All advances in science were proscribed as innovations. They pretended to praise and encourage education, but it was to be the educa-tion of our ancestors. We were to look backwards, not forwards, for im-provement; the President himself declaring, in one of his answers to ad-dresses, that we were never to expect to go beyond them in real science. This was the real ground of all the attacks on you. Those who live by mys-tery & *charlatanerie*, fearing you would render them useless by simplifying the Christian philosophy,—the most sublime & benevolent, but most per-verted system that ever shone on man,—endeavored to crush your well-earnt & well-deserved fame. But it was the Lilliputians upon Gulliver. Our countrymen have recovered from the alarm into which art & industry had thrown them; science & honesty are replaced on their high ground; and you, my dear Sir, as their great apostle, are on it's pinnacle. It is with heartfelt satisfaction that, in the first moments of my public action, I can hail you with welcome to our land, tender to you the homage of it's respect & esteem, cover you under the protection of those laws which were made for the wise and good like you, and disdain the legitimacy of that libel on legislation, which under the form of a law, was for some time placed among them.

As the storm is now subsiding, and the horizon becoming serene, it is pleasant to consider the phenomenon with attention. We can no longer say there is nothing new under the sun. For this whole chapter in the history of man is new. The great extent of our Republic is new. Its sparse habitation is new. The mighty wave of public opinion which has rolled over it is new. But the most pleasing novelty is, it's so quickly subsiding over such an extent of surface to it's true level again. The order & good sense displayed in this recovery from delusion, and in the momentous crisis which lately arose, really bespeak a strength of character in our nation which augurs well for the duration of our Republic; & I am much better satisfied now of it's stability than I was before it was tried. I have been, above all things, solaced by the prospect which opened on us, in the event of a non-election of a President; in which case, the federal government would have been in the situation of a clock or watch run down. There was no idea of force, nor of any occasion for it. A convention, invited by the Republican members of Congress, with the virtual President & Vice President, would have been on the ground in 8. weeks, would have repaired the Constitution where it was defective, & wound it up again. This peaceable & legitimate resource, to which we are in the habit of implicit obedience, superseding all appeal to force, and being always within our reach, shows a precious principle of self-preservation in our composition, till a change of circumstances shall take place, which is not within prospect at any definite period.

3. To Governor James Monroe of Virginia, Washington, 24 November 1801. *Before being elected governor of Virginia in 1799, James Monroe (1758–1831), TJ's longtime protégé and political ally, had served from 1790 to 1794 as senator from Virginia and from 1794 to 1796 as American minister in Paris during a tumultuous phase of the French Revolution. In responding to Gabriel's Rebellion, an insurrectionary plot involving an extensive network of Virginia slaves that was uncovered in September 1800, Governor Monroe faced one of the biggest challenges of his career. The dilemma of how to dispose of slaves implicated in the rebellion raised to the fore the possibility of colonization, the putative solution to the slavery problem that TJ had advocated in his* Notes on Virginia *(see Chapter 2, document 7). The Virginia House looked to the new President for assistance and direction.*

I had not been unmindful of your letter of June 15, covering a resolution of the House of Representatives of Virginia [*concerning the colonization of rebellious slaves*]. . . . You will perceive that some circumstances connected with the subject, & necessarily presenting themselves to view, would be improper but for yours' & the legislative ear. Their publication might have an ill effect in more than one quarter. In confidence of attention to this, shall indulge greater freedom in writing. Common malefactors, I presume, make no part of the object of that resolution. Neither their numbers, nor the nature of their offences, seem to require any provisions beyond those practised heretofore, & found adequate to the repression of ordinary crimes. Conspiracy, insurgency, treason, rebellion, among that description of persons who brought on us the alarm, and on themselves the tragedy, of 1800, were doubtless within the view of every one; but many perhaps contemplated, and one expression of the resolution might comprehend, a much larger scope. Respect to both opinions makes it my duty to understand the resolution in all the extent of which it is susceptible.

The idea seems to be to provide for these people by a purchase of lands; and it is asked whether such a purchase can be made of the U S in their western territory? A very great extent of country, north of the Ohio, has been laid off into townships, and is now at market, according to the provisions of the acts of Congress, with which you are acquainted. There is nothing which would restrain the State of Virginia either in the purchase or the application of these lands; but a purchase, by the acre, might perhaps be a more expensive provision than the H of Representatives contemplated. Questions would also arise whether the establishment of such a colony within our limits, and to become a part of our union, would be desirable to the State of Virginia itself, or to the other States—especially those who would be in its vicinity?

Could we procure lands beyond the limits of the U S to form a receptacle for these people? On our northern boundary, the country not occupied by British subjects, is the property of Indian nations, whose title would be to be extinguished, with the consent of Great Britain; & the new settlers would be British subjects. It is hardly to be believed that either Great Britain or the Indian proprietors have so disinterested a regard for us, as to be willing to relieve us, by receiving such a colony themselves; and as much to be doubted whether that race of men could long exist in so rigorous a climate. On our western & southern frontiers, Spain holds an immense country, the occupancy of which, however, is in the Indian natives, except a few insulated spots possessed by Spanish subjects. It is very questionable, indeed, whether the Indians would sell? whether Spain would be willing to receive these people? and nearly certain that she would not alienate the sovereignty. The same question to ourselves would recur here also, as did in the first case: should we be willing to have such a colony in contact with us? However our present interests may restrain us within our own limits, it is impossible not to look forward to distant times, when our rapid multiplication will expand itself beyond those limits, & cover the whole northern, if not the southern continent, with a people speaking the same language, governed in similar forms, & by similar laws; nor can we contemplate with satisfaction either blot or mixture on that surface. Spain, France, and Portugal hold possessions on the southern continent, as to which I am not well enough informed to say how far they might meet our views. But either there or in the northern continent, should the constituted authorities of Virginia fix their attention, of preference, I will have the dispositions of those powers sounded in the first instance.

The West Indies offer a more probable & practicable retreat for them. Inhabited already by a people of their own race & color; climates congenial with their natural constitution; insulated from the other descriptions of men; nature seems to have formed these islands to become the receptacle of the blacks transplanted into this hemisphere. Whether we could obtain from the European sovereigns of those islands leave to send thither the persons under consideration, I cannot say; but I think it more probable than the former propositions, because of their being already inhabited more or less by the same race. The most promising portion of them is the island of St. Domingo, where the blacks are established into a sovereignty de facto, & have organized themselves under regular laws & government. I should conjecture that their present ruler might be willing, on many considerations, to receive even that description which would be exiled for acts deemed criminal by us, but meritorious, perhaps, by him. The possibility that these exiles might stimulate & conduct vindicative or predatory descents on our coasts, & facilitate concert with their brethren remaining here, looks to a state of things between that island & us not probable on a contemplation of our relative strength, and of the disproportion daily growing; and it is overweighed by the humanity of the measures proposed, & the advantages of disembarrassing ourselves of such dangerous characters. Africa would offer a last & undoubted resort, if all others more desirable should fail us. Whenever the Legislature of Virginia shall have brought it's mind to a point, so that I may know exactly what to propose to foreign authorities, I will execute their wishes with fidelity & zeal. I hope, however, they will pardon me for suggesting a single question for their own consideration. When we contemplate the variety of countries & of sovereigns towards which we may direct our views, the vast revolutions & changes of circumstances which are now in a course of progression, the possibilities that arrangements now to be made, with a view to any particular plan, may, at no great distance of time, be totally deranged by a change of sovereignty, of government, or of other circumstances, it will be for the Legislature to consider whether, after they shall have made all those general provisions which may be fixed by legislative authority, it would be reposing too much confidence in their Executive to leave the place of relegation to be decided on by them. They could accommodate their arrangements to the actual state of things, in which countries or powers may be found to exist at the day; and may prevent the effect of the law from being defeated by intervening changes. This, however, is for them to decide. Our duty will be to respect their decision.

4. To Messrs. Nehemiah Dodge and Others, a Committee of the Danbury Baptist Association, in the State of Connecticut, 1 January 1802. *This brief response to a message from Baptists in Connecticut congratulating TJ on his election has been taken as a major statement of his position on church-state relations. For the leading role he took in dismantling Virginia's Anglican establishment (see*

Chapter 1, document 6G), TJ despite his own deistic persuasion was a favorite among evangelical Christians across the country. Baptist dissenters against the Congregational Standing Order in Connecticut constituted an important element in that state's Republican Party.

The affectionate sentiments of esteem and approbation which you are so good as to express towards me, on behalf of the Danbury Baptist Association, give me the highest satisfaction. My duties dictate a faithful and zealous pursuit of the interests of my constituents, and in proportion as they are persuaded of my fidelity to those duties, the discharge of them becomes more and more pleasing.

Believing with you that religion is a matter which lies solely between man and his God, that he owes account to none other for his faith or his worship, that the legislative powers of government reach actions only, and not opinions, I contemplate with sovereign reverence that act of the whole American people which declared that their legislature should "make no law respecting an establishment of religion, or prohibiting the free exercise thereof," thus building a wall of separation between church and State. Adhering to this expression of the supreme will of the nation in behalf of the rights of conscience, I shall see with sincere satisfaction the progress of those sentiments which tend to restore to man all his natural rights, convinced he has no natural right in opposition to his social duties.

I reciprocate your kind prayers for the protection and blessing of the common Father and Creator of man, and tender you for yourselves and your religious association, assurances of my high respect and esteem.

5. To Robert R. Livingston, U.S. Minister to France, Washington, 18 April 1802. *Robert R. Livingston (1746–1813) was Chancellor of New York from 1777 to 1801. He broke with the Federalists over Jay's Treaty and as a reward TJ made him minister to France. Negotiations leading up to the Louisiana Purchase, completed by Livingston and Minister Plenipotentiary James Monroe in May 1803, were precipitated by the projected retrocession of this vast region from Spain to France in the secret Treaty of San Ildefonso of October 1800. TJ was most concerned about control of the mouth of the Mississippi; when in October 1802 the Spanish intendant prohibited shippers in the United States from depositing their goods in New Orleans, the crisis escalated, and westerners called for a preemptive strike on the city before the French could establish their authority there. Napoleon had a grand design for French empire in the American heartland, but when a French expeditionary force failed to suppress the Haitian revolution, he decided to sell the Americans the entire Louisiana Territory.*

The cession of Louisiana and the Floridas by Spain to France works most sorely on the U. S. On this subject the Secretary of State has written to you fully. Yet cannot forbear recurring to it personally, so deep is the impression it makes in my mind. It compleatly reverses all the political relations of the U. S. and will form a new epoch in our political course. Of all nations of any consideration France is the one which hitherto has offered the fewest points on which we could have any conflict of right, and the most points of a communion of interests. From these causes we have ever looked to her as our *natural friend*, as one with which we never could have an occasion of difference. Her growth therefore we viewed as our own, her misfortunes ours. There is on the globe one single spot, the possessor of which is our natural and habitual enemy. It is New Orleans, through which the produce of three-eighths of our territory must pass to market, and from its fertility it will ere long yield more than half of our whole produce and contain more than half our inhabitants. France placing herself in that door assumes to us the attitude of defiance. Spain might have retained it quietly for years. Her pacific dispositions, her feeble state, would induce her to increase our facilities there, so that her possession of the place would be hardly felt by us, and it would not perhaps be very long before some circumstance might arise which might make the cession of it to us the price of something of more worth to her. Not so can it ever be in the hands of France. The impetuosity of her temper, the energy and restlessness of her character, placed in a point of eternal friction with us, and our character, which though quiet, and loving peace and the pursuit of wealth, is high-minded, despising wealth in competition with insult or injury, enterprising and energetic as any nation on earth, these circumstances render it impossible that France and the U. S. can continue long friends when they meet in so irritable a position. They as well as we must be blind if they do not see this; and we must be very improvident if we do not begin to make arrangements on that hypothesis. The day that France takes possession of N. Orleans fixes the sentence which is to restrain her forever within her low water mark. It seals the union of two nations who in conjunction can maintain exclusive possession of the ocean. From that moment we must marry ourselves to the British fleet and nation. We must turn all our attentions to a maritime force, for which our resources place us on very high grounds: and having formed and cemented together a power which may render reinforcement of her settlements here impossible to France, make the first cannon, which shall be fired in Europe the signal for tearing up any settlement she may have made, and for holding the two continents of America in sequestration for the common purposes of the united British and American nations. This is not a state of things we seek or desire. It is one which this measure, if adopted by France, forces on us, as necessarily as any other cause, by the laws of nature, brings on its necessary effect. It is not from a fear of France that we deprecate this measure proposed by her. For however greater her force is than ours compared in the abstract, it is nothing in comparison of ours when to be exerted on our soil. But it is from a sincere love of peace, and a firm persuasion that bound to France by the interests and the strong sympathies still existing in the minds of our citizens, and holding relative positions which ensure their continuance we are secure of a long course of peace. Whereas the change of friends, which will be rendered necessary if France changes that position, embarks us necessarily as a belligerent power in the first war of Europe. In that case France will have held possession of New Orleans during the interval of a peace, long or short, at the end of which it will be wrested from her. Will this short-lived possession have been an equivalent to her for the transfer of such a weight into the scale of her enemy? Will not the amalgamation of a young, thriving, nation continue to that enemy the health and force which are at present so evidently on the decline? And will a few years possession of N. Orleans add equally to the strength of France? She may say she needs Louisiana for the supply of her West Indies. She does not need it in time of peace. And in war she could not depend on them because they would be so easily intercepted. I should suppose that all these considerations might in some proper form be brought into view of the government of France. Tho' stated by us, it ought not to give offence; because we do not bring them forward as a menace, but as consequences not controulable by us, but inevitable from the course of things. We mention them not as things which we desire by any means, but as things we deprecate; and we beseech a friend to look forward and to prevent them for our common interests.

If France considers Louisiana however as indispensable for her views she might perhaps be willing to look about for arrangements which might reconcile it to our interests. If anything could do this it would be the ceding to us the island of New Orleans and the Floridas. This would certainly in a great degree remove the causes of jarring and irritation between us, and perhaps for such a length of time as might produce other means of making the measure permanently conciliatory to our interests and friendships. It would at any rate relieve us from the necessity of taking immediate measures for countervailing such an operation by arrangements in another quarter. Still we should consider N. Orleans and the Floridas as equivalent for the risk of a quarrel with France produced by her vicinage. I have no doubt you have urged these considerations on every proper occasion with the government where you are. They are such as must have effect if you can find the means of producing thorough reflection on them by that government. The idea here is that the troops sent to St. Domingo, were to proceed to Louisiana after finishing their work in that island. If this were the arrangement, it will give you time to return again and again to the charge, for the conquest of St. Domingo will not be a short work. It will take considerable time to wear down a great number of souldiers. Every eye in the U. S. is now fixed on this affair of Louisiana. Perhaps nothing since the revolutionary war has produced more uneasy sensations through the body of the nation. Notwithstanding temporary bickerings have taken place with France, she has still a strong hold on the affections of our citizens generally.

6. To Governor William H. Harrison, Washington, 27 February 1803.

After service in the army, William Henry Harrison (1773–1841) of Virginia accepted an appointment as secretary of the Northwest Territory in 1798 and was territorial delegate to Congress in 1799. Harrison was subsequently named by President John Adams as first governor of the new Indiana Territory, holding that office from 1801 to 1812. TJ elaborates here an approach to Indian affairs designed to push forward the boundary of white settlement with as little expense and bloodshed as possible, and with at least a semblance of legal propriety. This strategically impor-

tant territory, lying between British Canada and the young republic's settlements, remained volatile through the War of 1812.

From the Secretary of War you receive from time to time information and instructions as to our Indian affairs. These communications being for the public records, are restrained always to particular objects and occasions; but this letter being unofficial and private, I may with safety give you a more extensive view of our policy respecting the Indians, that you may the better comprehend the parts dealt out to you in detail through the official channel, and observing the system of which they make a part, conduct yourself in unison with it in cases where you are obliged to act without instruction. Our system is to live in perpetual peace with the Indians, to cultivate an affectionate attachment from them, by everything just and liberal which we can do for them within the bounds of reason, and by giving them effectual protection against wrongs from our own people. The decrease of game rendering their subsistence by hunting insufficient, we wish to draw them to agriculture, to spinning and weaving. The latter branches they take up with great readiness, because they fall to the women, who gain by quitting the labors of the field for those which are exercised within doors. When they withdraw themselves to the culture of a small piece of land, they will perceive how useless to them are their extensive forests, and will be willing to pare them off from time to time in exchange for necessaries for their farms and families. To promote this disposition to exchange lands, which they have to spare and we want, for necessaries, which we have to spare and they want, we shall push our trading uses, and be glad to see the good and influential individuals among them run in debt, because we observe that when these debts get beyond what the individuals can pay, they become willing to lop them off by a cession of lands. At our trading houses, too, we mean to sell so low as merely to repay us cost and charges, so as neither to lessen or enlarge our capital. This is what private traders cannot do, for they must gain; they will consequently retire from the competition, and we shall thus get clear of this pest without giving offence or umbrage to the Indians. In this way our settlements will gradually circumscribe and approach the Indians, and they will in time either incorporate with us as citizens of the United States, or remove beyond the Mississippi. The former is certainly the termination of their history most happy for themselves; but, in the whole course of this, it is essential to cultivate their love. As to their fear, we presume that our strength and their weakness is now so visible that they must see we have only to shut our hand to crush them, and that all our liberalities to them proceed from motives of pure humanity only. Should any tribe be fool-hardy enough to take up the hatchet at any time, the seizing the whole country of that tribe, and driving them across the Mississippi, as the only condition of peace, would be an example to others, and a furtherance of our final consolidation.

Combined with these views, and to be prepared against the occupation of Louisiana by a powerful and enterprising people, it is important that, setting less value on interior extension of purchases from the Indians, we bend our whole views to the purchase and settlement of the country on the Mississippi, from its mouth to its northern regions, that we may be able to present as strong a front on our western as on our eastern border, and plant on the Mississippi itself the means of its own defence. We now own from 31 to the Yazoo, and hope this summer to purchase what belongs to the Choctaws from the Yazoo up to their boundary, supposed to be about opposite the mouth of Acanza. We wish at the same time to begin in your quarter, for which there is at present a favorable opening. The Cahokias extinct, we are entitled to their country by our paramount sovereignty. The Piorias, we understand, have all been driven off from their country, and we might claim it in the same way; but as we understand there is one chief remaining, who would, as the survivor of the tribe, sell the right, it is better to give him such terms as will make him easy for life, and take a conveyance from him. The Kaskaskias being reduced to a few families, I presume we may purchase their whole country for what would place every individual of them at his ease, and be a small price to us,—say by laying off for each family, whenever they would choose it, as much rich land as they could cultivate, adjacent to each other, enclosing the whole in a single fence, and giving them such an annuity in money or goods forever as would place them in happiness; and we might take them also under the protection of the United States. Thus possessed of the rights of these tribes, we should proceed to the settling their boundaries with the Poutewatamies and Kickapoos; claiming all doubtful territory, but paying them a price for the relinquishment of their concurrent claim, and even prevailing on them, if possible, to cede, for a price, such of their own unquestioned territory as would give us a convenient northern boundary. Before broaching this, and while we are bargaining with the Kaskaskias, the minds of the Poutewatamies and Kickapoos should be soothed and conciliated by liberalities and sincere assurances of friendship. Perhaps by sending a well-qualified character to stay some time in Decoigne's village, as if on other business, and to sound him and introduce the subject by degrees to his mind and that of the other heads of families, inculcating in the way of conversation, all those considerations which prove the advantages they would receive by a cession on these terms, the object might be more easily and effectually obtained than by abruptly proposing it to them at a formal treaty. Of the means, however, of obtaining what we wish, you will be the best judge; and I have given you this view of the system which we suppose will best promote the interests of the Indians and ourselves, and finally consolidate our whole country to one nation only; that you may be enabled the better to adapt your means to the object, for this purpose we have given you a general commission for treating. The crisis is pressing: whatever can now be obtained must be obtained quickly. The occupation of New Orleans, hourly expected, by the French, is already felt like a light breeze by the Indians. You know the sentiments they entertain of that nation; under the hope of their protection they will immediately stiffen against cessions of lands to us. We had better, therefore, do at once what can now be done.

I must repeat that this letter is to be considered as private and friendly, and is not to control any particular instructions which you may receive through official channel. You will also perceive how sacredly it must be kept within your own breast, and especially how improper to be understood by the Indians. For their interests and their tranquillity it is best they should see only the present age of their history.

7. To Dr. Benjamin Rush, Washington, 21 April 1803, with a "Syllabus . . . of the Merit of the Doctrines of Jesus." *Dr. Benjamin Rush (1745–1813) studied medicine at Edinburgh before becoming a professor of chemistry at the College of Philadelphia in 1769. A prominent patriot and civic leader during the Revolution, Rush published widely on medical topics. Rush was appointed treasurer of the mint by John Adams in 1797, serving in this position under subsequent Republican administrations. A close friend of both TJ and John Adams, Rush was instrumental in effecting a late-life reconciliation between the two old patriots. At this time, TJ resumed earlier conversations with the Calvinist Rush, seeking to explain his religious position. During the 1800 election season, TJ had been assailed by Federalist clergy for his unconventional beliefs; he now proclaimed, "I am a Christian," albeit of a very idiosyncratic kind.*

In some of the delightful conversations with you, in the evenings of 1798–99, and which served as an anodyne to the afflictions of the crisis through which our country was then laboring, the Christian religion was sometimes our topic; and I then promised you, that one day or other, would give you my views of it. They are the result of a life of inquiry & reflection, and very different from that anti-Christian system imputed to me by those who know nothing of my opinions. To the corruptions of Christianity I am indeed opposed; but not to the genuine precepts of Jesus himself. I am a Christian, in the only sense he wished any one to be; sincerely attached to his doctrines, in preference to all others; ascribing to himself every human excellence; & believing he never claimed any other. At the short intervals since these conversations, when I could justifiably abstract my mind from public affairs, the subject has been under my contemplation. But the more considered it, the more it expanded beyond the measure of either my time or information. In the moment of my late departure from Monticello, I received from Doctr Priestley, his little treatise of "Socrates & Jesus compared." This being a section of the general view I had taken of the field, it became a subject of reflection while on the road, and unoccupied otherwise. The result was, to arrange in my mind a syllabus, or outline of such an estimate of the comparative merits of Christianity, as wished to see executed by some one of more leisure and information for the task, than myself. This I now send you, as the only discharge of my promise I can probably ever execute. And in confiding it to you, I know it will not be exposed to the malignant perversions of those who make every word from me a text for new misrepresentations & calumnies. I am moreover averse to the communication of my religious tenets to the public; because it would countenance the presumption of those who have endeavored to draw them before that tribunal, and to seduce public opinion to erect itself into that inquisition over the rights of conscience, which the laws have so justly proscribed. It behoves every man who values liberty of conscience for himself, to resist invasions of it in the case of others; or their case may, by change of circumstances, become his own. It behoves him, too, in his own case, to give no example of concession, betraying the common right of independent opinion, by answering questions of faith, which the laws have left between God & himself. Accept my affectionate salutations.

SYLLABUS OF AN ESTIMATE OF THE
MERIT OF THE DOCTRINES OF JESUS,
COMPARED WITH THOSE OF OTHERS,
April, 1803

In a comparative view of the Ethics of the enlightened nations of antiquity, of the Jews and of Jesus, no notice should be taken of the corruptions of reason among the ancients, to wit, the idolatry & superstition of the vulgar, nor of the corruptions of Christianity by the learned among its professors.

Let a just view be taken of the moral principles inculcated by the most esteemed of the sects of ancient philosophy, or of their individuals; particularly Pythagoras, Socrates, Epicurus, Cicero, Epictetus, Seneca, Antoninus.

I. PHILOSOPHERS. 1. Their precepts related chiefly to ourselves, and the government of those passions which, unrestrained, would disturb our tranquillity of mind. In this branch of philosophy they were really great.

2. In developing our duties to others, they were short and defective. They embraced, indeed, the circles of kindred & friends, and inculcated patriotism, or the love of our country in the aggregate, as a primary obligation: toward our neighbors & countrymen they taught justice, but scarcely viewed them as within the circle of benevolence. Still less have they inculcated peace, charity & love to our fellow men, or embraced with benevolence the whole family of mankind.

II. JEWS. 1. Their system was Deism; that is, the belief of one only God. But their ideas of him & of his attributes were degrading & injurious.

2. Their Ethics were not only imperfect, but often irreconcilable with the sound dictates of reason & morality, as they respect intercourse with those around us; & repulsive & anti-social, as respecting other nations. They needed reformation, therefore, in an eminent degree.

III. JESUS. In this state of things among the Jews, Jesus appeared. His parentage was obscure; his condition poor; his education null; his natural endowments great; his life correct and innocent: he was meek, benevolent, patient, firm, disinterested, & of the sublimest eloquence.

The disadvantages under which his doctrines appear are remarkable.

1. Like Socrates & Epictetus, he wrote nothing himself.

2. But he had not, like them, a Xenophon or an Arrian to write for him. On the contrary, all the learned of his country, entrenched in its power and riches, were opposed to him, lest his labors should undermine their advantages; and the committing to writing his life & doctrines fell on

the most unlettered & ignorant men; who wrote, too, from memory, & not till long after the transactions had passed.

3. According to the ordinary fate of those who attempt to enlighten and reform mankind, he fell an early victim to the jealousy & combination of the altar and the throne, at about 33. years of age, his reason having not yet attained the maximum of its energy, nor the course of his preaching, which was but of 3. years at most, presented occasions for developing a complete system of morals.

4. Hence the doctrines which he really delivered were defective as a whole, and fragments only of what he did deliver have come to us mutilated, misstated, & often unintelligible.

5. They have been still more disfigured by the corruptions of schismatising followers, who have found an interest in sophisticating & perverting the simple doctrines he taught by engrafting on them the mysticisms of a Grecian sophist, frittering them into subtleties, & obscuring them with jargon, until they have caused good men to reject the whole in disgust, & to view Jesus himself as an impostor.

Notwithstanding these disadvantages, a system of morals is presented to us, which, if filled up in the true style and spirit of the rich fragments he left us, would be the most perfect and sublime that has ever been taught by man.

The question of his being a member of the Godhead, or in direct communication with it, claimed for him by some of his followers, and denied by others, is foreign to the present view, which is merely an estimate of the intrinsic merit of his doctrines.

1. He corrected the Deism of the Jews, confirming them in their belief of one only God, and giving them juster notions of his attributes and government.

2. His moral doctrines, relating to kindred & friends, were more pure & perfect than those of the most correct of the philosophers, and greatly more so than those of the Jews; and they went far beyond both in inculcating universal philanthropy, not only to kindred and friends, to neighbors and countrymen, but to all mankind, gathering all into one family, under the bonds of love, charity, peace, common wants and common aids. A development of this head will evince the peculiar superiority of the system of Jesus over all others.

3. The precepts of philosophy, & of the Hebrew code, laid hold of actions only. He pushed his scrutinies into the heart of man; erected his tribunal in the region of his thoughts, and purified the waters at the fountain head.

4. He taught, emphatically, the doctrines of a future state, which was either doubted, or disbelieved by the Jews; and wielded it with efficacy, as an important incentive, supplementary to the other motives to moral conduct.

8. Second Inaugural Address, 4 March 1805. *Jefferson's successful first term led to his landslide reelection in 1804, when he received 162 out of 176 electoral votes; Republicans dominated both houses of Congress. TJ surveyed the na-*

tion's accomplishments and prospects with satisfaction, but troubles associated with the resumption of the Napoleonic wars in Europe lay not far ahead.

Proceeding, fellow citizens, to that qualification which the constitution requires, before my entrance on the charge again conferred upon me, it is my duty to express the deep sense entertain of this new proof of confidence from my fellow citizens at large, and the zeal with which it inspires me, so to conduct myself as may best satisfy their just expectations.

On taking this station on a former occasion, I declared the principles on which I believed it my duty to administer the affairs of our commonwealth. My conscience tells me that I have, on every occasion, acted up to that declaration, according to its obvious import, and to the understanding of every candid mind.

In the transaction of your foreign affairs, we have endeavored to cultivate the friendship of all nations, and especially of those with which we have the most important relations. We have done them justice on all occasions, favored where favor was lawful, and cherished mutual interests and intercourse on fair and equal terms. We are firmly convinced, and we act on that conviction, that with nations, as with individuals, our interests soundly calculated, will ever be found inseparable from our moral duties; and history bears witness to the fact, that a just nation is taken on its word, when recourse is had to armaments and wars to bridle others.

At home, fellow citizens, you best know whether we have done well or ill. The suppression of unnecessary offices, of useless establishments and expenses, enabled us to discontinue our internal taxes. These covering our land with officers, and opening our doors to their intrusions, had already begun that process of domiciliary vexation which, once entered, is scarcely to be restrained from reaching successively every article of produce and property. If among these taxes some minor ones fell which had not been inconvenient, it was because their amount would not have paid the officers who collected them, and because, if they had any merit, the state authorities might adopt them, instead of others less approved.

The remaining revenue on the consumption of foreign articles, is paid cheerfully by those who can afford to add foreign luxuries to domestic comforts, being collected on our seaboards and frontiers only, and incorporated with the transactions of our mercantile citizens, it may be the pleasure and pride of an American to ask, what farmer, what mechanic, what laborer, ever sees a tax-gatherer of the United States? These contributions enable us to support the current expenses of the government, to fulfil contracts with foreign nations, to extinguish the native right of soil within our limits, to extend those limits, and to apply such a surplus to our public debts, as places at a short day their final redemption, and that redemption once effected, the revenue thereby liberated may, by a just repartition among the states, and a corresponding amendment of the constitution, be applied, *in time of peace,* to rivers, canals, roads, arts, manufactures, education, and other great objects within each state. *In time of war,* if injustice, by ourselves or others, must sometimes produce war, increased as the same revenue will be increased by population and consumption, and aided by other resources reserved for that crisis, it may meet within the year all the

expenses of the year, without encroaching on the rights of future generations, by burdening them with the debts of the past. War will then be but
a suspension of useful works, and a return to a state of peace, a return to
the progress of improvement.

I have said, fellow citizens, that the income reserved had enabled us to
extend our limits; but that extension may possibly pay for itself before we
are called on, and in the meantime, may keep down the accruing interest;
in all events, it will repay the advances we have made. I know that the acquisition of Louisiana has been disapproved by some, from a candid apprehension that the enlargement of our territory would endanger its union.
But who can limit the extent to which the federative principle may operate effectively? The larger our association, the less will it be shaken by local passions; and in any view, is it not better that the opposite bank of the
Mississippi should be settled by our own brethren and children, than by
strangers of another family? With which shall we be most likely to live in
harmony and friendly intercourse?

In matters of religion, I have considered that its free exercise is placed
by the constitution independent of the powers of the general government.
I have therefore undertaken, on no occasion, to prescribe the religious
exercises suited to it; but have left them, as the constitution found them,
under the direction and discipline of state or church authorities acknowledged by the several religious societies.

The aboriginal inhabitants of these countries I have regarded with the
commiseration their history inspires. Endowed with the faculties and the
rights of men, breathing an ardent love of liberty and independence, and
occupying a country which left them no desire but to be undisturbed, the
stream of overflowing population from other regions directed itself on
these shores; without power to divert, or habits to contend against, they
have been overwhelmed by the current, or driven before it; now reduced
within limits too narrow for the hunter's state, humanity enjoins us to
teach them agriculture and the domestic arts; to encourage them to that
industry which alone can enable them to maintain their place in existence,
and to prepare them in time for that state of society, which to bodily comforts adds the improvement of the mind and morals. We have therefore
liberally furnished them with the implements of husbandry and household
use; we have placed among them instructors in the arts of first necessity;
and they are covered with the aegis of the law against aggressors from
among ourselves.

But the endeavors to enlighten them on the fate which awaits their
present course of life, to induce them to exercise their reason, follow its
dictates, and change their pursuits with the change of circumstances, have
powerful obstacles to encounter; they are combated by the habits of their
bodies, prejudice of their minds, ignorance, pride, and the influence of
interested and crafty individuals among them, who feel themselves something in the present order of things, and fear to become nothing in any
other. These persons inculcate a sanctimonious reverence for the customs
of their ancestors; that whatsoever they did, must be done through all
time; that reason is a false guide, and to advance under its counsel, in their
physical, moral, or political condition, is perilous innovation; that their

duty is to remain as their Creator made them, ignorance being safety, and knowledge full of danger; in short, my friends, among them is seen the action and counteraction of good sense and bigotry; they, too, have their anti-philosophers, who find an interest in keeping things in their present state, who dread reformation, and exert all their faculties to maintain the ascendency of habit over the duty of improving our reason, and obeying its mandates.

In giving these outlines, I do not mean, fellow citizens, to arrogate to myself the merit of the measures; that is due, in the first place, to the reflecting character of our citizens at large, who, by the weight of public opinion, influence and strengthen the public measures; it is due to the sound discretion with which they select from among themselves those to whom they confide the legislative duties; it is due to the zeal and wisdom of the characters thus selected, who lay the foundations of public happiness in wholesome laws, the execution of which alone remains for others; and it is due to the able and faithful auxiliaries, whose patriotism has associated with me in the executive functions.

During this course of administration, and in order to disturb it, the artillery of the press has been levelled against us, charged with whatsoever its licentiousness could devise or dare. These abuses of an institution so important to freedom and science, are deeply to be regretted, inasmuch as they tend to lessen its usefulness, and to sap its safety; they might, indeed, have been corrected by the wholesome punishments reserved and provided by the laws of the several States against falsehood and defamation; but public duties more urgent press on the time of public servants, and the offenders have therefore been left to find their punishment in the public indignation.

Nor was it uninteresting to the world, that an experiment should be fairly and fully made, whether freedom of discussion, unaided by power, is not sufficient for the propagation and protection of truth—whether a government, conducting itself in the true spirit of its constitution, with zeal and purity, and doing no act which it would be unwilling the whole world should witness, can be written down by falsehood and defamation. The experiment has been tried; you have witnessed the scene; our fellow citizens have looked on, cool and collected; they saw the latent source from which these outrages proceeded; they gathered around their public functionaries, and when the constitution called them to the decision by suffrage, they pronounced their verdict, honorable to those who had served them, and consolatory to the friend of man, who believes he may be intrusted with his own affairs.

No inference is here intended, that the laws, provided by the State against false and defamatory publications, should not be enforced; he who has time, renders a service to public morals and public tranquillity, in reforming these abuses by the salutary coercions of the law; but the experiment is noted, to prove that, since truth and reason have maintained their ground against false opinions in league with false facts, the press, confined to truth, needs no other legal restraint; the public judgment will correct false reasonings and opinions, on a full hearing of all parties; and no other definite line can be drawn between the inestimable liberty of the press and its demoralizing licentiousness. If there be still improprieties which this rule would not restrain, its supplement must be sought in the censorship of public opinion.

Contemplating the union of sentiment now manifested so generally, as auguring harmony and happiness to our future course, offer to our country sincere congratulations. With those, too, not yet rallied to the same point, the disposition to do so is gaining strength; facts are piercing through the veil drawn over them; and our doubting brethren will at length see, that the mass of their fellow citizens, with whom they cannot yet resolve to act, as to principles and measures, think as they think, and desire what they desire; that our wish, as well as theirs, is, that the public efforts may be directed honestly to the public good, that peace be cultivated, civil and religious liberty unassailed, law and order preserved; equality of rights maintained, and that state of property, equal or unequal, which results to every man from his own industry, or that of his fathers. When satisfied of these views, it is not in human nature that they should not approve and support them; in the meantime, let us cherish them with patient affection; let us do them justice, and more than justice, in all competitions of interest; and we need not doubt that truth, reason, and their own interests, will at length prevail, will gather them into the fold of their country, and will complete their entire union of opinion, which gives to a nation the blessing of harmony, and the benefit of all its strength.

I shall now enter on the duties to which my fellow citizens have again called me, and shall proceed in the spirit of those principles which they have approved. I fear not that any motives of interest may lead me astray; I am sensible of no passion which could seduce me knowingly from the path of justice; but the weakness of human nature, and the limits of my own understanding, will produce errors of judgment sometimes injurious to your interests. I shall need, therefore, all the indulgence I have heretofore experienced—the want of it will certainly not lessen with increasing years. Shall need, too, the favor of that Being in whose hands we are, who led our forefathers, as Israel of old, from their native land, and planted them in a country flowing with all the necessaries and comforts of life; who has covered our infancy with his providence, and our riper years with his wisdom and power; and to whose goodness I ask you to join with me in supplications, that he will so enlighten the minds of your servants, guide their councils, and prosper their measures, that whatsoever they do, shall result in your good, and shall secure to you the peace, friendship, and approbation of all nations.

9. To the Chiefs of the Cherokee Nation, Washington, 10 January 1806. *TJ drafted numerous addresses like this one to various Indian delegations that came to negotiate with federal officials in the nation's capital. TJ applauds the Cherokees' advances toward "civilization," comparing them favorably with the tribes Governor Harrison dealt with in the Northwest (see document 6 above).*

MY FRIENDS AND CHILDREN. . . . Having now finished our business and finished it I hope to mutual satisfaction, I cannot take leave of you without expressing the satisfaction I have received from your visit. I see with my own eyes that the endeavors we have been making to encourage and lead you in the way of improving your situation have not been unsuccessful; it has been like grain sown in good ground, producing abundantly. You are becoming farmers, learning the use of the plough and the hoe, enclosing your grounds and employing that labor in their cultivation which you formerly employed in hunting and in war; and I see handsome specimens of cotton cloth raised, spun and wove by yourselves. You are also raising cattle and hogs for your food, and horses to assist your labors. Go on, my children, in the same way and be assured the further you advance in it the happier and more respectable you will be.

Our brethren, whom you have happened to meet here from the West and Northwest, have enabled you to compare your situation now with what it was formerly. They also make the comparison, and they see how far you are ahead of them, and seeing what you are they are encouraged to do as you have done. You will find your next want to be mills to grind your corn, which by relieving your women from the loss of time in beating it into meal, will enable them to spin and weave more. When a man has enclosed and improved his farm, builds a good house on it and raised plentiful stocks of animals, he will wish when he dies that these things shall go to his wife and children, whom he loves more than he does his other relations, and for whom he will work with pleasure during his life. You will, therefore, find it necessary to establish laws for this. When a man has property, earned by his own labor, he will not like to see another come and take it from him because he happens to be stronger, or else to defend it by spilling blood. You will find it necessary then to appoint good men, as judges, to decide contests between man and man, according to reason and to the rules you shall establish. If you wish to be aided by our counsel and experience in these things we shall always be ready to assist you with our advice.

My children, it is unnecessary for me to advise you against spending all your time and labor in warring with and destroying your fellow-men, and wasting your own members. You already see the folly and iniquity of it. Your young men, however, are not yet sufficiently sensible of it. Some of them cross the Mississippi to go and destroy people who have never done them an injury. My children, this is wrong and must not be; if we permit them to cross the Mississippi to war with the Indians on the other side of that river, we must let those Indians cross the river to take revenge on you. I say again, this must not be. The Mississippi now belongs to us. It must not be a river of blood. It is now the water-path along which all our people of Natchez, St. Louis, Indiana, Ohio, Tennessee, Kentucky and the western parts of Pennsylvania and Virginia are constantly passing with their property, to and from New Orleans. Young men going to war are not easily restrained. Finding our people on the river they will rob them, perhaps kill them. This would bring on a war between us and you. It is better to stop this in time by forbidding your young men to go across the river to make war. If they go to visit or to live with the Cherokees on the other side of the river we shall not object to that. That country is ours. We will permit them to live in it.

My children, this is what I wished to say to you. To go on in learning to cultivate the earth and to avoid war. If any of your neighbors injure you, our beloved men whom we place with you will endeavor to obtain justice for you and we will support them in it. If any of your bad people injure your neighbors, be ready to acknowledge it and to do them justice. It is more honorable to repair a wrong than to persist in it. Tell all your chiefs, your men, women and children, that I take them by the hand and hold it fast. That I am their father, wish their happiness and well-being, and am always ready to promote their good.

My children, I thank you for your visit and pray to the Great Spirit who made us all and planted us all in this land to live together like brothers that He will conduct you safely to your homes, and grant you to find your families and your friends in good health.

10. To Barnabas Bidwell, Washington, 5 July 1806. *Barnabas Bidwell (1763–1833) was a staunch Republican loyalist who ably promoted the administration's interests in the House of Representatives from 1805 until his resignation in 1807. The rising Republican tide in Massachusetts culminated in the election of James Sullivan as governor in 1807. Under him Bidwell served as state attorney general. The reference to "schism" is to the Quids, a small group of Republican dissidents, led by John Randolph of Roanoke, who defied the administration—and locked horns with Bidwell—on the recent settlement of the Yazoo land controversy, questioned TJ's foreign policy, and challenged James Madison's position of heir apparent to the presidency.*

I sincerely congratulate you on the triumph of republicanism in Massachusetts. The Hydra of federalism has now lost all its heads but two. Connecticut think will soon follow Massachusetts. Delaware will probably remain what it ever has been, a mere county of England, conquered indeed, and held under by force, but always disposed to counter-revolution. I speak of its majority only.

Our information from London continues to give us hopes of an accommodation there on both the points of 'accustomed commerce and impressment.' In this there must probably be some mutual concession, because we cannot expect to obtain every thing and yield nothing. But I hope it will be such an one as may be accepted. The arrival of the Hornet in France is so recently known, that it will yet be some time before we learn our prospects there. Notwithstanding the efforts made here, and made professedly to assassinate that negotiation in embryo, if the good sense of Buonaparte should prevail over his temper, the present state of things in Europe may induce him to require of Spain that she should do us justice at least. That he should require her to sell us East Florida, we have no right to insist: yet there are not wanting considerations which may induce him to wish a permanent foundation for peace laid between us. In this treaty, whatever it shall be, our old enemies the federalists, and their new friends, will find enough to carp at. This is a thing of course, and I should suspect error where they found no fault. The buzzard feeds on carrion only. Their rallying point is 'war with France and Spain, and alliance with Great

Britain:' and every thing is wrong with them which checks their new ardor to be fighting for the liberties of mankind; on the sea always excepted. There one nation is to monopolise all the liberties of the others.

I read, with extreme regret, the expressions of an inclination on your part to retire from Congress. I will not say that this time, more than all others, calls for the service of every man; but I will say, there never was a time when the services of those who possess talents, integrity, firmness and sound judgment, were more wanted in Congress. Some one of that description is particularly wanted to take the lead in the House of Representatives, to consider the business of the nation as his own business, to take it up as if he were singly charged with it, and carry it through. I do not mean that any gentleman, relinquishing his own judgment, should implicitly support all the measures of the administration; but that, where he does not disapprove of them, he should not suffer them to go off in sleep, but bring them to the attention of the House, and give them a fair chance. Where he disapproves, he will of course leave them to be brought forward by those who concur in the sentiment. Shall I explain my idea by an example? The classification of the militia was communicated to General Varnum and yourself merely as a proposition, which, if you approved, it was trusted you would support. I knew, indeed, that General Varnum was opposed to any thing which might break up the present organization of the militia: but when so modified as to avoid this, I thought he might, perhaps, be reconciled to it. As soon as I found it did not coincide with your sentiments, I could not wish you to support it; but using the same freedom of opinion, procured it to be brought forward elsewhere. It failed there also, and for a time perhaps, may not prevail: but a militia can never be used for distant service on any other plan; and Buonaparte will conquer the world, if they do not learn his secret of composing armies of young men only, whose enthusiasm and health enable them to surmount all obstacles. When a gentleman, through zeal for the public service, undertakes to do the public business, we know that we shall hear the cant of backstairs counsellors. But we never heard this while the declaimer was himself a backstairs man, as he calls it, but in the confidence and views of the administration, as may more properly and respectfully be said. But if the members are to know nothing but what is important enough to be put into a public message, and indifferent enough to be made known to all the world; if the executive is to keep all other information to himself, and the House to plunge on in the dark, it becomes a government of chance and not of design. The imputation was one of those artifices used to despoil an adversary of his most effectual arms; and men of mind will place themselves above a gabble of this order. The last session of Congress was indeed an uneasy one for a time: but as soon as the members penetrated into the views of those who were taking a new course, they rallied in as solid a phalanx as I have ever seen act together. Indeed have never seen a House of better dispositions. They want only a man of business & in whom they can confide to conduct things in the house; and they are as much disposed to support him as can be wished. It is only speaking a truth to say that all eyes look to you. It was not perhaps expected from a new member, at his first session, & before the forms & style of doing business were familiar. But it would be a subject of deep regret were you to refuse yourself to the conspicuous part in the business of the house which all assign you. Perhaps I am not entitled to speak with so much frankness; but it proceeds from no motive which has not a right to your forgiveness. Opportunities of candid explanation are so seldom afforded me, that I must not lose them when they occur.

The information I receive from your quarter agrees with that from the south; that the late schism has made not the smallest impression on the public, and that the seceders are obliged to give to it other grounds than those which we know to be the true ones. All we have to wish is, that at the ensuing session, every one may take the part openly which he secretly befriends. I recollect nothing new and true, worthy communicating to you. As for what is not true, you will always find abundance in the newspapers. Among other things, are those perpetual alarms as to the Indians, for no one of which has there ever been the slightest ground. They are the suggestions of hostile traders, always wishing to embroil us with the Indians, to perpetuate their own extortionate commerce.

11. Sixth Annual Message, 2 December 1806. *Though new entanglements in the widening European conflict were imminent, TJ's attention was here riveted on the West. Even as reports of the success of the expedition of Lewis and Clark, lasting from 1803 to 1806 provided a glimpse of the vast potential of the Louisiana Purchase and adjacent territories, TJ sought to head off a purported plot by Burr to separate the western states from the union, or to move against adjacent Spanish territories. In August Aaron Burr (1756–1836), TJ's Vice President during his first term, had launched an expedition down the Ohio and Mississippi rivers, recruiting a small expeditionary force whose ultimate object remained—and remains— unclear. On 27 November TJ issued a proclamation warning citizens against participating in any unauthorized campaign against any nation with which the United States was then at peace. Burr was apprehended in the Mississippi Territory in February and was subsequently transported to Richmond, where he stood trial for treason.*

It would have given me, fellow citizens, great satisfaction to announce in the moment of your meeting that the difficulties in our foreign relations, existing at the time of your last separation, had been amicably and justly terminated. I lost no time in taking those measures which were most likely to bring them to such a termination, by special missions charged with such powers and instructions as in the event of failure could leave no imputation on either our moderation or forbearance. The delays which have since taken place in our negotiations with the British government appears to have proceeded from causes which do not forbid the expectation that during the course of the session I may be enabled to lay before you their final issue. What will be that of the negotiations for settling our differences with Spain, nothing which had taken place at the date of the last despatches enables us to pronounce. On the western side of the Mississippi she advanced in considerable force, and took post at the settlement of Bayou Pierre, on the Red river. This village was originally settled by France, was held by her as long as she held Louisiana, and was delivered to Spain only as a part of Louisiana. Being small, insulated, and distant, it was not observed, at the moment of redelivery to France and the United States, that she continued a guard of half a dozen men which had been stationed there. A proposition, however, having been lately made by our commander-in-chief, to assume the Sabine river as a temporary line of separation between the troops of the two nations until the issue of our negotiations shall be known; this has been referred by the Spanish commandant to his superior, and in the meantime, he has withdrawn his force to the western side of the Sabine river. The correspondence on this subject, now communicated, will exhibit more particularly the present state of things in that quarter.

The nature of that country requires indispensably that an unusual proportion of the force employed there should be cavalry or mounted infantry. In order, therefore, that the commanding officer might be enabled to act with effect, I had authorized him to call on the governors of Orleans and Mississippi for a corps of five hundred volunteer cavalry. The temporary arrangement he has proposed may perhaps render this unnecessary. But I inform you with great pleasure of the promptitude with which the inhabitants of those territories have tendered their services in defence of their country. It has done honor to themselves, entitled them to the confidence of their fellow-citizens in every part of the Union, and must strengthen the general determination to protect them efficaciously under all circumstances which may occur.

Having received information that in another part of the United States a great number of private individuals were combining together, arming and organizing themselves contrary to law, to carry on military expeditions against the territories of Spain, I thought it necessary, by proclamations as well as by special orders, to take measures for preventing and suppressing this enterprise, for seizing the vessels, arms, and other means provided for it, and for arresting and bringing to justice its authors and abettors. It was due to that good faith which ought ever to be the rule of action in public as well as in private transactions; it was due to good order and regular government, that while the public force was acting strictly on the defensive and merely to protect our citizens from aggression, the criminal attempts of private individuals to decide for their country the question of peace or war, by commencing active and unauthorized hostilities, should be promptly and efficaciously suppressed.

Whether it will be necessary to enlarge our regular force will depend on the result of our negotiation with Spain; but as it is uncertain when that result will be known, the provisional measures requisite for that, and to meet any pressure intervening in that quarter, will be a subject for your early consideration.

The possession of both banks of the Mississippi reducing to a single point the defence of that river, its waters, and the country adjacent, it becomes highly necessary to provide for that point a more adequate security. Some position above its mouth, commanding the passage of the river, should be rendered sufficiently strong to cover the armed vessels which may be stationed there for defence, and in conjunction with them to present an insuperable obstacle to any force attempting to pass. The approaches to the city of New Orleans, from the eastern quarter also, will require to be examined, and more effectually guarded. For the internal support of the country, the encouragement of a strong settlement on the western side of the Mississippi, within reach of New Orleans, will be worthy the consideration of the legislature.

The gun-boats authorized by an act of the last session are so advanced that they will be ready for service in the ensuing spring. Circumstances permitted us to allow the time necessary for their more solid construction. As a much larger number will still be wanting to place our seaport towns and waters in that state of defence to which we are competent and they entitled, a similar appropriation for a further provision for them is recommended for the ensuing year.

A further appropriation will also be necessary for repairing fortifications already established, and the erection of such works as may have real effect in obstructing the approach of an enemy to our seaport towns, or their remaining before them.

In a country whose constitution is derived from the will of the people, directly expressed by their free suffrages; where the principal executive functionaries, and those of the legislature, are renewed by them at short periods; where under the characters of jurors, they exercise in person the greatest portion of the judiciary powers; where the laws are consequently so formed and administered as to bear with equal weight and favor on all, restraining no man in the pursuits of honest industry, and securing to every one the property which that acquires, it would not be supposed that any safeguards could be needed against insurrection or enterprise on the public peace or authority. The laws, however, aware that these should not be trusted to moral restraints only, have wisely provided punishments for these crimes when committed. But would it not be salutary to give also the means of preventing their commission? Where an enterprise is meditated by private individuals against a foreign nation in amity with the United States, powers of prevention to a certain extent are given by the laws; would they not be as reasonable and useful were the enterprise preparing against the United States? While adverting to this branch of the law, it is proper to observe, that in enterprises meditated against foreign nations, the ordinary process of binding to the observance of the peace and good behavior, could it be extended to acts to be done out of the jurisdiction of the United States, would be effectual in some cases where the offender is able to keep out of sight every indication of his purpose which could draw on him the exercise of the powers now given by law.

The states on the coast of Barbary seem generally disposed at present to respect our peace and friendship; with Tunis alone some uncertainty remains. Persuaded that it is our interest to maintain our peace with them on equal terms, or not at all, propose to send in due time a reinforcement into the Mediterranean, unless previous information shall show it to be unnecessary.

We continue to receive proofs of the growing attachment of our Indian neighbors, and of their disposition to place all their interests under the patronage of the United States. These dispositions are inspired by their confidence in our justice, and in the sincere concern we feel for their welfare; and as long as we discharge these high and honorable functions with the integrity and good faith which alone can entitle us to their continuance, we may expect to reap the just reward in their peace and friendship.

The expedition of Messrs. Lewis and Clarke, for exploring the river Missouri, and the best communication from that to the Pacific ocean, has had all the success which could have been expected. They have traced the Missouri nearly to its source, descended the Columbia to the Pacific ocean, ascertained with accuracy the geography of that interesting communication across our continent, learned the character of the country, of its commerce, and inhabitants; and it is but justice to say that Messrs. Lewis and Clarke, and their brave companions, have by this arduous service deserved well of their country.

The attempt to explore the Red river, under the direction of Mr. Freeman, though conducted with a zeal and prudence meriting entire approbation, has not been equally successful. After proceeding up it about six hundred miles, nearly as far as the French settlements had extended while the country was in their possession, our geographers were obliged to return without completing their work. ·

Very useful additions have also been made to our knowledge of the Mississippi by Lieutenant Pike, who has ascended to its source, and whose journal and map, giving the details of the journey, will shortly be ready for communication to both houses of Congress. Those of Messrs. Lewis and Clarke, and Freeman, will require further time to be digested and prepared. These important surveys, in addition to those before possessed, furnish materials for commencing an accurate map of the Mississippi, and its western waters. Some principal rivers, however, remain still to be explored, toward which the authorization of Congress, by moderate appropriations, will be requisite.

I congratulate you, fellow-citizens, on the approach of the period at which you may interpose your authority constitutionally, to withdraw the citizens of the United States from all further participation in those violations of human rights which have been so long continued on the unoffending inhabitants of Africa, and which the morality, the reputation, and the best interests of our country, have long been eager to proscribe. Although no law you may pass can take prohibitory effect till the first day of the year one thousand eight hundred and eight, yet the intervening period is not too long to prevent, by timely notice, expeditions which cannot be completed before that day.

The receipts at the treasury during the year ending on the 30th of September last, have amounted to near fifteen millions of dollars, which have enabled us, after meeting the current demands, to pay two millions seven hundred thousand dollars of the American claims, in part of the price of Louisiana; to pay of the funded debt upward of three millions of principal, and nearly four of interest; and in addition, to reimburse, in the course of the present month, near two millions of five and a half per cent. stock. These payments and reimbursements of the funded debt, with those which have been made in the four years and a half preceding, will, at the close of the present year, have extinguished upwards of twenty-three millions of principal.

The duties composing the Mediterranean fund will cease by law at the end of the present season. Considering, however, that they are levied chiefly on luxuries, and that we have an impost on salt, a necessary of life, the free use of which other-wise is so important, I recommend to your consideration the suppression of the duties on salt, and the continuation of the Mediterranean fund, instead thereof, for a short time, after which that also will become unnecessary for any purpose now within contemplation.

When both of these branches of revenue shall in this way be relinquished, there will still ere long be an accumulation of moneys in the treasury beyond the instalments of public debt which we are permitted by contract to pay. They cannot, then, without a modification assented to by the public creditors, be applied to the extinguishment of this debt, and the complete liberation of our revenues—the most desirable of all objects; nor, if our peace continues, will they be wanting for any other existing purpose. The question, therefore, now comes forward,—to what other objects shall these surpluses be appropriated, and the whole surplus of impost, after the entire discharge of the public debt, and during those intervals when the purposes of war shall not call for them? Shall we suppress the impost and give that advantage to foreign over domestic manufactures? On a few articles of more general and necessary use, the suppression in due season will doubtless be right, but the great mass of the articles on which impost is paid is foreign luxuries, purchased by those only who are rich enough to afford themselves the use of them. Their patriotism would certainly prefer its continuance and application to the great purposes of the public education, roads, rivers, canals, and such other objects of public improvement as it may be thought proper to add to the constitutional enumeration of federal powers. By these operations new channels of communication will be opened between the States; the lines of separation will disappear, their interests will be identified, and their union cemented by new and indissoluble ties. Education is here placed among the articles of public care, not that it would be proposed to take its ordinary branches out of the hands of private enterprise, which manages so much better all the concerns to which it is equal; but a public institution can alone supply those sciences which, though rarely called for, are yet necessary to complete the circle, all the parts of which contribute to the improvement of the country, and some of them to its preservation. The subject is now proposed for the consideration of Congress, because, if approved by the time the State legislatures shall have deliberated on this extension of the federal trusts, and the laws shall be passed, and other arrangements made for their execution, the necessary funds will be on hand and without employment. I suppose an amendment to the constitution, by consent of the States, necessary, because the objects now recommended are not among those enumerated in the constitution, and to which it permits the public moneys to be applied.

The present consideration of a national establishment for education, particularly, is rendered proper by this circumstance also, that if Congress, approving the proposition, shall yet think it more eligible to found it on a donation of lands, they have it now in their power to endow it with those which will be among the earliest to produce the necessary income. This foundation would have the advantage of being independent on war, which may suspend other improvements by requiring for its own purposes the resources destined for them.

This, fellow citizens, is the state of the public interest at the present moment, and according to the information now possessed. But such is the situation of the nations of Europe, and such too the predicament in which we stand with some of them, that we cannot rely with certainty on the present aspect of our affairs that may change from moment to moment, during the course of your session or after you shall have separated. Our duty is, therefore, to act upon things as they are, and to make a reasonable provision for whatever they may be. Were armies to be raised whenever a speck of war is visible in our horizon, we never should have been without them. Our resources would have been exhausted on dangers which have never happened, instead of being reserved for what is really to take place. A steady, perhaps a quickened pace in preparations for the defence of our seaport towns and waters; an early settlement of the most exposed and vulnerable parts of our country; a militia so organized that its effective portions can be called to any point in the Union, or volunteers instead of them to serve a sufficient time, are means which may always be ready yet never preying on our resources until actually called into use. They will maintain the public interests while a more permanent force shall be in course of preparation. But much will depend on the promptitude with which these means can be brought into activity. If war be forced upon us in spite of our long and vain appeals to the justice of nations, rapid and vigorous movements in its outset will go far toward securing us in its course and issue, and toward throwing its burdens on those who render necessary the resort from reason to force.

The result of our negotiations, or such incidents in their course as may enable us to infer their probable issue; such further movements also on our western frontiers as may show whether war is to be pressed there while negotiation is protracted elsewhere, shall be communicated to you from time to time as they become known to me, with whatever other information I possess or may receive, which may aid your deliberations on the great national interests committed to your charge.

12. To William Branch Giles, Monticello, 20 April 1807. *William Branch Giles (1762–1830) served from 1790 to 1798 and again from 1801 to 1803 as a Republican member of Congress from Virginia and between 1803 and 1815 as a senator. Aaron Burr had been captured in February and transported to Richmond, where on 30 March he was brought before Chief Justice John Marshall, presiding over the federal Circuit Court. Burr was at first held on a misdemeanor charge for his alleged expedition against Spain, but at TJ's instigation was indicted for treason on 24 June. In the ensuing trial, Burr and his associates were acquitted.*

Your favor . . . on the subject of Burr's offences, was received only 4 days ago. That there should be anxiety & doubt in the public mind, in the present defective state of the proof, is not wonderful; and this has been sedulously encouraged by the tricks of the judges to force trials before it is possible to collect the evidence, dispersed through a line of 2000 miles from Maine to Orleans. The federalists, too, give all their aid, making Burr's cause their own, mortified only that he did not separate the Union or overturn the government, & proving, that had he had a little dawn of success, they would have joined him to introduce his object, their favorite monarchy, as they would any other enemy, foreign or domestic, who could rid them of this hateful republic for any other government in exchange.

The first ground of complaint was the supine inattention of the administration to a treason stalking through the land in open day. The present one, that they have crushed it before it was ripe for execution, so that no overt acts can be produced. This last may be true; tho' I believe it is not. Our information having been chiefly by way of letter, we do not know of a certainty yet what will be proved. We have set on foot an inquiry through the whole of the country which has been the scene of these trans-actions, to be able to prove to the courts, if they will give time, or to the public by way of communication to Congress, what the real facts have been. For obtaining this, we are obliged to appeal to the patriotism of par-ticular persons in different places, of whom we have requested to make the inquiry in their neighborhood, and on such information as shall be vol-untarily offered. Aided by no process or facilities from the federal courts, but frowned on by their new born zeal for the liberty of those whom we would not permit to overthrow the liberties of their country, we can expect no revealments from the accomplices of the chief offender. Of treasonable intentions, the judges have been obliged to confess there is probable ap-pearance. What loophole they will find in it, when it comes to trial, we can-not foresee. Eaton, Stoddart, Wilkinson, and two others whom I must not name, will satisfy the world, if not the judges, on that head. And I do sup-pose the following overt acts will be proved. 1. The enlistment of men in a regular way. 2. The regular mounting of guard round Blennerhassett's island when they expected Governor Tiffin's men to be on them, *modo guerrino arraiali.* 3. The rendezvous of Burr with his men at the mouth of the Cumberland. 4. His letter to the acting Governor of Mississippi, hold-ing up the prospect of civil war. 5. His capitulation regularly signed with the aids of the Governor, as between two independent & hostile com-manders.

But a moment's calculation will shew that this evidence cannot be col-lected under 4 months, probably 5. from the moment of deciding when & where the trial shall be. I desired Mr. Rodney expressly to inform the Chief Justice of this, inofficially. But Mr. Marshall says, "more than 5 weeks have elapsed since the opinion of the Supreme court has declared the necessity of proving the overt acts, if they exist. Why are they not proved?" In what terms of decency can we speak of this? As if an express could go to Natchez, or the mouth of Cumberland, & return in 5 weeks, to do which has never taken less than twelve. Again, "If, in Nov. or Dec. last, a body of troops had been assembled on the Ohio, it is impossible to suppose the affidavits establishing the fact could not have been obtained by the last of March." But I ask the judge where they should have been lodged? At Frankfort? at Cincinnati? at Nashville? St. Louis? Natchez? New Orleans? These were the probable places of apprehension & examination. It was not known at *Washington* till the 26th of March that Burr would escape from the

Western tribunals, be retaken & brought to an Eastern one; and in 5 days after, (neither 5. months nor 5. weeks, as the judge calculated,) he says, it is "impossible to suppose the affidavits could not have been obtained." Where? At Richmond he certainly meant, or meant only to throw dust in the eyes of his audience. But all the principles of law are to be perverted which would bear on the favorite offenders who endeavor to overrun this odious Republic. "I understand," sais the judge, "*probable* cause of guilt to be a case made out by *proof* furnishing good reason to believe," &c. Speaking as a lawyer, he must mean legal proof, i.e., proof on oath, at least. But this is confounding *probability* and *proof*. We had always before understood that where there was reasonable ground to believe guilt, the offender must be put on his trial. That guilty intentions were probable, the judge believed. And as to the overt acts, were not the bundle of letters of information in Mr. Rodney's hands, the letters and facts published in the local newspapers, Burr's flight, & the universal belief or rumor of his guilt, probable ground for presuming the facts of enlistment, military guard, rendezvous, threats of civil war, or capitulation, so as to put him on trial? Is there a candid man in the U S who does not believe some one, if not all, of these overt acts to have taken place?

If there ever had been an instance in this or the preceding administrations, of federal judges so applying principles of law as to condemn a federal or acquit a republican offender, I should have judged them in the present case with more charity. All this, however, will work well. The nation will judge both the offender & judges for themselves. If a member of the Executive or Legislature does wrong, the day is never far distant when the people will remove him. They will see then & amend the error in our Constitution, which makes any branch independent of the nation. They will see that one of the great co-ordinate branches of the government, setting itself in opposition to the other two, and to the common sense of the nation, proclaims impunity to that class of offenders which endeavors to overturn the Constitution, and are themselves protected in it by the Constitution itself; for impeachment is a farce which will not be tried again. If their protection of Burr produces this amendment, it will do more good than his condemnation would have done. Against Burr, personally, I never had one hostile sentiment. I never indeed thought him an honest, frank-dealing man, but considered him as a crooked gun, or other perverted machine, whose aim or stroke you could never be sure of. Still, while he possessed the confidence of the nation, thought it my duty to respect in him their confidence, & to treat him as if he deserved it; and if this punishment can be commuted now for any useful amendment of the Constitution, shall rejoice in it.

13. Eighth Annual Message, 8 November 1808. *As TJ's second term drew to an end, American relations with both Britain and France had deteriorated badly. Efforts to secure neutral rights of American carriers and the freedom of American sailors from impressment had proven ineffective. In the course of a search for alleged deserters near the Norfolk Roads off Virginia, the* Leopard, *a British Navy frigate, attacked the United States Navy frigate, the* Chesapeake, *in June 1807, sparking widespread demands for retaliation. Diplomatic initiatives failed to yield satisfactory*

*reparations in this case, or to secure American shipping from the continuing depre-
dations of both belligerent powers. In a desperate move to extricate the United States
from the widening European conflict, TJ induced the Republican Congress to enact
an embargo, effective 22 December 1807, on all American vessels sailing for foreign
ports. Here was the great test of TJ's commercial diplomacy: would the loss of American trade lead the belligerent powers to assume a more conciliatory posture? In any
case, TJ reasoned, the embargo would facilitate ongoing preparations for war,
should diplomacy fail. Enforcement of the ban on shipping stretched to the breaking point the administrative and political resources of the administration. Evasion
of the embargo led to increasingly severe sanctions that fostered a Federalist revival,
particularly in the Northeast.*

It would have been a source, fellow citizens, of much gratification, if
our last communications from Europe had enabled me to inform you that
the belligerent nations, whose disregard of neutral rights has been so
destructive to our commerce, had become awakened to the duty and true
policy of revoking their unrighteous edicts. That no means might be omit-
ted to produce this salutary effect, I lost no time in availing myself of the
act authorizing a suspension, in whole or in part, of the several embargo
laws. Our ministers at London and Paris were instructed to explain to the
respective governments there, our disposition to exercise the authority in
such manner as would withdraw the pretext on which the aggressions were
originally founded, and open a way for a renewal of that commercial intercourse which it was alleged on all sides had been reluctantly obstructed.
As each of those governments had pledged its readiness to concur in
renouncing a measure which reached its adversary through the incon-
testable rights of neutrals only, and as the measure had been assumed by
each as a retaliation for an asserted acquiescence in the aggressions of the
other, it was reasonably expected that the occasion would have been seized
by both for evincing the sincerity of their profession, and for restoring to
the commerce of the United States its legitimate freedom. The instructions to our ministers with respect to the different belligerents were necessarily modified with reference to their different circumstances, and to
the condition annexed by law to the executive power of suspension, requiring a degree of security to our commerce which would not result from a
repeal of the decrees of France. Instead of a pledge, therefore, of a suspension of the embargo as to her in case of such a repeal, it was presumed that
a sufficient inducement might be found in other considerations, and particularly in the change produced by a compliance with our just demands
by one belligerent, and a refusal by the other, in the relations between the
other and the United States. To Great Britain, whose power on the ocean
is so ascendant, it was deemed not inconsistent with that condition to state
explicitly, that on her rescinding her orders in relation to the United
States their trade would be opened with her, and remain shut to her enemy, in case of his failure to rescind his decrees also. From France no
answer has been received, nor any indication that the requisite change in
her decrees is contemplated. The favorable reception of the proposition
to Great Britain was the less to be doubted, as her orders of council had
not only been referred for their vindication to an acquiescence on the
part of the United States no longer to be pretended, but as the arrange-

ment proposed, while it resisted the illegal decrees of France, involved, moreover, substantially, the precise advantages professedly aimed at by the British orders. The arrangement has nevertheless been rejected.

This candid and liberal experiment having thus failed, and no other event having occurred on which a suspension of the embargo by the executive was authorized, it necessarily remains in the extent originally given to it. We have the satisfaction, however, to reflect, that in return for the privations by the measure, and which our fellow citizens in general have borne with patriotism, it has had the important effects of saving our mariners and our vast mercantile property, as well as of affording time for prosecuting the defensive and provisional measures called for by the occasion. It has demonstrated to foreign nations the moderation and firmness which govern our councils, and to our citizens the necessity of uniting in support of the laws and the rights of their country, and has thus long frustrated those usurpations and spoliations which, if resisted, involve war; if submitted to, sacrificed a vital principle of our national independence.

Under a continuance of the belligerent measures which, in defiance of laws which consecrate the rights of neutrals, overspread the ocean with danger, it will rest with the wisdom of Congress to decide on the course best adapted to such a state of things; and bringing with them, as they do, from every part of the Union, the sentiments of our constituents, my confidence is strengthened, that in forming this decision they will, with an unerring regard to the essential rights and interests of the nation, weigh and compare the painful alternatives out of which a choice is to be made. Nor should I do justice to the virtues which on other occasions have marked the character of our fellow citizens, if I did not cherish an equal confidence that the alternative chosen, whatever it may be, will be maintained with all the fortitude and patriotism which the crisis ought to inspire.

The documents containing the correspondences on the subject of the foreign edicts against our commerce, with the instructions given to our ministers at London and Paris, are now laid before you.

The communications made to Congress at their last session explained the posture in which the close of the discussion relating to the attack by a British ship of war on the frigate Chesapeake left a subject on which the nation had manifested so honorable a sensibility. Every view of what had passed authorized a belief that immediate steps would be taken by the British government for redressing a wrong, which, the more it was investigated, appeared the more clearly to require what had not been provided for in the special mission. It is found that no steps have been taken for the purpose. On the contrary, it will be seen, in the documents laid before you, that the inadmissible preliminary which obstructed the adjustment is still adhered to; and, moreover, that it is now brought into connection with the distinct and irrelative case of the orders in council. The instructions which had been given to our ministers at London with a view to facilitate, if necessary, the reparation claimed by the United States, are included in the documents communicated.

Our relations with the other powers of Europe have undergone no material changes since your last session. The important negotiations with Spain, which had been alternately suspended and resumed, necessarily experience a pause under the extraordinary and interesting crisis which distinguished her internal situation.

With the Barbary powers we continue in harmony, with the exception of an unjustifiable proceeding of the dey of Algiers toward our consul to that regency. Its character and circumstances are now laid before you, and will enable you to decide how far it may, either now or hereafter, call for any measures not within the limits of the executive authority. With our Indian neighbors the public peace has been steadily maintained. Some instances of individual wrong have, as at other times, taken place, but in nowise implicating the will of the nation. Beyond the Mississippi, the Iowas, the Sacs, and the Alabamas, have delivered up for trial and punishment individuals from among themselves accused of murdering citizens of the United States. On this side of the Mississippi, the Creeks are exerting themselves to arrest offenders of the same kind; and the Choctaws have manifested their readiness and desire for amicable and just arrangements respecting depredations committed by disorderly persons of their tribe. And, generally, from a conviction that we consider them as part of ourselves, and cherish with sincerity their rights and interests, the attachment of the Indian tribes is gaining strength daily—is extending from the nearer to the more remote, and will amply requite us for the justice and friendship practised towards them. Husbandry and household manufacture are advancing among them, more rapidly with the southern than the northern tribes, from circumstances of soil and climate; and one of the two great divisions of the Cherokee nation have now under consideration to solicit the citizenship of the United States, and to be identified with us in laws and government, in such progressive manner as we shall think best. In consequence of the appropriations of the last session of Congress for the security of our seaport towns and harbors, such works of defence have been erected as seemed to be called for by the situation of the several places, their relative importance, and the scale of expense indicated by the amount of the appropriation. These works will chiefly be finished in the course of the present season, except at New York and New Orleans, where most was to be done; and although a great proportion of the last appropriation has been expended on the former place, yet some further views will be submitted by Congress for rendering its security entirely adequate against naval enterprise. A view of what has been done at the several places, and of what is proposed to be done, shall be communicated as soon as the several reports are received.

Of the gun-boats authorized by the act of December last, it has been thought necessary to build only one hundred and three in the present year. These, with those before possessed, are sufficient for the harbors and waters exposed, and the residue will require little time for their construction when it is deemed necessary.

Under the act of the last session for raising an additional military force, so many officers were immediately appointed as were necessary for carrying on the business of recruiting, and in proportion as it advanced, others have been added. We have reason to believe their success has been satisfactory, although such returns have not yet been received as enable me to present to you a statement of the numbers engaged.

I have not thought it necessary in the course of the last season to call for any general detachments of militia or volunteers under the law passed for that purpose. For the ensuing season, however, they will require to be in readiness should their services be wanted. Some small and special detachments have been necessary to maintain the laws of embargo on that portion of our northern frontier which offered peculiar facilities for evasion, but these were replaced as soon as it could be done by bodies of new recruits. By the aid of these, and of the armed vessels called into actual service in other quarters, the spirit of disobedience and abuse which manifested itself early, and with sensible effect while we were unprepared to meet it, has been considerably repressed.

Considering the extraordinary character of the times in which we live, our attention should unremittingly be fixed on the safety of our country. For a people who are free, and who mean to remain so, a well-organized and armed militia is their best security. It is, therefore, incumbent on us, at every meeting, to revise the condition of the militia, and to ask ourselves if it is prepared to repel a powerful enemy at every point of our territories exposed to invasion. Some of the States have paid a laudable attention to this object; but every degree of neglect is to be found among others. Congress alone have power to produce a uniform state of preparation in this great organ of defence; the interests which they so deeply feel in their own and their country's security will present this as among the most important objects of their deliberation.

Under the acts of March 11th and April 23d, respecting arms, the difficulty of procuring them from abroad, during the present situation and dispositions of Europe, induced us to direct our whole efforts to the means of internal supply. The public factories have, therefore, been enlarged, additional machineries erected, and in proportion as artificers can be found or formed, their effect, already more than doubled, may be increased so as to keep pace with the yearly increase of the militia. The annual sums appropriated by the latter act, have been directed to the encouragement of private factories of arms, and contracts have been entered into with individual undertakers to nearly the amount of the first year's appropriation.

The suspension of our foreign commerce, produced by the injustice of the belligerent powers, and the consequent losses and sacrifices of our citizens, are subjects of just concern. The situation into which we have thus been forced, has impelled us to apply a portion of our industry and capital to internal manufactures and improvements. The extent of this conversion is daily increasing, and little doubt remains that the establishments formed and forming will—under the auspices of cheaper materials and subsistence, the freedom of labor from taxation with us, and of protecting duties and prohibitions—become permanent. The commerce with the Indians, too, within our own boundaries, is likely to receive abundant aliment from the same internal source, and will secure to them peace and the progress of civilization, undisturbed by practices hostile to both.

The accounts of the receipts and expenditures during the year ending on the 30th day of September last, being not yet made up, a correct statement will hereafter be transmitted from the Treasury. In the meantime, it is ascertained that the receipts have amounted to near eighteen millions of dollars, which, with the eight millions and a half in the treasury at the beginning of the year, have enabled us, after meeting the current demands and interest incurred, to pay two millions three hundred thousand dollars of the principal of our funded debt, and left us in the treasury, on that day, near fourteen millions of dollars. Of these, five millions three hundred and fifty thousand dollars will be necessary to pay what will be due on the first day of January next, which will complete the reimbursement of the eight per cent. stock. These payments, with those made in the six years and a half preceding, will have extinguished thirty-three millions five hundred and eighty thousand dollars of the principal of the funded debt, being the whole which could be paid or purchased within the limits of the law and our contracts; and the amount of principal thus discharged will have liberated the revenue from about two millions of dollars of interest, and added that sum annually to the disposable surplus. The probable accumulation of the surpluses of revenue beyond what can be applied to the payment of the public debt, whenever the freedom and safety of our commerce shall be restored, merits the consideration of Congress. Shall it lie unproductive in the public vaults? Shall the revenue be reduced? Or shall it rather be appropriated to the improvements of roads, canals, rivers, education, and other great foundations of prosperity and union, under the powers which Congress may already possess, or such amendment of the constitution as may be approved by the States? While uncertain of the course of things, the time may be advantageously employed in obtaining the powers necessary for a system of improvement, should that be thought best.

Availing myself of this the last occasion which will occur of addressing the two houses of the legislature at their meeting, cannot omit the expression of my sincere gratitude for the repeated proofs of confidence manifested to me by themselves and their predecessors since my call to the administration, and the many indulgences experienced at their hands. The same grateful acknowledgments are due to my fellow citizens generally, whose support has been my great encouragement under all embarrassments. In the transaction of their business I cannot have escaped error. It is incident to our imperfect nature. But I may say with truth, my errors have been of the understanding, not of intention; and that the advancement of their rights and interests has been the constant motive for every measure. On these considerations I solicit their indulgence. Looking forward with anxiety to their future destinies, I trust that, in their steady character unshaken by difficulties, in their love of liberty, obedience to law, and support of the public authorities, I see a sure guaranty of the permanence of our republic; and retiring from the charge of their affairs, I carry with me the consolation of a firm persuasion that Heaven has in store for our beloved country long ages to come of prosperity and happiness.

14. To Thomas Jefferson Randolph, Washington, 24 November 1808.
Thomas Jefferson Randolph (1792–1875), one of the twelve children of TJ's daughter Martha and Thomas Mann Randolph, was a particular favorite of his grandfather. Young "Jefferson," as he was called, had recently visited TJ in Washington en route to Philadelphia, where he was now preparing to begin studies at the Uni-

versity of Pennsylvania. On the eve of his retirement from office, TJ recalls the temptations and opportunities of his youth.

Your situation, thrown at such a distance from us and alone, cannot but give us all, great anxieties for you. As much has been secured for you, by your particular position and the acquaintance to which you have been recommended, as could be done towards shielding you from the dangers which surround you. But thrown on a wide world, among entire strangers without a friend or guardian to advise so young too and with so little experience of mankind, your dangers are great, and still your safety must rest on yourself. A determination never to do what is wrong, prudence, and good humor, will go far towards securing to you the estimation of the world. When I recollect that at 14. years of age, the whole care and direction of my self was thrown on my self entirely, without a relation or friend qualified to advise or guide me, and recollect the various sorts of bad company with which I associated from time to time, I am astonished I did not turn off with some of them, and become as worthless to society as they were. I had the good fortune to become acquainted very early with some characters of very high standing, and to feel the incessant wish that I could even become what they were. Under temptations and difficulties, I could ask myself what would Dr. Small, Mr. Wythe, Peyton Randolph do in this situation? What course in it will ensure me their approbation? I am certain that this mode of deciding on my conduct tended more to it's correctness than any reasoning powers I possessed. Knowing the even and dignified line they pursued, could never doubt for a moment which of two courses would be in character for them. Whereas seeking the same object through a process of moral reasoning, and with the jaundiced eye of youth, I should often have erred. From the circumstances of my position I was often thrown into the society of horseracers, cardplayers, Foxhunters, scientific and professional men, and of dignified men; and many a time have I asked myself, in the enthusiastic moment of the death of a fox, the victory of a favorite horse, the issue of a question eloquently argued at the bar or in the great Council of the nation, well, which of these kinds of reputation should I prefer? That of a horse jockey? A foxhunter? An Orator? Or the honest advocate of my country's rights? Be assured my dear Jefferson, that these little returns into ourselves, this self-cathechising habit, is not trifling, nor useless, but leads to the prudent selection and steady pursuits of what is right? I have mentioned good humor as one of the preservatives of our peace and tranquillity. It is among the most effectual, and it's effect is so well imitated and aided artificially by politeness, that this also becomes an acquisition of first rate value. In truth, politeness is artificial good humor, it covers the natural want of it, and ends by rendering habitual a substitute nearly equivalent to the real virtue. It is the practice of sacrificing to those whom we meet in society all the little conveniences and preferences which will gratify them, and deprive us of nothing worth a moment's consideration; it is the giving a pleasing and flattering turn to our expressions which will conciliate others, and make them pleased with us as well as themselves. How cheap a price for the good will of another! When this is in return for a rude thing said by another, it brings him to his senses, it mortifies and corrects him in the most salutary way, and places him at the feet of your good nature in the eyes of the company. But in stating prudential rules for our government in society I must not omit the important one of never entering into dispute or argument with another. I never yet saw an instance of one of two disputants convincing the other by argument. I have seen many on their getting warm, becoming rude, and shooting one another. Conviction is the effect of our own dispassionate reasoning, either in solitude, or weighing within ourselves dispassionately what we hear from others standing uncommitted in argument ourselves. It was one of the rules which above all others made Doctr. Franklin the most amiable of men in society, 'never to contradict any body.' If he was urged to anounce an opinion, he did it rather by asking questions, as if for information, or by suggesting doubts. When I hear another express an opinion, which is not mine, I say to myself, He has a right to his opinion, as to mine; why should I question it. His error does me no injury, and shall I become a Don Quixote to bring all men by force of argument, to one opinion? If a fact be misstated, it is probable he is gratified by a belief of it, and I have no right to deprive him of the gratification. If he wants information he will ask it, and then I will give it in measured terms; but if he still believes his own story, and shows a desire to dispute the fact with me, I hear him and say nothing. It is his affair, not mine, if he prefers error. There are two classes of disputants most frequently to be met with among us. The first is of young students just entered the threshold of science, with a first view of it's outlines, not yet filled up with the details and modifications which a further progress would bring to their knowledge. The other consists of the ill-tempered and rude men in society who have taken up a passion for politics. (Good humor and politeness never introduce into mixed society a question on which they foresee there will be a difference of opinion.) From both of these classes of disputants, my dear Jefferson, keep aloof, as you would from the infected subjects of yellow fever or pestilence. Consider yourself, when with them, as among the patients of Bedlam needing medical more than moral counsel. Be a listener only, keep within yourself, and endeavor to establish with yourself the habit of silence, especially in politics. In the fevered state of our country, no good can ever result from any attempt to set one of these fiery zealots to rights either in fact or principle. They are determined as to the facts they will believe, and the opinions on which they will act. Get by them, therefore as you would by an angry bull: it is not for a man of sense to dispute the road with such an animal. You will be more exposed than others to have these animals shaking their horns at you, because of the relation in which you stand with me and to hate me as a chief in the antagonist party your presence will be to them what the vomit-grass is to the sick dog a nostrum for producing an ejaculation. Look upon them exactly with that eye, and pity them as objects to whom you can administer only occasional ease. My character is not within their power. It is in the hands of my fellow citizens at large, and will be consigned to honor or infamy by the verdict of the republican mass of our country, according to what themselves will have seen, not what their enemies and mine shall have said. Never therefore consider these puppies in politics as requiring any notice from you, and always shew that you are not afraid to leave my character to the umpirage of public opinion. Look steadily to the pursuits which have carried you to Philadelphia, be very select in the society you attach yourself to; avoid taverns, drinkers, smoakers, and idlers and dissipated persons generally; for it is with such that broils and contentions arise, and you will find your path more easy and tranquil.

15. To P. S. Dupont de Nemours, Washington, 2 March 1809. *During his Paris years, TJ had befriended Pierre Samuel Dupont de Nemours (1739–1817), the prominent French economist and banker. Dupont emigrated to the United States in 1799, returning to France in 1802. On March 1809, Jefferson signed the Non-Intercourse Act. American trade would be reopened with the rest of the world, except for Britain and France; should either agree to respect America's neutral rights, the President could lift the ban on that nation.*

After using every effort which could prevent or delay our being entangled in the war of Europe, that seems now our only resource. The edicts of the two belligerents, forbidding us to be seen on the ocean, we met by an embargo. This gave us time to call home our seamen, ships and property, to levy men and put our sea ports into a certain state of defence. We have now taken off the embargo, except as to France and England and their territories, because fifty millions of exports, annually sacrificed, are the treble of what war would cost us; besides, that by war we should take something, and lose less than at present. But to give you a true description of the state of things here, I must refer you to Mr. Coles, the bearer of this, my secretary, a most worthy, intelligent and well informed young man, whom I recommend to your notice, and conversation on our affairs. His discretion and fidelity may be relied on. I expect he will find you with Spain at your feet, but England still afloat, and a barrier to the Spanish colonies. But all these concerns I am now leaving to be settled by my friend Mr. Madison. Within a few days I retire to my family, my books and farms; and having gained the harbor myself, I shall look on my friends still buffeting the storm, with anxiety indeed, but not with envy. Never did a prisoner, released from his chains, feel such relief as I shall on shaking off the shackles of power. Nature intended me for the tranquil pursuits of science, by rendering them my supreme delight. But the enormities of the times in which I have lived, have forced me to take a part in resisting them, and to commit myself on the boisterous ocean of political passions. Thank God for the opportunity of retiring from them without censure, and carrying with me the most consoling proofs of public approbation. I leave every thing in the hands of men so able to take care of them, that if we are destined to meet misfortunes, it will be because no human wisdom could avert them. Should you return to the United States, perhaps your curiosity may lead you to visit the hermit of Monticello. He will receive you with affection and delight; hailing you in the mean time with his affectionate salutations, and assurances of constant esteem and respect.

P. S. If you return to us, bring a couple of pair of true-bred shepherd's dogs. You will add a valuable possession to a country now beginning to pay great attention to the raising sheep.

CHAPTER SIX

Retirement Years

After retiring in March 1809 to Monticello, his mountaintop home, Jefferson never left Virginia. Although he kept up a far-flung correspondence and took a keen interest in national politics under the administrations of his Virginian allies James Monroe and James Madison, who together kept the presidency in Republican hands from 1809 to 1825, Jefferson focused his energies on his home, his ever-expanding family, and his agricultural enterprises. The vindication of American independence in the War of 1812 and the consolidation of the Republican ascendancy initiated by the "Revolution of 1800" quickly revived Jefferson's reputation from the political and diplomatic setbacks of his second term. Swarms of admiring visitors came to pay homage, driving the Sage of Monticello into periodic exile at his Poplar Forest plantation in Bedford County, seventy miles away.

Popular adulation was undoubtedly gratifying to Jefferson: ambitious young public men sought his counsel, aspiring authors sent their books for his endorsement, and an adoring family basked in his genial presence (daughter Martha and her husband Thomas Mann Randolph provided Jefferson with twelve grandchildren, eleven still living at his death). Despite recurrent physical complaints, these were among Jefferson's happiest years. For the first time since serving as American minister in Paris, Jefferson could indulge his many intellectual interests. Rising above partisan conflict, he could take a more dispassionate, philosophical view of the controversial questions—for instance, were social divisions natural in modern societies?—that had led to his estrangement from fellow revolutionaries such as John Adams who had betrayed "aristocratic" tendencies. The correspondence of the two old patriots following their reconciliation in 1812, one of the most celebrated in American letters (documents 3 and 4), is distinguished by extraordinary generosity and tact, a willingness to accommodate differences of opinion rarely apparent during the heat of party strife. But Jefferson did not lose his intellectual edge in these years. To the contrary, his reflections on political and constitutional theory (documents 1 and 10), and on morality and religion (documents 6 and 15), offered him the opportunity to reaffirm and deepen his commitment to the fundamental principles that had guided him throughout his career. Jefferson's retrospective view was often distorted and self-serving, but the story he told about the new nation's history and about his own participation in nation making was inspiring and influential. The strength of Jefferson's prophetic vision, reflected in his country's glorious ascent, transformed him into an American icon in his own lifetime.

Yet all was not well in Jefferson's world. His determination to rise

213

above the political fray was periodically challenged by ominous developments that seemed to threaten the survival of the union, and thus to reverse the outcome of the American Revolution. Sectional divisions during the Missouri Controversy from 1819 to 1821 over the spread of slavery presented the most obvious danger, but Jefferson was equally troubled by Supreme Court decisions such as *McCulloch v. Maryland* in 1819 that pointed toward the consolidation of power in the federal government (documents 12, 14, and 19). Jefferson's dire financial situation, exacerbated by a depression in 1819 that was particularly devastating to overextended staple producers, made him acutely sensitive to threats to the economic interests and political power of his class and region. Jefferson's solicitude for his fellow slaveholders made him increasingly suspicious of the motives of antislavery activists whose humanitarian professions masked a greater danger, that Virginia and the other slave states would themselves be enslaved by an all-powerful central government. Jefferson continued to advocate the compensated emancipation and colonization of slaves (document 17), but his hopes for this great panacea were undercut by doubts about the good faith of his fellow Americans.

When Jefferson confronted fundamental challenges to the republican legacy of the American Revolution, he was forced to question the value and purpose of his whole public life. The prevailing tone of his retirement years was of personal contentment and philosophical detachment, but his equanimity was often sorely tested. The oscillation between vaulting hopes and bleak moments of despair that characterized his political life thus echoed through his retirement. Yet there was always consolation in the long historical perspective: the sons of Virginia educated at Jefferson's new University would redeem the revolutionary legacy (document 11); the rising generation would, somehow, deal with the problem of slavery (document 7); American independence would be an inspiration to oppressed peoples everywhere, "arousing men to burst the chains under which monkish ignorance and superstition had persuaded them to bind themselves" (document 20).

Jefferson was eighty-three years old when he died at Monticello on July 4th, 1826, the fiftieth anniversary of American independence. At his direction, the following epitaph was inscribed on his tombstone: "Here was buried Thomas Jefferson, Author of the Declaration of American Independence, of the Statute of Virginia for religious freedom & Father of the University of Virginia."

* * * * * * * * * *

1. To A. L. C. Destutt de Tracy, Monticello, 26 January 1811. *The French philosopher Comte Louis Claude Destutt de Tracy (1754–1836) was, as TJ wrote John Adams in 1816, "the ablest writer living on intellectual subjects, or the operations of the understanding." TJ supervised the translation of Destutt's Commentary & Review of Montesquieu's Spirit of the Laws, published in Philadelphia in 1811. In this congratulatory letter, TJ emphasizes the American contribution to constitutional thought and practice; the French revolutionaries, he believed, had erred in failing to recognize the importance of decentralizing power in a genuinely federal system.*

I cannot express to you the satisfaction which I received from [*your commentaries on* The Spirit of the Laws]. I had, with the world, deemed Montesquieu's work of much merit; but saw in it, with every thinking man, so much of paradox, of false principle and misapplied fact, as to render its value equivocal on the whole. . . . A radical correction of them, therefore, was a great desideratum. This want is now supplied, and with a depth of thought, precision of idea, of language and of logic, which will force conviction into every mind. I declare to you, Sir, in the spirit of truth and sincerity, that I consider it the most precious gift the present age has received. But what would it have been, had the author, or would the author, take up the whole scheme of Montesquieu's work, and following the correct analysis he has here developed, fill up all its parts according to his sound views of them? Montesquieu's celebrity would be but a small portion of that which would immortalize the author. And with whom? With the rational and high-minded spirits of the present and all future ages. With those whose approbation is both incitement and reward to virtue and ambition. Is then the hope desperate? To what object can the occupation of his future life be devoted so usefully to the world, so splendidly to himself? But I must leave to others who have higher claims on his attention, to press these considerations. . . .

One of its doctrines, indeed, the preference of a plural over a singular executive, will probably not be assented to here. When our present government was first established, we had many doubts on this question, and many leanings towards a supreme executive council. It happened that at that time the experiment of such an one was commenced in France, while the single executive was under trial here. We watched the motions and effects of these two rival plans, with an interest and anxiety proportioned to the importance of a choice between them. The experiment in France failed after a short course, and not from any circumstance peculiar to the times or nation, but from those internal jealousies and dissensions in the Directory, which will ever arise among men equal in power, without a principal to decide and control their differences. We had tried a similar experiment in 1784, by establishing a committee of the States, composed of a member from every State, then thirteen, to exercise the executive functions during the recess of Congress. They fell immediately into schisms and dissensions, which became at length so inveterate as to render all cooperation among them impracticable: they dissolved themselves, abandoning the helm of government, and it continued without a head, until Congress met the ensuing winter. This was then imputed to the temper of two or three individuals; but the wise ascribed it to the nature of man. The failure of the French Directory, and from the same cause, seems to have authorized a belief that the form of a plurality, however promising in theory, is impracticable with men constituted with the ordinary passions. While the tranquil and steady tenor of our single executive, during a course of twenty-two years of the most tempestuous times the history of the world has ever presented, gives a rational hope that this important problem is at length solved. Aided by the counsels of a cabinet of heads of departments, originally four, but now five, with whom the President consults, either singly or altogether, he has the benefit of their wisdom and information, brings their views to one centre, and produces an unity of action and direction in all the branches of the government. The excellence of this construction of the executive power has already manifested itself here under very opposite circumstances. During the administration of our first President, his cabinet of four members was equally divided by as marked an opposition of principle as monarchism and republicanism could bring into conflict. Had that cabinet been a directory, like positive and negative quantities in algebra, the opposing wills would have balanced each other and produced a state of absolute inaction. But the President heard with calmness the opinions and reasons of each, decided the course to be pursued, and kept the government steadily in it, unaffected by the agitation. The public knew well the dissensions of the cabinet, but never had an uneasy thought on their account, because they knew also they had provided a regulating power which would keep the machine in steady movement. I speak with an intimate knowledge of these scenes, *quorum pars fui;* as I may of others of a character entirely opposite. The third administration, which was of eight years, presented an example of harmony in a cabinet of six person, to which perhaps history has furnished no parallel. There never arose, during the whole time, an instance of an unpleasant thought or word between the members. We sometimes met under differences of opinion, but scarcely ever failed, by conversing and reasoning, so to modify each other's ideas, as to produce an unanimous result. Yet, able and amicable as these members were, I am not certain this would have been the case, had each possessed equal and independent powers. Ill-defined limits of their respective departments, jealousies, trifling at first, but nourished and strengthened by repetition of occasions, intrigues without doors of designing persons to build an importance to themselves on the divisions of others, might, from small beginnings, have produced persevering oppositions. But the power of decision in the President left no object for internal dissension, and external intrigue was stifled in embryo by the knowledge which incendiaries possessed, that no division they could foment would change the course of the executive power. I am not conscious that my participations in executive authority have produced any bias in favor of the single executive; because the parts I have acted have been in the subordinate, as well as superior stations, and because, if I know myself, what I have felt, and what I have wished, I know that have never been so well pleased, as when I could shift power from my own, on the shoulders of others; nor have I ever been able to conceive how any rational being could propose happiness to himself from the exercise of power over others.

I am still, however, sensible of the solidity of your principle, that, to insure the safety of the public liberty, its depository should be subject to be changed with the greatest ease possible, and without suspending or disturbing for a moment the movements of the machine of government. You apprehend that a single executive, with eminence of talent, and destitution of principle, equal to the object, might, by usurpation, render his powers hereditary. Yet I think history furnishes as many examples of a single usurper arising out of a government by a plurality, as of temporary trusts of power in a single hand rendered permanent by usurpation. I do not believe, therefore, that this danger is lessened in the hands of a plural executive. Perhaps it is greatly increased, by the state of inefficiency to which they are liable from feuds and divisions among themselves. The conservative body you propose might be so constituted, as, while it would be an admirable sedative in a variety of smaller cases, might also be a valuable sentinel and check on the liberticide views of an ambitious individual. I am friendly to this idea. But the true barriers of our liberty in this country are our State governments; and the wisest conservative power ever contrived by man, is that of which our Revolution and present government found us possessed. Seventeen distinct States, amalgamated into one as to their foreign concerns, but single and independent as to their internal administration, regularly organized with legislature and governor resting on the choice of the people, and enlightened by a free press, can never be so fascinated by the arts of one man, as to submit voluntarily to his usurpation. Nor can they be constrained to it by any force he can possess. While that may paralyze the single State in which it happens to be encamped, sixteen others, spread over a country of two thousand miles diameter, rise up on every side, ready organized for deliberation by a constitutional legislature, and for action by their governor, constitutionally the commander of the militia of the State, that is to say, of every man in it able to bear arms; and that militia, too, regularly formed into regiments and battalions, into infantry, cavalry and artillery, trained under officers general and subordinate, legally appointed, always in readiness, and to whom they are already in habits of obedience. The republican government of France was lost without a struggle, because the party of "*un et indivisible*" had prevailed; no provincial organizations existed to which the people might rally under authority of the laws, the seats of the directory were virtually vacant, and a small force sufficed to turn the legislature out of their chamber, and to salute its leader chief of the nation. But with us, sixteen out of seventeen States rising in mass, under regular organization, and legal commanders, united in object and action by their Congress, or, if that be in duresse, by a special convention, present such obstacles to an usurper as forever to stifle ambition in the first conception of that object.

Dangers of another kind might more reasonably be apprehended from this perfect and distinct organization, civil and military, of the States; to wit, that certain States from local and occasional discontents, might attempt to secede from the Union. This is certainly possible; and would be befriended by this regular organization. But it is not probable that local discontents can spread to such an extent, as to be able to face the sound parts of so extensive an Union; and if ever they should reach the majority, they would then become the regular government, acquire the ascendency in Congress, and be able to redress their own grievances by laws peaceably and constitutionally passed. And even the States in which local discontents might engender a commencement of fermentation, would be paralyzed and self-checked by that very division into parties into which we have fallen, into which all States must fall wherein men are at liberty to think, speak, and act freely, according to the diversities of their individual conformations, and which are, perhaps, essential to preserve the purity of the government, by the censorship which these parties habitually exercise over each other.

2. To William Duane, Monticello, 28 March 1811. *William Duane (1760–1835) became editor of the Philadelphia* Aurora *in 1798 after the death of Benjamin Franklin Bache, Benjamin Franklin's grandson. Throughout the party battles of the 1790s, the* Aurora *was the flagship Republican newspaper, one of very few to survive Federalist efforts to muzzle the opposition press under the Sedition Act of 1798. Duane's role of party spokesman was eclipsed after TJ's election, when the* National Intelligencer *of Washington D.C. became the administration's leading organ. The radical Duane remained a key figure in Republican factional politics in Pennsylvania, one of the many sources of "schism" in the national party.*

I do not know whether I am able at present to form a just idea of the situation of our country. If I am, it is such as, during the bellum omnium in omnia in Europe, will require the union of all its friends to resist its enemies within and without. If we schismatize on either men or measures, if we do not act in phalanx, as when we rescued it from the satellites of monarchism, I will not say our party, the term is false and degrading, but our nation will be undone. For the republicans are the nation. Their opponents are but a faction, weak in numbers, but powerful and profuse in the command of money, and backed by a nation, powerful also and profuse, in the use of the same means; and the more profuse, in both cases, as the money they thus employ is not their own but their creditors', to be paid off by a bankruptcy, which whether it pays a dollar or a shilling in the pound is of little concern with them. The last hope of human liberty in the world rests on us. We ought, for so dear a state, to sacrifice every attachment and every enmity. Leave the President free to choose his own coadjutors, to pursue his own measures, and support him and them, even if we think we are wiser than they, honester than they are, or possessing of more enlarged information of the state of things. If we move in mass, be it ever so circuitously, we shall attain our object; but if we break into squads, every one pursuing the path he thinks most direct, we become an easy conquest to those who can now barely hold us in check. I repeat again, that we ought not to schismatize on either men or measures. Principles alone can justify that. If we find our government in all its branches rushing headlong, like, our predecessors, into the arms of monarchy if we find them violating our dearest rights, the trial by jury, the freedom of the press, the freedom of opinion, civil or religious, or opening on our peace of mind or personal safety the sluices of terrorism, if we see them raising standing armies, when the absence of all other danger points to these as the sole objects on which they are to be employed, then indeed let us withdraw and call the nation to its tents. But while our functionaries are wise, and honest, and vigilant, let us move compactly under their guidance, and we have nothing to fear. Things may here and there go a little wrong. It is not in their power to prevent it. But all will be right in the end, though not perhaps by the shortest means.

You know, my dear Sir, that this union of republicans has been the constant theme of my exhortations, that I have ever refused to know any sub-divisions among them, to take part in any personal differences; and therefore you will not give to the present observations any other than general application. I may sometimes differ in opinion from some of my friends, from those whose views are as pure and sound as my own. I censure none, but do homage to every one's right of opinion. If I have indulged my pen, therefore, a little further than the occasion called for, you will ascribe it to a sermonizing habit, to the anxieties of age, perhaps to its garrulity, or to any other motive rather than the want of the esteem and confidence of which I pray you to accept sincere assurances.

3. To John Adams, 21 January 1812. *Thanks to the intercession of their mutual friend Benjamin Rush of Pennsylvania, TJ and his revolutionary colleague John Adams (1735–1826) were reconciled in this year after a long estrangement dating back to the American publication of Thomas Paine's* Rights of Man *in 1791. In a prefatory note to Paine's sensational treatise, which TJ insisted had not been intended for publication, the secretary of state referred to the "political heresies which have sprung up among us," strongly implying that Adams and other supposed advocates of "aristocratic" principles were apostates from the true republican standard. This letter was TJ's first contribution to a rich correspondence that continued into 1826; both men died on July 4th of that year, on the fiftieth anniversary of American independence.*

I thank you before hand (for they are not yet arrived) for the specimens of homespun you have been so kind as to forward me by post. I doubt not their excellence, knowing how far you are advanced in these things in your quarter. Here we do little in the fine way, but in coarse and midling goods a great deal. Every family in the country is a manufactory within itself, and is very generally able to make within itself all the stouter and midling stuffs for it's own cloathing and household use. We consider a sheep for every person in the family as sufficient to clothe it, in addition to the cotton, hemp and flax which we raise ourselves. For fine stuff we shall depend on your Northern manufactures. Of these, that is to say, of company establishments, we have none. We use little machinery. The Spinning Jenny and loom with the flying shuttle can be managed in a family; but nothing more complicated. The economy and thriftiness resulting from our household manufactures are such that they will never again be laid aside; and nothing more salutary for us has ever happened than the British obstructions to our demands for their manufactures. Restore free intercourse when they will, their commerce with us will have totally changed it's form, and the articles we shall in future want from them will not exceed their own consumption of our produce.

A letter from you calls up recollections very dear to my mind. It carries me back to the times when, beset with difficulties and dangers, we were fellow laborers in the same cause, struggling for what is most valuable to man, his right of self-government. Laboring always at the same oar, with some wave ever ahead threatening to overwhelm us and yet passing harmless under our bark, we knew not how, we rode through the storm with heart and hand, and made a happy port. Still we did not expect to be without rubs and difficulties; and we have had them. First the detention of the Western posts: then the coalition of Pilnitz, outlawing our commerce with France, and the British enforcement of the outlawry. In your day French depredations: in mine English, and the Berlin and Milan decrees: now the English orders of council, and the piracies they authorise: when these shall be over, it will be the impressment of our seamen, or something else: and so we have gone on, and so we shall go on, puzzled and prospering beyond example in the history of man. And I do believe we shall continue to grow, to multiply and prosper until we exhibit an association, powerful, wise and happy, beyond what has yet been seen by men. As for France and England, with all their pre-eminence in science, the one is a den of robbers, and the other of pirates. And if science produces no better fruits than tyranny, murder, rapine and destitution of national morality, I would rather wish our country to be ignorant, honest and estimable as our neighboring savages are.

But whither is senile garrulity leading me? Into politics, of which I have taken final leave. I think little of them, and say less. I have given up newspapers in exchange for Tacitus and Thucydides, for Newton and Euclid; and I find myself much the happier. Sometimes indeed I look back to former occurrences, in remembrance of our old friends and fellow laborers, who have fallen before us. Of the signers of the Declaration of Independance I see now living not more than half a dozen on your side of the Potomak, and, on this side, myself alone. You and I have been wonderfully spared, and myself with remarkable health, and a considerable activity of body and mind. I am on horseback 3. or 4. hours of every day; visit 3. or 4. times a year a possession I have 90 miles distance, performing the winter journey on horseback. I walk little however; a single mile being too much for me; and I live in the midst of my grandchildren, one of whom has lately promoted me to be a great grandfather. I have heard with pleasure that you also retain good health, and a greater power of exercise in walking than do. But I would rather have heard this from yourself, and that, writing a letter, like mine, full of egotisms, and of details of your health, your habits, occupations and enjoyments, I should have the pleasure of knowing that, in the race of life, you do not keep, in it's physical decline, the same distance ahead of me which you have done in political honors and achievements. No circumstances have lessened the interest I feel in these particulars respecting yourself; none have suspended for one moment my sincere esteem for you; and I now salute you with unchanged affections and respect.

4. To John Adams, Monticello, 28 October 1813. *In this famous letter on "natural aristocracy," TJ offers a philosophical—and conciliatory—perspective on what he understood to be the conflicting principles animating the party battles of the 1790s.*

[*TJ translates a passage from Ocellus, a Greek philosopher.*] " . . . The powers, the organs and desires for coition have not been given by god to man for the sake of pleasure, but for the procreation of the race. For as it were incongruous for a mortal born to partake of divine life, the immortality of the race being taken away, god fulfilled the purpose by making the generations uninterrupted and continuous. This therefore we are especially to lay down as a principle, that coition is not for the sake of pleasure." But Nature, not trusting to this moral and abstract motive, seems to have provided more securely for the perpetuation of the species by making it the effect of the oestrum implanted in the constitution of both sexes. And not only has the commerce of love been indulged on this unhallowed impulse, but made subservient also to wealth and ambition by marriages without regard to the beauty, the healthiness, the understanding, or virtue of the subject from which we are to breed. The selecting the best male for a Haram of well chosen females also, which Theognis seems to recommend from the example of our sheep and asses, would doubtless improve the human, as it does the brute animal, and produce a race of veritable *aristoi* ["aristocrats"]. For experience proves that the moral and physical qualities of man, whether good or evil, are transmissible in a certain degree from father to son. But suspect that the equal rights of men will rise up against this privileged Solomon, and oblige us to continue acquiescence under "the degeneration of the race of men" which Theognis complains of, and to content ourselves with the accidental aristoi produced by the fortuitous concourse of breeders. For I agree with you that there is a natural aristocracy among men. The grounds of this are virtue and talents. Formerly bodily powers gave place among the aristoi. But since the invention of gunpowder has armed the weak as well as the strong with missile death, bodily strength, like beauty, good humor, politeness and other accomplishments, has become but an auxiliary ground of distinction. There is also an artificial aristocracy founded on wealth and birth, without either virtue or talents; for with these it would belong to the first class. The natural aristocracy I consider as the most precious gift of nature for the instruction, the trusts, and government of society. And indeed it would have been inconsistent in creation to have formed man for the social state, and not to have provided virtue and wisdom enough to manage the concerns of the society. May we not even say that that form of government is the best which provides the most effectually for a pure selection of these natural aristoi into the offices of government? The artificial aristocracy is a mischievous ingredient in government, and provision should be made to prevent it's ascendancy. On the question, What is the best provision, you and I differ; but we differ as rational friends, using the free exercise of our own reason, and mutually indulging it's errors. You think it best to put the Pseudo-aristoi into a separate chamber of legislation where they may be hindered from doing mischief by their coordinate branches, and where also they may be a protection to wealth against the Agrarian and plundering enterprises of the Majority of the people. I think that to give them power in order to prevent them from doing mischief, is arming them for it, and increasing instead of remedying the evil. For if the coordinate branches can arrest their action, so may they that of the coordinates. Mischief may be done negatively as well as positively. Of this a cabal in the Senate of the U. S. has furnished many proofs. Nor do I believe them necessary to protect the wealthy; because enough of these will find their way into every branch of the legislation to protect themselves. From 15. to 20. legislatures of our own, in action for 30. years past, have proved that no fears of an equalisation of property are to be apprehended from them.

I think the best remedy is exactly that provided by all our constitutions, to leave to the citizens the free election and separation of the aristoi from the pseudo-aristoi, of the wheat from the chaff. In general they will elect the real good and wise. In some instances, wealth may corrupt, and birth blind them; but not in sufficient degree to endanger the society.

It is probable that our difference of opinion may in some measure be produced by a difference of character in those among whom we live. From what I have seen of Massachusets and Connecticut myself, and still more from what have heard, and the character given of the former by yourself, [vol. 1. pa. 111.] who know them so much better, there seems to be in those two states a traditionary reverence for certain families, which has rendered the offices of the government nearly hereditary in those families. I presume that from an early period of your history, members of these families happening to possess virtue and talents, have honestly exercised them for the good of the people, and by their services have endeared their names to them.

In coupling Connecticut with you, I mean it politically only, not morally. For having made the Bible the Common law of their land they seem to have modelled their morality on the story of Jacob and Laban. But altho' this hereditary succession to office with you may in some degree be founded in real family merit, yet in a much higher degree it has proceeded from your strict alliance of church and state. These families are canonised in the eyes of the people on the common principle "you tickle me, and I will tickle you." In Virginia we have nothing of this. Our clergy, before the revolution, having been secured against rivalship by fixed salaries, did not give themselves the trouble of acquiring influence over the people. Of wealth, there were great accumulations in particular families, handed down from generation to generation under the English law of entails. But the only object of ambition for the wealthy was a seat in the king's council. All their court then was paid to the crown and it's creatures; and they Philipised in all collisions between the king and people. Hence they were unpopular; and that unpopularity continues attached to their names. A Randolph, a Carter, or a Burwell must have great personal superiority over a common competitor to be elected by the people, even at this day.

At the first session of our legislature after the Declaration of Independance, we passed a law abolishing entails. And this was followed by one abolishing the privilege of Primogeniture, and dividing the lands of intestates equally among all their children, or other representatives. These laws, drawn by myself, laid the axe to the root of Pseudo-aristocracy. And had another which I prepared been adopted by the legislature, our work would have been compleat. It was a Bill for the more general diffusion of learning. This proposed to divide every county into wards of 5. or 6. miles square, like your townships; to establish in each ward a free school for reading, writing and common arithmetic; to provide for the annual selection of the best subjects from these schools who might recieve at the public expence a higher degree of education at a district school; and from these district schools to select a certain number of the most promising subjects to be compleated at an University, where all the useful sciences should be taught. Worth and genius would thus have been sought out from every condition of life, and compleatly prepared by education for defeating the competition of wealth and birth for public trusts.

My proposition had for a further object to impart to these wards those portions of self-government for which they are best qualified, by confiding to them the care of their poor, their roads, police, elections, the nomination of jurors, administration of justice in small cases, elementary exercises of militia, in short, to have made them little republics, with a Warden at the head of each, for all those concerns which, being under their eye, they would better manage than the larger republics of the county or state. A general call of ward-meetings by their Wardens on the same day thro' the state would at any time produce the genuine sense of the people on any required point, and would enable the state to act in mass, as your people have so often done, and with so much effect, by their town meetings. The law for religious freedom, which made a part of this system, having put down the aristocracy of the clergy, and restored to the citizen the freedom of the mind, and those of entails and descents nurturing an equality of condition among them, this on Education would have raised the mass of the people to the high ground of moral respectability necessary to their own safety, and to orderly government; and would have compleated the great object of qualifying them to select the veritable aristoi, for the trusts of government, to the exclusion of the Pseudalists: and the same Theognis who has furnished the epigraphs of your two letters assures us that "Curnis, good men have never harmed any city." Altho' this law has not yet been acted on but in a small and inefficient degree, it is still considered as before the legislature, with other bills of the revised code, not yet taken up, and I have great hope that some patriotic spirit will, at a favorable moment, call it up, and make it the key-stone of the arch of our government.

With respect to Aristocracy, we should further consider that, before the establishment of the American states, nothing was known to History but the Man of the old world, crouded within limits either small or overcharged, and steeped in the vices which that situation generates. A government adapted to such men would be one thing; but a very different one that for the Man of these states. Here every one may have land to labor for himself if he chuses; or, preferring the exercise of any other industry, may exact for it such compensation as not only to afford a comfortable subsistence, but where-with to provide for a cessation from labor in old age. Every one, by his property, or by his satisfactory situation, is interested in the support of law and order. And such men may safely and advantageously reserve to themselves a wholsome controul over their public affairs, and a degree of freedom, which in the hands of the Canaille of the cities of Europe, would be instantly perverted to the demolition and destruction of every thing public and private. The history of the last 25. years of France, and of the last 40. years in America, nay of it's last 200. years, proves the truth of both parts of this observation.

But even in Europe a change has sensibly taken place in the mind of Man. Science had liberated the ideas of those who read and reflect, and the American example had kindled feelings of right in the people. An insurrection has consequently begun, of science, talents and courage against rank and birth, which have fallen into contempt. It has failed in it's first effort, because the mobs of the cities, the instrument used for it's accomplishment, debased by ignorance, poverty and vice, could not be restrained to rational action. But the world will recover from the panic of this first catastrophe. Science is progressive, and talents and enterprize on the alert. Resort may be had to the people of the country, a more governable power from their principles and subordination; and rank, and birth, and tinsel-aristocracy will finally shrink into insignificance, even there. This however we have no right to meddle with. It suffices for us, if the moral and physical condition of our own citizens qualifies them to select the able and good for the direction of their government, with a recurrence of elections at such short periods as will enable them to displace an unfaithful servant before the mischief he meditates may be irremediable.

5. To Baron Alexander von Humboldt, Montpelier, 6 December 1813.

Baron Friedrich Wilhelm Heinrich Alexander von Humboldt (1769–1859), the great German naturalist, traveled through Spanish America from 1799 to 1804. On his return to Europe he visited TJ in Washington D.C. Von Humboldt's many writings, including his Political Essay on the Kingdom of New Spain, *published in English translation in New York in 1811, established him as a leading European authority on the New World. TJ was visiting Montpelier, James Madison's home in Orange County.*

The European nations constitute a separate division of the globe; their localities make them part of a distinct system; they have a set of interests of their own in which it is our business never to engage ourselves. America has a hemisphere to itself. It must have its separate system of interests, which must not be subordinated to those of Europe. The insulated state in which nature has placed the American continent, should so far avail it that no spark of war kindled in the other quarters of the globe should be wafted across the wide oceans which separate us from them. And it will be so. In fifty years more the United States alone will contain fifty millions of inhabitants, and fifty years are soon gone over. The peace of 1763 is within that period. I was then twenty years old, and of course remember well all the transactions of the war preceding it. And you will live to see the epoch now equally ahead of us; and the numbers which will then be spread over the other parts of the American hemisphere, catching long before that the principles of our portion of it, and concurring with us in the maintenance of the same system. You see how readily we run into ages beyond the grave; and even those of us to whom that grave is already opening its quiet bosom. I am anticipating events of which you will be the bearer to me in the Elsyian fields fifty years hence.

You know, my friend, the benevolent plan we were pursuing here for the happiness of the aboriginal inhabitants in our vicinities. We spared nothing to keep them at peace with one another. To teach them agriculture and the rudiments of the most necessary arts, and to encourage industry by establishing among them separate property. In this way they would have been enabled to subsist and multiply on a moderate scale of landed possession. They would have mixed their blood with ours, and been amalgamated and identified with us within no distant period of time. On the commencement of our present war, we pressed on them the observance of peace and neutrality, but the interested and unprincipled policy of England has defeated all our labors for the salvation of these unfortunate people. They have seduced the greater part of the tribes within our neighborhood, to take up the hatchet against us, and the cruel massacres they have committed on the women and children of our frontiers taken by surprise, will oblige us now to pursue them to extermination, or drive them to new seats beyond our reach. Already we have driven their patrons and seducers into Montreal, and the opening season will force them to their last refuge, the walls of Quebec. We have cut off all possibility of intercourse and of mutual aid, and may pursue at our leisure whatever plan we find necessary to secure ourselves against the future effects of their savage and ruthless warfare. The confirmed brutalization, if not the extermination of this race in our America, is therefore to form an additional chapter in the English history of the same colored man in Asia, and of the brethren of their own color in Ireland, and wherever else Anglo-mercantile cupidity can find a two-penny interest in deluging the earth with human blood. But let us turn from the loathsome contemplation of the degrading effects of commercial avarice.

6. To Thomas Law, Poplar Forest, 13 June 1814. *Thomas Law (1756–1834), a prolific writer on scientific and philosophical questions, sent TJ copies of several of his works, including the one that prompted this response. TJ's exposition of his thinking about the "moral sense" is the most elaborate—and illuminating—in all his writings.*

The copy of your Second Thoughts on Instinctive Impulses, with the letter accompanying it, was received just as I was setting out on a journey to this place, two or three days' distant from Monticello. I brought it with me and read it with great satisfaction, and with the more as it contained exactly my own creed on the foundation of morality in man. It is really curious that on a question so fundamental, such a variety of opinions should have prevailed among men, and those, too, of the most exemplary virtue and first order of understanding. It shows how necessary was the care of the Creator in making the moral principle so much a part of our constitution as that no errors of reasoning or of speculation might lead us astray from its observance in practice. Of all the theories on this question, the most whimsical seems to have been that of Wollaston, who considers truth as the foundation of morality. The thief who steals your guinea does wrong only inasmuch as he acts a lie in using your guinea as if it were his own. Truth is certainly a branch of morality, and a very important one to society. But presented as its foundation, it is as if a tree taken up by the roots, had its stem reversed in the air, and one of its branches planted in the ground. Some have made the love of God the foundation of morality.

This, too, is but a branch of our moral duties, which are generally divided into duties to God and duties to man. If we did a good act merely from the *love of God* and a belief that it is pleasing to Him, whence arises the morality of the Atheist? It is idle to say, as some do, that no such being exists. We have the same evidence of the fact as of most of those we act on, to-wit: their own affirmations, and their reasonings in support of them. Have observed, indeed, generally, that while in protestant countries the defections from the Platonic Christianity of the priests is to Deism, in catholic countries they are to Atheism. Diderot, D'Alembert, D'Holbach, Condorcet, are known to have been among the most virtuous of men. Their virtue, then, must have had some other foundation than the love of God. . . .

We have indeed an innate sense of what we call beautiful, but that is exercised chiefly on subjects addressed to the fancy, whether through the eye in visible forms, as landscape, animal figure, dress, drapery, architecture, the composition of colors, &c., or to the imagination directly, as imagery, style, or measure in prose or poetry, or whatever else constitutes the domain of criticism or taste, a faculty entirely distinct from the moral one. Self-interest, or rather self-love, or *egoism*, has been more plausibly substituted as the basis of morality. But I consider our relations with others as constituting the boundaries of morality. With ourselves we stand on the ground of identity, not of relation, which last, requiring two subjects, excludes self-love confined to a single one. To ourselves, in strict language, we can owe no duties, obligation requiring also two parties. Self-love, therefore, is no part of morality. Indeed it is exactly its counterpart. It is the sole antagonist of virtue, leading us constantly by our propensities to self-gratification in violation of our moral duties to others. Accordingly, it is against this enemy that are erected the batteries of moralists and religionists, as the only obstacle to the practice of morality. Take from man his selfish propensities, and he can have nothing to seduce him from the practice of virtue. Or subdue those propensities by education, instruction or restraint, and virtue remains without a competitor. Egoism, in a broader sense, has been thus presented as the source of moral action. It has been said that we feed the hungry, clothe the naked, bind up the wounds of the man beaten by thieves, pour oil and wine into them, set him on our own beast and bring him to the inn, because we receive ourselves pleasure from these acts. So Helvetius, one of the best men on earth, and the most ingenious advocate of this principle, after defining "interest" to mean not merely that which is pecuniary, but whatever may procure us pleasure or withdraw us from pain, says, "the humane man is he to whom the sight of misfortune is insupportable, and who to rescue himself from this spectacle, is forced to succor the unfortunate object." This indeed is true. But it is one step short of the ultimate question. These good acts give us pleasure, but how happens it that they give us pleasure? Because nature hath implanted in our breasts a love of others, a sense of duty to them, a moral instinct, in short, which prompts us irresistibly to feel and to succor their distresses, and protests against the language of Helvetius, "what other motive than self-interest could determine a man to generous actions? It is as impossible for him to love what is good for the sake of good, as to love evil for the sake of evil." The Creator would indeed have been a bungling artist, had he intended man for a social animal, without planting in him social dispositions. It is true they are not planted in every man, because there is no rule without exceptions; but it is false reasoning which converts exceptions into the general rule. Some men are born without the organs of sight, or of hearing, or without hands. Yet it would be wrong to say that man is born without these faculties, and sight, hearing, and hands may with truth enter into the general definition of man. The want or imperfection of the moral sense in some men, like the want or imperfection of the senses of sight and hearing in others, is no proof that it is a general characteristic of the species. When it is wanting, we endeavor to supply the defect by education, by appeals to reason and calculation, by presenting to the being so unhappily conformed, other motives to do good and to eschew evil, such as the love, or the hatred, or rejection of those among whom he lives, and whose society is necessary to his happiness and even existence; demonstrations by sound calculation that honesty promotes interest in the long run; the rewards and penalties established by the laws; and ultimately the prospects of a future state of retribution for the evil as well as the good done while here. These are the correctives which are supplied by education, and which exercise the functions of the moralist, the preacher, and legislator; and they lead into a course of correct action all those whose disparity is not too profound to be eradicated. Some have argued against the existence of a moral sense, by saying that if nature had given us such a sense, impelling us to virtuous actions, and warning us against those which are vicious, then nature would also have designated, by some particular ear-marks, the two sets of actions which are, in themselves, the one virtuous and the other vicious. Whereas, we find, in fact, that the same actions are deemed virtuous in one country and vicious in another. The answer is that nature has constituted utility to man the standard and best of virtue. Men living in different countries, under different circumstances, different habits and regimens, may have different utilities; the same act, therefore, may be useful, and consequently virtuous in one country which is injurious and vicious in another differently circumstanced. I sincerely, then, believe with you in the general existence of a moral instinct. I think it the brightest gem with which the human character is studded, and the want of it as more degrading than the most hideous of the bodily deformities. I am happy in reviewing the roll of associates in this principle which you present in your second letter, some of which I had not before met with. To these might be added Lord Kaims, one of the ablest of our advocates, who goes so far as to say, in his Principles of Natural Religion, that a man owes no duty to which he is not urged by some impulsive feeling. This is correct, if referred to the standard of general feeling in the given case, and not to the feeling of a single individual. Perhaps I may misquote him, it being fifty years since I read his book.

7. To Edward Coles, Monticello, 25 August 1814. *Edward Coles (1786–1868), TJ's young Albemarle County neighbor, was from 1809 to 1815 private secretary to President Madison. Coles had urged TJ to take a leading role in working for the emancipation of Virginia's slaves. TJ's evasive response reveals the practical* *limits to his opposition to the institution. Despairing of any progress toward eman-cipation in his native state, Coles liberated his own slaves and emigrated to the free Illinois Territory in 1819.*

Your favour of July 31, was duly received, and was read with peculiar pleasure. The sentiments breathed through the whole do honor to both the head and heart of the writer. Mine on the subject of slavery of negroes have long since been in possession of the public, and time has only served to give them stronger root. The love of justice and the love of country plead equally the cause of these people, and it is a moral reproach to us that they should have pleaded it so long in vain, and should have produced not a single effort, nay fear not much serious willingness to relieve them & ourselves from our present condition of moral & political reprobation. From those of the former generation who were in the fulness of age when I came into public life, which was while our controversy with England was on paper only, I soon saw that nothing was to be hoped. Nursed and edu-cated in the daily habit of seeing the degraded condition, both bodily and mental, of those unfortunate beings, not reflecting that that degradation was very much the work of themselves & their fathers, few minds have yet doubted but that they were as legitimate subjects of property as their horses and cattle. The quiet and monotonous course of colonial life has been disturbed by no alarm, and little reflection on the value of liberty. And when alarm was taken at an enterprize on their own, it was not easy to carry them to the whole length of the principles which they invoked for themselves. In the first or second session of the Legislature after I became a member, drew to this subject the attention of Col. Bland, one of the old-est, ablest, & most respected members, and he undertook to move for cer-tain moderate extensions of the protection of the laws to these people. I seconded his motion, and, as a younger member, was more spared in the debate; but he was denounced as an enemy of his country, & was treated with the grossest indecorum. From an early stage of our revolution other & more distant duties were assigned to me, so that from that time till my return from Europe in 1789, and I may say till I returned to reside at home in 1809, I had little opportunity of knowing the progress of public senti-ment here on this subject. I had always hoped that the younger generation receiving their early impressions after the flame of liberty had been kin-dled in every breast, & had become as it were the vital spirit of every Amer-ican, that the generous temperament of youth, analogous to the motion of their blood, and above the suggestions of avarice, would have sympathized with oppression wherever found, and proved their love of liberty beyond their own share of it. But my intercourse with them, since my return has not been sufficient to ascertain that they had made towards this point the progress I had hoped. Your solitary but welcome voice is the first which has brought this sound to my ear; and I have considered the general silence which prevails on this subject as indicating an apathy unfavorable to every hope. Yet the hour of emancipation is advancing, in the march of time. It will come; and whether brought on by the generous energy of our own minds; or by the bloody process of St Domingo, excited and conducted by the power of our present enemy, if once stationed permanently within our Country, and offering asylum & arms to the oppressed, is a leaf of our history not yet turned over. As to the method by which this difficult work is to be effected, if permitted to be done by ourselves, I have seen no proposition so expedient on the whole, as that as emancipation of those born after a given day, and of their education and expatriation after a given age. This would give time for a gradual extinction of that species of labour & substitution of another, and lessen the severity of the shock which an operation so fundamental cannot fail to produce. For men probably of any color, but of this color we know, brought from their infancy without necessity for thought or forecast, are by their habits rendered as incapable as children of taking care of themselves, and are extinguished promptly wherever industry is necessary for raising young. In the mean time they are pests in society by their idleness, and the depredations to which this leads them. Their amalgamation with the other color produces a degradation to which no lover of his country, no lover of excellence in the human character can innocently consent. I am sensible of the partialities with which you have looked towards me as the person who should undertake this salutary but arduous work. But this, my dear sir, is like bidding old Priam to buckle the armour of Hector "trementibus aequo humeris et inutile ferruncingi." No, I have overlived the generation with which mutual labors & perils begat mutual confidence and influence. This enterprise is for the young; for those who can follow it up, and bear it through to its consummation. It shall have all my prayers, & these are the only weapons of an old man. But in the mean time are you right in abandoning this property, and your country with it? I think not. My opinion has ever been that, until more can be done for them, we should endeavor, with those whom fortune has thrown on our hands, to feed and clothe them well, protect them from all ill usage, require such reasonable labor only as is performed voluntarily by freemen, & be led by no repugnancies to abdicate them, and our duties to them. The laws do not permit us to turn them loose, if that were for their good: and to commute them for other property is to commit them to those whose usage of them we cannot control. I hope then, my dear sir, you will reconcile yourself to your country and its unfortunate condition; that you will not lessen its stock of sound disposition by withdrawing your portion from the mass. That, on the contrary you will come forward in the public councils, become the missionary of this doctrine truly christian; insinuate & inculcate it softly but steadily, through the medium of writing and conversation; associate others in your labors, and when the phalanx is formed, bring on and press the proposition perseveringly until its accomplishment. It is an encouraging observation that no good measure was ever proposed, which, if duly pursued, failed to prevail in the end. We have proof of this in the history of the endeavors in the English parliament to suppress that very trade which brought this evil on us. And you will be supported by the religious precept, "be not weary in well-doing." That your success may be as speedy & complete, as it will be of honorable & immortal consolation to yourself, I shall as fervently and sincerely pray as I assure you of my great friendship and respect.

8. To William Short, Monticello, 28 November 1814. *William Short (1759–1849), TJ's private secretary in Paris and "adoptive son," relocated in Philadelphia after returning to America. TJ's analysis of the War of 1812 reveals his profound animosity to Federalist New England. Agitation there against the American war effort led to the anticlimactic Hartford Convention that met from 15 December to 5 January 1815: the Peace of Ghent, signed on 24 December, and Andrew Jackson's great victory at New Orleans, on 8 January 1815, took the wind out of the Convention's sails. Federalism would never again be a force in national politics.*

Although withdrawn from all anxious attention to political concerns, yet I will state my impressions as to the present war, because your letter leads to the subject. The essential grounds of the war were, 1st, the orders of council; and 2d, the impressment of our citizens; (for I put out of sight from the love of peace the multiplied insults on our government and aggressions on our commerce, with which our pouch, like the Indian's, had long been filled to the mouth.) What immediately produced the declaration was, 1st, the proclamation of the Prince Regent that he would never repeal the orders of council as to us, until Bonaparte should have revoked his decrees as to all other nations as well as ours; and 2d, the declaration of his minister to ours that no arrangement whatever could be devised admissible in lieu of impressment. It was certainly a misfortune that they did not know themselves at the date of this silly and insolent proclamation, that within one month they would repeal the orders, and that we, at the date of our declaration, could not know of the repeal which was then going on one thousand leagues distant. Their determinations, as declared by themselves, could alone guide us, and they shut the door on all further negotiation, throwing down to us the gauntlet of war or submission as the only alternatives. We cannot blame the government for choosing that of war, because certainly the great majority of the nation thought it ought to be chosen, not that they were to gain by it in dollars and cents; all men know that war is a losing game to both parties. But they know also that if they do not resist encroachment at some point, all will be taken from them, and that more would then be lost even in dollars and cents by submission than resistance. It is the case of giving a part to save the whole, a limb to save life. It is the melancholy law of human societies to be compelled sometimes to choose a great evil in order to ward off a greater; to deter their neighbors from rapine by making it cost them more than honest gains. The enemy are accordingly now disgorging what they had so ravenously swallowed. The orders of council had taken from us near one thousand vessels. Our list of captures from them is now one thousand three hundred, and, just become sensible that it is small and not large ships which gall them most, we shall probably add one thousand prizes a year to their past losses. Again, supposing that, according to the confession of their own minister in parliament, the Americans they had impressed were something short of two thousand, the war against us alone cannot cost them less than twenty millions of dollars a year, so that each American impressed has already cost them ten thousand dollars, and every year will add five thousand dollars more to his price. We, I suppose, expend more; but had we adopted the other alternative of submission, no mortal can tell what the cost would have been. I consider the war then as entirely justifiable on our part, although I am still sensible it is a deplorable misfortune to us. It has arrested the course of the most remarkable tide of prosperity any nation ever experienced, and has closed such prospects of future improvement as were never before in the view of any people. Farewell all hopes of extinguishing public debt! farewell all visions of applying surpluses of revenue to the improvements of peace rather than the ravages of war. Our enemy has indeed the consolation of Satan on removing our first parents from Paradise: from a peaceable and agricultural nation, he makes us a military and manufacturing one. We shall indeed survive the conflict. Breeders enough will remain to carry on population. We shall retain our country, and rapid advances in the art of war will soon enable us to beat our enemy, and probably drive him from the continent. We have men enough, and I am in hopes the present session of Congress will provide the means of commanding their services. But I wish I could see them get into a better train of finance. Their banking projects are like dosing dropsy with more water. If anything could revolt our citizens against the war, it would be the extravagance with which they are about to be taxed. It is strange indeed that at this day, and in a country where English proceedings are so familiar, the principles and advantages of funding should be neglected, and expedients resorted to. Their new bank, if not abortive at its birth, will not last through one campaign; and the taxes proposed cannot be paid. How can a people who cannot get fifty cents a bushel for their wheat, while they pay twelve dollars a bushel for their salt, pay five times the amount of taxes they ever paid before? Yet that will be the case in all the States south of the Potomac. Our resources are competent to the maintenance of the war if duly economized and skillfuly employed in the way of anticipation. However, we must suffer, I suppose, from our ignorance in funding, as we did from that of fighting, until necessity teaches us both; and, fortunately, our stamina are so vigorous as to rise superior to great mismanagement. This year I think we shall have learnt how to call forth our force, and by the next hope our funds, and even if the state of Europe should not by that time give the enemy employment enough nearer home, we shall leave him nothing to fight for here. These are my views of the war. They embrace a great deal of sufferance, trying privations, and no benefit but that of teaching our enemy that he is never to gain by wanton injuries on us. To me this state of things brings a sacrifice of all tranquillity and comfort through the residue of life. For although the debility of age disables me from the services and sufferings of the field, yet, by the total annihilation in value of the produce which was to give me subsistence and independence, I shall be like Tantalus, up to the shoulders in water, yet dying with thirst. We can make indeed enough to eat, drink and clothe ourselves; but nothing for our salt, iron, groceries and taxes, which must be paid in money. For what can we raise for the market? Wheat? we can only give it to our horses, as we have been doing ever since harvest. Tobacco? it is not worth the pipe it is smoked in. Some say Whiskey; but all mankind must become drunkards to consume it. But although we feel, we shall not flinch. We must consider now, as in the revolutionary war, that although the evils of resistance are great, those of submission would be greater. We must meet, therefore, the former as the casualties of tempests and earthquakes, and like them necessarily resulting from the constitution of the world. Your situation, my dear friend, is much better. For, although I do not know with certainty the nature of your investments, yet I presume they are not in banks, insurance companies, or any other of those gossamer castles. If in ground-rents, they are solid; if in stock of the United States, they are equally so. I once thought that in the event of a war we should be obliged to suspend paying the interest of the public debt. But a dozen years more of experience and observation on our people and government, have satisfied me it will never be done. The sense of the necessity of public credit is so universal and so deeply rooted, that no other necessity will prevail against it; and I am glad to see that while the former eight millions are steadfastly applied to the sinking of the old debt, the Senate have lately insisted on a sinking fund for the new. This is the dawn of that improvement in the management of our finances which I look to for salvation; and I trust that the light will continue to advance, and point out their way to our legislators. They will soon see that instead of taxes for the whole year's expenses, which the people cannot pay, a tax to the amount of the interest and a reasonable portion of the principal will command the whole sum, and throw a part of the burthens of war on times of peace and prosperity. A sacred payment of interest is the only way to make the most of their resources, and a sense of that renders your income from our funds more certain than mine from lands. Some apprehend danger from the defection of Massachusetts. It is a disagreeable circumstance, but not a dangerous one. If they become neutral, we are sufficient for one enemy without them, and in fact we get no aid from them now. If their administration determines to join the enemy, their force will be annihilated by equality of division among themselves. Their federalists will then call in the English army, the republicans ours, and it will only be a transfer of the scene of war from Canada to Massachusetts; and we can get ten men to go to Massachusetts for one who will go to Canada. Every one, too, must know that we can at any moment make peace with England at the expense of the navigation and fisheries of Massachusetts. But it will not come to this. Their own people will put down these factionists as soon as they see the real object of their opposition; and of this Vermont, New Hampshire, and even Connecticut itself, furnish proofs.

9. To Benjamin Austin, Monticello, 9 January 1816. *Benjamin Austin, a prominent Massachusetts Republican politician and writer, urged that the federal government by levying a protective tariff on imports foster the manufacturing enterprises that had sprouted up during TJ's embargo and the War of 1812. These developments prompted TJ to reconsider the hostility to American manufactures expressed in the* Notes on Virginia *(see Chapter 2, document 10).*

Your favor of December 21st has been received, and I am first to thank you for the pamphlet it covered. The same description of persons which is the subject of that is so much multiplied here too, as to be almost a grievance, and by their numbers in the public councils, have wrested from the public hand the direction of the pruning knife. But with us as a body, they are republican, and mostly moderate in their views; so far, therefore, less objects of jealousy than with you. Your opinions on the events which have taken place in France, are entirely just, so far as these events are yet developed. But they have not reached their ultimate termination. There is still an awful void between the present and what is to be the last chapter of that history; and I fear it is to be filled with abominations as frightful as those which have already disgraced it. That nation is too high-minded, has too much innate force, intelligence and elasticity, to remain under its present compression. Samson will arise in his strength, as of old, and as of old will burst asunder the withes and the cords, and the webs of the Philistines. But what are to be the scenes of havoc and horror, and how widely they may spread between brethren of the same house, our ignorance of the interior feuds and antipathies of the country places beyond our ken. It will end, nevertheless, in a representative government, in a government in which the will of the people will be an effective ingredient. This important element has taken root in the European mind, and will have its growth; their despots, sensible of this, are already offering this modification of their governments, as if on their own accord. Instead of the parricide treason of Bonaparte, in perverting the means confided to him as a republican magistrate, to the subversion of that republic and erection of a military despotism for himself and his family, had he used it honestly for the establishment and support of a free government in his own country, France would now have been in freedom and rest; and her example operating in a contrary direction, every nation in Europe would have had a government over which the will of the people would have had some control. His atrocious egotism has checked the salutary progress of principle, and deluged it with rivers of blood which are not yet run out. To the vast sum of devastation and of human misery, of which he has been the guilty cause, much is still to be added. But the object is fixed in the eye of nations, and they will press on to its accomplishment and to the general amelioration of the condition of man. What a germ have we planted, and how faithfully should we cherish the parent tree at home!

You tell me I am quoted by those who wish to continue our dependence on England for manufactures. There was a time when I might have been so quoted with more candor, but within the thirty years which have since elapsed, how are circumstances changed! We were then in peace. Our independent place among nations was acknowledged. A commerce which offered the raw material in exchange for the same material after receiving the last touch of industry, was worthy of welcome to all nations. It was expected that those especially to whom manufacturing industry was important, would cherish the friendship of such customers by every favor, by every inducement, and particularly cultivate their peace by every act of justice and friendship. Under this prospect the question seemed legitimate, whether, with such an immensity of unimproved land, courting the hand of husbandry, the industry of agriculture, or that of manufactures, would add most to the national wealth? And the doubt was entertained on this consideration chiefly, that to the labor of the husbandman a vast addition is made by the spontaneous energies of the earth on which it is employed: for one grain of wheat committed to the earth, she renders twenty, thirty, and even fifty fold, whereas to the labor of the manufacturer nothing is added. Pounds of flax, in his hands, yield, on the contrary, but penny-weights of lace. This exchange, too, laborious as it might seem, what a field did it promise for the occupations of the ocean; what a nursery for that class of citizens who were to exercise and maintain our equal rights on that element? This was the state of things in 1785, when the "Notes on Virginia" were first printed; when, the ocean being open to all nations, and their common right in it acknowledged and exercised under regulations sanctioned by the assent and usage of all, it was thought that the doubt might claim some consideration. But who in 1785 could foresee the rapid depravity which was to render the close of that century the disgrace of the history of man? Who could have imagined that the two most distinguished in the rank of nations, for science and civilization, would have suddenly descended from that honorable eminence, and setting at defiance all those moral laws established by the Author of nature between nation and nation, as between man and man, would cover earth and sea with robberies and piracies, merely because strong enough to do it with temporal impunity; and that under this disbandment of nations from social order, we should have been despoiled of a thousand ships, and have thousands of our citizens reduced to Algerine slavery. Yet all this has taken place. One of these nations interdicted to our vessels all harbors of the globe without having first proceeded to some one of hers, there paid a tribute proportioned to the cargo, and obtained her license to proceed to the port of destination. The other declared them to be lawful prize if they had touched at the port, or been visited by a ship of the enemy nation. Thus were we completely excluded from the ocean. Compare this state of things with that of '85, and say whether an opinion founded in the circumstances of that day can be fairly applied to those of the present. We have experienced what we did not then believe, that there exists both profligacy and power enough to exclude us from the field of interchange with other nations: that to be independent for the comforts of life we must fabricate them ourselves. We must now place the manufacturer by the side of the agriculturist. The former question is suppressed, or rather assumes a new form. Shall we make our own comforts, or go without them, at the will of a foreign nation? He, therefore, who is now against domestic manufacture, must be for reducing us either to dependence on that foreign nation, or to be clothed in skins, and to live like wild beasts in dens and caverns. I am not one of these; experience has taught me that manufactures are now as necessary to our independence as to our comfort; and if those who quote me as of a different opinion, will keep pace with me in purchasing nothing foreign where an equivalent of domestic fabric can be obtained, without regard to difference of price, it will not be our fault if we do not soon have a supply at home equal to our demand, and wrest that weapon of distress from the hand which has wielded it. If it shall be proposed to go beyond our own supply, the question of '85 will then recur, will our surplus labor be then most beneficially employed in the culture of the earth, or in the fabrications of art? We have time yet for consideration, before that question will press upon us; and the maxim to be applied will depend on the circumstances which shall then exist; for in so complicated a science as political economy, no one axiom can be laid down as wise and expedient for all times and circumstances, and for their contraries. Inattention to this is what has called for this explanation, which reflection would have rendered unnecessary with the candid, while nothing will do it with those who use the former opinion only as a stalking horse, to cover their disloyal propensities to keep us in eternal vassalage to a foreign and unfriendly people.

10. To Samuel Kercheval, Monticello, 12 July 1816. *Samuel Kercheval, a leader from the Shenandoah Valley of the state constitutional reform movement, had sent TJ a pamphlet calling for a constitutional convention. Westerners resented the disproportionate representation of Tidewater counties under the 1776 Constitution, echoing criticisms TJ made in his* Notes on Virginia *(see Chapter 2, document 6). In this famous letter TJ elaborates his mature constitutional theory, connecting to his concern with equitable representation a conception of state government organized along federal lines. The basic unit of self-government should be the township or "ward."*

At the birth of our republic, I committed that opinion to the world, in the draught of a constitution annexed to the "Notes on Virginia," in which a provision was inserted for a representation permanently equal. The infancy of the subject at that moment, and our inexperience of self-government, occasioned gross departures in that draught from genuine republican canons. In truth, the abuses of monarchy had so much filled all the space of political contemplation, that we imagined everything republican which was not monarchy. We had not yet penetrated to the mother principle, that "governments are republican only in proportion as they embody the will of their people, and execute it." Hence, our first constitutions had really no leading principles in them. But experience and reflection have but more and more confirmed me in the particular importance of the equal representation then proposed. On that point, then, I am entirely in sentiment with your letters; and only lament that a copyright of your pamphlet prevents their appearance in the newspapers, where alone they would be generally read, and produce general effect. The present vacancy too, of other matter, would give them place in every paper, and bring the question home to every man's conscience.

But inequality of representation in both Houses of our legislature, is not the only republican heresy in this first essay of our revolutionary patriots at forming a constitution. For let it be agreed that a government is republican in proportion as every member composing it has his equal voice in the direction of its concerns (not indeed in person, which would be impracticable beyond the limits of a city, or small township, but) by representatives chosen by himself, and responsible to him at short periods, and let us bring to the test of this canon every branch of our constitution.

In the legislature, the House of Representatives is chosen by less than half the people, and not at all in proportion to those who do choose. The Senate are still more disproportionate, and for long terms of irresponsibility. In the Executive, the Governor is entirely independent of the choice of the people, and of their control; his Council equally so, and at best but a fifth wheel to a wagon. In the Judiciary, the judges of the highest courts are dependent on none but themselves. In England, where judges were named and removable at the will of an hereditary executive, from which branch most misrule was feared, and has flowed, it was a great point gained, by fixing them for life, to make them independent of that executive. But in a government founded on the public will, this principle operates in an opposite direction, and against that will. There, too, they were still removable on a concurrence of the executive and legislative branches. But we have made them independent of the nation itself. They are irremovable, but by their own body, for any depravities of conduct, and even by their own body for the imbecilities of dotage. The justices of the inferior courts are self-chosen, are for life, and perpetuate their own body in succession forever, so that a faction once possessing themselves of the bench of a county, can never be broken up, but hold their county in chains, forever indissoluble. Yet these justices are the real executive as well as judiciary, in all our minor and most ordinary concerns. They tax us at will; fill the office of sheriff, the most important of all the executive officers of the county; name nearly all our military leaders, which leaders, once named, are removable but by themselves. The juries, our judges of all fact, and of law when they choose it, are not selected by the people, nor amenable to them. They are chosen by an officer named by the court and executive. Chosen, did I say? Picked up by the sheriff from the loungings of the court yard, after everything respectable has retired from it. Where then is our republicanism to be found? Not in our constitution certainly, but merely in the spirit of our people. That would oblige even a despot to govern us republicanly. Owing to this spirit, and to nothing in the form of our constitution, all things have gone well. But this fact, so triumphantly misquoted by the enemies of reformation, is not the fruit of our constitution, but has prevailed in spite of it. Our functionaries have done well, because generally honest men. If any were not so, they feared to show it.

But it will be said, it is easier to find faults than to amend them. I do not think their amendment so difficult as is pretended. Only lay down true principles, and adhere to them inflexibly. Do not be frightened into their surrender by the alarms of the timid, or the croakings of wealth against the ascendency of the people. If experience be called for, appeal to that of our fifteen or twenty governments for forty years, and show me where the people have done half the mischief in these forty years, that a single despot would have done in a single year; or show half the riots and rebellions, the crimes and the punishments, which have taken place in any single nation, under kingly government, during the same period. The true foundation of republican government is the equal right of every citizen, in his person and property, and in their management. Try by this, as a tally, every provision of our constitution, and see if it hangs directly on the will of the people. Reduce your legislature to a convenient number for full, but orderly discussion. Let every man who fights or pays, exercise his just and equal right in their election. Submit them to approbation or rejection at short intervals. Let the executive be chosen in the same way, and for the same term, by those whose agent he is to be; and leave no screen of a council behind which to skulk from responsibility. It has been thought that the people are not competent electors of judges learned in the law. But I do not know that this is true, and, if doubtful, we should follow principle. In this, as in many other elections, they would be guided by reputation, which would not err oftener, perhaps, than the present mode of appointment. In one State of the Union, at least, it has long been tried, and with the most satisfactory success. The judges of Connecticut have been chosen by the people every six months, for nearly two centuries, and believe there has hardly ever been an instance of change; so powerful is the curb of incessant responsibility. If prejudice, however, derived from a monarchical institution, is still to prevail against the vital elective principle of our own, and if the existing example among ourselves of periodical election of judges by the people be still mistrusted, let us at least not adopt the evil, and reject the good, of the English precedent; let us retain amovability on the concurrence of the executive and legislative branches, and nomination by the executive alone. Nomination to office is an executive function. To give it to the legislature, as we do, is a violation of the principle of the separation of powers. It swerves the members from correctness, by temptations to intrigue for office themselves, and to a corrupt barter of votes; and destroys responsibility by dividing it among a multitude. By leaving nomination in its proper place, among executive functions, the principle of the distribution of power is preserved, and responsibility weighs with its heaviest force on a single head.

The organization of our county administrations may be thought more difficult. But follow principle, and the knot unties itself. Divide the counties into wards of such size as that every citizen can attend, when called on, and act in person. Ascribe to them the government of their wards in all things relating to themselves exclusively. A justice, chosen by themselves, in each, a constable, a military company, a patrol, a school, the care of their own poor, their own portion of the public roads, the choice of one or more jurors to serve in some court, and the delivery, within their own wards, of their own votes for all elective officers of higher sphere, will relieve the county administration of nearly all its business, will have it better done, and by making every citizen an acting member of the government, and in the offices nearest and most interesting to him, will attach him by his strongest feelings to the independence of his country, and its republican constitution. The justices thus chosen by every ward, would constitute the county court, would do its judiciary business, direct roads and bridges, levy county and poor rates, and administer all the matters of common interest to the whole country. These wards, called townships in New England, are the vital principle of their governments, and have proved themselves the wisest invention ever devised by the wit of man for the perfect exercise of self-government, and for its preservation. We should thus marshal our government into, 1, the general federal republic, for all concerns foreign and federal; 2, that of the State, for what relates to our own citizens exclusively; 3, the county republics, for the duties and concerns of the county; and 4, the ward republics, for the small, and yet numerous and interesting concerns of the neighborhood; and in government, as well as in every other business of life, it is by division and subdivision of duties alone, that all matters, great and small, can be managed to perfection. And the whole is cemented by giving to every citizen, personally, a part in the administration of the public affairs

The sum of these amendments is, 1. General Suffrage. 2. Equal representation in the legislature. 3. An executive chosen by the people. 4. Judges elective or amovable. 5. Justices, jurors, and sheriffs elective. 6. Ward divisions. And 7. Periodical amendments of the constitution.

I have thrown out these as loose heads of amendment, for consideration and correction; and their object is to secure self-government by the republicanism of our constitution, as well as by the spirit of the people; and to nourish and perpetuate that spirit. I am not among those who fear the people. They, and not the rich, are our dependence for continued freedom. And to preserve their independence, we must not let our rulers load us with perpetual debt. We must make our election between *economy and liberty*, or *profusion and servitude*. If we run into such debts, as that we must be taxed in our meat and in our drink, in our necessaries and our comforts, in our labors and our amusements, for our callings and our creeds, as the people of England are, our people, like them, must come to labor sixteen hours in the twenty-four, give the earnings of fifteen of these to the government for their debts and daily expenses; and the sixteenth being insufficient to afford us bread, we must live, as they now do, on oatmeal and potatoes; have no time to think, no means of calling the mismanagers to account; but be glad to obtain subsistence by hiring ourselves to rivet their chains on the necks of our fellow-sufferers. Our landholders, too, like theirs, retaining indeed the title and stewardship of estates called theirs, but held really in trust for the treasury, must wander, like theirs, in foreign countries, and be contented with penury, obscurity, exile, and the glory of the nation. This example reads to us the salutary lesson, that private fortunes are destroyed by public as well as by private extravagance. And this is the tendency of all human governments. A departure from principle in one instance becomes a precedent for a second; that second for a third; and so on, till the bulk of the society is reduced to be mere automatons of misery, and to have no sensibilities left but for sinning and suffering. Then begins, indeed, the *bellum omnium in omnia*, which some philosophers observing to be so general in this world, have mistaken it for the natural, instead of the abusive state of man. And the fore horse of this frightful team is public debt. Taxation follows that, and in its train wretchedness and oppression.

Some men look at constitutions with sanctimonious reverence, and deem them like the arc of the covenant, too sacred to be touched. They ascribe to the men of the preceding age a wisdom more than human, and suppose what they did to be beyond amendment. I knew that age well; I belonged to it, and labored with it. It deserved well of its country. It was very like the present, but without the experience of the present; and forty years of experience in government is worth a century of book-reading; and this they would say themselves, were they to rise from the dead. I am certainly not an advocate for frequent and untried changes in laws and constitutions. I think moderate imperfections had better be borne with; because, when once known, we accommodate ourselves to them, and find practical means of correcting their ill effects. But I know also, that laws and institutions must go hand in hand with the progress of the human mind. As that becomes more developed, more enlightened, as new discoveries are made, new truths disclosed, and manners and opinions change with the change of circumstances, institutions must advance also, and keep pace with the times. We might as well require a man to wear still the coat which fitted him when a boy, as civilized society to remain ever under the regimen of their barbarous ancestors. It is this preposterous idea which has lately deluged Europe in blood. Their monarchs, instead of wisely yielding to the gradual change of circumstances, of favoring progressive accommodation to progressive improvement, have clung to old abuses, entrenched themselves behind steady habits, and obliged their subjects to seek through blood and violence rash and ruinous innovations, which, had they been referred to the peaceful deliberations and collected wisdom of the nation, would have been put into acceptable and salutary forms. Let us follow no such examples, nor weakly believe that one generation is not as capable as another of taking care of itself, and of ordering its own affairs. Let us, as our sister States have done, avail ourselves of our reason and experience, to correct the crude essays of our first and unexperienced, although wise, virtuous, and well-meaning councils. And lastly, let us provide in our constitution for its revision at stated periods. What these periods should be, nature herself indicates. By the European tables of mortality, of the adults living at any one moment of time, a majority will be dead in about nineteen years. At the end of that period, then, a new majority is come into place; or, in other words, a new generation. Each generation is as independent as the one preceding, as that was of all which had gone before. It has then, like them, a right to choose for itself the form of government it believes most promotive of its own happiness; consequently, to accommodate to the circumstances in which it finds itself, that received from its predecessors; and it is for the peace and good of mankind, that a solemn opportunity of doing this every nineteen or twenty years, should be provided by the constitution; so that it may be handed on, with periodical repairs, from generation to generation, to the end of time, if anything human can so long endure. It is now forty years since the constitution of Virginia was formed. The same tables inform us, that, within that period, two-thirds of the adults then living are now dead. Have then the remaining third, even if they had the wish, the right to hold in obedience to their will, and to laws heretofore made by them, the other two-thirds, who, with themselves, compose the present mass of adults? If they have not, who has? The dead? But the dead have no rights. They are nothing; and nothing cannot own something. Where there is no substance, there can be no accident. This corporeal globe, and everything upon it, belong to its present corporeal inhabitants, during their generation. They alone have a right to direct what is the concern of themselves alone, and to declare the law of that direction; and this declaration can only be made by their majority. That majority, then, has a right to depute representatives to a convention, and to make the constitution what they think will be the best for themselves. But how collect their voice? This is the real difficulty. If invited by private authority, or county or district meetings, these divisions are so large that few will attend; and their voice will be imperfectly, or falsely pronounced. Here, then, would be one of the advantages of the ward divisions I have proposed. The mayor of every ward, on a question like the present, would call his ward together, take the simple yea or nay of its members, convey these to the county court, who would hand on those of all its wards to the proper general authority; and the voice of the whole people would be thus fairly, fully, and peaceably expressed, discussed, and decided by the common reason of the society. If this avenue be shut to the call of sufferance, it will make itself heard through that of force, and we shall go on, as other nations are doing, in the endless circle of oppression, rebellion, reformation; and oppression, rebellion, reformation, again; and so on forever.

11. Report of the Commissioners for the University of Virginia, 4 August 1818. *TJ presided at a meeting of a special commission, including representatives from all of Virginia's senatorial districts, at Rockfish Gap in the Blue Ridge, thirty miles west of Charlottesville, to resolve the controversial question of where to locate the new University of Virginia. The commission's twenty-one members unanimously supported TJ's recommendation of Central College in Charlottesville as the most central and salubrious site. After some debate (westerners favored Staunton in the Shenandoah Valley), the Virginia House and Senate approved the Rockfish Gap Report in January 1819, establishing the University and fulfilling TJ's long-cherished ambition. Beyond resolving the site controversy, the Rockfish Gap Report articulates TJ's vision of the University's curriculum and educational philosophy.*

The commissioners for the University of Virginia, having met, as by law required, at the tavern, in Rockfish Gap, on the Blue Ridge, on the first day of August, of this present year, 1818; and having formed a board, proceeded on that day to the discharge of the duties assigned to them by the act of the Legislature, entitled "An act, appropriating part of the revenue of the literary fund, and for other purposes;" and having continued their proceedings by adjournment, from day to day, to Tuesday, the 4th day of August, have agreed to a report on the several matters with which they were charged, which report they now respectfully address and submit to the Legislature of the State.

The first duty enjoined on them, was to enquire and report a site, in some convenient and proper part of the State, for an university, to be called the "University of Virginia." In this enquiry, they supposed that the governing considerations should be the healthiness of the site, the fertility of the neighboring country, and its centrality to the white population of the whole State. For, although the act authorized and required them to receive any voluntary contributions, whether conditional or absolute, which might be offered through them to the President and Directors of the Literary Fund, for the benefit of the University, yet they did not consider this as establishing an auction, or as pledging the location to the highest bidder.

Three places were proposed, to wit: Lexington, in the county of Rockbridge, Staunton, in the county of Augusta, and the Central College, in the county of Albemarle. Each of these was unexceptionable as to healthiness and fertility. It was the degree of centrality to the white population of the State which alone then constituted the important point of comparison between these places; and the Board, after full enquiry, and impartial and mature consideration, are of opinion, that the central point of the white population of the State is nearer to the Central College than to either Lexington or Staunton, by great and important differences; and all other circumstances of the place in general being favorable to it, as a position for an university, they do report the Central College, in Albemarle, to be a convenient and proper part of the State for the University of Virginia.

2. The Board having thus agreed on a proper site for the University, to be reported to the Legislature, proceed to the second of the duties assigned to them—that of proposing a plan for its buildings—and they are of opinion that it should consist of distinct houses or pavilions, arranged at proper distances on each side of a lawn of a proper breadth, and of indefinite extent, in one direction, at least; in each of which should be a lecturing room, with from two to four apartments, for the accommodation of a professor and his family; that these pavilions should be united by a range of dormitories, sufficient each for the accommodation of two students only, this provision being deemed advantageous to morals, to order, and to uninterrupted study; and that a passage of some kind, under cover from the weather, should give a communication along the whole range. It is supposed that such pavilions, on an average of the larger and smaller, will cost each about $5,000; each dormitory about $350, and hotels of a single room, for a refectory, and two rooms for the tenant, necessary for dieting the students, will cost about $3500 each. The number of these pavilions will depend on the number of professors, and that of the dormitories and hotels on the number of students to be lodged and dieted. The advantages of this plan are: greater security against fire and infection; tranquillity and comfort to the professors and their families thus insulated; retirement to the students; and the admission of enlargement to any degree to which the institution may extend in future times. It is supposed probable, that a building of somewhat more size in the middle of the grounds may be called for in time, in which may be rooms for religious worship, under such impartial regulations as the Visitors shall prescribe, for public examinations, for a library, for the schools of music, drawing, and other associated purposes.

3, 4. In proceeding to the third and fourth duties prescribed by the Legislature, of reporting "the branches of learning, which should be taught in the University, and the number and description of the professorships they will require," the Commissioners were first to consider at what point it was understood that university education should commence? Certainly not with the alphabet, for reasons of expediency and impracticability, as well from the obvious sense of the Legislature, who, in the same act, make other provision for the primary instruction of the poor children, expecting, doubtless, that in other cases it would be provided by the parent, or become, perhaps, subject of future and further attention of the Legislature. The objects of this primary education determine its character and limits. These objects would be,

To give to every citizen the information he needs for the transaction of his own business;

To enable him to calculate for himself, and to express and preserve his ideas, his contracts and accounts, in writing;

To improve, by reading, his morals and faculties;

To understand his duties to his neighbors and country, and to discharge with competence the functions confided to him by either;

To know his rights; to exercise with order and justice those he retains; to choose with discretion the fiduciary of those he delegates; and to notice their conduct with diligence, with candor, and judgment;

And, in general, to observe with intelligence and faithfulness all the social relations under which he shall be placed.

To instruct the mass of our citizens in these, their rights, interests and duties, as men and citizens, being then the objects of education in the primary schools, whether private or public, in them should be taught reading, writing and numerical arithmetic, the elements of mensuration, (useful in so many callings,) and the outlines of geography and history. And this brings us to the point at which are to commence the higher branches of education, of which the Legislature require the development; those, for example, which are,

To form the statesmen, legislators and judges, on whom public prosperity and individual happiness are so much to depend;

To expound the principles and structure of government, the laws which regulate the intercourse of nations, those formed municipally for our own government, and a sound spirit of legislation, which, banishing all arbitrary and unnecessary restraint on individual action, shall leave us free to do whatever does not violate the equal rights of another;

To harmonize and promote the interests of agriculture, manufactures and commerce, and by well informed views of political economy to give a free scope to the public industry;

To develop the reasoning faculties of our youth, enlarge their minds, cultivate their morals, and instill into them the precepts of virtue and order;

To enlighten them with mathematical and physical sciences, which advance the arts, and administer to the health, the subsistence, and comforts of human life;

And, generally, to form them to habits of reflection and correct action, rendering them examples of virtue to others, and of happiness within themselves.

These are the objects of that higher grade of education, the benefits and blessings of which the Legislature now propose to provide for the good and ornament of their country, the gratification and happiness of their fellow-citizens, of the parent especially, and his progeny, on which all his affections are concentrated.

In entering on this field, the Commissioners are aware that they have to encounter much difference of opinion as to the extent which it is expedient that this institution should occupy. Some good men, and even of respectable information, consider the learned sciences as useless acquirements; some think that they do not better the condition of man; and others that education, like private and individual concerns, should be left to private individual effort; not reflecting that an establishment embracing all the sciences which may be useful and even necessary in the various vocations of life, with the buildings and apparatus belonging to each, are far beyond the reach of individual means, and must either derive existence from public patronage, or not exist at all. This would leave us, then, without those callings which depend on education, or send us to other countries to seek the instruction they require. But the Commissioners are happy in considering the statute under which they are assembled as proof that the Legislature is far from the abandonment of objects so interesting. They are sensible that the advantages of well-directed education, moral, political and economical, are truly above all estimate. Education generates habits of application, of order, and the love of virtue; and controls, by the force of habit, any innate obliquities in our moral organization. We should be far, too, from the discouraging persuasion that man is fixed, by the law of his nature, at a given point; that his improvement is a chimera, and the hope delusive of rendering ourselves wiser, happier or better than our forefathers were. As well might it be urged that the wild and uncultivated tree, hitherto yielding sour and bitter fruit only, can never be made to yield better; yet we know that the grafting art implants a new tree on the savage stock, producing what is most estimable both in kind and degree. Education, in like manner, engrafts a new man on the native stock, and improves what in his nature was vicious and perverse into qualities of virtue and social worth. And it cannot be but that each generation succeeding to the knowledge acquired by all those who preceded it, adding to it their own acquisitions and discoveries, and handing the mass down for successive and constant accumulation, must advance the knowledge and well-being of mankind, not *infinitely*, as some have said, but *indefinitely*, and to a term which no one can fix and foresee. Indeed, we need look back half a century, to times which many now living remember well, and see the wonderful advances in the sciences and arts which have been made within that period. Some of these have rendered the elements themselves subservient to the purposes of man, have harnessed them to the yoke of his labors, and effected the great blessings of moderating his own, of accomplishing what was beyond his feeble force, and extending the comforts of life to a much enlarged circle, to those who had before known its necessaries only. That these are not the vain dreams of sanguine hope, we have before our eyes real and living examples. What, but education, has advanced us beyond the condition of our indigenous neighbors? And what chains them to their present state of barbarism and wretchedness, but a bigotted veneration for the supposed superlative wisdom of their fathers, and the preposterous idea that they are to look backward for better things, and not forward, longing, as it should seem, to return to the days of eating acorns and roots, rather than indulge in the degeneracies of civilization? And how much more encouraging to the achievements of science and improvement is this, than the desponding view that the condition of man cannot be ameliorated, that what has been must ever be, and that to secure ourselves where we are, we must tread with awful reverence in the footsteps of our fathers. This doctrine is the genuine fruit of the alliance between Church and State; the tenants of which, finding themselves but too well in their present condition, oppose all advances which might unmask their usurpations, and monopolies of honors, wealth, and power, and fear every change, as endangering the comforts they now hold. Nor must we omit to mention, among the benefits of education, the incalculable advantage of training up able counsellors to administer the affairs of our country in all its departments, legislative, executive and judiciary, and to bear their proper share in the councils of our national government; nothing more than education advancing the prosperity, the power, and the happiness of a nation.

12. To John Holmes, Monticello, 22 April 1820. *John Holmes (1773–1843), recently a Republican congressman from Maine, risked the disfavor of his constituents by supporting the admission of the new state of Missouri without any restriction regarding slavery. James Tallmadge, a Republican from New York, initiated the Missouri Controversy on 13 February 1819 by proposing that Missouri prohibit further slave importations as a condition of statehood. The failure of the Tallmadge Amendment led to a protracted impasse, resolved in March 1820 when the admission of Missouri without restrictions was hooked to the admission of the Maine District of Massachusetts as a free state. Holmes resigned from Congress to participate in his state's constitutional convention, returning to Washington later in the year as one of Maine's first United States senators. TJ's famous "fire bell in the night" letter applauded Holmes's stand, emphasizing that the only alternative to this "compromise" was the breakup of the union.*

I thank you, dear Sir, for the copy you have been so kind as to send me of the letter to your constituents on the Missouri question. It is a perfect justification to them. I had for a long time ceased to read newspapers, or pay any attention to public affairs, confident they were in good hands, and content to be a passenger in our bark to the shore from which I am not distant. But this momentous question, like a fire bell in the night, awakened and filled me with terror. I considered it at once as the knell of the Union. It is hushed, indeed, for the moment. But this is a reprieve only, not a final sentence. A geographical line, coinciding with a marked principle, moral and political, once conceived and held up to the angry passions of men, will never be obliterated; and every new irritation will mark it deeper and deeper. I can say, with conscious truth, that there is not a man on earth who would sacrifice more than I would to relieve us from this heavy reproach, in any *practicable* way. The cession of that kind of property, for so it is misnamed, is a bagatelle which would not cost me a second thought, if, in that way, a general emancipation and *expatriation* could be effected; and gradually, and with due sacrifices, I think it might be. But as it is, we have the wolf by the ears, and we can neither hold him, nor safely let him go. Justice is in one scale, and self-preservation in the other. Of one thing I am certain, that as the passage of slaves from one State to another, would not make a slave of a single human being who would not be so without it, so their diffusion over a greater surface would make them individually happier, and proportionally facilitate the accomplishment of their emancipation, by dividing the burthen on a greater number of coadjutors. An abstinence too, from this act of power, would remove the jealousy excited by the undertaking of Congress to regulate the condition of the different descriptions of men composing a State. This certainly is the exclusive right of every State, which nothing in the constitution has taken from them and given to the General Government. Could Congress, for example, say, that the non-freemen of Connecticut shall be freemen, or that they shall not emigrate into any other State?

I regret that I am now to die in the belief, that the useless sacrifice of themselves by the generation of 1776, to acquire self-government and happiness to their country, is to be thrown away by the unwise and unworthy passions of their sons, and that my only consolation is to be, that I live not to weep over it. If they would but dispassionately weigh the blessings they will throw away, against an abstract principle more likely to be effected by union than by scission, they would pause before they would perpetrate this act of suicide on themselves, and of treason against the hopes of the world. To yourself, as the faithful advocate of the Union, I tender the offering of my high esteem and respect.

13. To Richard Rush, Monticello, 20 October 1820. *Richard Rush (1780–1859), son of TJ's old friend Benjamin Rush, was the American minister to Great Britain. TJ emphasizes here the magnitude of the danger from the Missouri Controversy to the progress of political enlightenment in Europe as well as the survival of the American union.*

The important news lies now on your side of the Atlantic. England, in throes from a trifle, as it would seem, but that trifle the symptom of an irremediable disease proceeding from a long course of exhaustion by efforts and burdens beyond her natural strength; France agonizing between royalists and constitutionalists; the other States of Europe pressing on to revolution and the rights of man, and the colossal powers of Russia and Austria marshalled against them. These are more than specks of hurricane in the horizon of the world. You, who are young, may live to see its issue; the beginning only is for my time. Nor is our side of the water entirely untroubled, the boisterous sea of liberty is never without a wave. A hideous evil, the magnitude of which is seen, and at a distance only, by the one party, and more sorely felt and sincerely deplored by the other, from the difficulty of the cure, divides us at this moment too angrily. The attempt by one party to prohibit willing States from sharing the evil, is thought by the other to render desperate, by accumulation, the hope of its final eradication. If a little time, however, is given to both parties to cool, and to dispel their visionary fears, they will see that concurring in sentiment as to the evil, moral and political, the duty and interest of both is to concur also in divining a practicable process of cure. Should time not be given, and the schism be pushed to separation, it will be for a short term only; two or three years' trial will bring them back, like quarrelling lovers to renewed embraces, and increased affections. The experiment of separation would soon prove to both that they had mutually miscalculated their best interests. And even were the parties in Congress to secede in a passion, the soberer people would call a convention and cement again the severance attempted by the insanity of their functionaries. With this consoling view, my greatest grief would be for the fatal effect of such an event on the hopes and happiness of the world. We exist, and are quoted, as standing proofs that a government, so modelled as to rest continually on the will of the whole society, is a practicable government. Were we to break to pieces, it would damp the hopes and the efforts of the good, and give triumph to those of the bad through the whole enslaved world. As members, therefore, of the universal society of mankind, and standing in high and responsible relation with them, it is our sacred duty to suppress passion among ourselves, and not to blast the confidence we have inspired of proof that a government of reason is better than one of force.

14. To Judge Spencer Roane, Monticello, 27 June 1821. *Spencer Roane (1762–1822), judge of the General Court of Virginia and the state Supreme Court of Appeals, was a distinguished jurist and Republican defender of states' rights against the judicial nationalism of the Supreme Court under Chief Justice John Marshall. Roane asked TJ to endorse John Taylor's latest broadside against "consolidationism,"* Constructions Construed, and Constitutions Vindicated, *published in Richmond in 1820.*

It is with extreme reluctance that I permit myself to usurp the office of an adviser of the public, what books they should read, and what not. [*However, TJ has worked up the following passage, which he says may be published as "an extract of a letter from Th: J. to—;"*] . . . I have read Colonel Taylor's book of "Constructions Construed," with great satisfaction, and, I will say, with edification; for I acknowledge it corrected some errors of opinion into which I had slidden without sufficient examination. It is the most logical retraction of our governments to the original and true principles of the Constitution creating them, which has appeared since the adoption of that instrument. I may not perhaps concur in all its opinions, great and small; for no two men ever thought alike on so many points. But on all its important questions, it contains the true political faith, to which every catholic republican should steadfastly hold. It should be put into the hands of all our functionaries, authoritatively, as a standing instruction, and true exposition of our Constitution, as understood at the time we agreed to it. It is a fatal heresy to suppose that either our State governments are superior to the federal, or the federal to the States. The people, to whom all authority belongs, have divided the powers of government into two distinct departments, the leading characters of which are *foreign* and domestic; and they have appointed for each a distinct set of functionaries. These they have made co-ordinate, checking and balancing each other, like the three cardinal departments in the individual States: each equally supreme as to the powers delegated to itself, and neither authorized ultimately to decide what belongs to itself, or to its coparcenor in government. As independent, in fact, as different nations, a spirit of forbearance and compromise, therefore, and not of encroachment and usurpation, is the healing balm of such a Constitution; and each party should prudently shrink from all approach to the line of demarcation, instead of rashly overleaping it, or throwing grapples ahead to haul to hereafter. But, finally, the peculiar happiness of our blessed system is, that in differences of opinion between these different sets of servants, the appeal is to neither, but to their employers peaceably assembled by their representatives in convention. This is more rational than the *jus fortioris,* or the cannon's mouth, the *ultima et sola ratio regnum.*

15. To Dr. Benjamin Waterhouse, Monticello, 26 June 1822. *In this letter to physician Benjamin Waterhouse (1754–1846), who had made his mark as a pioneering vaccinator, Jefferson presents his fundamental religious beliefs. TJ's prediction that Unitarianism ultimately would triumph in America showed how far out of touch he was with religious developments.*

I have received and read with thankfulness and pleasure your denunciation of the abuses of tobacco and wine. Yet, however sound in its principles, I expect it will be but a sermon to the wind. You will find it as difficult to inculcate these sanative precepts on the sensualities of the present day, as to convince an Athanasian that there is but one God. I wish success to both attempts, and am happy to learn from you that the latter, at least, is making progress, and the more rapidly in proportion as our Platonizing Christians make more stir and noise about it. The doctrines of Jesus are simple, and tend all to the happiness of man.

1. That there is one only God, and he all perfect.
2. That there is a future state of rewards and punishments.
3. That to love God with all thy heart and thy neighbor as thyself, is the sum of religion. These are the great points on which he endeavored to reform the religion of the Jews. But compare with these the demoralizing dogmas of Calvin.

1. That there are three Gods.
2. That good works, or the love of our neighbor, are nothing.
3. That faith is every thing, and the more incomprehensible the proposition, the more merit in its faith.
4. That reason in religion is of unlawful use.
5. That God, from the beginning, elected certain individuals to be saved, and certain others to be damned; and that no crimes of the former can damn them; no virtues of the latter save.

Now, which of these is the true and charitable Christian? He who believes and acts on the simple doctrines of Jesus? Or the impious dogmatists, as Athanasius and Calvin? Verily I say these are the false shepherds foretold as to enter not by the door into the sheepfold, but to climb up some other way. They are mere usurpers of the Christian name, teaching a counter-religion made up of the *deliria* of crazy imaginations, as foreign from Christianity as is that of Mahomet. Their blasphemies have driven thinking men into infidelity, who have too hastily rejected the supposed author himself, with the horrors so falsely imputed to him. Had the doctrines of Jesus been preached always as pure as they came from his lips, the whole civilized world would now have been Christian. I rejoice that in this blessed country of free inquiry and belief, which has surrendered its creed and conscience to neither kings nor priests, the genuine doctrine of one only God is reviving, and trust that there is not a *young man* now living in the United States who will not die an Unitarian.

But much I fear, that when this great truth shall be re-established, its votaries will fall into the fatal error of fabricating formulas of creed and confessions of faith, the engines which so soon destroyed the religion of Jesus, and made of Christendom a mere Aceldama; that they will give up morals for mysteries, and Jesus for Plato. How much wiser are the Quakers, who, agreeing in the fundamental doctrines of the gospel, schismatize about no mysteries, and, keeping within the pale of common sense, suffer no speculative differences of opinion, any more than of feature, to impair the love of their brethren. Be this the wisdom of Unitarians, this the holy mantle which shall cover within its charitable circumference all who believe in one God, and who love their neighbor! I conclude my sermon with sincere assurances of my friendly esteem and respect.

16. To President James Monroe, Monticello, 11 June 1823. *TJ's protégé James Monroe (1758–1831) succeeded James Madison to the presidency in 1817. TJ expresses here the broad outlines of his geopolitical perspective: the new nations of the Western Hemisphere must avoid entanglement in the affairs of Europe. As in the case of the Louisiana crisis two decades earlier, TJ was prepared to consider an alliance with Britain to secure Cuban independence against intervention by the Holy Alliance. Monroe and his secretary of state John Quincy Adams opted for an independent policy instead, announcing in the Monroe Doctrine of 2 December 1823 that the Western Hemisphere would be off limits to future interventions by all European powers. The "matter" now embroiling Europe was the Alliance's restoration of Ferdinand VII's authority in Spain: the question was whether this intervention would be a prelude to further action in Spain's remaining American dominions.*

The matter which now embroils Europe, the presumption of dictating to an independent nation the form of its government, is so arrogant, so atrocious, that indignation, as well as moral sentiment, enlists all our partialities and prayers in favor of one, and our equal execrations against the other. I do not know, indeed, whether all nations do not owe to one another a bold and open declaration of their sympathies, with the one party, and their detestation of the conduct of the other. But farther than this we are not bound to go; and indeed, for the sake of the world, we ought not to increase the jealousies, or draw on ourselves the power of this formidable confederacy. I have ever deemed it fundamental for the United States, never to take active part in the quarrels of Europe. Their political interests are entirely distinct from ours. Their mutual jealousies, their balance of power, their complicated alliances, their forms and principles of government, are all foreign to us. They are nations of eternal war.

All their energies are expended in the destruction of the labor, property and lives of their people. On our part, never had a people so favorable a chance of trying the opposite system, of peace and fraternity with mankind, and the direction of all our means and faculties to the purposes of improvement instead of destruction. With Europe we have few occasions of collision, and these, with a little prudence and forbearance, may be generally accommodated. Of the brethren of our own hemisphere, none are yet, or for an age to come will be, in a shape, condition, or disposition to war against us. And the foothold which the nations of Europe had in either America, is slipping from under them, so that we shall soon be rid of their neighborhood. Cuba alone seems at present to hold up a speck of war to us. Its possession by Great Britain would indeed be a great calamity to us. Could we induce her to join us in guaranteeing its independence against all the world, *except* Spain, it would be nearly as valuable to us as if it were our own. But should she take it, I would not immediately go to war for it; because the first war on other accounts will give it to us or the island will give itself to us, when able to do so. While no duty, therefore, calls on us to take part in the present war of Europe, and a golden harvest offers itself in reward for doing nothing, peace and neutrality seem to be our duty and interest. We may gratify ourselves, indeed, with a neutrality as partial to Spain as would be justifiable without giving cause of war to her adversary; we might and ought to avail ourselves of the happy occasion of procuring and cementing a cordial reconciliation with her, by giving assurance of every friendly office which neutrality admits, and especially, against all apprehension of our intermeddling in the quarrel with her colonies. And I expect daily and confidently to hear of a spark kindled in France, which will employ her at home, and relieve Spain from all further apprehensions of danger.

That England is playing false with Spain cannot be doubted. Her government is looking one way and rowing another. It is curious to look back a little on past events. During the ascendancy of Bonaparte, the word among the herd of kings, was "*sauve qui peut.*" Each shifted for himself, and left his brethren to squander and do the same as they could. After the battle of Waterloo, and the military possession of France, they rallied and combined in common cause, to maintain each other against any similar and future danger. And in this alliance, Louis, now avowedly, and George, secretly but solidly, were of the contracting parties; and there can be no doubt that the allies are bound by treaty to aid England with their armies, should insurrection take place among her people. The coquetry she is now playing off between her people and her allies is perfectly understood by the latter, and accordingly gives no apprehensions to France, to whom it is all explained. The diplomatic correspondence she is now displaying, these double papers, fabricated merely for exhibition, in which she makes herself talk of morals and principle, as if her qualms of conscience would not permit her to go all lengths with her Holy Allies, are all to gull her own people. It is a theatrical farce, in which the five powers are the actors, England the Tartuffe, and her people, the dupe. Playing thus so dextrously into each others' hands, and their own persons seeming secured, they are now looking to their privileged orders. These faithful auxiliaries, or accomplices, must be saved. This war is evidently that of the general body of the aristocracy, in which England is also acting her part. "Save but the nobles and there shall be no war," says she, masking her measures at the same time under the form of friendship and mediation, and hypocritically, while a party, offering herself as a judge, to betray those whom she is not openly to oppose. A fraudulent neutrality, if neutrality at all, is all Spain will get from her. And Spain, probably, perceives this, and willingly winks at it rather than have her weight thrown openly into the other scale.

17. To Jared Sparks, Monticello, 4 February 1824. *Jared Sparks (1789–1866) was editor of the* North American Review, *a leading literary and political journal published in Boston to which TJ subscribed. From the time he drafted the* Notes on Virginia *(see Chapter 2, document 7), TJ had advocated the colonization of emancipated slaves. The scheme presented here reveals the effects of long-standing intersectional tensions on the slavery issue that had recently erupted in the Missouri Controversy. While TJ has no wish that the federal government interfere with the institution of slavery within Missouri or other slave states, he argues that the nation as a whole must bear the costs of emancipation and colonization.*

The article on the African colonization of the people of color, to which you invite my attention, I have read with great consideration. It is, indeed, a fine one, and will do much good. I learn from it more, too, than I had before known, of the degree of success and promise of that colony.

In the disposition of these unfortunate people, there are two rational objects to be distinctly kept in view. First. The establishment of a colony on the coast of Africa, which may introduce among the aborigines the arts of cultivated life, and the blessings of civilization and science. By doing this, we may make to them some retribution for the long course of injuries we have been committing on their population. And considering that these blessings will descend to the *"nati natorum, et qui nascentur ab illis,"* we shall in the long run have rendered them perhaps more good than evil. To fulfil this object, the colony of Sierra Leone promises well, and that of Mesurado adds to our prospect of success. Under this view, the colonization society is to be considered as a missionary society, having in view, however, objects more humane, more justifiable, and less aggressive on the peace of other nations, than the others of that appellation.

The subject object, and the most interesting to us, as coming home to our physical and moral characters, to our happiness and safety, is to provide an asylum to which we can, by degrees, send the whole of that population from among us, and establish them under our patronage and protection, as a separate, free and independent people, in some country and climate friendly to human life and happiness. That any place on the coast of Africa should answer the latter purpose, I have ever deemed entirely impossible. And without repeating the other arguments which have been urged by others, I will appeal to figures only, which admit no controversy. I shall speak in round numbers, not absolutely accurate, yet not so wide from truth as to vary the result materially. There are in the United States a million and a half of people of color in slavery. To send off the whole of these at once, nobody conceives to be practicable for us, or expedient for them. Let us take twenty-five years for its accomplishment, within which time they will be doubled. Their estimated value as property, in the first place, (for actual property has been lawfully vested in that form, and who can lawfully take it from the possessors?) at an average of two hundred dollars each, young and old, would amount to six hundred millions of dollars, which must be paid or lost by somebody. To this, add the cost of their transportation by land and sea to Mesurado, a year's provision of food and clothing, implements of husbandry and of their trades, which will amount to three hundred millions more, making thirty-six millions of dollars a year for twenty-five years, with insurance of peace all that time, and it is impossible to look at the question a second time. I am aware that at the end of about sixteen years, a gradual detraction from this sum will commence, from the gradual diminution of breeders, and go on during the remaining nine years. Calculate this deduction, and it is still impossible to look at the enterprise a second time. I do not say this to induce an inference that the getting rid of them is forever impossible. For that is neither my opinion nor my hope. But only that it cannot be done in this way. There is, I think, a way in which it can be done; that is, by emancipating the after-born, leaving them, on due compensation, with their mothers, until their services are worth their maintenance, and then putting them to industrious occupations, until a proper age for deportation. This was the result of my reflections on the subject five and forty years ago, and I have never yet been able to conceive any other practicable plan. It was sketched in the Notes on Virginia, under the fourteenth query. The estimated value of the new-born infant is so low, (say twelve dollars and fifty cents,) that it would probably be yielded by the owner gratis, and would thus reduce the six hundred millions of dollars, the first head of expense, to thirty-seven millions and a half; leaving only the expense of nourishment while with the mother, and of transportation. And from what fund are these expenses to be furnished? Why not from that of the lands which have been ceded by the very States now needing this relief? And ceded on no consideration, for the most part, but that of the general good of the whole. These cessions already constitute one fourth of the States of the Union. It may be said that these lands have been sold; are now the property of the citizens composing those States; and the money long ago received and expended. But an equivalent of lands in the territories since acquired, may be appropriated to that object, or so much, at least, as may be sufficient; and the object, although more important to the slave States, is highly so to the others also, if they were serious in their arguments on the Missouri question. The slave States, too, if more interested, would also contribute more by their gratuitous liberation, thus taking on themselves alone the first and heaviest item of expense.

In the plan sketched in the Notes on Virginia, no particular place of asylum was specified; because it was thought possible, that in the revolutionary state of America, then commenced, events might open to us some one within practicable distance. This has now happened. St. Domingo has become independent, and with a population of that color only; and if the public papers are to be credited, their Chief offers to pay their passage, to receive them as free citizens, and to provide them employment. This leaves, then, for the general confederacy, no expense but of nurture with the mother a few years, and would call, of course, for a very moderate appropriation of the vacant lands. Suppose the whole annual increase to be of sixty thousand effective births, fifty vessels, of four hundred tons burthen each, constantly employed in that short run, would carry off the increase of every year, and the old stock would die off in the ordinary course of nature, lessening from the commencement until its final disappearance. In this way no violation of private right is proposed. Voluntary surrenders would probably come in as fast as the means to be provided for their care would be competent to it. Looking at my own State only, and I presume not to speak for the others, I verily believe that this surrender of property would not amount to more, annually, than half our present direct taxes, to be continued fully about twenty or twenty-five years, and then gradually diminishing for as many more until their final extinction; and even this half tax would not be paid in cash, but by the delivery of an object which they have never yet known or counted as part of their property; and those not possessing the object will be called on for nothing. I do not go into all the details of the burthens and benefits of this operation. And who could estimate its blessed effects? I leave this to those who will live to see their accomplishment, and to enjoy a beatitude forbidden to my age. But I leave it with this admonition, to rise and be doing. A million and a half are within their control; but six millions, (which a majority of those now living will see them attain,) and one million of these fighting men, will say, "we will not go."

I am aware that this subject involves some constitutional scruples. But a liberal construction, justified by the object, may go far, and an amendment of the constitution, the whole length necessary. The separation of infants from their mothers, too, would produce some scruples of humanity. But this would be straining at a gnat, and swallowing a camel.

18. To William Ludlow, Monticello, 6 September 1824. *In this frequently cited evocation of the progress of civilization across the continent TJ's historical and geographical perspectives converge. I have been unable to identify the correspondent.*

Let a philosophic observer commence a journey from the savages of the Rocky Mountains, eastwardly towards our sea-coast. These he would observe in the earliest stage of association living under no law but that of nature, subscribing and covering themselves with the flesh and skins of wild beasts. He would next find those on our frontiers in the pastoral state, raising domestic animals to supply the defects of hunting. Then succeed our own semi-barbarous citizens, the pioneers of the advance of civilization, and so in his progress he would meet the gradual shades of improving man until he would reach his, as yet, most improved state in our sea-port towns. This, in fact, is equivalent to a survey, in time, of the progress of man from the infancy of creation to the present day. I am eighty-one years of age, born where I now live, in the first range of mountains in the interior of our country. And I have observed this march of civilization advancing from the sea coast, passing over us like a cloud of light, increasing our knowledge and improving our condition, insomuch as that we are at this time more advanced in civilization here than the seaports were when was a boy. And where this progress will stop no one can say. Barbarism has, in the meantime, been receding before the steady step of amelioration; and will in time, I trust, disappear from the earth. You seem to think that this advance has brought on too complicated a state of society, and that we should gain in happiness by treading back our steps a little way. I think, myself, that we have more machinery of government than is necessary, too many parasites living on the labor of the industrious. I believe it might be much simplified to the relief of those who maintain it. Your experiment seems to have this in view. A society of seventy families, the number you name, may very possibly be governed as a single family, subsisting on their common industry, and holding all things in common. Some regulators of the family you still must have, and it remains to be seen at what period of your increasing population your simple regulations will cease to be sufficient to preserve order, peace, and justice. The experiment is interesting; I shall not live to see its issue, but I wish it success equal to your hopes, and to yourself and society prosperity and happiness.

19. To William Branch Giles, Monticello, 26 December 1825. *Before failing in a bid in 1825 to regain a seat in the federal Senate, William Branch Giles (1762–1830) had served in that body from 1803 to 1815 and the Virginia House of Delegates in 1816 and 1817. TJ shared Giles's concerns about the consolidationist tendencies of the federal government under John Quincy Adams, the first non-Virginian to ascend to the presidency since his father John Adams. That the nationalist Marshall Court now had powerful allies in the other branches threatened to reverse the outcome of TJ's Revolution of 1800. TJ yet again counsels patience, as he had done during the "reign of the witches" in the late 1790s. But he also contemplates the possibility of disunion: if union requires "submission to a government without limitation of powers," "there can be no hesitation" in opting for liberty.*

I see, as you do, and with the deepest affliction, the rapid strides with which the federal branch of our government is advancing towards the usurpation of all the rights reserved to the States, and the consolidation in itself of all powers, foreign and domestic; and that, too, by constructions which, if legitimate, leave no limits to their power. Take together the decisions of the federal court, the doctrines of the President, and the misconstructions of the constitutional compact acted on by the legislature of the federal branch, and it is but too evident, that the three ruling branches of that department are in combination to strip their colleagues, the State authorities, of the powers reserved by them, and to exercise themselves all functions foreign and domestic. Under the power to regulate commerce, they assume indefinitely that also over agriculture and manufactures, and call it regulation to take the earnings of one of these branches of industry, and that too the most depressed, and put them into the pockets of the other, the most flourishing of all. Under the authority to establish post roads, they claim that of cutting down mountains for the construction of roads, of digging canals, and aided by a little sophistry on the words "general welfare," a right to do, not only the acts to effect that, which are specifically enumerated and permitted, but whatsoever they shall think, or pretend will be for the general welfare. And what is our resource for the preservation of the constitution? Reason and argument? You might as well reason and argue with the marble columns encircling them. The representatives chosen by ourselves? They are joined in the combination, some from incorrect views of government, some from corrupt ones, sufficient voting together to out-number the sound parts; and with majorities only of one, two, or three, bold enough to go forward in defiance. Are we then to *stand to our arms,* with the hot-headed Georgian? No. That must be the last resource, not to be thought of until much longer and greater sufferings. If every infraction of a compact of so many parties is to be resisted at once, as a dissolution of it, none can ever be formed which would last one year. We must have patience and longer endurance then with our brethren while under delusion; give them time for reflection and experience of consequences; keep ourselves in a situation to profit by the chapter of accidents; and separate from our companions only when the sole alternatives left, are the dissolution of our Union with them, or submission to a government without limitation of powers. Between these two evils, when we must make a choice, there can be no hesitation. But in the meanwhile, the States should be watchful to note every material usurpation on their rights; to denounce them as they occur in the most peremptory terms; to protest against them as wrongs to which our present submission shall be considered, not as acknowledgments or precedents of right, but as a temporary yielding to the lesser evil, until their accumulation shall outweigh that of separation. I would go still further, and give to ther federal member, by a regular amendment of the constitution, a right to make roads and canals of intercommunication between the states, providing sufficiently against corrupt practices in Congress, (log-rolling, &c.,) by declaring that the federal proportion of each State of the moneys so employed, shall be in works within the State, or elsewhere with its consent, and with a due *salvo* of jurisdiction. . . .

Our University has been most fortunate in the five professors procured from England. A finer selection could not have been made. Besides their being of a grade of science which has left little superior behind, the correctness of their moral character, their accommodating dispositions, and zeal for the prosperity of the institution, leave us nothing more to wish. I verily believe that as high a degree of education can now be obtained here, as in the country they left. And a finer set of youths I never saw assembled for instruction. They committed some irregularities at first, until they learned the lawful length of their tether; since which it has never been transgressed in the smallest degree. A great proportion of them are severely devoted to study, and I fear not to say that within twelve or fifteen years from this time, a majority of the rulers of our State will have been educated here. They shall carry hence the correct principles of our day, and you may count assuredly that they will exhibit their country in a degree of sound respectability it has never known, either in our days, or those

of our forefathers. I cannot live to see it. My joy must only be that of anticipation. But that you may see it in full fruition, is the probable consequence of the twenty years I am ahead of you in time, and is the sincere
prayer of your affectionate and constant friend.

20. To Roger C. Weightman, Monticello, 24 June 1826. *Roger C. Weightman, a bookseller, had written TJ on behalf of the citizens of Washington, D.C., inviting the author of the Declaration of Independence to join in their celebration of the
fiftieth anniversary of American independence. Despite profound misgivings about
the political tendencies of the day (see document 19), TJ in this eloquent letter, the
last he ever wrote, testifies to his faith in the ultimate triumph of republicanism.*

The kind invitation I receive from you, on the part of the citizens of
the city of Washington, to be present with them at their celebration on the
fiftieth anniversary of American Independence, as one of the surviving
signers of an instrument pregnant with our own, and the fate of the world,
is most flattering to myself, and heightened by the honorable accompaniment proposed for the comfort of such a journey. It adds sensibly to the
sufferings of sickness, to be deprived by it of a personal participation in the
rejoicings of that day. But acquiescence is a duty, under circumstances not
placed among those we are permitted to control. I should, indeed, with
peculiar delight, have met and exchanged there congratulations personally with the small band, the remnant of that host of worthies, who joined
with us on that day, in the bold and doubtful election we were to make
for our country, between submission or the sword; and to have enjoyed
with them the consolatory fact, that our fellow citizens, after half a century
of experience and prosperity, continue to approve the choice we made.
May it be to the world, what I believe it will be, (to some parts sooner, to
others later, but finally to all,) the signal of arousing men to burst the
chains under which monkish ignorance and superstition had persuaded
them to bind themselves, and to assume the blessings and security of self-
government. That form which we have substituted, restores the free right to
the unbounded exercise of reason and freedom of opinion. All eyes are
opened, or opening, to the rights of man. The general spread of the light
of science has already laid open to every view the palpable truth, that the
mass of mankind has not been born with saddles on their backs, nor a
favored few booted and spurred, ready to ride them legitimately, by the
grace of God. These are grounds of hope for others. For ourselves, let the
annual return of this day forever refresh our recollections of these rights,
and an undiminished devotion to them.

I will ask permission here to express the pleasure with which I should
have met my ancient neighbors of the city of Washington and its vicinities,
with whom I passed so many years of a pleasing social intercourse; an intercourse which so much relieved the anxieties of the public cares, and left
impressions so deeply engraved in my affections, as never to be forgotten.
With my regret that ill health forbids me the gratification of an acceptance, be pleased to receive for yourself, and those for whom you write, the
assurance of my highest respect and friendly attachments.